CALIFORNIA GOVERNMENT TODAY

Politics of Reform

FIFTH EDITION

Charles M. Price

California State University, Chico

Charles G. Bell

Harcourt Brace College Publishers
Fort Worth   Philadelphia   San Diego
New York   Orlando   Austin   San Antonio
Toronto   Montreal   London   Sydney   Tokyo

Political Science Editor: Tammy Goldfeld
Editorial Assistants: Kelly Zavislak, Heide Chavez
Copy Editor: Jennifer Lindsey
Production, Design, Illustration, Photo Research, & Composition: Summerlight Creative
Print Buyer: Diana Spence
Cover Design: Cuttriss & Hambleton
Cover Photo: © Philip Harvey Photography, San Francisco
Printer: Malloy Lithographing, Inc.

Printed in the United States of America
ISBN 0-534-25998-7

6 7 8 9 0 1 2 3 4 5 066 9 8 7 6 5 4 3 2 1

Library of Congress Cataloging-in-Publication Data

Price, Charles M.
        California government today : politics of reform / Charles M.
    Price, Charles G. Bell. — 5th ed.
            p.   cm.
        Bell's name appears first on the previous editions.
        Includes bibliographic references and index.
        ISBN 0-534-25998-7 (paper bound)
            1. California—Politics and government—1951–   I. Bell, Charles
    G. (Charles Gordon), 1929–   II. Title.
    JK8716.P75   1995
    320.9794—dc20   95-13452
                                                     CIP

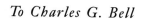

To Charles G. Bell

CONTENTS

PREFACE

The one constant in California politics is change. Once again, in this fifth edition, we must update material and reassess trends and developments. Trying to grasp the truth of California politics is like trying to grab lightning: It is fascinating, ephemeral, brilliant, electric (perhaps shocking), and, most of all, elusive. It is the inevitable task of text authors who write about California government and politics to be consigned to constant revision—or become hopelessly out of date.

Although many significant changes and new trends in California politics are discussed in the chapters ahead, we note a few at the outset. First, term limits are having, and will continue to have, an enormous impact on the California legislature, its leaders, lobbyists, staff, and other state elected officials. Second, the California legislature, once the model for professionalism, is now evolving into a more nonprofessional, citizen legislature. Third, Republican fortunes in the state are definitely on the upswing. Although Democrats have had solid majorities in the California legislature since the 1960s, Republicans today are on the verge of capturing control of both houses of the California legislature. Fourth, California's racial demographics are undergoing rapid change. The Latino and Asian portion of the population is increasing substantially. Fifth, with this ethnic growth, racism has reemerged as an important issue in the 1990s. The Los Angeles riots that broke out after a jury acquitted police officers of beating African American Rodney King; the bitter controversy over Proposition 187, the illegal immigrants initiative of 1994; and the looming civil rights initiative slated for the

1996 ballot, which would eliminate affirmative action programs in the state, are indicative of this renewed racial tension. And sixth, the California electorate (and U.S. as well) seems angrier, more cynical, and less tied to traditional politics than ever in this past century.

In revising this text I am indebted to Tom Hoeber, publisher, and Rich Zeiger, editor, of the *California Journal* for their keen insights into California politics. I was aided in this effort by the surveys and political analyses of the California electorate of Mervin Field and Mark DiCamillo. Mark Powers, chief of staff to former California assemblymember Stan Statham, offered sage comments on Chapter 7, the California legislature. Peter Detwiler, consultant to the Senate Committee on Local Government, provided many suggestions for Chapter 12, local government. Thanks also to the following critics—Lydia Andrade, San Jose State University; Gene Geisler, San Francisco State University; Kenneth D. Kennedy, College of San Mateo; Barbara Stone, California State University at Fullerton; Mark Weaver, Glendale Community College; and Lance Widman, El Camino College—who provided guidance to the author in proceeding with this new edition. Additional thanks go to Wadsworth editor Tammy Goldfeld, production editor S.M. Summerlight, and copy editor Jennifer Lindsey. Bob Ross, chair of the political science department at California State University at Chico, provided assistance in the arcane world of computers. My colleagues in the department have, over the years, provided me with many keen insights into California politics.

Lastly, in 1992 after an extended illness, Charles Bell, my coauthor, died. Charles and I worked closely on this text in its first four editions as well as on many other research ventures. Charles had a love and zest for studying California politics that was unmatched. Over our many years of collaboration, we developed a close working relationship. This text is dedicated to him. He was sorely missed in the rewrite of this new edition.

Charles M. Price
Chico, California

CALIFORNIA:
CRITICAL STATE

California is, without question, one of the most important states in the nation. The state's significance is based on a number of factors, including size, location, resources, people, climate, and economy.

THE DUALITY OF CALIFORNIA'S "GOOD LIFE"

California, the proverbial "Land of Plenty," represents what many Americans see as the "good life"—sprawling ranch-style homes, swimming pools, shopping centers, backyard patios, outdoor living, and, above all, affluence. Paradoxically, California is also a prime technological society run amok: smog, water pollution, toxic waste, threatened redwoods, bulldozed orchards, prime soil and farmlands lost to shopping centers and apartment complexes, crowded and violent freeways, high unemployment, expensive housing, drive-by shootings, and assembly-line food in plastic, franchise restaurants. A recent *Newsweek* article was aptly titled, "California: American Dream, American Nightmare" (July 31, 1989). This duality of promise and peril is part of the California enigma.

George Leonard, describing California in 1962, proclaimed:

> Here is the most fertile soil for new ideas in the U.S. The migrating millions who vote with their wheels for California are responding not only to the lure of sunny skies, but to the lure of opportunity. Already, this state shows the way with a revolutionary master plan of higher education for practically everybody; with an increasingly egalitarian society; with unprecedented opportunities for personal pleasure and fulfillment. Most important of all, California presents the promise and the challenge contained at the very heart of the original American dream; here, probably more than at any other place or time, the shackles of the past are broken.

Although Leonard's comments are overblown, California is still viewed by its own citizens and others as a relatively good place to live. "Given a choice," wrote Ed Salzman (1977), "most of us who live in San Diego, Los Angeles, San Francisco, and Sacramento would not trade places with fellow Americans in New York, Washington, Philadelphia, and Chicago, and that's probably the best test of the quality of life in California today." Even after the big earthquake of October 1989, few San Franciscans wanted to move elsewhere. Most are likely to rebuild where they are; living in the Bay Area is worth the risk. And a new study by G. Scott Thomas (1994) ranks California tenth among the fifty states for its overall quality of life—Vermont ranked first and Louisiana fiftieth.

However, the sense that all is not right is reflected in three recent Mervin Field surveys. In 1985, 78 percent of Californians rated the state as "one of the best places to live"; in 1989, only 58 percent did. But in 1994, only 41 percent thought so. In fact, Field found that one-third of all Californians said they would rather live elsewhere, and, indeed, many have been pulling up stakes and moving out of the state in the 1990s. The dream of California as the "Land of Plenty" is heard less often these days. Of course, foreign immigrants and undocumented workers are still dazzled by the state's beauty, wealth, and opportunities and are eager to come to the state. But most Californians are far more pessimistic these days about their quality of life. Natural disasters—fires, floods, droughts, and earthquakes—have become tiresomely commonplace, and environmental concerns are legion. Human disasters have become increasingly plentiful, from the 1991 Los Angeles race riots to drive-by shootings, gang warfare, serial killers, and violent carjackings. Public schools and state universities have declined in quality, public services have been reduced, government has become gridlocked, and the economy seems, at best, to have bottomed out; and genuine recovery is years away. Indeed, Michael Huffington, the Republican candidate for U.S. Senate in 1994, highlighted the problems of the state when he tried to deflect criticism that he was a Texas carpetbagger (Lapin, 1994). A Huffington television spot stated that despite the recession, fires, and earthquakes that have prompted many Californians to leave, "Mike Huffington and his wife came back to the state that educated him and is the birthplace of his two daughters."

California is also steadily becoming more Latino and Asian in population. Yet political power continues to reside within the Anglo community. Anglos, unlike ethnic minorities, have a relatively high voter turnout. As political columnist Dan Walters (p. 20) hypothesized, "The most likely political scenario for California in the 1990s and at least in the early years of the 21st century is for dominance by an affluent, politically active overclass using its position to protect its wealth and privileges against the larger but weaker underclass." Dozens of articles have appeared in the popular press over the last several years chronicling the state's fall from grace. In short, all is not well; the Golden State is tarnished.

Geography

California is the third largest state in the nation, encompassing some 164,000 square miles. A trip from San Diego at the state's southern end north along the coast to Crescent City near the Oregon border is an 876-mile drive—greater than the distance between New York and Chicago! On the eastern side of California, the Sierra Nevada range stretches some 400 miles. These mountains (many with peaks more than 13,000 feet above sea level) presented a formidable barrier to explorers and early settlers attempting to enter the state. The Sierra Nevada along with the Cascade and Klamath ranges in the north, the Coastal Range on the west, and the Tehachapis in the south enclose one of the world's most fertile agricultural regions—the Central Valley. These mountains trap much of the snow and rain that enter from the northwest. Thus, Northern California usually has ample water, sometimes floods, while Central and Southern California have to import water. In an average year, California receives 193 million acre-feet of water as rain or snow; three-fourths of this precipitation falls north of Sacramento. Since the mid-1980s, California has been suffering through a prolonged drought. Fortunately for Californians, 1995 was a bountiful year for precipitation. However, new studies using radiocarbon isotope dating indicate that droughts of 100 to 200 years occurred on several occasions in the state less than 1,000 years ago. Because the water supply system is based on dams, reservoirs, and aqueducts transporting "surplus" water southward to California's ever-burgeoning population, these historical implications are ominous. Use of state water—its allocation for agriculture and its transport—has been one of the most consistently controversial regional issues dividing Northern and Southern Californians. Finally, California usually leads the nation in a rather dubious category: number of significant (above 3.0 on the Richter scale) earthquakes per year. Indeed, Southern California averages more than 11,000 yearly; pollster Mervin Field reports that a growing number of Californians (67 percent) are concerned about them.

Climate

For many Californians, the state's climate is its most admirable feature. Despite widely varying temperature extremes—the harsh cold and deep snows of the Sierra Nevada and the blistering heat of Death Valley—the mild weather of coastal regions has lured millions to California. Dry, moderate warmth in the summer contrasts markedly with the muggy heat of the Southern and Central

California State Library

UPI / Bettmann

In search of the golden dream. Whether they have arrived by covered wagon, by Dust Bowl auto, or over the border illegally (right page), those who have come to California have looked to the state for a new start.

Jim Wilson / NYT Pictures

states and much of the Atlantic seaboard. The warm, sunny days of winter in the state's south contrast dramatically with much of the rest of the country.

Population

As of 1994, according to the state's Demographic Research Unit, California's population was approximately 32 million (see Figure 1.1, page 6). In addition, the U.S. Bureau of the Census has acknowledged an undercount of approximately 1 million residents in the state. Some of those uncounted are the homeless, drug addicts, and gang members; others are undocumented workers.

Size and Growth   Between 1980 and 1990, California's official population grew by more than 5 million people, and by 2000 the state will gain an additional 6 million. The 5 million gain in the 1980s equals the current population of Missouri (the fifteenth most populous of the 50 states). California's yearly gain in population is approximately 620,000, or roughly the size of Alaska's population. In 1940, Californians constituted about 5 percent of the total U.S. population; today it's nearly 13 percent. By 2020, the state may have a population of 50 million!

What is California's carrying capacity? How many more people can be accommodated before the dream of the "good life" becomes a myth? Have we already reached that point? Obviously, rapid population growth puts increasing

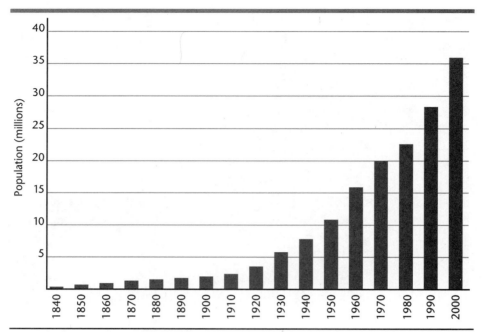

FIGURE 1.1 CALIFORNIA'S POPULATION BY DECADES
Source: U.S. Bureau of the Census; California Department of Finance, Demographic Research Unit

demands on the supply of energy, water resources, maintenance of prime agricultural land, use of wild and scenic rivers, use of urban parks and recreation facilities, and school and highway construction, among others. California, in fact, has the dubious distinction in the 1990s of leading the nation in the number of metropolitan areas that failed to meet federal air-quality standards.

Explosive population growth exacerbates these problems. But population concerns are seldom referred to by state political leaders—the subject is too sensitive.[1] California's rate of natural increase (births over deaths) was about on a par with the national rate of increase for this century until the 1980s, but over the last several decades the state's birthrate has increased substantially from 1.9 per average California woman to 2.3. The natural increase in the 1990s has been averaging about 390,000 annually (about 300,000 abortions take place each year as well). Why has there been such growth in natural increase? Demographers contend that young Latino and Asian immigrants who come from cultures where large families are the rule are major contributors to the spiraling birthrate.

Population growth has also been triggered by immigration to the state from other states and from foreign countries. In the 1970s and 1980s, California averaged a net gain yearly of about 100,000 from population inflow from other states. Because of all of California's recent problems, this inflow has declined dramatically in the 1990s. Indeed, since 1992 California has been exporting more citizens than importing them; the state has experienced a net outflow of about 150,000 yearly. But California's population surge is likely to continue well into the twenty-first century because: (1) About 35 percent of all legally admitted foreign immigrants coming to the United States want to live in California (over the last five years, about 370,000 annually); (2) 50 percent of all refugees settle here; (3) nearly 50 percent of all illegal immigrants (approximately 100,000) come here yearly; and (4) the state has a high birthrate. Foreign immigrants choose California for the same reasons that Americans historically have and because they have families here or ethnic communities to help them. While legal foreign immigrants moving to California come from many different nations, in the 1990s most come from: (1) Mexico, (2) Vietnam, (3) Philippines, and (4) former republics of the Soviet Union.

What, if anything, can be done to slow the pace of population increase? Trying to persuade Californians to limit family size would incur the wrath of some religious leaders and others who object to governmental intrusion into the private lives of citizens. Indeed, if the Christian right and Catholic church had their way, abortions would be sharply restricted or denied, and hundreds of thousands of additional babies would be born in California every year.

Attempting to stem the tide of foreign immigrants and refugees would entail, in part, reducing the number legally admitted to this country. But this runs counter to our "Statue of Liberty" tradition, and, obviously, we are virtually all immigrants ourselves. We are descendants of immigrants who came to the United States seeking work, land, and a better life. Immigrants also have greatly enriched the quality of American life. And so, some question, can we in good conscience deny or restrict this opportunity to others? Mervin Field reported in 1993 that 81 percent of Californians believed that foreign immigrants make just as good or better citizens than U.S.-born citizens. However, Field also notes that 58 percent of Californians want to reduce the number of legal immigrants and refugees admitted. In any case, immigration quotas are established at the federal level, and California public officials have only limited influence on the issue.

However, consensus is growing among Republican and Democratic politicians and the general public that the nation must do a better job of preventing illegal immigration. California and other states sharing a common border with Mexico and coastal states are particularly vulnerable. In 1993, a Field Poll reported that 76 percent of Californians viewed illegal immigration as a serious issue and that it had an unfavorable effect on the state. Proposition 187, the illegal-immigration initiative (nicknamed SOS, "Save Our State") on the November 1994 ballot, sought to bar education, health, and welfare benefits to illegal immigrants. It was strongly approved by the California electorate, 59 to 41 percent. The initiative was immediately challenged in state and federal courts, and an injunction was issued barring its implementation until the courts can rule on its constitutionality.

Whatever the reality, there is much hypocrisy on this subject. Illegals pay sales and Social Security taxes, accept few social services, and take jobs Americans refuse. Many in California (and other states) benefit from illegal workers accepting minimum-wage jobs, such as farmers, factory owners, apparel manufacturers, motel and hotel managers, fast-food restaurants, and amusement park owners. Others hire illegals for personal services at their homes to do the gardening, take care of young children, or prepare meals. Indeed, one day after Republican U.S. Senate candidate Michael Huffington announced his strong support for Proposition 187, the press reported that the Huffington family had employed an illegal Guatemalan woman to care for the Huffington children from 1988 to 1993. The ensuing scandal contributed to Huffington's defeat in the 1994 election.

Proponents of Proposition 187 have already succeeded on one dimension: They have forced President Bill Clinton to deal with the illegal immigration issue seriously. The U.S. Border Patrol has been increased, modern high-tech surveillance equipment is now being used, and the Department of Labor is cracking down on employers who hire illegals.

Urban–Suburban Patterns   California is an urban state. In fact, with 93 percent of the population living in various urban concentrations, it is the most urbanized state in the nation. But this urban pattern is substantially different than most other large industrial states. With relatively low land costs (historically, at least), a desire for room, an extensive freeway system, and a willingness to commute long distances to work, Californians have spread across the landscape. More than half of all Californians live in suburbs.

In the 1950s and 1960s, California's suburban growth was massive; whole counties mushroomed overnight. Orange County, south of Los Angeles, and Santa Clara County, south of San Francisco, grew at a dizzying rate.

In the 1980s and 1990s, this suburbanization pattern has changed. Instead of rapid growth taking place in areas close to major cities, the most significant gains in population have been in rural areas away from the major cities. In particular, some rural counties in the Sierra foothills and other bucolic northern areas have experienced massive growth: The populations of Amador, Calaveras, San Luis Obispo, Lake, Merced, Placer, and Nevada counties have increased substantially.

Here and there, pleasant, quiet, semirural towns suddenly attracted thousands of new settlers fleeing the urban or suburban "rat race." Redding, Santa Rosa,

Doug Menuez / Reportage

Passengers departing a BART (Bay Area Rapid Transit) train. BART serves the San Francisco Bay Area. The overwhelming majority of Californians, however, get to work by private automobiles, not public transit.

and Napa in Northern California and Corona, San Juan Capistrano, Yorba Linda, Palmdale, and Oceanside in Southern California are good examples of this changing pattern.

In Southern California, although Los Angeles, Orange, and San Diego counties have continued to grow steadily, the largest percentage increases have come in adjoining counties such as Riverside, San Bernardino, Imperial, and Ventura, where relatively cheap land and housing encourage people to make long freeway commutes. A similar pattern of urban sprawl is found in counties within commuting distance of the San Francisco Bay Area in Northern California.

CALIFORNIA'S ECONOMIC SIGNIFICANCE

The unique feature of the California economy is its diversity. The state grows more crops, produces more food, builds more airplanes, and manufactures more

RANK ($)	ENTITY	GROSS PRODUCT OR SALES ($ MILLIONS)
1.	United States	5,237,707
2.	Japan	2,920,310
3.	Germany	1,272,959
4.	France	1,000,866
5.	Italy	871,955
6.	United Kingdom	834,166
7.	California	697,381
8.	Canada	500,337
9.	New York	441,068
10.	China	393,006

TABLE 1.1 CALIFORNIA'S LEADING ECONOMIC INDICATORS, 1992
Source: "State Stats," *The Journal of State Government* (Summer 1992), p. 127.

computers and space and military hardware than any other in the nation. Unlike many of the major industrial states of the Eastern seaboard, California has an exceedingly important and varied agricultural sector. And distinct from the major industrial states of the Midwest, which do have an important agricultural base, the California economy includes other diverse activities such as mining, communications, finance, lumber, and petroleum.

Overall, when we consider the major factors shaping the state's economy— rapid population growth, climate, a broad range of industrial activity (with emphasis on communications, electronics, and space and defense), percentage of work force in defense-related jobs, importance of tourism, and number of retirees—California's economy most resembles Southern or Southwestern states such as Florida, Texas, and Arizona. However, the diversity of California agriculture; the affluence of its petroleum industry; the importance of the motion-picture, record, and television industries headquartered in the state; and trade and exporting make the state unique economically.[2]

California ranks first among the states in manufacturing, employment, tourism, aerospace, agriculture, retail, and savings assets. Business leaders and politicians have long boasted that the Golden State surpasses most countries of the world in gross national product (GNP). The state's 1992 gross products, or sales of leading economic entities, are shown in Table 1.1.

Indeed, one recently filed initiative proposes that California should declare independence from the United States and become an independent nation!

Leading Economic Sectors and Trends

Land Ownership and Use As in most Western states, a large percentage of California land is federally owned (45.2 percent). When state and county land is added to the federal total, more than half of California (50.2 percent) is owned by government. Table 1.2 (page 12) also shows that a few major corporations control vast tracts of California's private lands. In fact, the great majority of the state's population lives on only a small percentage of the land.

However, there has been a persistent trend in California for prime agricultural land to be gobbled up by new shopping centers, housing developments, and freeways. California is currently losing about 50,000 acres of prime agricultural land and another 100,000 acres of nonprime land a year to development. Although some experts claim this is not a problem, because hundreds of thousands of acres of potential farmland could be converted to agricultural use if needed or if water were available, agricultural experts and environmentalists worry that the most productive lands are being lost to development. Between 1987 and 1992, farm acreage in the state declined by 5.3 percent.

Agriculture Agriculture—or, perhaps more accurately, agribusiness—is an important pillar of the state's economy. Although California has relatively few farms, and only a small percentage of its population lives in rural areas, it is the nation's leading farm state (Texas ranks second).

According to a 1993 report by the state Department of Food and Agriculture, California produced crops valued at $18.1 billion on some 85,000 farms. California, Oregon, and Washington have the largest percentage (22.9 percent) of large farms ($500,000-plus annual sales volume) in the nation. Key features of California farming include: large acreages, mechanization, extensive use of pesticides, a sizable percentage of prime agricultural land owned by foreign conglomerates, some unionization of poorly paid farm workers organized by the United Farm Workers Union, extensive use of temporary legal workers and undocumented workers, and futuristic farming techniques (cloning, genetic engineering, and computerization). Calgene, a California genetic-engineering firm, test-marketed in 1994 in select supermarkets a new tomato (the Flav'r Sav'r) with a reversed PG gene that represses the natural PG gene's production of fruit-rotting enzymes. The aim was to allow tomatoes to ripen on the vine and acquire their full flavor and then be shipped to markets before they spoil. This is the first genetically engineered whole food ever to reach consumers.

With just 3 percent of the nation's farmland, California produces 10 percent of national gross farm receipts and 50 percent of U.S. fruits, nuts, and vegetables. More than 250 crop and livestock commodities are produced here. California

CLASS OF LAND	NUMBER OF ACRES	PERCENT OF STATE AREA	
Total	100,185,000		100.00
Forest land	42,416,000	42.3	
Agricultural	35,722,000	35.7	
Urban and suburban land	2,200,000	2.2	
Other land	19,847,000	19.8	
GOVERNMENT-OWNED			
Total	50,335,946		50.2
Federal	45,251,036	45.2	
State	2,437,809	2.4	
Cities	865,895	.86	
Counties	691,827	.69	
Special districts	461,868	.46	
Indian land	540,471	.54	
School districts	80,025	.08	
Junior college districts	7,012	.01	
PRIVATELY OWNED			
Total	49,847,735		49.8
Southern Pacific	2,411,000	2.4	
Newhall Land Co.	1,590,00	1.6	
Shasta Forest Co.	479,196	.4	
Tenneco Inc.	362,843	.4	
Tejon Ranch Co.	348,000	.3	
Standard Oil of California	306,000	.3	
Boise Cascade	303,000	.3	
Georgia Pacific	278,000	.3	
Pacific Gas and Electric Co.	250,000	.2	
Occidental Petroleum	200,000	.2	
Sunkist Corporation	192,000	.2	
Other "smaller holdings"	43,127,714	43.0	

TABLE 1.2   CALIFORNIA LAND USE AND OWNERSHIP
Source: California Land Use Task Force, Department of Finance, *California Statistical Abstract,* and Ralph Nader's *Who Owns California?* (Washington, D.C., Center for Study of Responsive Law).

© Jon Brenneis / Photo 20-20

California's massive agriculture industry applies sophisticated technology in marketing its bounty.

ranks first among the states in 66 different crop and livestock commodities, and more are being added to the list each year.[3] For example, in 1994 California surpassed Wisconsin in milk production. In addition, 8 California counties rank among the top 10 in the country in total value of agricultural production.

California's agricultural exports amount to about $5.1 billion annually. More than half goes to Pacific Rim nations, and another third to Europe. More than half of California's cotton, rice, wheat, and almond crops are also exported.

California farmers, however, face such imponderables as the availability of cheap water (85 percent of state water resources go to agriculture), pesticide regulations, soil salinity, overmortgaged land, and an inadequate labor supply.

Uncounted in the lush agricultural California bounty is probably the single most important cash crop in the state: illegally grown marijuana. State and federal drug agents report that marijuana is grown in at least forty-three of California's fifty-eight counties. The total yearly California harvest is estimated to be worth more than $3 billion! In terms of cash value, no other crop grown surpasses marijuana in California.

SECTOR	PERCENTAGE OF EMPLOYMENT
Services	28
Trade	17
Government	17
Manufacturing	16
Finance, insurance, and real estate	7
Trade	6
Transportation and utilities	5
Construction/mining	4

TABLE 1.3   CALIFORNIA'S NONAGRICULTURAL EMPLOYMENT BY SECTOR
Source: California Statistical Abstract, State of California, 1993.

Postindustrial Economics   One expert, Ted Bradshaw (1976), has contended that California is the world's most advanced industrial society because of its high-technology industry, heavy concentration of workers in services, rapid change, and innovation. In this same vein, Todd La Porte and C. J. Abrams (1976) argue that California is one of the world's best examples of a postindustrial society. They note that the state's innovations in petrochemicals, agriculture, transport, aerospace, electronics, nuclear energy, medicine, education, and biology indicate the sophisticated nature of the California economy.

The computer industry began here. California is also the broadcast media state: Hollywood is the center of the nation's film industry, and television, radio, and the music industry are major state industries. It is the critical state for aerospace and advanced weapons systems. Finally, major California research institutions—the UC system, state universities, Stanford, Cal Tech, USC, the Claremont Graduate School, and think tanks such as the Rand Corporation—are significant contributors to California's technological prowess.

The percentage of Californians employed in manufacturing and agriculture has declined steadily over the past several decades, while jobs in services and trade have increased substantially. However, according to Stern and Taylor (1990, p. 86), manufacturing still provides jobs for approximately 20 percent of California workers and generates more than $150 billion in production annually. Dan Walters (1986) notes that "the new industrial jobs that have been created, especially those in high-tech and services, are overwhelmingly non-union with non-professional wage scales in the sub-$10-per-hour range." Types of employment are listed in Table 1.3.

CALIFORNIA LEADS THE NATION IN:	PERCENTAGE OF NATION
Microcomputer-related companies—2,081	29
Microcomputer production—$3 billion	26
Value of computer shipments—$10 billion	36
Computer employment—115,800	11
Peripheral equipment manufacturing—$3.1 billion	11
Semiconductor manufacturers—94	46
Value of semiconductor shipments—$4 billion	32
Semiconductor employment—52,500	38
Independent software production—$1.8 billion	20
Software employment—32,000	20
Total electronics industry employment—598,000	24

TABLE 1.4   THE CALIFORNIA DIFFERENCE
Source: California Department of Commerce Governor's Budget Summary, 1990–1991.

Electronics   Much of the world's research in microelectronics is conducted in Santa Clara County's "Silicon Valley," which has the highest concentration of high-tech electronics companies in the nation. Not surprisingly, California leads in the number of personal computers—more than 20 percent of the nation's total—and in other high-tech categories (see Table 1.4).

International Trade and Foreign Investment   One of the stronger sectors in the California economy is foreign trade. California exports about $70 billion yearly in manufactured goods, agriculture, and lumber. The state's top three international trading partners—Japan, Canada, and Mexico—account for more than one-third of total exports. And trade with Mexico will probably increase now that NAFTA (North American Free Trade Agreement) is in place. To promote exports, California has established trade offices in Mexico City, Tokyo, Hong Kong, Frankfurt, London, Jerusalem, Taipei, and South Africa. Also, nearly 80 percent of California imports come from Pacific Rim countries—Japan alone accounts for 37 percent of state imports.

Foreign commercial interests have invested heavily in California farmland and purchased major businesses and property in the state's urban centers. Indeed, 64 percent of downtown Los Angeles is owned by foreign investors! And of the top ten banks in California, Japan owns five: Union, Mitsubishi, Sanwa, Sumitomo, and Tokai. Some 285,000 Californians work for foreign-owned corporations (Japan is the leading foreign employer in the state). In terms of foreign investment in California, European countries account for 48 percent, Canada 24 percent, Japan 15 percent, the Middle East 3 percent, Latin America 3 percent, and others 7 percent.

Aerospace and Defense   California's aerospace and defense industry has always depended heavily on the federal government for health and vitality. California ranks among the top ten military powers of the world. Nearly 33 percent of the nation's aerospace companies, 20 percent of aircraft manufacturing, and 60 percent of missile- and space-equipment manufacturing companies are located in California, and there are more engineers here than in any other state.

From the end of World War II until the mid-1980s, California's economy boomed. Federal dollars spent on space and defense projects and military bases were a major component of the state's buoyant economy. However, the collapse of communism in the former Soviet Union and Eastern Europe has allowed the Clinton administration to scale back defense spending. Proposed weapons systems have been scrapped, aircraft production pared back, Strategic Defense Initiative spending eliminated, space research funding reduced, and dozens of California Air Force, Navy, Marine, and Army bases closed. Thousands of defense-related jobs have been lost in the process. In 1994, Lockheed, California's preeminent defense corporation, announced that it was merging with Martin Marietta and moving its corporate headquarters to Bethesda, Maryland, to be closer to Washington, D.C. Defense cutbacks have had a staggering impact on the California economy.

Of course, there is hope that some engineers and other technical specialists displaced in this downsizing will eventually find employment in the production of high-speed rail systems, electric cars, or wind turbines, but for the short run the impact has been devastating. Converting military bases to civilian use will have a high priority in the coming years.

More than half of the 90,000 jobs lost annually in California during the 1990s have been in electronics and defense industries. Although high-tech research and development will continue, some assembly and production will shift out of state or out of the country over the next several years.

Finally, though world communism is dead, new world "hot spot" problems in places such as Bosnia, Kosovo, Rwanda, Haiti, Iraq, Ukraine, North Korea, and the Sudan may force the Clinton administration to augment defense and military spending in the years ahead. This could be to California's economic advantage.

Tourism and Show Business   Tourism and travel are strong components of the state's economy. Thirty million Americans and 6 million foreigners visit California annually. Travel-related spending accounts for $54 billion yearly in the state.

The Sacramento Bee

Energy from the wind. Whirling windmills are a high-tech nonpolluting energy source that can serve the needs of California's millions.

California continues to be a vacation mecca for Americans and international tourists: world-famous national parks and forests, spectacular mountain ranges and desert scenery, the coast, the Napa–Sonoma wine country, Lake Tahoe, Hollywood, the San Diego Zoo and Wildlife Park, Disneyland, and other amusement parks are but a few of the attractions.

In addition, Hollywood is the center of American filmmaking, generating $6 billion in revenues and employing 80,000 Californians. Nearly 70 percent of all feature films are produced in the Golden State. Ties between the political world and show business are becoming ever closer. Many politicians have persuaded film stars to join them at fund-raisers (to pull in a crowd) or to contribute. Show business celebrities frequently visit the capital to testify on issues of concern.

Other Manufacturing and Construction The California recession has hurt the construction industry. Residential homebuilding has declined. According to the state Department of Economic Development, only film production, apparel, and textiles have registered job gains in the 1990s. In its own assessment of the California economy in the mid-1990s, Wells Fargo Bank comments, "The decline in (California) employment is already the steepest since the Great

Depression of the 1930s, and it will take several years for California's labor market to fully recover. Under this scenario, even if job growth resumes at a 2% annual rate starting in 1996, California will not reach its pre-recession peak in employment until 1998."

Financial Services Employment in finance, insurance, and real estate declined in the early 1990s, although bank profits have begun to improve in the mid-1990s.

Economic Malaise Defense cutbacks, the social and economic costs of massive foreign immigration (legal and illegal), workers' compensation system excesses, businesses moving to less tax-stringent states, and a cascade of recent natural calamities have put California in an economic tailspin over the last several years. Mervin Field reported that 84 percent of Californians surveyed in 1994 described California as being in bad economic times. Through the early 1990s, unemployment ran well ahead of the national average.

CALIFORNIA'S SOCIAL SIGNIFICANCE

Two prominent features of the California social potpourri deserve comment. First, the state has been the haven for and sometimes the birthplace of a variety of exotic religious cults, offbeat political movements, and extremist groups. Second, it has been a major contributor to American "pop" culture. Though the endless discussion of the zany California social milieu has been exaggerated by its critics—after all, a large, diverse, and populous state is sure to have a certain number of eccentrics—much of this nation's sociopolitical exotica either started in California or took root here.

Diversity and Extremes

Historically, groups on the far left and far right of the American political spectrum have found California fertile recruiting ground for members, and this has contributed to the state's quirky political reputation. However, no far-left or far-right fringe group has ever been a significant factor in state politics.

The John Birch Society, a rabidly anticommunist and ultraconservative group formed in the "red scare" days of the 1950s, at one time had thousands of California followers. Today, the Birch Society has become irrelevant, particularly with the collapse of world communism.

Another fringe right-wing group on the contemporary California political scene is the Lyndon LaRouche National Democratic Policy Committee. (Earlier in his career, LaRouche had been a far-left extremist.) Among his zanier beliefs is that the Queen of England is the chief mastermind of the world's illegal drug trade. None of LaRouche's California followers has won nomination in the Democratic primaries they have entered. However, his California supporters were able to qualify two different AIDS initiatives for the ballot, in November 1986 and June 1988. Both were rejected by the California electorate. Today, LaRouche's political influence is on the wane.

Neo-Nazi, Aryan hate groups, and skinheads, though an infinitesimal part of the California population, have stirred up trouble on occasion in prisons and public schools, and incidents of gay-bashing are not uncommon. Synagogues and NAACP (National Association for the Advancement of Colored People) offices have been favorite targets for firebombings and cross burnings. Several family planning clinics also have been fire- or stinkbombed by antiabortion fanatics. In addition, several self-styled militia groups are part of the California far-right political scene. The members of these paramilitary groups are convinced that U.N. troops are poised to conquer the United States.

Of course, extremism is in the eye of the beholder. As an example, in 1994 Democratic Assembly member Richard Katz introduced Assembly Bill 2810. The bill would have allowed nonmarried couples sharing a common residence and expenses and who were not related to register their relationship with the secretary of state. By so doing, these domestic partners (1) would have hospital visitation rights and (2) could act as conservators if one became incapacitated. The bill was supported by senior citizen groups and homosexual organizations and strongly endorsed by Democrats and moderate Republicans. Yet, this seemingly innocuous bill was attacked by archconservative Republican legislators for "leading to gay marriages" and being "catastrophic to the survival of our civilization." The Katz bill was vetoed by Governor Pete Wilson because he contended "government should encourage and reward marriage."

Left-wing extremism has virtually disappeared from the contemporary California political scene. In the 1960s and 1970s, the Black Panther party emerged from the black ghettos of Oakland to become the defiant voice of African American militancy in the state. Today, the Black Panthers are only a memory. Now Louis Farrakhan, chief minister for the Nation of Islam, is the major exponent of black rage in the United States. Nation of Islam temples can be found in some of California's larger cities. The Symbionese Liberation "Army" (which never had more than a dozen or so members) emerged in the early 1970s. Group members kidnapped heiress Patty Hearst, a major news event of the time, but most of its members were later killed in a police shootout in Los Angeles. The tiny and inconsequential Peace and Freedom Party and the now largely defunct Campaign California of State Senator Tom Hayden are among the last remnants of leftist protest in the state.

Another example of the unique California political milieu has been the growing political power of the state's homosexual community. Although gays have organized politically throughout the nation, in California they have had their greatest impact. According to *Newsweek* ("Battle over Gay Rights," June 6, 1977), no city has a larger homosexual population proportionally than San Francisco (a reported 120,000 out of a total 680,000), and no city has adopted a more tolerant view of homosexuals. San Francisco is home to openly gay Democratic clubs, office holders, and police officers. Gay supervisor Harvey Milk became a symbol of gay pride after he was assassinated in 1978. Mayoral candidates in San Francisco must seek support from the gay community to have a chance of winning. In 1994, the first openly gay statewide candidate for office, Tony Miller, captured the Democratic nomination for secretary of state in the June primary but was defeated in the November general election. Miller's sexual orientation was not a campaign issue. Moreover, in 1994 Sheila James Kuehl of Los Angeles—an attorney and former television actor (girlfriend of "Dobie Gillis" in the old TV sitcom)—became the first open lesbian elected to the state legislature. However, gays have not been welcomed into state Republican ranks. Republican and Christian conservatives contend that the gay lifestyle undercuts traditional family structure and that homosexual sex is condemned in the Bible. Indeed, more extreme conservatives contend that AIDS is God's plan for punishing gays and intravenous drug users for their lifestyles. Republican moderates argue their party should be open to all and warn that exclusion can lead to lost election opportunities.

California has also served as sanctuary for a wide variety of unusual religious cults and sects from Aimee Semple McPherson and the Foursquare Gospel Church in the 1930s to Hare Krishna disciples, the Church of Scientology, Synanon, and the "Moonies" of the 1990s. The 1978 mass suicide of hundreds of members of the People's Temple Church, a California-based cult, in Guyana, South America, became an international incident. The notorious Branch Davidians of Waco, Texas, infamy also had a California connection: They were a cult offshoot of the Seventh Day Adventists, who were first established in California under the leadership of Victor Houteff, a former school teacher in a Los Angeles Adventist grade school. After being expelled from the Adventist Church for his heretical views, Houteff led his California flock to Waco to establish their new home. David Koresh, a Bible-quoting rock musician, joined the group in the early 1980s and assumed leadership after Houteff's death. In 1994, Koresh led most of his followers into a mass suicide, shoot-out, and fiery conflagration with federal authorities. Gurus, con artists, and fanatical leaders have always found willing followers in the Golden State.

AP / Wide World Photos

Gay support parade. Gays in California are a significant political force.

Window on the Future

California inevitably seems to be in the center of the American political–social swirl: the Watts race riots, the 1960s student protest movement, the anti–Vietnam War crusade, the environmental movement, the antienvironmental movement, the Jarvis–Gann property tax revolt, the term limits crusade, the illegal immigrant issue highlighted by Proposition 187 of November 1994, and a pending civil rights initiative in 1996 that would eliminate all state affirmative action programs. Bradshaw (1976, p. 1) observes that "new issues often seem to demand attention in California long before they emerge in other places." Kenneth Lamott (1971, p. 4) writes, "California is our distant warning system for the rest of the United States. California is our window into the future."

Clearly, a great many features of American social life and "pop" culture are California-inspired—fashions, sports, music, food, movies, and television programs. California is frequently the springboard for national trends —hang gliding, scuba diving, surfing, snowboarding, hot air balloons, off-road vehicles, hot tubs, and bungee jumping (first done off the Golden Gate Bridge). The "drive-in" phenomenon—movies, restaurants, banks, photo processing, and now supermarkets—is particularly Californian. Walt Disney's Disneyland in Anaheim, California, was the first of the modern theme amusement parks that have sprung up around the country. Glendora in Southern California is famous as the site of the first McDonald's.

Much of what has been written about California pokes fun at the Golden State: "California's major export to the rest of the country has not been its fruits and vegetables; it has been craziness. . . . You name it: if it babbles and its eyeballs are glazed, it probably comes from California" (Royko, 1979). In a less critical vein, John Naisbitt (1982, p. 6) writes:

> We have learned that there are five states in which most social invention occurs in this country. The other forty-five are in effect followers. . . . Not surprisingly, California is the key indicator state; Florida is second, although not too far behind; the other three trend-setter states are Washington, Colorado, and Connecticut. . . . When we trace back new trends or positions on issues eventually adopted by most of the fifty states, we find that these five states are again and again the places where new trends began.

California has always been a public policy innovator and leader among the states. One of the best examples of this was the pioneering legislation in the 1970s that promoted clean-air-quality standards. Many of its provisions were later formulated into federal air-quality standards.

California seems to be in the forefront of two major domestic policy issues: health care and welfare reform. Francy Blanchard (p. 63) comments, "Whatever Washington finally decides, the prescription for health care reform will have been written in the golden state. . . . California is on the cutting edge with models that offer a glimpse of what America's health care system will look like under national health care reform." So, too, on welfare reform, the innovative GAIN (Greater Avenues for Independence) program developed in this state to get recipients off welfare and into jobs has been cited by the Clinton administration as a prototype for its federal welfare reform effort.

Some of America's leading authors—Walt Whitman, Mark Twain, John Steinbeck, and contemporary novelist Joan Didion—have written about the Golden State. On one point they all agree: California is indeed fascinating.

California has long served as a haven for senior retirees seeking mild, balmy weather. Many Californians fight the aging process with ferocious determination: Jogging, aerobics, fat farms, health-food stores, iron-pumping emporiums, and exercise salons are all very much a part of the state social scene. Physical fitness entrepreneurs such as Jack LaLanne, Vic Tanney, and Jane Fonda are state folk heroes. Zsa Zsa Gabor, George Burns, and Lauren Bacall are examples of senior Californians who seem ageless. California leads the way in restoring sagging bodies: 20 percent of all U.S. plastic surgeons have their practices in California! And when death can no longer be denied, there is Forest Lawn Cemetery, yet another prime tourist attraction. Finally, for those unwilling to accept death from modern disease, California is the home of the world's only two cryonics companies, Trans Time and Alcor. For a fee, one can have his or her body frozen in the hope that future advances in medical science will allow doctors to cure the clients' diseases and revive them for a new life in newly cloned bodies!

Some of this country's most famous personalities have been Californians: ex-presidents Ronald Reagan, Gerald Ford, and the late Richard Nixon; nationally known politicians such as Republican Governor Pete Wilson, Democratic U.S. Senators Dianne Feinstein and Barbara Boxer, and Speaker Willie Brown. Many famous movie stars, television personalities, and sports figures also live in California. Indeed, some in the entertainment industry have become quite involved in politics—Charlton Heston, Jane Fonda, Ed Asner, Clint Eastwood, Sonny Bono, and Ronald Reagan are examples. Conversely, some in the political realm go into entertainment: Both former Governor Jerry Brown and Speaker Willie Brown have their own talk shows. And don't forget national conservative radio talk show host Rush Limbaugh. He got his start and developed his show's format at Sacramento radio station KBFK. Of course, the state has more than its fair share of infamous personalities, including Charles Manson, Sirhan Sirhan, "Nightstalker" Richard Ramirez, and other serial killers.

No person better symbolizes the California dream gone awry, however, than O. J. Simpson. From football megastar to product endorser, sports announcer, and movie star with fabulous wealth and a loving family, Simpson had it all. Now, he's being tried for the murder of his ex-wife and her friend. Innocent or guilty, his life will never be the same. Political columnist Mary McGrory (1994), decrying California attitudes, comments:

> Never mind, for the moment Simpson's blazing celebrity. California juries, in recent bizarre verdicts, have exhibited an aversion to holding human beings responsible for their actions. Juries are supposed to collect facts; California juries shop for atmospherics, for extenuating context.
>
> In the case of the Menendez brothers, who shot both their parents . . . [j]urors thought the poor kids had no choice because of various injuries mother and father had inflicted on them. In the case of Reginald Denny, the jury saw two victims neither of them Denny. The aggressors had simply been swept up in the fury of the Los Angeles riots. In the state that gave us the self-esteem commission and the cult of victimology, Simpson could expect every consideration.

Although other states have their personalities, unusual cults, extremist political groups, and fads, in overall magnitude California remains in a class by itself.

CALIFORNIA'S POLITICAL SIGNIFICANCE

As the most populous state in the nation, California has more voters and potential voters than any other state. Presidential candidates have also found the state irresistible because of its importance in campaign fund-raising.

Presidential Nomination Process

Nineteenth-century delegates to national presidential nominating conventions were handpicked by party leaders. These delegates did the bidding of their respective leaders at the convention. Early in this century, in California and other (mainly Western) states, reform-oriented Progressives came to political power. Among the various reforms they advocated (see Chapter 2 for a more complete discussion) was the presidential primary system of *electing* delegates. California, Oregon, Washington, Wisconsin, New Hampshire, and a half dozen other states adopted the presidential primary system early in the twentieth century.

Through much of this century, two states, New Hampshire and California, had the most important presidential preference primaries. The New Hampshire primary, traditionally the first scheduled in presidential election years, has played a decisive role in providing momentum to presidential candidates and, conversely, in torpedoing the plans of other presidential hopefuls. The California June primary was traditionally the last major battleground test for presidential candidates before the national party conventions. Sizable Republican and Democratic delegations also made the state a great prize for presidential candidates. Winning the California primary could give a presidential candidate a helpful last-minute surge. William J. Crotty (1977, p. 214) noted, "The Golden State's primary was easily the most significant and decisive of all."[4] Further adding to its historical importance was the fact it was "winner take all." The candidate receiving the most votes in the primary elected the entire delegation to the national convention. Democrats changed to a proportional system in 1976, but Republican primary winners still take it all.

Over the last several decades, however, California's presidential primary has become less important. Most states now have presidential primaries, so California's is no longer unique. But more important, in the contemporary setting, the early calendar primary states such as New Hampshire and the Southern states' collective primary (Super Tuesday) have become the key battlegrounds for presidential candidates. Getting off to a good start in these states (building momentum) is more than half the battle. Eventual nominees have had their nominations wrapped up by the end of March or early April, long before California's June primary was held. The California presidential primary had become completely irrelevant.

The only way to provide California voters a voice in the nomination process was to hold an earlier presidential primary. But doing so has always been fraught with political uncertainty. Which party in a particular presidential year had the most to gain from moving it ahead? Should only the presidential primary be moved ahead? Many state politicians prefer to retain the later June primary for other offices, but a separate presidential primary would cost state taxpayers $40 million. If only the presidential primary is moved ahead, should ballot propositions be included? If so, whichever party had a contested primary could determine the success of a liberal or conservative ballot proposition.

A legislative compromise was achieved for the 1996 presidential primary. On a one-time experimental basis, the entire California primary has been moved from the first Tuesday in June to the fourth Tuesday in March 1996. California Republicans will probably benefit because their party is almost sure to have a spirited nomination contest. Incumbent President Bill Clinton, humiliated in the congressional elections of 1994, could conceivably face opposition for the Democratic presidential nomination. However, one problem remains: California's earlier than ever 1996 primary will still take place *after* many other states' presidential primaries. The Iowa caucuses, the New Hampshire primary, junior Tuesday (several mountain states), Super Tuesday (Southern states), and now the Illinois, Ohio, and Michigan primaries all come weeks or days before California's. Significant momentum toward a presidential nomination will probably have developed before Californians even vote. California's March primary may still be too late for Californians to have much effect on the nomination. Given the "front-loading" of so many states eager to move their delegate selection ahead on the calendar, California officials may have to push their primary even earlier in 2000 and thereafter for California voters to have an impact.

Presidential Elections

California has more electoral votes, 54 (the total number of congressmembers and senators), than any other state. It has almost as many electoral votes as the fifteen smallest states —Alaska, Delaware, Hawaii, Idaho, Maine, Montana, Nebraska, Nevada, New Hampshire, New Mexico, North Dakota, Rhode Island, South Dakota, Vermont, and Wyoming (55)—combined. California's 54 votes constitute 20 percent of the total 270 needed for a presidential candidate to win election! California also tends to be a bellwether state in presidential elections. From 1920 to 1992, California has gone with the presidential winner seventeen times in nineteen elections (1960 and 1976 are the exceptions).

Because of the state's electoral importance and the high visibility of its major officeholders, over the past several decades California politicians have been key players in the presidential and vice-presidential nomination process. California Republican nominees have included Earl Warren, vice-presidential candidate (1948); Richard M. Nixon, vice-president (1952 and 1956), presidential candidate (1960), and president (1968 and 1972); Ronald Reagan, presidential candidate (1968 and 1976) and president (1980 and 1984).[5] On the Democratic side, Jerry Brown ran unsuccessfully for the presidency in 1976, 1980, and 1992. Republican Pete Wilson's decisive 1994 reelection as governor has made him a prospect for the 1996 presidential or vice-presidential contests, although he would be replaced as governor by Democrat Gray Davis if he left office. This may change if Republicans win approval of a potential initiative that would require a special election to replace the governor rather than retaining the current practice of allowing the lieutenant governor to fill the vacancy.

Congressional Politics

As California's population has spiraled, the state has, with each new census, been allocated more new seats in the House of Representatives. In the 1970 census, California became the largest state delegation in the House (43). Two more seats were added in the 1980s, and seven more were allocated in the 1990s, for a total today of 52 (12 percent of all House members) of a total 435. And the state may be allocated one additional House seat this decade. In a pending lawsuit, the Supreme Court must determine whether the census bureau should be required to use its own population projections for states in 1990 (there was an acknowledged undercount of about one million in California) instead of the actual count for determining the state's official population.

It has become a cliché to state that power in Congress resides in its committees and committee chairs. Traditionally, seniority has been the main criterion for determining committee membership and chairs. Until the mid-1970s, the majority party member with the longest continuous service on a committee automatically became its chair. In 1970, Democrats modified their seniority rule by requiring that all chairs be ratified by their respective chambers' caucuses. The Democratic House and Senate caucuses (made up of all Democrat members) usually confirmed the senior member of their party with the longest continuous service on a committee to the chair position, but on a few occasions veteran chairs lost their positions.

In the early 1990s, California Democrats had attained several key committee chair positions—George Brown, Space and Technology; Ron Dellums, Armed Services; George Miller, Natural Resources; Norm Mineta, Public Works and Transportation; and Pete Stark, District of Columbia governance committee—or in party leadership positions (Vic Fazio is Democratic Caucus chair). However, because of the overwhelming Republican vote in 1994, the GOP for the first time in 40 years captured control of both houses of Congress. Indeed, Republicans achieved near parity in the 52-member California House delegation (27 Democrats, 25 Republicans). Because of their new majority status, Republican chairs replaced all the former Democrat chairs. However, only one California Republican House member, Bill Thomas, will chair a standing committee. Other California Republicans became subcommittee chairs.

Until May 1995, term limits further complicated the picture. California voters approved term limits for state officials in 1990, and two years later approved term limits for congressmembers. Under Proposition 164, California's congressional officers were to be limited to six years in the House (three terms) and twelve years in the U.S. Senate (two terms). In a split decision (5–4), however, the Supreme Court ruled that the states have no constitutional power to limit the terms of federal officeholders. Such limits could only be set nationally and by amendment to the Constitution; two months earlier, Republican House leaders failed to get such an amendment through the House with the necessary two-thirds vote. The California congressional delegation would have become less influential had term limits been allowed to stand: Our congressmembers would probably never have become committee chairs because of their inability to accrue seniority, and the state's influence in Congress would have been sharply reduced.

The fifty-two–member California House delegation has frequently been wracked by strong internal political feuds. Not unexpectedly, staunch liberal Democratic representatives from the Bay Area have little in common with archconservative Republican congressmembers from Orange and San Diego counties, and this antagonism has dissipated California's overall influence in the House (Bottoroff, 1986). In addition, other state delegations fear and resent the sheer numbers and potential power of California's House members.[6] Compounding these sentiments is the fact that the Golden State has historically been the prime recipient of federal largesse for space and defense projects. Indicative of this resentment, Buffalo, New York, not Los Angeles, was selected as the site of a federal research facility for an earthquake study in 1989.

On those rare occasions when the California House delegation is unified, it can be a formidable force. After the San Francisco earthquake of 1989 and the Northridge earthquake of 1994, California House members worked cooperatively and effectively to secure federal emergency funds for the state. State officials have also unified in efforts to get more federal money to pay California for foreign immigrant costs.

In 1992, California made U.S. Senate history. For the first time ever, a state elected two women to the Senate: Dianne Feinstein and Barbara Boxer (for a total of six women U.S. senators). Although neither has much seniority, they have been placed on key policy committees. Senator Feinstein skillfully steered the landmark Desert Protection Act through Congress and secured President Clinton's signature. The act establishes several new national parks in the Mojave Desert and places other desert country under federal protection.

Supreme Court Politics

California's impact on the U.S. Supreme Court is more difficult to gauge, although four of the nine justices are Stanford University alumni: William Rehnquist, Sandra Day O'Connor, Anthony Kennedy, and Stephen Breyer.

Former California Governor Earl Warren served as Chief Justice in the 1950s and 1960s. The Warren court issued many critical decisions on a variety of topics, including school desegregation, voting rights, reapportionment, and the rights of defendants. In addition, several significant California-generated legal controversies have served as a backdrop for major Supreme Court decisions. The Bakke case is an example. Alan Bakke, a white male, contended that he had been denied admission to the University of California at Davis Medical School because of reverse discrimination. In 1978, the Court ruled that Bakke had been wrongfully denied admission to the medical school under an unconstitutional quota system, but it also said that race could be used as a criterion for admission to assist minority applicants. In 1996, a civil rights anti–affirmative action initiative is likely to be on the state ballot; if approved, it surely will be challenged in the courts. Or, another example, the U.S. Supreme Court in 1992 let stand a state Supreme Court ruling, *California Legislature v. March Fong Eu, Secretary of State*, 1991, that upheld Proposition 140's term limits for state elected officials.

During the 1950s and 1960s, the Court followed the lead of the California Supreme Court on several legal issues. Ronald Blubaugh in the *Sacramento Bee* (October 6, 1974, sec. P, p. 1) recalled:

> In 1961, when the U.S. Supreme Court held that all states were forbidden to use illegally seized evidence in a criminal trial, it cited a 1955 California decision. In 1965, the U.S. Supreme Court struck down Arizona and New York Supreme Court decisions when it announced the Miranda rule against confessions from a suspect not informed of his rights. . . . California has led, too, in civil rights cases. In 1948, California was the first to strike down a statute prohibiting interracial marriage. Nineteen years later the U.S. Supreme Court followed the California example.

However, the California Supreme Court's once prestigious reputation has declined over the past several decades. Ideological conflict, partisan pressures, a public investigation of the Court for allegedly delaying the announcement of a

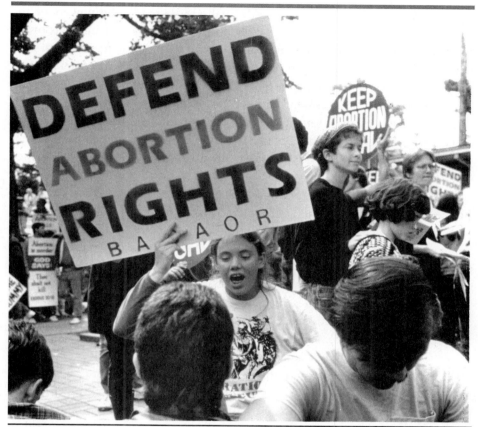

Skip Shuman / *The Sacramento Bee*

The politics of abortion politically divides Californians.

decision, the defeat in confirmation elections of three Court members in 1986, and a rapid turnover in membership has diminished its stature.

CALIFORNIA AND THE FEDERAL SYSTEM

California was officially admitted to statehood in 1850. It was the first noncontiguous American territory to become a state. Debate over California's admission as a free state was intense because of the slavery issue and Southern fears that political power would tip to the north.

In theory, within the American federal system, the national government has only those few powers that are explicitly delegated to it in the U.S. Constitution; all other powers are reserved to the states. In fact, under the early leadership of

Supreme Court Chief Justice John Marshall (1801–1853), the powers of the national government were vastly expanded through the use of the implied powers doctrine. Sharing governmental functions among national, state, and local governments has been our tradition. While Marshall's immediate successors shifted away from federal supremacy to a states' rights position, in the 1930s, during the Great Depression and President Franklin Delano Roosevelt's New Deal, a new court majority eventually returned to the strong national government position. Since 1937, the Court has usually upheld the right of the national government to act in most areas. Today, there are virtually no limits on the subjects on which Congress may legislate.

The balance between national and state government powers has always been a bone of contention in the federal system. Although various issues have exacerbated national–state tensions over the years, one issue in particular generated much early conflict: race. From debates at the constitutional convention over the continued importation of slaves to the Civil War, Reconstruction, the Plessy decision, the "separate but equal" doctrine, and the civil rights struggles of the 1960s and 1970s, one of the chief legacies of federalism was that it allowed Southern states a legal rationale for maintaining white supremacy. However, in 1954 the U.S. Supreme Court reversed itself and ruled in *Brown v. Board of Education* that "separate but equal" was unconstitutional and that public school officials would have to integrate their schools "with all deliberate speed." This decision was extended in later Court rulings to all public facilities. In 1964, Congress passed the Civil Rights Act, which forbade discrimination in hiring by governmental or private employers engaged in interstate commerce. And in 1965, Congress passed the Voting Rights Act, which mandated federal intervention in states to guarantee voting access. Today, racial issues tend to be more national in scope—school busing and affirmative action are examples—and the strong states' rights stance of the old confederate states is in sharp decline.

Indeed, the states' rights battle cry is heard more these days in Western than in Southern states. In the late 1970s, California, Nevada, Alaska, Montana, and Idaho were in the forefront of what came to be dubbed the Sagebrush Rebellion. At the heart of this squabble was federal ownership of a large percentage of Western land (including 45 percent of California); most Midwestern, Southern, and Eastern states have miniscule federal landholdings. Many conservative Western state officials resented federal rules and regulations dealing with this land and other policy matters. During the Carter presidency, the federal government mandated a 55-miles-per-hour speed limit on interstate highways to promote fuel conservation and safety. To "encourage" Western states (the measure's chief opponents) to comply, the federal government threatened to withhold portions of federal highway funds from those that failed to enforce the new speed limit. Many Western politicians argued that the limit made little sense in the vast expanses of the West. The Reagan administration and Congress agreed to modify this policy in 1986 primarily because of Western pressure.

Throughout his two terms as president, Ronald Reagan steadfastly promoted a "New Federalism," advocating a shift of powers and responsibilities from Washington, D.C., to state and local governments. Reagan had modest successes in promoting this goal. Though a staunch advocate of states' rights, Reagan took a national stance on (1) a federal 21-year-old drinking age (comply or else the state's highway funds would be reduced) and (2) federal offshore oil exploration and drilling (many coastal states were bitterly opposed). When Vice President George Bush succeeded Reagan as president, he continued the pro–states' rights stance of his predecessor, although with less enthusiasm. Ex-Arkansas Governor and now President Bill Clinton currently supports states having major policy roles, but he clearly wants the federal government to be the dominant partner. However, given the overwhelming Democratic congressional defeats in 1994, he may be willing to shift more responsibilities to state and local government in 1995–96. Renewing Reagan's New Federalism stance, Republican Speaker Newt Gingrich and his GOP majority have raised the states' rights banner once again on issues such as no more unfunded mandates, shifting federal programs to block grants to states, and welfare reform to be undertaken by the states.

Dividing California

Ever since California became a state in 1850, there have been efforts to divide it. In the first half of this century, division efforts were launched by Southern California politicians unhappy that northern interests dominated state government in Sacramento. However, ever since the U.S. Supreme Court ruled in 1964 that both houses of American state legislatures would have to be apportioned on the basis of population—"one person, one vote"—Southern California interests have had solid majorities in both houses. Resentment toward southern control of state government has simmered ever since in Northern California, where sporadic attempts to divide the state were launched. None have succeeded.

In 1991, Republican Assemblymember Stan Statham, representing the far northeast portion of the state, proposed that California be divided north and south (the dividing line would have run west to east from just north of San Francisco). Rural Northern Californians, however, did not want liberal San Francisco or Sacramento counties included in Northern California. Statham favored division for several reasons. First, northern rural counties were in a desperate financial situation (partly caused by state mandates), and yet urban-dominated Southern California government didn't seem to care. Second, he contended that California had become too big and populous for one state government. California government was simply not working. And third, splitting the state would give California additional U.S. senators.

In pursuing his vision, Statham persuaded thirty-one of fifty-eight counties (nearly all northern and a few central) to put a nonbinding advisory question to voters in 1992: Would you favor dividing California? Twenty-seven of the thirty-one counties approved (some more northerly, rural, sparsely populated counties gave more than 80 percent support to the proposal). But the twenty-seven approving counties constituted only 5 percent of the state's population.

After considering the county votes, Statham proposed that California be divided into three states. Under this proposal, Northern California would run from the Oregon border to Marin County's southern border and eastward; Central California would have included San Francisco, Solano, Sacramento, Mariposa, and Mono counties south to Kern County; and Southern California would comprise Santa Barbara, Ventura, Los Angeles, San Bernardino, Orange, Riverside, San Diego, and Imperial counties. Southern California alone would still be the most populous state in the nation with some 18.7 million as of 1994 (New York would rank second with about 18.3 million). Statham favored a three-state format because many San Franciscans and Sacramentans did not want to be lumped in a two-way split with Southern California and Los Angeles; besides, a three-state California plan would mean six U.S. senators.

To win approval for his plan, Statham needed the approval of both the California legislature and Congress. To provide momentum for his plan, Statham proposed a concurrent resolution to place the state-split question on the California ballot. Both houses of the legislature, however, would have to approve the measure before it could be placed on the ballot for public vote. If the public approved, the plan would then be sent to Congress for its approval. The resolution was voted out of the Assembly in 1993 but failed to clear the Senate.

Prospects for dividing the state seem remote at best for several reasons. First, we're used to thinking of California as a single state. The last state split occurred long ago—Virginia and West Virginia during the Civil War. Second, Governor Wilson and many central and southern elected officials of both parties are opposed. Third, pollster Mervin Field reported in 1993 that 79 percent of Californians oppose division. Fourth, U.S. senators would not want to expand membership in their 100-member exclusive club. Fifth, U.S. House members would be concerned that other states might want to split, which could lead to instability. And sixth, many complicated legal issues would have to be resolved in determining rights and ownership.

Stan Statham has been the driving force behind division, but he failed in his bid to win the Republican nomination for lieutenant governor in 1994 and is no longer an elected official.

POLITICAL REFORM LEADERSHIP

For much of this century, California has been in the vanguard of states promoting political reform. At the turn of the century, reform-oriented Progressives throughout the West came to political power, promoting honest, open, efficient, and responsive government. They saw as their enemies party bosses, party machines, tainted public officials, and avaricious special interests. Central to the Progressive philosophy was the belief that the public—not politicians or corporate interests—should wield ultimate political power through the ballot box. William J. Crotty (1977, p. 214) describes this Western reform mentality:

> The weight of public opinion in the western states was overwhelmingly against any property limitations on the vote. . . . The contrast between the western states and those in the East was pronounced. . . . Not surprisingly, voting rights for women were granted in the western states first.

Some Progressive reform ideas, such as the direct primary, presidential primary, and direct-democracy devices (initiative, referendum, and recall), were adopted later in some states east of the Mississippi River. Although these reforms were not a panacea, on the whole they did for a time promote more honest and responsive state government.

In addition, through the leadership of Speaker Jess Unruh, the California legislature in the 1960s was modernized and reformed (see Chapter 7) by raising legislators' salaries, adding professional staff, and refurbishing offices. Unruh argued that state legislatures should set their own salaries and determine their own schedules. By the late 1960s, the California legislature had again become the reform model for other states. And in 1974, when voters approved the Political Reform Act initiative—which sought to regulate lobbyists, limit campaign contributions, and require all political candidates to report periodically on campaign contributions and expenditures—California again was on the cutting edge of political reform.

In November 1990, California voters approved Proposition 140, which set term limits for state officeholders. California was one of the first three states in the nation to approve this concept. In 1992, voters easily approved term limits for California congressmembers through Proposition 164, and at the local level term limits for elected officials have been adopted by cities and counties across the state. California has gone from being the leader among the states in the professional legislature movement to being the leader in returning to amateur lawmaking—a citizen legislature (see Chapter 7).

The most critical political reform issue of the 1990s is finding a way to stop the ever-mounting costs of political campaigns and the attendant advantages gained by major special-interest campaign contributors or wealthy candidates. FBI investigations of California government in the 1980s and 1990s led to convictions of legislators, lobbyists, and staff. Scandals highlighted the need for a solution to "Big Money" in election campaigns. Although California has been a political reform leader on many issues this century, it has not provided leadership in campaign finance reform. Indeed, a host of other states have adopted laws to cope with this problem. The initiative process (not the governor and legislature) probably offers the best hope for resolving this issue.

William Crotty (1977, p. 293) wisely observed some years ago:

> The need for reform has to be demonstrated over and over again, and most frequently it takes a crisis situation to arouse broad public concern and responsible official action. Even then, reforms once made are never secure. Often, the changes do not accomplish the desired end. Always, they introduce new problems. And the effort to repeal and render them impotent continues unabated by their critics, comfortable and powerful within a system that has rewarded them generously.

SUMMARY

Economically, socially, and politically, California is one of the most influential states in the nation. Technologically, it is the most advanced. Historically, it has been a leader among the states in reform and policy issues. By understanding something about the issues and political crosscurrents in California today, we may discern something about future trends in national politics.

NOTES

1. Former Governor Jerry Brown's resources secretary, Huey Johnson, raised the issue of population growth and its impact on state resources during Brown's second term. Johnson was bitterly criticized from many quarters for his comments, and Brown came under intense pressure to fire Johnson.

2. According to *California Business* ("California's Top 500 Companies," June–July 1993), the top ten public corporations in California are: (1) Chevron, (2) Atlantic Richfield, (3) Hewlett-Packard, (4) Safeway, (5) Bank of America, (6) McKesson, (7) Rockwell Intl., (8) Pacific Gas and Electric, (9) Lockheed, and (10) Pacific Telesis. Bechtel Corporation and Levi Strauss are the two largest private companies in the state.

3. According to a 1992 report of the state Food and Agriculture Department, California leads all other states in the following crops and livestock commodities:

Leads in Production	Percent of U.S. Production	Leads in Production	Percent of U.S. Production
Alfalfa seed	38	Indoor plants	17
Almonds	100	Kiwifruit	100
Apricots	94	Kumquats	47
Artichokes	100	Ladino clover seed	*
Asparagus	42	Lemons	74
Avocados	85	Lettuce	73
Bedding plants	18	Mustard greens	17
Bell peppers	40	Nectarines	93
Bermuda grass seed	76	Olives	100
Broccoli	89	Onions	26
Brussels sprouts	95	Oriental vegetables	43
Bulbs	22	Parsley	30
Cabbage	19	Peaches	69
Cantaloupes	67	Pears, Bartlett	56
Carrots	53	Persian melons	*
Casaba melons	*	Persimmons	98
Cauliflower	79	Pigeons and squabs	62
Celery	73	Pistachios	100
Chinchillas	20	Plums	87
Cowpeas	46	Pomegranates	100
Crenshaw melons	*	Prunes	100
Cut flowers	59	Rabbits	20
Dates	100	Raisins	99
Eggs	10	Safflower	77
Figs	100	Spinach	51
Garlic	81	Strawberries	79
Goats milk	22	Sudan grass	89
Green lima beans	28	Table grapes	97
Green onions	48	Tomatoes, processing	90
Greenhouse vegetables	26	Vegetable and flower seeds	38
Herbs	61	Walnuts	99
Honey	14	Wild rice	*
Honeydew melons	72	Wine and juice grapes	85

*Data not available

Source: California Department of Food and Agriculture. "California Agriculture: 1992 Statistics." Sacramento: 1993.

4. From *Political Reform and the American Experiment,* by William J. Crotty. Copyright 1977 by Thomas Y. Crowell. This and all other quotations from this source are reprinted by permission of the author.

5. In 1980, after receiving the Republican presidential nomination, Ronald Reagan seriously considered naming Gerald Ford, a former Michigan politician living in retirement in Palm Springs, California, as his running mate. A president and vice-president coming from the same state would have been unprecedented.

6. Conceivably, California could receive another House seat (53 in all). In August 1994, a U.S. Appeals Court ruled that the Bush administration was wrong not to adjust upward an acknowledged census undercount. (The Bush administration decided to use the official count and not the census bureau's projection.) California and Arizona will both add one House member, and Wisconsin and Pennsylvania will each lose one if the Appeals Court decision stands.

REFERENCES

"Battle over Gay Rights." *Newsweek*, June 6, 1977, pp. 16–26.

Blanchard, Francy. "The California Cure." *California Business* 28 (September 1993), pp. 63–71.

Bradshaw, Ted K. "New Issues for California, the World's Most Advanced Industrial Society." *Public Affairs Report* 17 (August 1976), pp. 1–6.

California Department of Food and Agriculture. "California Agriculture: 1992 Statistics." Sacramento, 1993.

California Employment Development Department. "California Nonagricultural Wage and Salary Employment by Industry." Sacramento, 1993.

"California: 1994–95 Outlook." *The Wells Fargo Economic Monitor* (December 10, 1993), pp. 1–8.

"California's Largest Companies." *California Business* 28 (June–July 1993), pp. 25–36.

"California's Unemployment Rate Drops to 8.3%." News release, Economic Development Department (June 1994).

Cory, Ann. "Calgene's Tomato to Leap from Lab into Salad Bowl." *Sacramento Bee* (September 27, 1993), p. A1.

Cox, John D. "Epic Droughts in Past Suggest Harsh Future in State." Sacramento Bee (June 16, 1994), p. B1.

Crotty, William J. *Political Reform and the American Experiment.* New York: Thomas Y. Crowell, 1977.

Department of Finance. "California Economic Indicators." (March/April 1994), pp. 1–30.

———. Demographic Research Unit, "Official Population Projections." (April 1993).

Field Institute. California Opinion Index (1985, November). "Living in California." *California Opinion Index*. San Francisco.

———. (1989, May). "Living in California." *California Opinion Index*. San Francisco.

———. (November 2, 1993). "Large Majority Against Splitting State in Two. 79% Disapprove of Three-Way Division."

———. (November 24, 1993). "Californians Extremely Concerned About a Wide Variety of Problems; Crime Is Now State's Top Issue."

———. (February 4, 1994). "Greater Level of Worry About Earthquakes. More Residents Considering Moving out of the State Because of Quake Fears."

———. (February 10, 1994). "Californians' Once Golden Image of the State Has Palled Considerably in Recent Years."

———. (August 19, 1993). "Californians Have Favorable View of Legal Immigrants. However, Ready to Support Some Proposals Which Would Restrict and Penalize Illegal Immigrants."

———. (February 16, 1994)."Californians Remain Gloomy About Their Personal Financial Condition, Increased Concern about Job Security.

"How the Water Flows." *Sacramento Bee* (March 17, 1991), pp. A10–11.

Lamott, Kenneth. *Anti-California: Report from Our First Parafascist State.* Boston: Little, Brown, 1971.

Lapin, Lisa. "Huffington, Feinstein Enlist New Ads in Fray." *Sacramento Bee* (September 20, 1994), p. A4.

La Porte, Todd, and C. J. Abrams. "Alternative Patterns of Post Industria: The California Experience." In *Politics and the Future of Industrial Society*, edited by Leon Lindberg. New York: McKay, 1976.

Leonard, George. "California: A Promised Land for Millions of Migrating Americans." *Look*, 1962, p. 27.

McGrory, Mary. "O. J. Simpson the Victim?" *Sacramento Bee* (June 22, 1994), p. D3.

Naisbitt, John. *Megatrends.* New York: Warner Books, 1982.

Price, Charles M. "The Longshot Bid to Split California." *California Journal* 23 (August 1992), pp. 387–392.

Reese, Michael, and Jennifer Foote. "California: American Dream, American Nightmare." *Newsweek*, July 31, 1989, pp. 23–26.

"State Stats." *The Journal of State Government* (Summer 1992), p. 127.

Stern, Richard L., and John H. Taylor. "California's Fading Boom." *Forbes*, November 1990, pp. 86–90.

Thomas, G. Scott. *The Rating Guide to Life in America's 50 States.* Amherst, NY: Prometheus Books, 1994.

Walters, Dan. *The New California.* Sacramento: California Journal, 1986, p. 14.

CALIFORNIA:

ITS PEOPLE AND POLITICS

THE LAST FRONTIER

For years, California has been the last physical and psychological frontier in America. Many people without hope came to the Golden State, and many others who came only brought hope. Between 1850 and 1995, the state's population grew 194 times—from 165,000 to nearly 32 million—while the population of the United States grew only 9 times. Had the nation grown at California's pace, there would be more than 3 billion Americans today rather than 250 million. What makes California's growth so startling is its continuous high rate.

For many, California was more than a "last frontier"—it was a last chance. Long after the Old West was gone, California remained a place where the young, the poor, and the adventurous had a chance to make it. It was also a place to retire, if you'd made it someplace else.

THE EARLY EXPLORERS

The first people to live in present-day California were Indians—descendants of nomadic tribes who crossed the Bering Strait 25,000 years ago. When Spain began its effort to colonize California in the 1760s, the indigenous population was about 140,000.

THE SPANISH–MEXICAN ERA
Early European Explorers

The Spaniards came to the New World looking for riches that had been described by Garci Ordonez de Montalvo in *Las Sergas de Esplandian*, a fanciful tale of adventure published about 1498. Montalvo noted, "at the right hand of the Indies there is an island named California, [which] abounds with gold and precious stones." Of course, no one had ever seen California: It was a myth.

Spain conquered Mexico in 1519, nearly a century before Jamestown, the first permanent English colony, was established in Virginia. Spain's occupation of Mexico also gave it claim to much of present-day Southwestern United States.

In 1542, Portuguese explorer Juan Rodriquez Cabrillo was the first European to reach California. He sailed along the California coast, passing by areas known today as San Diego, Catalina Island, Ventura, Monterey, and Fort Ross. After Cabrillo's death, Bartolome Ferrelo took command and sailed farther north along the coast to about the Oregon border. Sir Francis Drake, another early explorer, landed north of San Francisco Bay in 1579, named the land Nova Albion ("New England"), and claimed it for England. For the most part, California was ignored by Spain and other European nations until 1768, when Russian hunters began to move down the coast from Alaska in search of sea otters. Their presence was a threat to Spain's territorial claims; the Spanish decided to solidify their claims by establishing missions in California.

The Mission Period

Missions had been used extensively in the 1600s and 1700s as an expansion device for Spain's colonies. Under the command of Gaspar de Portola, soldiers and Franciscan priests, including Father Junipero Serra, reached San Diego in 1769 and established the first of a string of missions along or near the California coastline. Under Serra's direction, missions combined religious conversion of Indians with practical instruction in agriculture and building.[1] The last mission was established at Sonoma in 1823.

Little attention was given to, or control exercised over, this vast territory by the royal viceroy in Mexico City. At most, only 3,000 Spanish citizens, soldiers, and missionaries were in California during this period.

The Mexican Period

In 1822, Mexicans successfully overthrew the Spanish and attained independence. California then became part of the Mexican Empire. But preoccupied by internal conflict, the new Mexican government devoted even less attention to California than the Spanish had.

Under anticlerical Mexican rule, the missions were dismantled and replaced by rancheros. Mission properties were sold or given in grants to favored individuals. During this period, a trickle of American outsiders (the first illegals) came to the state. Most visited California and returned home, but a few stayed. Richard H. Dana wrote his famous *Two Years Before the Mast* after sailing to California in 1834. And in 1841, the Bidwell party arrived by land from the Middle West, opening a new route for thousands of Americans.

Encouraged by the weakness of the Mexican government, anticipating war between Mexico and the United States, and concerned about British designs on California, a few Americans staged a brief revolt in June 1846. Led by adventurer John C. Fremont, they seized a herd of horses, captured two Mexican generals, and raised a flag displaying a grizzly bear. Known as the Bear Flag revolt, this uprising was cut short by the war between Mexico and the United States. The bear emblem on the California state flag is the one legacy of the revolt.

In 1845, Texas, which had successfully fought a war for independence against Mexico in the 1830s, applied for admission to the United States. Southern states supported Texas because, under the terms of the Missouri Compromise, it would enter as a slave state. President James K. Polk believed his election in 1844 was a mandate for the annexation of both Texas and much of the Southwest. Angered by Texas's admission into the United States and insistent that its border with Texas was many miles north of the Rio Grande at the Nueces River, Mexico moved troops into the disputed area. After less than two years of bloody conflict, the U. S. Army captured Mexico City, and the provisional government of Mexico signed the Treaty of Guadalupe Hidalgo. Mexico agreed to the Rio Grande boundary and ceded much of present-day New Mexico, Arizona, Colorado, Utah, Nevada, and California to the United States for $15 million.

THE AMERICAN ERA
The Gold Rush

The discovery of gold in January 1848 at Sutter's Mill on the American River launched the American era. News of the find spread, and by late May 1848, San Francisco, Monterey, and San Jose were largely deserted as residents flocked to the goldfields on the American River. By 1849, the news had spread around the world, and the Gold Rush was on. In the mid-1850s, perhaps as many as 100,000 people were at the diggings—more than one-third of the state's population! The gold mined was worth millions of dollars.

Most miners came to make their fortune and then return home. Many left penniless, but a few made fortunes. Even more money was made by those who served

California State Library

Early California goldminers hoped to strike it rich.

the mining camps. But the miners of 1849 came to a state whose potential wealth in agriculture, timber, and trade would far exceed the riches of the mother lode.

In 1848, California's population was about 116,000, most of which (110,000) was Indian. Three decades after the Gold Rush, the population was one-half million, but the Indians had been reduced to about 30,000. To some extent, the number of Indians in California had declined during the Spanish and Mexican periods from diseases brought by the colonizers, but the Indian population plummeted in the early years of U.S. occupation through massacres. One of Fremont's expeditions reported, "We killed plenty of game and an occasional Indian. We made it a rule to spare none of the bucks."

Almost all of the Indian, Spanish, and Mexican cultures were swept aside by the onrushing American civilization. The most obvious remnants today are the names of some of our major cities: San Francisco, San Jose, Monterey, Santa Barbara, Los Angeles, San Bernardino, and San Diego. The missions, Old Town in San Diego, Olvera Street in Los Angeles, old Monterey, and some Indian reservations are reminders of the past. Although the first constitution of 1849 required that all laws be published in Spanish as well as English, that requirement was dropped in the second constitution of 1879. California quickly became part of the American culture.

The Railroad-Land Boom

When the Central Pacific Railroad joined the Union Pacific at Promontory Point, Utah, in May 1869, California was finally linked by land to the rest of the nation. Before this, travelers to California journeyed by sailing ship, stagecoach, wagon, horse, or foot. Most trade was carried by sail south around Cape Horn or across the Isthmus of Panama. But the ocean route was slow and dangerous. At best, in the mid-1860s, it took twenty-one days to get from the Atlantic coast to California by ship. The overland stage from Tipton, Missouri, to San Francisco took twenty-five days—subject to delays from Indian attacks or floods.

On completion of the railroad, California was open to massive migration. Many immigrants were drawn to Southern California by the promise of its healthful climate. One writer of the time noted, "The purity of the air of Los Angeles is remarkable. . . . The air . . . gives to the individual a stimulus and vital force which only an atmosphere so pure can ever communicate" (Dumke, 1944, p. 32). But most came in search of inexpensive land. The railroad received more than 10 million acres of land from the federal government as a construction reward, much of it in Southern California. Wanting to "cash out" its holdings, Southern Pacific flooded the country with sales propaganda. If a person were willing to buy Southern Pacific land in California, the railroad paid for the trip.

The land boom was significant in developing Southern California because, until then, most migration had been to the northern part of the state—first for gold, later for jobs. Los Angeles was a tough cow town in the mid-1850s; the murder rate was one a day—an ominous figure when we consider the county only had 5,000 people! But the land boom brought thousands of people to Southern California in the 1870s–1880s. By the 1890s, the region had begun to grow at a much faster rate than Northern California, and this pattern continued through much of this century. (Today, the two regions are growing commensurately.) The California land boom collapsed suddenly in 1888. Inflated prices, speculation, and the beginning of a national depression ended Southern California's first real estate boom.

Black Gold

The first oil rig drilled in California was in Petrolia in Humboldt County in the far northwestern part of the state. Between 1900 and 1940, a series of oil discoveries in Southern California stimulated land speculation and population growth. And in the late 1920s, offshore drilling and production began at Summerland, near Santa Barbara. Until the 1960s, California's oil production exceeded state needs; millions of barrels were exported each year to other states. Since 1968, however, production has declined while demand has increased.

California State Library

Chinese labor built much of the railroad that linked California to the rest of the nation. These workers are riding a woodburning train in the Bloomer cut, Placer County, California.

Today, only about half (47 percent) the oil consumed in the state is produced here; the remainder is imported from Alaska (46 percent) and Indonesia (7 percent). California imports no oil from the Middle East. Most of California's own oil production is found in Kern, Los Angeles, and Ventura counties (71, 13, and 4 percent, respectively).

The Military–Defense Industry Boom

Before World War II, the military had not been a significant presence in the state. But during the war, hundreds of thousands of soldiers were trained and stationed here, and of even greater importance, California became a major war-production and shipping center. More than a half million people were drawn by work opportunities in the war plants, and others came to take new jobs created by a booming economy.

After the end of the war in 1945, hundreds of thousands of servicemen discharged from military duty decided to stay in the Golden State, and thousands of others who went home soon returned.

POPULATION DIVERSITY

From the early years of California statehood to the present, California has always had a diverse ethnic mix.

Native Americans

California is home to more than 200,000 Native Americans, the second largest American Indian population of any state (Oklahoma is first). Some live on reservations in remote areas, such as the Hoopa of Humboldt and Trinity counties and the Wintu of Colusa County; others live in or near major urban areas. Poverty, unemployment, illiteracy, alcoholism, and poor health care remain significant problems. Many Indians have been largely assimilated or intermarried with non-native Americans. And tribes struggle to maintain their language, customs, and traditions in modern California. Legalized gambling has become a major revenue source for many tribes. At issue are state gambling regulations versus Indian gaming rights on federal lands. Another issue of concern to Native Americans is their ancestors' sacred skeletal remains, which are frequently housed in museums and university laboratories. Under prodding by Indian groups and recent legislation, these laboratories and museums have begun repatriating collections of bones unearthed in various archaeological digs.

Asians

People of Asian ancestry now constitute about 9 percent of the state's population, and their overall percentage will continue to grow based on population projections. This diverse Asian population includes many nationalities.

Filipinos Filipinos constitute the single largest Asian group in California: about 27 percent of all Asians in the state. Thousands of Filipinos emigrated to California during the early part of the twentieth century seeking work on farms or in factories, and many continue to come. The Philippines ranks second only to Mexico as a source of foreign immigration to California.

Chinese During the Gold Rush, some 25,000 Chinese came to California. Thousands more were brought in the 1860s to work on railroad-construction crews under labor contracts that nearly constituted a debt-bondage system. The growing Chinese population created concern among unemployed whites. Sub-

Library of Congress

Japanese American children wait to be sent to an Owens Valley relocation center.

jected to brutal harassment and discrimination, many Chinese returned to China, and the Chinese Exclusion Act of 1881 stopped further immigration for a time. Since the 1920s, however, California's Chinese population has grown steadily, today making up about 26 percent of the state's Asian population. Former Democrat Secretary of State March Fong Eu, now ambassador to Micronesia, and her son, Republican State Treasurer Matt Fong, are the state's leading Chinese American politicians.

Japanese The numbers of Japanese immigrants increased dramatically in the early part of this century, and racist pressures for their expulsion soon began. What particularly irritated many white Californians was Japanese success in agriculture. In 1924, Congress excluded further Japanese immigration.

After the imperial Japanese attack on Pearl Harbor in 1941 and U.S. entrance into World War II, and because of the perceived threat of a Japanese invasion of the U.S. mainland, many Americans believed that Japanese Americans were a potential enemy within. In 1942, under the authority of the national War Relocation Authority, some 112,000 Japanese (71,000 of them U.S. citizens) living on the West Coast were uprooted to remote relocation centers and confined behind barbed wire. Many lost homes, businesses, and farms in the abrupt evacuation. During the war, some young Japanese American men volunteered for service in the U.S. Army. A special Nisei unit serving in Europe was one of the most decorated in the U.S. Army. At the end of the war, the relocation centers were closed and camp inmates began the difficult process of rebuilding their shattered lives. In 1988, the U.S. government officially apologized for its disgraceful treatment of Japanese Americans during the war and agreed to compensate those interned or their family survivors $20,000 per internee.

Japanese Americans now constitute 11 percent of the state's Asian population. They are among the best educated and most affluent nationality groups in California. Two Japanese Americans, Democrats Bob Matsui and Norm Mineta, are California congressmembers.

Koreans   Korean Americans are a significant part of the state's Asian population at some 10 percent. Korean immigration to California increased sharply after the Korean War. Much of the wrath of black rioters in the 1991 Los Angeles conflagration was directed toward Korean shopkeepers, who were often reluctant to hire local African Americans to work in their stores in the black ghetto.

Vietnamese   Few Vietnamese lived in this country before 1970, but U.S. involvement in the Vietnam War, the need to save thousands of South Vietnamese allies from communist capture after our forced withdrawal from that country, and an exodus of thousands of "boat people" fleeing postwar Vietnam produced hundreds of thousands of new immigrants to the United States—with the great majority settling in California. About 10 percent of the state's Asian population is Vietnamese. Thousands of refugees from Cambodia and Laos, also uprooted by the Vietnam War and its aftermath, have come to California as well (7 percent of the state's Asian population).

Other Asians   In addition to the groups above, California has sizable numbers of Taiwanese, East Asian Indian, Thai, and Pacific Islander residents.

Latinos

According to the California Department of Finance, as of 1994 about 32 percent of the state's population was Latino—nearly 8 million people (about 75 percent are of Mexican origin). Mexican Americans constitute the largest single minority in California. In addition, thousands of other Latinos have immigrated from Central American countries, particularly Guatemala, El Salvador, and Nicaragua. These countries faced considerable turmoil in the late 1980s and early 1990s with civil wars, death squads, and economic disintegration.

Although a few thousand Mexicans lived in California when it was part of Mexico, the first major wave of Mexican immigrants came to California (and other Southwestern states) as a result of the Mexican Revolution in 1910. Exclusion of Japanese and Chinese migrants created a demand for cheap farm labor, which was filled by Mexicans.

World War II created a tremendous need for new farm labor again, and more Mexicans came to California—some illegally. These workers were often subjected to abuse and prejudicial actions. In 1951, the Mexican and U.S. governments signed an agreement to regulate migration and protect Mexican workers. Under this agreement, hundreds of thousands of "braceros" worked as laborers on California farms. But under pressure from organized labor, the bracero agreement was terminated in 1964. The anti-Latino prejudice was apparent in voter approval of Proposition 38 in 1984, which required that all voting materials be printed in English only in the state. (Federal law supersedes this state law and the latter is not in effect.) And in a similar vein, in 1986 state voters massively approved Proposition 63, which mandated English as the state's official language. There have also been constant attacks on bilingual education programs across the state. Prejudice was also present in the battle over Proposition 187 of 1994 (to be discussed later).

In 1986 and after years of debate, Congress passed the Simpson Immigration Reform Act. The act provided for strict sanctions and fines against employers who hired undocumented workers. In addition, the law granted amnesty to illegals living in the country before 1982 and to seasonal agricultural workers who had worked a minimum of ninety days before May 1, 1986, enabling them to apply for citizenship. Finally, the act allowed for the admission of several hundred thousand temporary "green card" farm laborers to work for a specific time in the United States and then return to Mexico.

The Simpson Act only briefly slowed the flow of undocumented workers entering the United States, and their numbers are as great today as in 1985 before Simpson. Illegal immigration was at the center of debate in the 1994 governor's race. Governor Wilson brought suit in federal court demanding $14 billion from the federal government for the costs of educating, incarcerating, and providing emergency health care to foreign nationals since 1988. Wilson and most other Republican officeseekers in 1994 also supported Proposition 187, the illegal immigrant initiative. The proposition's main objective was to bar educational,

Mary Kate Denny / PhotoEdit

Latinos are the largest minority within the state population.

health, and welfare services to illegals and to require school administrators, health officials, and police to report suspected illegals to federal immigration authorities. Proponents argued that the measure would send a message to the federal government. Kathleen Brown, Democratic gubernatorial candidate, and other Democratic politicians conceded that illegal immigration had become a critical issue, but they characterized Proposition 187 as excessively repressive and blatantly racist. Democrats argued that more border patrol officers, stricter surveillance, and tougher fines on employers of illegals should be undertaken. In any case, Proposition 187 was overwhelmingly approved by voters, 59 to 41 percent. The illegal immigration issue contributed significantly to Wilson's gubernatorial defeat of Kathleen Brown. The initiative was quickly challenged in court, and its implementation, if ever, may involve years of legal wrangle. The U. S. Supreme Court had previously ruled in 1982 in *Plyler v. Doe* that all children living in the United States, legal or illegal, have a right to a public education under the equal protection clause of the Fourteenth Amendment.

Typical Latinos are young and have less formal education than the average California resident. Only 25 percent have finished high school. Relative to their population numbers, Latinos are underrepresented in the state's university sys-

YEAR	% ASIAN/ OTHER	% AFRICAN AMERICAN	% LATINO	% WHITE– ANGLO
1970	3	7	12	78
1980	7	8	19	66
1990	10	7	26	57
2000	10	7	32	51
2010	11	7	36	46
2020	12	6	41	41

TABLE 2.1 ETHNIC COMPOSITION OF THE CALIFORNIA POPULATION BY DECADE
Source: Department of Finance, Population Research Unit, 1993.

tem. They are also underrepresented in state and local elective positions. In 1994, for the first time this century, a Latino, Democrat Art Torres, was nominated for statewide office as insurance commissioner, although he lost in the general election to Republican Chuck Quackenbush. Growing numbers of Latinos have been elected to the state legislature over the last several years, however, and Latino political impact is definitely growing.

Dust Bowl Victims

Oklahoma, Arkansas, and other plains states were swept by drought in the 1930s. Many displaced "Okies" and "Arkies" came in search of jobs, which were scare everywhere. Some ended up toiling in the Central Valley's fields.

African Americans

World War II's booming economy lured millions of African Americans away from their Southern homes. Many thousands came to California during the 1940s to work in defense plants. The African American portion of the state's population grew steadily from the 1940s through the 1960s, but it has leveled off since 1970 to about 7 percent of the state's overall population. This percentage is projected to remain fairly stable for the foreseeable future (see Table 2.1).

Two of three African Americans live in central cities, and many reside in ghettos such as Watts or Hunter's Point. On average, African Americans have less formal education and earn substantially less than whites. Since the civil rights struggle of the 1960s, African Americans have succeeded in winning many seats on city councils and boards of supervisors, in the state legislature, and in the state congressional delegation. Willie Brown, the long-time speaker of the California assembly, is the most prominent African American politician in the state.

Carl Myers

Japanese autos and kosher burritos: California's cosmopolitan culture mix can be found in many of its urban areas.

Future Population Patterns

California continues to be the most popular haven for new immigrants to this nation. In the next century, the state will be the first on the mainland with a white–Anglo proportion less than 50 percent of total population. As the white percentage declines and the black percentage remains stable, explosive growth will come within the Asian and Latino communities triggered by high birthrates and sizable foreign immigration. The state's growing ethnic diversity is reflected in dozens of foreign-language newspapers and radio and television stations.

The spectacular population growth in California of non–English-speaking Latinos and Asians presents local and state governments with major challenges in providing essential services to these newcomers. New schools must be built and new teachers hired, programs must be launched to help immigrants learn

English and become acquainted with the American political and social culture, and more welfare assistance and job-training programs are needed. Money to pay for these additional costs must come out of a sorely strained state budget.

Finally, defining race can be complicated. How should the millions of children born of racially different parents—white–black, white–Asian, Latino–Native American, for example—define their own race? Are Arab-Americans white or Asian? Should Native Americans be considered Asian? Should Spanish or Portuguese Americans be considered Latino? Should California Supreme Court Judge Joyce Kennard—born in Indonesia to Dutch–Asian parents during World War II, raised in the Netherlands, and immigrating to the United States in her early adult life—be considered Asian or white? Is a person who is 1/16 Cherokee and 15/16 white a Native American? And given that affirmative action programs attempt to rebalance historic injustices, this is not simply a problem in semantics. Perhaps someday we'll need only one classification: human.

POLITICS OF THE PEOPLE

To understand California politics today, we must be aware of the past. The following brief historical overview describes significant historical events in the state that have had a lasting impact on its politics.

Throughout California's history, political power has shifted back and forth: Democrats have dominated politically in some periods, Republicans in others, and, for long stretches of time, the two parties have competed equally. We can divide California political history into eight periods:

1. Statehood, Democratic dominance (1850–1861)
2. Civil War, Republican dominance (1862–1867)
3. Two-party competition before reform (1868–1897)
4. Emerging Progressive–Republican reform (1898–1923)
5. Republican dominance (1924–1957)
6. Two-party competition (1958–1973)
7. Democratic dominance (1974–1982)
8. Two-party competition (1983–?)

1850–1867

The early years of California history had little impact on the contemporary world of state politics. The first constitution was approved, and battles between pro-and antislavery forces were an overridding concern. Democrats were the dominant party in the first decade after statehood, but Republicans took control in the 1860s during the Civil War.

1868–1897

In the latter half of the nineteenth century, the owners of the Southern Pacific Railroad (called the Central Pacific before 1884)—Leland Stanford, Charles Crocker, Mark Hopkins, and Collis Huntington, or the "Big Four"—dominated California's economy and government by controlling transportation into, out of, and within the state. All four men became major economic powers in the state. Today, their names are institutionalized in a major university, a bank chain, a leading art gallery, and hotels. Their greed and corrupt politics, however, contributed to the rise of two major nineteenth-century protest movements: the Workingman's party and Populism.

Chinese workers were brought to the state in the late 1800s to work on railroad construction. When the work was completed, the Chinese moved to various Western communities looking for work. Unemployed white workers resented the job competition, particularly because the Chinese were willing to work for lower wages. White animosity gave rise to a xenophobic fear that Asians would take Anglos' jobs and soon control the state. The Workingman's party, led by Denis Kearney, was a protest response.

Kearneyism (as it was known) promoted reformist goals such as state regulation of railroads, utilities, and banks; a fair tax system; an eight-hour workday; compulsory education; and the direct election of U.S. senators. But it also featured another plank in its platform: "The Chinese Must Go." As California's economy improved and some of Kearney's proposed reforms were adopted by state government, the Workingman's party soon disappeared.

The late nineteenth-century Populist party was a mixture of agrarian reformers, nonpartisans, and socialists. Though never achieving significant political power, they held the balance of power between Democrats and Republicans. Populists helped to make several reforms popular. They were early advocates of women's suffrage, railroad regulation, monetary reform ("free silver"), municipal ownership of utilities, the secret ballot, the initiative, the referendum, the recall, direct primaries, income tax, and unemployment relief. Many of their reforms were later incorporated by Progressives.

1898–1923

In 1898, California Republicans elected their candidate for governor and captured control of both houses of the legislature. However, their reign was short-lived. By the early 1900s, the Progressives, initially a reform faction of the GOP, became increasingly assertive in promoting their causes in the state.

In the early 1900s, the leadership of both the Republican and Democratic parties came under the influence of the Southern Pacific Railroad and its corporate allies. As Fremont Older noted (1926, p. 61), "In those days there was only one kind of politics and that was corrupt politics. It didn't matter whether a man was a Republican or a Democrat. The Southern Pacific Railroad controlled both parties. . . ."

Besides Southern Pacific's machinations, another corrupt force—the political boss—emerged in California during this era. Across the country—Boston, New York City, Chicago, Kansas City, and San Francisco—corrupt big-city bosses and their political machines controlled urban politics. Using ballot fraud, kickbacks, patronage, and extortion, these minidictator bosses plundered their cities. On occasion, they did distribute food baskets to the poor and provide assistance to foreign immigrants at a time when there were no federal or state public assistance programs.

In San Francisco, Boss Abe Ruef controlled the city and engaged in a variety of corrupt activities. Ruef was eventually indicted by San Francisco reformers. His bribery trial received heightened publicity when the prosecuting attorney was brazenly shot and killed in the courtroom by a prospective juror. Hiram Johnson, an obscure attorney at that time, replaced the slain prosecutor and helped secure Ruef's conviction.

Appalled by the extent of corruption in California politics and by the need for social and economic improvement, a small group of reform Republicans began a statewide campaign to eliminate Southern Pacific control and implement reforms. The Progressive reform movement was national in scope, but these reformers made their greatest gains in the newer, Western states where boss machines were not as deeply entrenched as in the East. From 1911 to 1923, Progressive Republicans controlled California; nationally, Theodore Roosevelt was their spiritual leader.

Under Progressive pressure, in 1909 the California legislature adopted a direct primary nomination system. This allowed party registrants to *elect* their party's nominees instead of having them chosen by party leaders at state conventions. In the spring of 1910, in the first primary election conducted in the state, four "regular" Republicans and a Progressive Republican, Hiram Johnson, all filed for governor in the GOP (Grand Old Party) primary. Building on his publicity from the Ruef trial and growing voter discontent with the railroad and its cronies, and because Southern Pacific failed to put its support behind one of the four regulars, Hiram Johnson captured the Republican nomination. In his fall campaign against his Democratic opponent, Johnson toured the state with his battle cry, "Kick the Southern Pacific machine out of California politics." He described Harrison Gray Otis, owner of the *Los Angeles Times*, this way: "He sits in senile dementia, with gangrened heart and rotting brain, grimacing at every reform and chattering in impotent rage against decency and morality, while he is going down to his grave in snarling infamy" (Delmatier, McIntosh, and Waters, 1970, p. 168).

Johnson won the race and was sworn in as governor. Equally important, Progressive candidates won control of the state assembly and state senate. This gave them the power to put into the state constitution the most comprehensive and far-reaching political reforms ever enacted in California history.

Though Progressives were in power for only a few years, their legacy is enormous. Among their social reforms were prohibiting child labor, instituting a workman's compensation system, providing free school texts, adopting the eight-hour workday, and expanding conservation programs. Even more important were their political reforms, which involved significant changes in the processes of government:

1. direct-democracy legislation—the initiative and referendum
2. the recall
3. the direct primary system and a presidential preference primary
4. nonpartisan local elections
5. political party organizations regulated by state election code
6. the civil service
7. cross-filing
8. the Australian secret ballot
9. the short ballot
10. women's suffrage
11. the direct election of U.S. senators
12. the establishment of a state railroad commission.

Of these reforms, only cross-filing has been eliminated, although recent court rulings give political parties greater control over their own organizational structure. The other reforms continue to exert substantial influence on state politics.

For a time, Progressive reforms reduced corruption and special-interest power in the state. But in 1916, Hiram Johnson was elected to the U.S. Senate. His departure from state government left Progressives leaderless. By 1921, regular Republicans regained control of the party. By the late 1920s, special interests were as active as ever, and by the 1930s and 1940s, they had reached new heights of power (see Chapter 5).

1924–1957

In the 1920s and early 1930s, Democrats continued as the minority party. They had less than 30 percent of the two-party registration and fewer than 10 percent of the state's legislative seats. All major statewide officers were Republicans.

California State Library

Hiram Johnson speaks on the campaign trail. Without television or radio in 1910, candidates appeared in person.

The mid-1930s and Great Depression brought massive economic, social, and political change to the nation and California. Democratic registration increased dramatically as millions of unemployed and blue-collar workers gave strong support to Democratic President Franklin Delano Roosevelt's New Deal Program. Democratic registration rose dramatically in the 1930s, but the increase in the number of Democratic voters did not translate into many election victories for California Democratic candidates from the 1930s into the 1950s.

Why were Democrats unable to take advantage of their registered voter majority? First, on average, Democrat voters do not turn out to vote as conscientiously as do Republicans. Second, many registered Democrats had moved to California from Southern and border states and tended to be conservative (Republican) philosophically. Third, some Democrats had moved to the state from cities where Democrats had strong local organizations to turn out the vote; there was little precinct organization to get out the vote in California. Fourth, many of the major newspapers of the state were Republican-owned, and they endorsed Republican candidates. Fifth, GOP candidates were often better financed or were incumbents with good name identification. And sixth, cross-filing, a Progressive reform, allowed candidates of one party to file also in the other's primary (the intent was to allow voters the opportunity to choose the "best person," not just candidates who happened to belong to a voter's party).

Although some Democratic incumbents took advantage of the process, Republican candidates overall tended to thrive under cross-filing. Moreover, because the ballot had no designation to inform voters which party a candidate was actually affiliated with, some uninformed Democrats merely voted for the familiar name among the candidates, unaware that they were voting for a Republican. By the 1940s and 1950s, approximately 75 percent of legislative candidates were able to win not only their own party's primary but also the other party's. These successful cross-filers had no opponents on the November general election ballot; they were listed as "John Doe Republican–Democratic Assembly candidate." So, even though Republican registration was well below Democratic registration during this era, GOP legislative and statewide candidates continued to win most of the elections. Cross-filing was eventually modified by initiative in 1952 and abolished in 1959 by a Democratic legislature and governor. However, a newly qualified initiative on the March 1996 ballot, the "open primary" law, would allow voters to choose any party's candidates in the primary.

1958–1973

The 1958 elections ended thirty-five years of Republican rule in California and launched a period of intense two-party competition. As noted, Democrats became more competitive with the demise of cross-filing (see Figure 2.1). During this period, Democrats had solid majorities in the legislature, but Republicans often scored victories in major statewide races. Moderate Republicans led the GOP during the 1930s and 1940s, but conservatives took control in the 1950s and have held on to power ever since.

In 1964, conservative U.S. Senator Barry Goldwater of Arizona beat moderate New York Governor Nelson Rockefeller in the California Republican primary. Goldwater captured the GOP nomination but lost to Democrat Lyndon Johnson in the general election. Actor Ronald Reagan traveled with the Goldwater campaign and quickly became one of the conservative movement's most prominent spokespersons. Reagan's affability, quick-study knowledge of the issues, Hollywood persona, and ability to project an image of righteous indignation were attractive to voters. After encouragement from party leaders and major contributors, Reagan filed as a Republican candidate for governor in the June 1966 primary. Though he had never run for public office, his "amateur" status became a political asset. Reagan ran as a citizen-candidate against the professional politicians in Sacramento. He won the Republican primary and went on to face

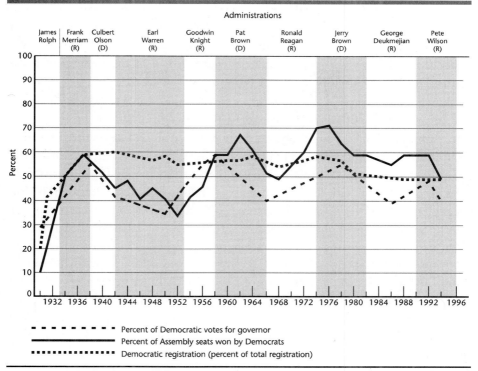

FIGURE 2.1   DEMOCRATIC PARTY STRENGTH, 1930–1994
Source: California Secretary of State, *Statement of Vote,* 1930–1994

incumbent Democratic Governor Pat Brown in the fall campaign. Unfortunately for Brown, California Democrats were badly divided over President Johnson's Vietnam policies, and race riots in Watts and Hunter's Point in 1965 created further tension in the state. Hurt by attacks from both left and right, Brown was no match for Ronald Reagan, but Democrats continued to control the legislature, the congressional delegation, and many other statewide offices.

Ironically, although pledging to "cut, trim, and squeeze" the state budget, Reagan presided over one of the largest tax increases in state history. Part of this increase was mandated by a state Supreme Court decision, *Serrano v. Priest,* to equalize public school funding. Additional tax revenues were required to meet the state's MediCal and welfare programs. Reagan's popularity with voters continued through his two terms from 1966–1974, but Democrats continued to maintain legislative majorities and control of most statewide offices.

In 1968, Democratic President Lyndon Johnson's decision not to seek reelection led to a nomination contest between Vice President Hubert Humphrey and

U.S. Senators Robert Kennedy and Eugene McCarthy. The conflict over the Vietnam War, the murder of Senator Kennedy on primary election night in California, and riots at the Democratic national convention helped pave the road to presidential victory for Californian Richard Nixon in the general election against Democratic nominee Hubert Humphrey.

Democratic Dominance: 1974–1982

The Watergate scandal engulfed and destroyed Nixon and devastated the state GOP in 1974. Republicans during this period held only twenty-three seats in the eighty-member assembly, and GOP party registration dropped to a historic low of 34 percent. Faced with the clear probability of impeachment, President Nixon resigned in August 1974, shattering state GOP election hopes.

Proposition 9, the Political Reform Act initiative of 1974, qualified for the ballot because of growing public concern over lobbying abuses, campaign contribution influence-peddling, and Watergate. The initiative was overwhelmingly approved by voters in November, even though both parties and virtually all special interests opposed it.

Democrat Jerry Brown (son of former Governor Pat Brown) was elected governor in 1974 (he had previously served as secretary of state). His campaign emphasized the need for cleaning up state politics, and he was a co-author of the Political Reform Act initiative.

In the 1970s, the state's growing nonwhite population began to assert itself politically. In 1970, Wilson Riles became the first African American to win election to a statewide office: superintendent of public instruction. He was joined in 1974 by Mervin Dymally, the state's first African American lieutenant governor and March Fong Eu, the first Asian elected to statewide office (secretary of state). Nearly a dozen African American, Latino, and women state legislators were elected in the mid-1970s.

Brown won reelection easily in 1978. However, the bigger story that year was the Howard Jarvis and Paul Gann Proposition 13 property-tax relief initiative, which qualified for the June primary ballot. Proposition 13 was opposed by most state political and economic leaders because they were convinced it would destroy local government's tax base, reduce or eliminate some local government services, and make local government dependent on state government for revenue. Most voters viewed Proposition 13 as needed relief from excessive taxes. Jarvis and Gann argued that essential services would not have to be cut if local governments would only cut the waste from their budgets. Proposition 13 was decisively approved by voters that June. After leading the opposition to Proposition 13, Governor Jerry Brown became zealous in implementing it. The proposition's popularity also helped elect a new contingent of eight ultraconservative Republican state legislators, the "Prop. 13 Babies." Republicans, though still a minority in the legislature, began to rebound from their Watergate low.

In 1980, former California Republican Governor Ronald Reagan easily defeated unpopular Democratic incumbent President Jimmy Carter. Reagan's victory was partly personal but also indicative of the growing popularity of conservative issues among the electorate in California and across the nation. Reagan ran as a proven tax cutter against "big government."

1983–?

Increasingly in the 1980s and 1990s, initiatives are center stage in California politics. Virtually all major issues of the day have been battled by initiative: reapportionment, term limits, AIDS, the homeless, welfare, taxes, the governor's budget powers, vouchers, handgun control, auto insurance, the environment, and lawyer fees. The November 1994 election was typical. Almost dwarfing the governor's contest were battles over initiatives dealing with illegal immigration, "three strikes" (that is, third-time felons are automatically sentenced to twenty-five years to life in prison), tobacco, and the single-payer health system.

In the 1980s and early 1990s, Republican party fortunes clearly revived. Democrats continue to hold a registration advantage over Republicans, but the difference has narrowed. For the first time since the 1950s, Democratic registration in the early 1990s dipped below 50 percent. However, because of partisan reapportioning in the 1980s and intraparty strife in Republican ranks between the Christian right and moderates, Democrats continued to win most elections to the state legislature, Congress, and lesser statewide offices—until 1994. Throughout this period, however, California Republicans did well in presidential contests (Reagan in 1980 and 1984 and Bush in 1988 captured the state's electoral votes) and were competitive in campaigns for major statewide office: governor, U.S. senator, and attorney general.

In 1990, moderate Pete Wilson continued Republican control of the governorship by beating Democrat Dianne Feinstein. Wilson's popularity was enhanced by his tough stance on crime and his support for the new political reform: term limits (Proposition 140). Democrats once again controlled the legislature, although conservative Republican Dan Lungren was elected attorney general.

In 1992, Democrat Bill Clinton decisively beat President George Bush. For the first time since 1964, California went Democratic in a presidential election. Clinton, however, won a plurality of the vote, not a majority, because independent presidential candidate Ross Perot captured almost 20 percent of the vote. The billionaire Perot spent lavishly in his losing effort. Many voters in California and

Campaign Committee for Proposition 9

across the nation were willing to abandon traditional party ties and cast protest votes for Perot. Republicans still failed to gain more state legislative or congressional seats in 1992, even though the Deukmejian–Wilson Supreme Court had reapportioned districts for the 1992 election.

After decades of political gridlock, scandals, expensive campaigns, and unrelenting media negativism, voter cynicism and anger were high in the early 1990s. Conspiracy theories were rampant. Many in the public responded by not voting, and others responded by voting "no" on most issues—particularly bond issues or tax increases. The ready acceptance California voters gave to two drastic term limits initiatives (Propositions 140 and 164) was expressive of this anger. So, too, was the large vote for Perot.

The conservative, Republican, antigovernment tide crested in the 1994 election. Pete Wilson, though unpopular with voters, was viewed as the "lesser of two evils" and easily defeated Democrat Kathleen Brown. Although Republican conservatives were angry about Wilson's acceptance of a 1991 state tax hike and for being prochoice, his dogged support for "three strikes," term limits, and the illegal-immigration initiative helped him win reelection. The major conservative issues of the day—"three strikes" and illegal immigration—passed easily, while the liberal issue—the single-payer health system—was overwhelmed. For the first time in forty years, majority control in Congress shifted to the Republicans. Not a single Republican incumbent running for federal office lost, but dozens of Democrats did. And those who survived the bloody onslaught found their winning margins reduced (Dianne Feinstein beat Michael Huffington 47 to 46 percent). Republicans took control of some statewide offices and achieved virtual parity in the assembly, senate, and congressional delegation. Given the mercurial nature of today's voters, it is uncertain whether the 1994 election was an anomaly or whether Republicans have long-term control in California.

SUMMARY

California's population growth and growing ethnic diversity have meant constantly changing social and political patterns. Latino and Asian populations have grown steadily, while the Anglo–white population has steadily declined.

In the early decades of this century, Republicans were dominant. Democratic strength began to build in the 1930s, but not until the late 1950s were they able to capture the legislature and elect many statewide officers. Democrats became the ascendant party in the 1960s and 1970s, particularly during the Watergate period, but more recently the parties have been relatively competitive.

As the population and economy changed during the Depression, World War II, the great postwar economic boom, and the economic doldrums of the 1980s and 1990s, the people's needs and issues also changed.

Two features are immutable in California politics: change and reform.

NOTE

1. Spanish treatment of Native Americans is a subject of ongoing controversy. On occasion, Indians were whipped, put in leg restraints, and locked up for various offenses, although these punishments were also found in British colonies of that era. Indeed, the military governor of California, Felipe de Neve, reported in 1780 that the Franciscans treated Indians so harshly that their situation was worse than slavery. Efforts are now underway by some in the Catholic community to make Father Serra, the founder of nine California missions, a saint. Many Indian activists, however, adamantly oppose his canonization.

REFERENCES

Bernstein, Dan. "Wilson Suit Claims Immigrant 'Invasion.'" *Sacramento Bee*, September 23, 1994, p. A6.

Delmatier, Royce D., Clarence F. McIntosh, and Earl G. Waters. *The Rumble of California Politics.* New York: Wiley, 1970.

Dumke, Glen S. *Boom of the Eighties in Southern California.* New York: Ward-Ritchie, 1944.

Mowry, George E. *The California Progressives.* Los Angeles: University of California Press, 1951.

Older, Fremont. *My Own Story.* New York: Macmillan, 1926.

ELECTIONS IN CALIFORNIA

VOTERS, CANDIDATES, AND CAMPAIGNS

WHO MAY VOTE

To be eligible to vote in California, first you must be a citizen of the United States. A U.S. citizen is anyone born in this country (Fourteenth Amendment) or born of a U.S. citizen abroad, or one who has been naturalized. Second, you must be a resident of California. Third, you must be at least 18 years old by the day of the election. Those in prison or on parole for felony convictions cannot vote. People convicted of lesser crimes do not lose their right to vote. Once a felon's parole period is completed, he or she is eligible to register to vote. In addition, appropriate courts determine on a case-by-case basis whether particular individuals with mental problems should be allowed to vote.

Citizens must register and list their residence at least twenty-nine days before the election to be eligible to vote. Registration is permanent in California. There is no purging of election rolls of citizens who don't vote in particular elections. However, if people move (millions do each year in this state), change their names, or shift party affiliation, they must re-register.

Before 1970, Californians had to prove they could read the Constitution and write their names before they could register. This discouraged some foreign-born citizens from registering. This is no longer the case. Indeed, the Elections Code now stipulates that non-English citizens "should be encouraged to vote." Yet in 1990, Orange County Republican leaders, fearing that noncitizens would attempt to vote (Democrat), sent uniformed private security officers to polling places to monitor voting. Democrats protested, contending that the presence of these officers was an attempt to discourage Latinos and Asians from voting.

Each county has a registrar of voters (smaller counties use the county clerk) to maintain a list of registered voters. Before the state primary and general elections, the registrar or clerk assigns deputies to supermarkets, shopping centers, churches, university and college campuses, sports events, and the like to register those interested. Civic groups such as the League of Women Voters also help register voters. One can even register by postcard. Department of Motor Vehicles (DMV) offices currently provide registration forms. Under new federal rules that began in 1995, DMV offices now ask those not registered if they would like to do so.[1]

Political parties also conduct registration drives. The National Republican and National Democratic party committees pump money to local state activists for drives to get "their" people registered. Such money does not count against the parties' federal spending limits (it's called "soft money"). In California, both parties often subcontract with companies to collect registrations for them—$3 to $5 per signing. Obviously, Democratic party officials won't pay for Republican signings, or vice versa. Fraud is possible with these "headhunter" entrepreneurs who seek to sign up people for profit.

Counties vary widely in the percentage of registered voters. In San Francisco, 89 percent of those eligible are registered, but in Tulare, Kings, and Imperial counties, less than 60 percent. Registration rate increases with education, income, and age.

WHO MAY RUN

To be eligible to run for public office in California one must:

1. **be a U.S. citizen.**
2. **be a resident of the state.** A candidate running for a district office, such as Board of Equalization or state legislature, must be a district resident. In the old days, one year of residency was required before a person could file to run in a particular district, but now the candidate must only be a district resident when receiving nomination papers.
3. **be a registered voter of the party whose nomination one seeks.** For nonpartisan offices (superintendent of public instruction or judge), party affiliation is not required. Independents, though, can run for partisan offices. If sufficient numbers of registered voters sign their petition papers, their names go on the general election ballot and they run against the nominees of the various parties for the particular office. Currently, two members of the state senate, Quentin Kopp and Lucy Killea, and one recently recalled assemblymember, Paul Horcher, are independents.

A potential candidate qualifies for the ballot by first filing a declaration of intent with the county clerk, in effect saying, "I intend to run for the office of ————." The potential candidate then must file a petition with a small number of signatures of registered voters who assert that they support the candidacy. For example, a candidate for the assembly needs the signatures of forty members of his or her political party in that district as sponsors. Finally, the potential candidate must pay a filing fee or substitute an additional petition with more signatures. The filing fee is 2 percent of the annual salary for statewide office, 1 percent for other offices. For example, 1 percent of an assemblymember's salary of $75,600 is $756. If a candidate either cannot afford to pay this fee or wants to indicate broad community support, then he or she can collect signatures of 1,500 registered voters in the district in lieu of the filing fee.

Getting on the ballot in California is easy, but getting elected is another matter. In an average election year in the 1990s, 330 candidates will file for the 80-member assembly. About 60 of these will be third-party candidates with no real chance of getting elected, and nearly all Democratic and Republican candidates running against incumbents will be eliminated in the June primary or the November general election (usually, several incumbents have no opponent). Given the electorate's angry mood, incumbency is not the advantage it once was. All state elected officials today are restricted by term limits, and in the future more districts will be open (no incumbent), encouraging more candidates to file for office.

THE BALLOT

Presidential Ballot

Under California law, the secretary of state compiles a list of presidential candidates for the primary. Those who have qualified for matching dollars under the Federal Election Campaign Act are sure to be included. If a presidential candidate is excluded from the secretary's list, then he or she can try to qualify for the ballot by petition. Usually, fourteen or fifteen presidential candidates are on the primary ballot.

Ballot Form

California uses the office block ballot, presenting competing candidates for each office (see Figure 3.1). This contrasts with the party column ballot used in some states, with competing candidates listed by party membership, and a single vote at the top of the column indicating a vote for all of a party's candidates. California's office block ballot discourages straight-ticket party voting by requiring a separate choice for each office.

A

OFFICIAL BALLOT
GENERAL ELECTION
BUTTE COUNTY
November 8, 1994

MARK YOUR CHOICE(S)
IN THIS MANNER ONLY:

This ballot stub shall be torn off by precinct board
member and handed to the voter.

STATE	
Governor	Vote for One
KATHLEEN BROWN, Democratic Treasurer, State of California	
PETE WILSON, Republican Governor	
RICHARD RIDER, Libertarian Stockbroker/Financial Planner	
JEROME "JERRY" MC CREADY, American Independent Businessman	
GLORIA ESTELA LA RIVA, Peace And Freedom Political Organizer/Printer	

FIGURE 3.1 AN OFFICE BLOCK BALLOT
Source: Butte County Clerk, sample ballot, November
1994

Ballot Position

Until 1974, incumbents were listed first in their office block, giving them an advantage because a few people merely vote for the first name on the ballot. Voter approval of the Political Reform Act initiative of June 1974 eliminated this incumbent advantage. Subsequent court cases and legislation have led to the current system of listing candidates in random order.

Absentee Ballots

Absentee ballots were first used in California during the Civil War by Union soldiers far away from the state on election day. Until 1978, only voters with a compelling excuse could apply for an absentee ballot. Usually, less than 1 percent of the electorate voted absentee. However, a 1978 law to encourage voting now allows anyone to vote absentee with no explanation needed. The number of voters exercising this option has grown steadily. In 1982, absentee ballots provided the winning margin (302,343 votes) for Republican Governor George Deukmejian in his close race with the Democratic candidate, Los Angeles Mayor Tom Bradley. In 1986, absentee ballots accounted for 9 percent of the total vote cast for governor. In 1990, 18 percent of the vote for governor was cast by absentee ballot. And in the 1993 special statewide election, nearly 22 percent voted by absentee ballot. Because of the closeness of several statewide races in 1994 (Feinstein vs. Huffington, Connell vs. McClintock, and Jones vs. Miller), absentee ballots had to be counted before winners were officially declared.

Voting by absentee ballot is more convenient for some people: no lines, less hassle, no worries about parking, and so on. Democratic and Republican party officials and some interest groups have encouraged absentee voting. Party precinct workers go to "their" neighborhoods and ask voters if they would like to vote absentee. If they do, they are provided the forms for and assistance in applying for absentee ballots. Party workers hope their solicitousness will pay off in voting dividends. Moreover, last-minute television campaign attack ads by an opposing party are of little consequence to most absentee voters because their ballots probably have already been mailed. But something is lost in the vote-by-mail procedure: the socializing benefits of voters going to the polls, meeting their neighbors, casting their ballots, and jointly doing their civic duty.

ELECTIONS
Primaries

The partisan primary is designed to select the political party's nominee for a particular office for the general election. Before the primary system was adopted, the state's political parties chose candidates at party conventions. At these conclaves, party leaders were often able to secure the nomination of their choices through manipulation or by packing meetings with supporters. California and many other Progressive Western states were the leaders early this century in promoting the direct primary to allow voters, not party leaders, to elect party nominees. Today, nearly all states use the primary system. However, a few states cling to the convention procedure. Thus, in 1994, Virginia Republicans nominated Oliver North as their U.S. Senate candidate at their state convention. North later lost to Democrat Charles Robb in the general election.

Primary elections are important because they determine not only the party's nominee but also, in many legislative races, the final outcome. Only about one-third of California legislative districts are truly competitive. In the other two-thirds of congressional, assembly, and state senate districts, either Republicans or Democrats have a decided registration advantage—winning the primary means, in effect, winning the election. California also has a closed primary; that is, only those registered in a particular party can vote for that party's candidates in the primary. However, an "open primary" initiative has qualified for the March 1996 ballot. It would allow voters to choose any candidate listed on the primary ballot regardless of party affiliation. Instead of candidates cross-filing, as they used to, voters would be able to do so. Also, under an open primary format, those registering as "decline to state" would be able to vote for party candidates in the primary. Democrats, and perhaps Republicans, might fear raiding by nonparty voters in "their" primary and are likely to be wary of this initiative. If approved and found constitutional, it will have a major impact on the nominating process.

The Green party provides its party registrants a "none of the above" option. If Green registrants don't know or like their party's candidates, they can vote "none of the above." Republicans complained in 1994 that Democrats contributed money in an effort to persuade Green voters to vote "none of the above" for governor in the primary. The Democratic strategy was based on the hope that if Green voters had no actual candidate to vote for as governor, they might vote for Democrat Kathleen Brown in the general election.

Currently, about 10 percent of voter registrants register as "decline to state" and, therefore, they cannot vote in any party's primary. "Decline to state" voters, however, can vote for nonpartisan officers—the superintendent of public instruction or judges—and for ballot measures in the primary.

When an incumbent decides not to seek reelection (or cannot because of term limits), there is usually considerable competition for nomination. Thus, in the 1994 June primary, assembly districts with incumbents averaged 2.3 Republican or Democratic candidates, while open seats attracted an average of six major party candidates. In many open primary contests with a half dozen or more Democratic and Republican candidates, the victor will usually win with a plurality, not a majority of the vote. For example, in the 1994 primary, Kevin Murrary became the Democratic nominee in Assembly District 47 (staunchly Democratic in registration) but received only 21 percent of his party's vote. In Assembly District 65 (a Republican stronghold), Bret Granlund won the GOP primary with only 31 percent of the Republican vote.

General Elections

Excitement is greater and turnout higher in the general election than in the primary. The general election is the payoff of a long, hard campaign. Instead of the primary's more muddled intraparty conflict, the issues are more clear-cut between Democratic and Republican candidates in the general election.

Over the last several decades, statewide campaigns for governor, attorney general, and the U.S. Senate have usually been hard-fought and competitive. The outcome is usually in doubt and the victory margin frequently narrow, particularly if there is no incumbent in the race. For example, in the 1992 U.S. Senate race, Democrat Barbara Boxer captured 48 percent of the vote to Republican Bruce Herschenson's 43 percent. The 1994 general election saw many close races. Because four third parties siphoned some of the vote in these races, plurality victories were common. The 1994 statewide victors who won by plurality were U.S. Senator Dianne Feinstein (D), Secretary of State Bill Jones (R), Controller Kathleen Connell (D), Treasurer Matt Fong (R), and Insurance Commissioner Chuck Quackenbush (R). Democrats had dominated lesser statewide offices until 1994, when Republicans swept many of them away.

Special Elections

A few governors have called special statewide elections, usually to provide momentum to favored issues. Such an election is expensive: about $40 million. Given that turnout tends to be very limited for these elections, and the few who do turn out are mainly white homeowners, conservative ballot measures are sometimes—but not always—helped by this type of election. For example, in 1993 Governor Pete Wilson called a special election for several measures, but voters soundly rejected the conservative Proposition 174 (school voucher).

Legislative special elections are called when an incumbent dies or retires in midterm. These legislative special elections are a kind of hybrid primary and general election. Voters choose from a list of candidates from all of the parties. If one candidate receives 50 percent plus one vote, he or she is elected immediately. If no one receives a majority, a runoff is held four weeks later between the top two vote-getters. The advent of term limits has encouraged some legislators to bail out early if other good job opportunities arise. This, in turn, means more and more costly special elections (an unanticipated consequence of reform).

THE ELECTORATE

Party Strength

Democratic and Republican party strength in California can be assessed in several different ways—registration numbers, public opinion polls, and vote results.

Registration Since 1934, California Democrats have had a decisive advantage in voter registration numbers. Although this advantage has narrowed in the

1990s, it is still clear-cut. The 1994 registration figures are as follows: Democrats, 48.9 percent; Republicans, 37.1 percent; "decline to state," 10.4 percent; and third parties (American Independent, Peace and Freedom, Libertarian, and Green), 3–4 percent. Those most likely to register "decline to state" (independents) are young, first-time voters who are uncertain or indifferent to party affiliation. Party registration numbers tend to overinflate Democratic strength, because (1) there is "deadwood" on the rolls (many people have moved but have not re-registered), (2) Democratic voters, on average, do not turn out as reliably as do Republicans, and (3) Democrats seem more willing than Republicans to cross party lines and vote for the other party.

Public Opinion Polls   The public opinion poll is a far more reliable barometer of Democratic–Republican voter strength. Pollster Mervin Field reports that California Democrats held a commanding numbers lead over Republicans from 1958 to 1985. Since then, the numbers of voters identifying with Democrats and Republicans have been very close, although Democrats retain a slight advantage.

Voting Behavior   Examining state assembly races is another way of assessing party strength. Because these contests are near the bottom of the state ticket, the effects of incumbency, personality, and issues are significantly reduced. Also, the court-designed reapportionment of 1991 was less partisan than previous reapportionments, and the districts have become more competitive. In any case, in the 1994 assembly contests, Republican candidates received 48.8 percent of the vote, Democratic candidates 48.6, and third-party filers 3.6 percent. Democrats won thirty-nine assembly races, Republicans forty, and one other Republican winner shifted to independent status after the election. In short, party strength in the mid-1990s is fairly even.

Ideology

Figure 3.2 (page 70) shows the ideological makeup of California voters. Most Republican voters, nearly five in ten, describe themselves as conservative, and another four in ten are middle-of-the-road. Republican liberals are a distinct minority. Democrats, on the other hand, lean slightly in the other direction: 36 percent are liberal, while almost one-half are middle-of-the-road. Democratic conservatives are more numerous than their counterpart Republican liberals.

Demographics

Examining party registration and self-identification by several demographic factors reveals some interesting patterns (see Table 3.1, page 71):

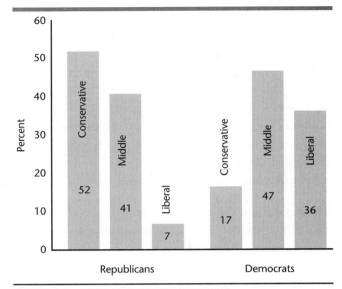

FIGURE 3.2   IDEOLOGY OF CALIFORNIANS
Source: "Political Demography," California Opinion Index, August 1992

1. Women are more likely to be Democrats, and men tend to be Republican. Women's increased support for the Democratic party results from its support for the Equal Rights Amendment (ERA), abortion rights, comparable worth, and child care.
2. African Americans, and to a lesser degree Latinos, tend to be loyal Democrats, whereas Asians lean toward the Democratic party. White–Anglos are evenly divided between Democrats and Republicans.
3. Democrats hold commanding leads over Republicans in virtually all age categories except the 25–29 age group.
4. In terms of education, those with a high school diploma or less and those with some college tend to identify themselves as Democrats as do those with a postgraduate education. Republicans hold a tenuous lead over Democrats among college graduates.
5. In terms of income, only among the wealthiest in California (incomes of $60,000 or more) do Republicans hold a lead over Democrats. Californians in the lower income groups are more likely to be Democrats. Those who rent are also more Democratically inclined.
6. Finally, in terms of religion, Republicans have the lead among Protestants, while Jewish and Catholic voters are more likely to be Democrats.

	REGISTRATION (%)		
	DEMOCRATS	REPUBLICANS	OTHER
SEX			
Male	43	43	14
Female	53	37	10
AGE			
18–24	44	37	19
25–29	39	47	14
30–39	50	38	12
40–49	52	36	12
50–59	48	44	8
60 or older	50	42	8
ETHNICITY			
White (non-Latino)	45	44	11
Latino	57	31	12
Black	85	7	8
Asian	48	35	17
EDUCATION			
High school graduate or less	52	36	12
Some college/trade school	48	42	10
College graduate	43	44	13
Postgraduate work	50	38	12
RELIGION			
Protestant	42	50	8
Catholic	52	37	11
Jewish	74	15	1
No preference	55	29	16
HOUSEHOLD INCOME			
Under $20,000	57	30	13
$20,000–$39,999	51	37	12
$40,000–$59,999	47	41	12
$60,000 or more	41	49	10
TENURE			
Homeowner	47	44	9
Rent	53	32	15

TABLE 3.1 PARTY DIFFERENCES BY SEX, AGE, ETHNICITY, AND OTHER DEMOGRAPHIC FACTORS

Source: "Political Demography." California Opinion Index, November 1992.

Regionalism

As in some other states, regional patterns can sometimes be discerned in California voting. In the Golden State, regionalism is typically north versus south; the south is usually considered to be the seven counties south of the Tehachapi Mountains, with the rest of the state making up the north. On rare occasions, a coastal-versus-inland dichotomy can occur: For example, farm interests in the Central Valley support pesticide use, whereas urban consumer interests oppose it. As previously noted (see Chapter 1), there have been constant efforts to divide the state throughout California's history.

Historically, water and gas tax allocations have been major regional issues dividing California. Both major political parties maintain state central committee offices in each of the two regions, and many state agencies and professional groups maintain northern and southern state offices.

Regionalism in voting occurs frequently as a political factor, sometimes in primary, nonpartisan, and partisan races and in ballot measures. The Bay Area and Los Angeles County tend to be liberal, whereas the other Southern California counties and much of rural Northern California tend to be conservative.

Pete Wilson's close victory in 1990 was based on his Southern California vote margin of 435,639, which overcame his Northern California deficit of 168,932 votes. In the 1986 reconfirmation election of Chief Justice Rose Bird, only two of fifty-eight counties gave her a majority—San Francisco and Alameda, two northern, liberal Bay Area counties. These two, plus adjoining Marin County, were the only counties to support Proposition 95, aid to the hungry and homeless, in November 1988. The school choice (voucher) initiative of November 1993, Proposition 174, was strongly promoted by conservative organizations and opposed by the California Teachers Association (CTA) and other liberal groups. It lost in all fifty-eight counties. However, assessing voting patterns on this initiative can provide a good indicator of the liberal or conservative attitude of a county's voters. The top ten anti-174 counties (liberal) and the top ten sympathetic to 174 (conservative) are listed in Table 3.2. In another example, U.S. Senator Dianne Feinstein's reelection race in 1994 garnered her highest support from the Bay Area counties of San Francisco (79%), Marin (71%), Alameda (68%), and San Mateo (64%). Huffington ran strongest in rural Northern California and Orange, San Diego, Riverside, and San Bernardino counties.

Voter Participation

Turnout Overall, turnout in California elections has been slightly below the national average. Over the last few presidential elections, about 54 percent of the

TOP TEN COUNTIES PRO-174	% YES	TOP TEN COUNTIES ANTI-174	% NO
1. Orange (southern)	38.7	1. San Francisco (north bay)	79.6
2. Madera (central)	37.0	2. Alameda (north bay)	77.3
3. Sutter (north central)	36.7	3. Marin (north bay)	75.6
4. Yuba (north central)	36.1	4. Yolo (north central)	75.5
5. San Diego (southern)	35.3	5. Contra Costa (north bay)	75.0
6. San Bernardino (southern)	34.4	6. Mendocino (north coast)	75.0
7. Glenn (north central)	34.4	7. Stanislaus (north central)	75.0
8. Butte (north central)	34.0	8. Sierra (north)	75.0
9. Kern (south central)	33.2	9. Sonoma (north bay)	74.5
10. Santa Barbara (southern)	32.9	10. Humboldt (north coast)	74.4

TABLE 3.2   CONSERVATIVE AND LIBERAL COUNTY VOTES ON PROPOSITION 174

potential voting population has voted, and in primaries it has been about one-third vote. Having DMV offices encouraging registration may help; also, if registration were allowed up to and including election day (as it is in some states), the percentage voting would inch up. Former Deputy Secretary of State Tony Miller proposed that a "None of the Above" option be permitted as a way of getting people to vote. Of course, if "None of the Above" won, this could mean many expensive special elections to elect someone to office.

Partisan Turnout   As a general rule, Democrats tend to participate politically less than Republicans, in part because they tend to come from lower socioeconomic groups. Citizens who are poor, have minimal education, hold unskilled jobs, or are young often do not see politics as being very important. Many do not have the time, skills, or energy to get politically involved. Many African Americans, Latinos, and poor whites are alienated from the system and often do not vote (see Figure 3.3, page 74). On the other hand, well-educated, wealthy, professional people usually see politics as important. They know they can have an impact on the system, and they vote and participate in politics in other ways.

This difference in voter turnout helps Republican candidates. In recent general elections, Republican voter turnout has exceeded Democratic turnout by about 5 percent. Republicans also tend to be more active in other forms of political effort: campaign work, financial contributions, and club membership.

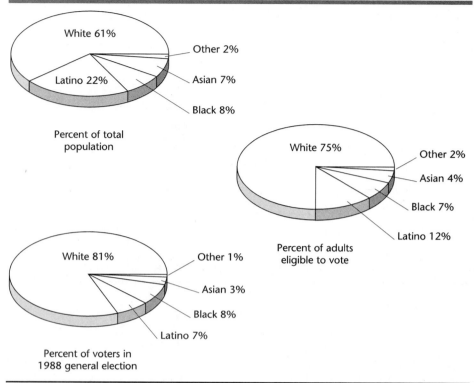

FIGURE 3.3   WHO VOTES IN CALIFORNIA?
Source: The Sacramento Bee, December 12, 1989, p. A 19. Copyright, The Sacramento Bee, 1989. Reprinted by permission.

RUNNING FOR OFFICE

Money

"Money is the mother's milk of politics," declared Jess Unruh, former California Assembly speaker and state treasurer. Any campaign for public office costs money. Even candidates running for minor office need printed literature. And for bigger campaigns, money is needed for postage, headquarters rent, telephones, bumper strips, billboards, polls, travel, advertisements in community newspapers, lawn signs, and staff. Candidates for state office and proponents and opponents of ballot measures also must pay large amounts for TV, radio, direct mail, campaign management fees, and attorneys' and accountants' salaries (to make sure that no campaign finance laws are broken). Inflation and state population growth also contribute to rising campaign costs. Equally important, California is a competi-

Dennis Renault / *The Sacramento Bee*

"Since we couldn't get the judges to recess the Simpson
trial on election day, we did the next best thing."

tive two-party state. Both parties believe they must spend more just to stay even, and an arms-race mentality develops.

The impact of personal fortune, "Big Money," was never more apparent than in the June 1994 primary. In the general election, political parties and interest groups provide money to the nominees. But in the primary, candidates must rely more on their own resources. Millionaire candidates have an enormous advantage. "Big Money" allows wealthy candidates to buy 30-second TV and radio spots to build name identification and to reach an increasingly hostile, cynical, and turned-off electorate. Using a spending game plan launched by billionaire

AP / Wide World Photos

Ross Perot in the 1992 presidential race, Republican millionaires Michael Huff-ington (U.S. Senate candidate) and Ron Unz (gubernatorial candidate) along with Democratic millionaires Dianne Feinstein (U.S. Senate candidate), Phil Angelides (lieutenant governor candidate), and Kathleen Connell (controller candidate) spent sizable portions of their own fortunes in winning their parties' nominations. Some voters prefer candidates to spend their own money rather than get it from interest groups and other millionaires.

Today, major statewide candidates may spend $20–30 million on their races, and in several initiative campaigns proponents or opponents have gone well beyond $20 million. Gubernatorial candidates Wilson and Feinstein spent a combined $43 million in their 1990 race. In 1994, Senate candidate Huffington spent nearly $30 million dollars of his own money in his losing effort. Spending in state legislative races has also exploded. Hundreds of thousands of dollars are spent in a typical state legislative race.

Carolyn Cole / *The Sacramento Bee*

Incumbent Governor Pete Wilson (Republican) (facing page) and hopeful challenger Kathleen Brown (Democrat) vote in June 1994. Both won their respective party primaries, and then Wilson came from behind in the polls to beat Brown and win reelection in November 1994.

Finally, some politicians take advantage of the campaign contribution system and use money raised to put wives, husbands, or other family members or friends on their payroll. Campaign funds have been used to pay for foreign travel, tickets to professional sporting events, and clothing. By law, campaign funds are supposed to be used only for professional, not personal, expenses. However, the line between personal and professional is not always clear.

Why People Give   Thousands of citizens (only a small percentage of the population) make modest (up to $100) campaign contributions. Most small contributors give because they believe in the candidate or issue. Unfortunately, only a small percentage of a typical candidate's budget comes from small contributions.

Some "fat cats" give for the same reasons small contributors give. For example, millionaire Harold Arbat gave more than $3 million to the yes on Proposition 130 (the Forests Forever initiative) campaign because of his concern for saving the last remnants of old-growth forests. However, most wealthy persons contribute for other reasons. Many of the superrich view their contributions as an investment, ensuring that their phone calls will be returned promptly by elected officials. Also, some wealthy contributors enjoy being fawned over by politicians seeking their financial help. Many politicians have formed clubs of their major contributors, and club members are invited to special briefing sessions or other exclusive social activities with the elected official.

Superrich candidates and their immediate families are not limited on what they can give or lend to their campaigns in state elections. Jane Fonda provided her then-husband, Tom Hayden, with more than $840,000 for his winning assembly race in 1982. Dianne Feinstein's husband, Richard Blum, lent her campaign $3 million to help win the June 1990 gubernatorial primary. However, because of federal restrictions, he could not give U.S. Senate candidate Feinstein the same kind of financial support in 1994.

Interest Group and PAC Contributions According to the Fair Political Practices Commission, interest groups and PACs (political action committees) contribute about 85 percent of a typical candidate's campaign war chest. PACs are organized by interest groups, trade associations, businesses, candidates, or ideological causes to collect and pool voluntary contributions from their members for candidates they support. Groups contribute to campaigns for many of the same reasons that fat cats contribute: as a reward for a "good" job and as an incentive for future decision making. Most groups and PACs claim that they give campaign money to ensure access to the official so that they can make their case, but critics say these campaign contributions are barely disguised bribes. Increasingly, incumbents hold fund-raisers in Sacramento where lobbyists and interest group officials buy $250 or $500 tickets to "Senator X's luau party" (these affairs invariably have some theme).

Political Party Contributions The Democratic and Republican party organizations provide funds for their candidates along with in-kind services—registration and "get out the vote" drives and campaign aides. Because the state Republican party is more successful in fund-raising, its funds are of greater significance to Republican candidates than are the Democratic party's contributions to its candidates. Adoption by voters in June 1988 of Proposition 73 established limits on how much political party campaign committees could contribute to individual candidates ($5,000 per race), and these limits were in effect for much of the 1990 campaign. However, a few weeks before the November general election, most of Proposition 73 was declared unconstitutional by a federal court.

An important state like California also attracts outside campaign money. Two 1982 ballot measures brought in significant out-of-state funds: Proposition 15 (handgun control) lured $1.2 million from the Washington, D.C., National Rifle Association, and out-of-state food packagers spent more than $1 million against

Proposition 11 (antilitter). Similarly, in 1988, $22 million spent to fight Proposition 99, the cigarette tax increase, came from Eastern tobacco corporations. This was also the case with Phillip Morris and other tobacco companies, who championed November 1994's Proposition 188, the smoking and tobacco products initiative.

Media

Television and Radio   California is a media state. It is one of the key centers of the nation's radio, television, and movie industries. More than 50 television and 400 radio stations serve the state.

"Media" in California has come to mean television, and television advertising is very expensive. Most TV money is spent on the thirty-second spot—selling the candidate's image, a slogan, and sometimes an issue. Costs vary with the size of the market (Los Angeles compared to Redding), the day (weekday or weekend), the time of day (3 A.M. or 7:30 P.M.), and the popularity of the program "next" to the spot. The going rate for a thirty-second spot (campaign commercial) during a top-rated prime time (7–10 P.M.) show in Los Angeles, San Diego, San Jose, San Francisco, or Sacramento can run as much as $35,000 or $40,000. Campaign commercials are often geared to the audience of the show: "Seinfeld," baby boomers and yuppies; "NFL Monday Night Football" or "Roseanne," blue-collar; "Fresh Prince of Bel Aire," African Americans; "Murder She Wrote," seniors; and "Beavis and Butthead," the academically challenged. Under federal law, radio stations must sell air time to federal candidates, but they do not have to sell time to state candidates. If they do, it must be at the lowest available rate. Therefore, when there are plenty of businesses willing to pay the normal rate, radio stations often prefer to sell time to private advertisers—it's more profitable. Some radio station managers also say they want to "protect" their listeners from the nasty and noisy political commercials.

Television reaches a wider audience than newspapers. Though virtually every home has a TV, newspapers reach only about eight of ten state households. Television newscasters, for the most part, have more credibility with the public than do politicians. Recent surveys indicate that the public has little faith in the accuracy of campaign spots (they are also suspicious of commercial ads). A recent Richard Hertz poll concludes that 71 percent of the public believes that most campaign ads are not truthful; 61 percent say they pay little attention to them.

Debates   Television debates are a feature of most major statewide campaigns and many legislative races as well. Over the years, a pattern has developed—the predebate debate. Candidates ahead in the polls are advised not to debate or to allow for only a limited number of debates. Candidates who are behind frequently challenge the front-runner by demanding ten or twenty debates. Charges of "chicken" abound. There is also predebate debate over the format: reporters asking questions? average citizens? candidates questioning each other? broadcast statewide or regionally? Usually, one or the other candidate feels more comfortable with a particular format. The problem is that debates often do not take place or are held only once during a campaign. (This was the case in 1994 between Wilson and Brown. In the 1994 senate race between Huffington and Feinstein, the candidates debated only once—on "Larry King Live.") The public is the loser.

Newspapers   Historically, the press has been a power in California state and local government. Before TV, a handful of newspapers—the *Los Angeles Times*, *San Francisco Chronicle*, *Oakland Tribune*, and the Hearst *Examiner* papers (San Francisco and Los Angeles)—were strong forces within the Republican party, lavishing their support on GOP candidates. Today, television provides substantial competition to newspapers throughout the state. Newspapers' impact on voters compared to television has declined, and some major dailies no longer make endorsements in major partisan campaigns. Some purposely present conflicting opinions on the editorial pages. The *Los Angeles Times* has developed into one of the nation's finest newspapers, and *The Sacramento Bee* has long enjoyed a solid reputation for its coverage of state politics.

Because of California's size and mountain ranges, California newspapers tend to be regional in scope. This fragmentation of media influence reduces the power of any one newspaper. The state's largest circulation newspaper, the *Los Angeles Times*, is read in about one in five California homes (in 1993, its daily circulation was 1,138,353). Yet even the *Times* has only one-third of the circulation in Los Angeles County. Political ads placed in newspapers can also be expensive depending in part on the newspaper's circulation. For example, a full-page political ad in *The Sacramento Bee* costs about $10,000 per day.

Talk Radio   The call-in talk radio phenomenon has taken the nation by storm over the last 10 to 15 years. Today, virtually every midsize city (50,000 or so) and all major cities have local talk shows. In addition, several talk hosts—including the controversial conservative Rush Limbaugh—are nationally syndicated. Hundreds of stations from the Pacific Coast to the Atlantic carry his show. In a sense, talk shows are the public town hall meeting of the 1990s: Callers express their viewpoints (they're frequently unhappy) on the events of the day. Talk shows can be informative, increase public awareness of issues, and encourage people to participate politically. Talk issues that seem to generate the most public interest and ire deal with subjects such as politicians' sexual indiscretions, pay raises for elected officials, and waste and fraud in government.

Talk show audiences appear to be skewed to the white, well-educated, and affluent in our society—people with the time to listen and with political interests. Thus, most (not all) radio talk hosts are conservative. Unlike town hall meetings, call-ins are screened and anonymous. Many talk hosts find it useful to be outrageous or humorous to build the largest listening audience possible. Entertainment is most important; political information is secondary. Unquestionably, radio talk shows are a growing political force in California and the rest of the country. They contributed to the Republican landslide victory in 1994. Indicative of his importance in the Republican House victories and in nationalizing these formerly parochial contests, Limbaugh was made an honorary member of the GOP House class of 1994.

Media Impact The multiplicity of newspapers and radio and TV stations serving each region is significant. Virtually all state residents have some choice of news source. And in the Los Angeles and San Francisco areas, the number and range of alternatives are staggering. Although most people read only one newspaper (if any), they have many TV stations, including cable, from which to choose. Interestingly, no Los Angeles, San Francisco, or San Diego television station still maintains a Sacramento bureau, unlike the 1960s and 1970s, when Governors Ronald Reagan and Jerry Brown were center stage. It's now too expensive. The attitude is that the public is not interested in state politics.

The precise impact of television, newspaper, and radio endorsements and news coverage is hard to assess, but a few studies suggest that newspapers and television appeal to different audiences. Newspaper readers tend to be high-income and better-educated voters; TV is more often the only news source for low-income and less-educated voters. The visual impact of television is a powerful influence on a viewer who has no other source of information about the subject.

The press has more influence in local and nonpartisan races than in national or partisan elections. There is evidence that radio and television have more impact on voting for or against ballot measures.

In the long run, media endorsements are probably less significant than day-to-day news coverage and content. Incumbents often get publicity; challengers usually do not. How an issue is presented (offshore oil spills, the state's annual budget, or an increase or decrease in the welfare load) affects voters' basic perceptions of the issues.

Public Opinion Polls

Public opinion polls are another key part of major campaigns for public office, and they can be expensive. A well-designed statewide poll can cost as much as $30,000 to $40,000. Serious candidates for major public office will try to take at least one public opinion survey early in the campaign. Such polls usually become the basis for a candidate's strategy. Candidates use such information to:

1. identify major issues,
2. assess their own and their opponent's strengths and weaknesses, and
3. help raise campaign funds and other support.

Candidates trailing in the polls often spend much of their campaign budget on a media "blitz" to generate increased name recognition before a scheduled Field Poll. The increased standing in the polls is used to convince potential contributors that the campaign is gaining momentum. It becomes a cycle of money leading to media, name recognition, increased support in the polls, more money, more media, more name recognition, and so on. This was the strategy used by Dianne Feinstein in her race for the Democratic gubernatorial nomination against John Van de Kamp in 1990. Trailing badly early on, she bought more than $500,000 worth of TV time in Southern California in January 1990 and shot into the lead. This made collecting campaign contributions much easier. Ironically, Michael Huffington used this same strategy running against Feinstein in the U.S. Senate race in 1994.

Initiative Championing

An increasingly popular tactic of California statewide candidates is to author or sponsor an initiative. In the 1990 race for governor in the June primary, winning Republican candidate Pete Wilson and losing Democratic candidate John Van de Kamp each authored initiatives (in fact, the latter was responsible for three initiatives that appeared on the November ballot). Instead of discussing what bills they will be presenting to the legislature, modern-day statewide candidates send out press releases and hold press conferences ballyhooing their initiative proposals. In the 1994 fall campaign, both Kathleen Brown and Governor Pete Wilson were major spokespersons for the "three strikes and you're out" initiative, Proposition 184. Wilson's endorsement of the 1990 term limits initiative, Proposition 140, was instrumental in the measure's election victory and helped Wilson, who was also the author of the budget powers and welfare reform initiative, Proposition 165, of November 1992. Finally, Wilson's reelection quest in 1994 was helped by his strong backing of the "save our state" illegal immigrants initiative, Proposition 187.

Incumbency

Over the last several decades, one feature of elective politics seemed unchangeable: Incumbents had enormous advantages and usually won easy reelection. Indeed, in the 1980s and early 1990s, sometimes virtually every incumbent running was reelected. Generally, only a major political scandal could dislodge an incumbent. Incumbency advantages were greatest in less visible offices (state legislature, board of equalization, or "lesser" statewide offices) because voters knew little about the candidates and often chose the familiar name. Incumbency was less critical in the major offices of governor and U.S. senator. The advent of term limits will dissipate the incumbent advantage.

What are the factors contributing to incumbent successes?

Money Incumbents usually have more campaign money (typically four to five times as much) because (1) they begin their fund-raising as soon as they are elected and (2) special interests want to be on the winning side. Here and there, a "cause" interest group (National Rifle Association, for example) may give money to the challenger, but generally the challenger must depend on friends, business or commercial contacts, or personal funds. Those with superior money resources can hire the best campaign management firms to run their campaigns.

Name Recognition Incumbents usually have superior name identification and years of publicity that challengers must overcome. Of course, sometimes non-incumbents are public figures who also enjoy name recognition. Actors (such as Ronald Reagan or Clint Eastwood), recording stars (such as Mike Curb or Sonny Bono), radio talk hosts, and sports figures can often build successful political careers on their own name recognition. And free-spending millionaire challengers can use their own money to build name identification.

The offspring of famous people also have advantages. Governor Jerry Brown's and Democratic candidate Kathleen Brown's campaigns for governor were substantially helped by the fact that their father (Pat Brown) had been governor. Republican candidate for Treasurer Matt Fong had name identification developed from his famous mother, former Secretary of State March Fong Eu. Most incumbents, though, do not have to worry about celebrity challengers.

Office Advantages All state legislators have district offices and staff who are busy year-round promoting the incumbent. District staff spend most of their time doing casework and assisting constituents who need help—and who often remember this when they vote. Problems range from lost Social Security checks to revoked drivers' licenses. Being in office means becoming more knowledgeable about issues and the legislative process than one's opponent—usually.

Lawmakers try to be in their districts on weekends when the legislature is in session and full-time during recess. Their days and nights are packed with breakfast, lunch, and dinner meetings; coffees and teas; Rotary, Kiwanis, chamber of commerce, and union meetings; visits to schools, churches, and PTAs; and speeches to groups such as the League of Women Voters. The incumbent "reports" on the Sacramento scene and soon builds an image as a hard-working, effective lawmaker.

Capitol staff of legislative incumbents constantly send out press releases informing district media of the latest activities of the members whom they serve. Until a few years ago, members were provided state funding to send out newsletters to their constituents to point out what they were doing. In both houses, majority and minority consultants in media operations videotape interviews with members. Staffers ask "their" members easy questions, and these taped interviews are then sent to TV and radio stations, where listeners may believe the incumbent is being questioned by reporters. Staff know that if they are to continue holding their positions, they must make sure "their" members get reelected.

Reapportionment State legislators customarily draw district lines each decade to guarantee easy elections for incumbents (see Chapter 7). Until the court-drawn 1991 reapportionment, there were only a handful of truly competitive districts in the state.

Incumbency and the 1994 Election The strong Republican tide running in the 1994 election swept an unprecedented number of incumbent Democrats in California (and nationwide as well) out of office. No Republican incumbent lost. Those Democratic incumbents who survived won by much narrower margins than usual. In addition to the Republican tide, the court-designed reapportionment of 1991 and the fact that few Democratic statewide incumbents were running for reelection also hurt the latter's efforts. Incumbency continues to be an advantage these days (particularly for Republicans), but an angry public seems less willing to give incumbents a blank check. For example, three conservative Supreme Court judges were up for reconfirmation in 1994. No issues, controversy, or emotions were involved in the contest, yet each received a 40 percent "no" vote!

PROCEDURAL REFORM

Reform has long been an integral part of California's political culture and history. There are two kinds of political reform: policy and procedure.

The state is best known for its procedural reforms, or those that have changed the way the political system functions—for example, the Progressive reforms of initiative, referendum, recall, and primaries, and now term limits. Having the initiative has allowed reformers to bypass the legislature and promote changes in the political system: the Political Reform Act initiative, Proposition 9 of June

1974, the campaign spending reform measures of June 1988, Propositions 68 and 73 (though struck down in the courts), or Proposition 140, term limits of November 1990. Yet one central reform issue continues to hound state government: the corrupting influence of megamillions in election campaigns and in lobbying. Chapter 5 examines the lobby role, but here we will consider campaign spending reform.

Hefty campaign contributions from interest group PACs and "Big Money" contributed by millionaires distort and corrupt the election process. Instead of "one person, one vote," those with large contributions have, in effect, multiple votes. Ideally, it would be far better for many people to contribute relatively small amounts (say $250 or less) to candidates to finance their campaigns than for a few people to make massive contributions. Large campaign contributions are given for a purpose: to influence. As campaigns become ever more expensive, it is critical that campaign finance reform be undertaken. Yet attempts by the legislature and governors to deal with the issue over the last three decades have failed. Partisan conflict, Republican opposition to publicly financed campaigns, Democrat reluctance to limit PAC contributions (as the legislative majority party, they have tended to collect more), court rulings emphasizing that a campaign contribution is a form of political expression protected under the First Amendment, and other factors have meant no institutional response to the issue. Two separate FBI investigations of the capitol in the 1980s and 1990s indicate a glaring problem: Five legislators, several legislative staff, one prominent lobbyist, local officials, and administrators have been convicted. Although some worry that these investigations are a form of entrapment (an FBI agent posed as a businessman who needed state financing assistance in his effort to bring a shrimp facility to the state), this is probably the only way to uncover this kind of capitol corruption. In any case, the only significant attempts to grapple with the subject have come through the initiative, outside the process. Let's consider them.

Political Reform Act of 1974

In 1974, in the post-Watergate era, Proposition 9, an initiative jointly sponsored by Common Cause, People's Lobby, and Secretary of State Jerry Brown, qualified for the June primary ballot. Although the reform measure was opposed by nearly all of the major interest groups operating in the state, it was overwhelmingly approved by voters.

The Political Reform Act (PRA) had four major goals: limiting campaign expenditures, requiring disclosure of campaign contributions and expenditures, limiting lobby gifting and entertaining (see Chapter 5), and prohibiting local officeholder conflicts of interest. In addition, the act established a Fair Political

Dennis Renault / *The Sacramento Bee*

L.A. judge rules against 1974 California
Political Reform Act.

—*News item*

Practices Commission (FPPC) to administer and enforce its provisions. After voter adoption, the act was immediately challenged in court. In 1977, the U.S. Supreme Court struck down the expenditure limits that had been established for statewide candidates and ballot propositions on First Amendment (free speech) grounds, but other PRA features, including disclosure and conflict of interest provisions, were upheld.

Disclosure Under PRA, campaign contributions and expenditures of $100 or more must be reported by candidates for state and local elective office. The contributor's name, address, occupation, and employer's name must be given. This information must be filed both forty and twelve days before and sixty-five days after election day. In addition, all state public officials are required to file annual income reports.

Fair Political Practices Commission The FPPC has five members: the chair and one other member appointed by the governor, plus one each appointed by the attorney general, secretary of state, and controller. Members serve four-year terms; only the chair is full-time.

The commission is empowered to establish rules to implement the act, hear complaints, hold hearings, issue fines, and investigate where needed. A major task of the commission is to receive and file reports from lobbyists and campaigns. Given the number of lobbyists, candidates, and ballot measure campaigns, the commission can reasonably expect more than 20,000 filings in an election year.

Impact Because of PRA, California citizens and the media can find out which individual or group is giving to a candidate or proposition, as well as how much and how this money is being expended. Voters can use this information as they see fit in determining their vote. However, for PRA to work, the media must report this information and the public must pay attention to it. Although most data have not been earthshaking, in a few campaigns candidates have been put on the defensive because of contributions from controversial sources. An unanticipated consequence of this reform is that some politicians have used these spending reports to pressure special interest groups for more campaign money. "You gave $5,000 to Assemblyman X and only $2,000 to me—what's the matter?"

Inexperienced candidates often find the paperwork (reports, records, etc.) a substantial burden on their small staffs. In contrast, experienced candidates (usually incumbents) have less difficulty with these requirements. The act has also had substantial impact on some specific campaign activities. Most notable has been the increased use of paid legal and accounting personnel.

Over the years, the FPPC has fined a variety of public officials for violations of the act—failing to file spending reports on time, failing to promptly report campaign contributions, and so on. Violators are fined for their transgressions, usually a few thousand dollars. However, in 1986 the FPPC filed suit against Sacramento County Supervisor William Bryan for $2.9 million, accusing him of "violating virtually every major provision of the act." Bryan was convicted.

On balance, the act has been a limited success. Having an FPPC and requiring disclosure of campaign funding can provide voters useful information. Unfortunately, the spending limits portion of PRA was declared unconstitutional.

Propositions 68, 73, and 131

Two separate and distinctive campaign finance reform initiatives were approved in June 1988. Proposition 73—jointly authored by Republican Assembly Leader

Ross Johnson, Independent Senator Quentin Kopp, and Democratic Senator Joe Montoya (since convicted of extortion and sent to prison)—received 58 percent approval, and Proposition 68—authored by Common Cause, a public interest lobby group—received 53 percent approval. Although the two initiatives had some similar features, such as limits on the size of campaign contributions to California politicians, banning transfers of campaign funds from one officeholder to another, and honoraria limits, Proposition 68 was more comprehensive. It provided for public financing of elections, established overall expenditure limits, and banned off-year fund raising.

Because Proposition 73 received more votes, under state law it had legal precedence over Proposition 68. Common Cause argued in court that state law stipulated that if provisions of two or more measures approved at the same election on the same topic were not in conflict, they too became law. After much study, the state Supreme Court ruled that Proposition 68 had been superseded by Proposition 73, and because each had its own set of regulations, they would not try to "graft" nonconflicting sections of Proposition 68 onto Proposition 73. However, a federal court struck down most of Proposition 73 five weeks before the November 1990 election. Federal judges argued that the funding provisions under Proposition 73 gave incumbents too much of an advantage (of course, they had an advantage also before Proposition 73). Special elections continue to operate under Proposition 73's regulations. Currently, the state Supreme Court is considering modifying the calendar guidelines of Proposition 73 to give challengers a better chance of being competitive and then seeing if this will be sufficient to mollify federal courts.

In November 1990, Common Cause placed Proposition 131 on the ballot, which was a combined term limits and campaign finance reform measure. This measure was overwhelmingly defeated by voters, 38 percent to 62 percent. Thus, campaign finance reform remains an unresolved issue in California.

Attempting to put together a public finance law that meets court and constitutional standards, does not alienate taxpayers ("My tax dollars will be going to provide money to that no-good crook!"), treats all candidates fairly, provides for assistance in primary and general elections, and encourages small contributors to participate is a complex task, but it must be done.

Other Reform Issues

Slate Mailers   Slate mailers are lists of endorsed candidates and propositions put together by various party groups, special interests, or "quick-buck" operators that can confuse voters (see Chapter 6).

Dirty Campaign Tactics Every two years, newspaper writers and television commentators are almost sure to say, "The election campaign this year is the dirtiest in our nation's history." The problem is that candidates and campaign consultants all understand one key facet of campaigning. Although voters say they don't like and are disgusted by mud-slinging campaigns, every study indicates that voters are far likelier to remember dirty campaign charges and attacks. Attack campaigns win. California's campaign innovation, the thirty-second spot, is the major attack vehicle. Candidates are advised, "If hit, hit back." Party leaders urge candidates to wage holy war so their party can control the legislature.

The pit bull mode of campaign attack was clearly evident in the general election campaign race between Democrat U.S. Senate incumbent Dianne Feinstein and Republican challenger Michael Huffington in their 1994 race (although virtually all other major political contests in this state and outside the state were similar, including the governor's race between Republican Pete Wilson and Democrat Kathleen Brown).

In the Republican primary contest, Huffington was ahead in the polls, so he exclusively focused his attack on Feinstein and didn't even refer to his Republican opponents. After his primary victory, Huffington hired Ed Rollins, a long-time Republican consultant, a clear sign that the Huffington campaign was going to play "hard ball." Rollins had become infamous running Republican New Jersey Governor Christine Whitman's campaign. After winning there, Rollins bragged that he had distributed $500,000 to black ministers in the state to urge their parishioners not to vote (they ostensibly would have voted Democrat). Though Rollins later repudiated his comments, the scar remained. The campaign between Feinstein and Huffington did not just *degenerate* into an attack campaign, it started that way in June and continued on to November.

This is part of the text of an early Feinstein spot:

Michael Huffington, stop the tap dancing and be honest with the people of California. Special interests? Your company, HuffCo, had its own special interest, big oil PAC to give away big bucks to push big oil's agenda in Congress. Californians are entitled to know where your money comes from. So disclose your state and federal taxes. . . .

This is part of the text of an early Huffington spot:

There's a lot flying through the air lately—mud from Dianne Feinstein. In 1990, Feinstein used a commercial that NBC News labeled as the meanest and sneakiest of the year. Feinstein complains about spending, but she's spent over $30 million running for office in the last four years. Where did Feinstein's $30 million come from? A big chunk of it came from special interests. . . .

Essentially, campaign dialogue is protected by First Amendment free speech guarantees. According to the U.S. Supreme Court, if state laws attempt to restrict political advertising, mailings, or other forms of communication, those restrictions must be narrowly and specifically aimed at false statements. Further, the Supreme Court has ruled that candidates for public office or elected public officials are in the public arena. They may be attacked and criticized to a far greater extent than private citizens.

There does not appear to be a way to legislate against false, misleading, or ego-inspired statements a candidate may make about him- or herself. The normal concept of "consumer protection" does not apply, again because of the prime importance in a democracy of the free and unrestricted flow of campaign materials. The old adage holds true, "Let the buyer beware."

SUMMARY

The ways in which election laws work are not neutral. Although any voter can file for public office in California, few have or can attract the resources required for victory.

Primary elections are sometimes more important than the general election, but turnout is lower in the former.

Many California Democrats and Republicans view themselves as middle-of-the-road, and a substantial number do not identify with either major party. Democrats and Republicans, at present, are at about equal strength in competing in California elections.

Although reforms have been instituted to improve the election process and provide for fairer elections, the continuing corrupting feature of super-rich and special-interest campaign contributions must be dealt with through further reforms.

NOTE

1. Governor Wilson complained that the federal government had not provided funds to implement this "motor voter" feature and threatened not to implement the DMV voter registration program unless funding was forthcoming.

REFERENCES

Field Institute. "Political Demography." (November 1992) San Francisco, pp. 1–6.

Green, Stephen. ed. *California Political Almanac, 1993–1994.* California Journal Press, Sacramento, 1993.

Price, Charles M. "Attack of the Radio Talk Show Hosts." *California Journal* 20 (November 1989), pp. 365–369.

Richardson, James. "Political Consultants." *California Journal* 21 (1990), pp. 385–389.

Simon, Mark. "Slate Mailers." *California Journal* 20 (1989), pp. 289–291.

Stemmler, Hal. "Absentee Ballots, a New Frontier in California Electoral Politics." *California Journal* 14 (1983), pp. 296–298.

Stern, Robert. "Voting in the 21st Century." *California Journal* 21 (1990), pp. 53–54.

DIRECT DEMOCRACY:

POWER TO THE PEOPLE?

In the early 1900s, the Progressive political reform movement swept the nation (see Chapter 2). Though the movement was national in scope, affecting to varying degrees cities and towns in nearly every state, the Progressive impact was felt most keenly in a few Midwestern states and in the West in former strongholds of Populism, a nineteenth-century political reform movement.

Progressives wanted to clean up politics, check politicians, and curb excessive special-interest power. In California, the chief special-interest target of Progressives was the Southern Pacific Railroad. According to Fremont Older (1926, p. 14), in 1896 Southern Pacific dominated the legislature, courts, municipal governments, county governments, and newspapers of California. Southern Pacific, in turn, was the recipient of state and federal largesse—cash subsidies, no rate regulation, massive land grants, and favorable loans.

To combat this political and economic power, California Progressives wanted to provide citizens with a greater voice in governmental decision making. No reform elements in the Progressive program were more important than their holy trinity: the initiative, referendum, and recall. Underlying these three reforms was the belief that ordinary citizens ought to have ultimate governmental decision-making power.

DIRECT DEMOCRACY: A WESTERN PHENOMENON

Currently, twenty-four states offer the initiative, and in many the referendum and recall are also provided. In addition, some of the other twenty-six states that offer no statewide direct-democracy options do allow them at the local level.

FIGURE 4.1   USAGE PATTERNS OF STATES PROVIDING FOR THE CONSTITUTIONAL INITIATIVE, THE STATUTE INITIATIVE, OR BOTH

Unlike some Progressive reforms (the secret ballot, direct primary, and presidential preference primary) that have since been adopted in the great majority of states, direct democracy enjoyed an initial burst of adoptions by states in the early part of this century. But only a few others have incorporated the initiative device in the intervening years (Alaska is one exception, but it just became a state in 1959). This is particularly striking in light of the enormous interest in the initiative process generated by Proposition 13, the Jarvis–Gann property-tax relief measure and various states' term limit initiatives in the 1990s. Most legislators in noninitiative states do not want to share lawmaking power with voters and oppose adding this feature to their constitutions. However, no state with the initiative has abandoned it. Once in place, it stays.

Direct-democracy devices have been adopted primarily in the West. Only seven of twenty-six states east of the Mississippi River now allow the initiative, compared to seventeen of twenty-four states to the west (see Figures 4.1 and 4.2).

Progressives' middle-class reformism, their antipathy toward the two major establishment parties, their suspicion of officeholders, and their reliance on ordinary citizens to exercise ultimate political power have helped shape the ebb and flow of California politics. California voters tend to be wary of "politicians,"

184	**INCREASED SENTENCES. REPEAT OF-FENDERS. INITIATIVE STATUTE.** Increases sentences for convicted felons who have previous convictions for certain serious or violent	Yes / No

felonies. Includes as prior convictions certain felonies committed by older juveniles. Fiscal Impact: Reaffirms existing law, which results in annual state costs initially of hundreds of millions increasing to multi-billion dollars. Unknown net impact on local governments. Unknown state and local savings for costs of crimes not committed. No direct fiscal impact resulting from measure.

185	**PUBLIC TRANSPORTATION TRUST FUNDS. GASOLINE SALES TAX. INITIATIVE STATUTE.** Provides for an additional 4%	Yes / No

tax on gasoline sales. Revenues for electric rail and clean fuel buses, light rail, commuter and intercity rail systems, and other transportation-related programs, including wetlands, riparian habitat and parks. Fiscal Impact: Increased gasoline sales tax revenues of about $630 million annually. Multimillion dollar annual increases in state and local costs for mass transportation services, potentially offset by unknown amount of revenues.

186	**HEALTH SERVICES. TAXES. INITIATIVE CONSTITUTIONAL AMENDMENT AND STATUE.** Establishes health services system,	Yes / No

defined benefits, for California residents to replace existing health insurance, premiums, programs. Costs/provider payments funded by employer, individual, tobacco taxes. Elected Health Commissioner administers Fund/system. Fiscal Impact: Potentially over $75 billion in government funds to provide health insurance. Costs could be greater or less than funds. Potential government savings over time. Impact on state revenues over time, uncertain, probably not major.

187	**ILLEGAL ALIENS. INITIATIVE STATUTE.** Makes illegal aliens ineligible for public social services, public health care services (unless emergency under federal law), and attendance	Yes / No

at public schools. Requires state/local agencies report suspected illegal aliens. Fiscal Impact: Annual state/local program savings of roughly $200 million, offset by administrative costs of tens of millions (potentially more than $100 million in first year). Places at possible risk billions of dollars in federal funding for California.

188	**SMOKING AND TOBACCO PRODUCTS. LOCAL PREEMPTION. STATEWIDE REGULATION. INITIATIVE STATUTE.** Preempts local smoking laws. Replaces existing regulations	Yes / No

with limited public smoking ban. Permits regulated smoking in most public places. Increases penalties for tobacco purchases by, and sales to, minors. Fiscal Impact: Likely, but unknown, annual increase in state and local government health care costs and state tobacco tax revenues. State enforcement costs of less than $1 million annually.

FIGURE 4.2   DIRECT DEMOCRACY IN ACTION   The November 1994 ballot contained five initiatives, Propositions 184–188. *Source:* Butte County Election Department

and though the Progressive movement has faded from the political stage, reformist public interest lobbies such as Common Cause, the Public Interest Research Group, and the League of Women Voters struggle today to promote reforms in tune with Progressive goals. In a sense, Paul Gann and Howard Jarvis, the late authors of Proposition 13 of June 1978 and other tax cut measures, struck a particularly Progressive theme in their Proposition 13 campaign: "Teach the politicians a lesson." That same theme was replicated in the winning campaign to approve Proposition 140, term limits, in November 1990.

None of these direct-democracy devices are allowed at the federal level. The framers of the U.S. Constitution were not enthusiastic about direct democracy.

PROCEDURES: DIRECT-DEMOCRACY DEVICES

The *initiative* gives citizens the right to propose laws and constitutional amendments using the petition process and to enact them using the voting booth. In California, 5 percent of the total number of votes cast for governor in the most recent election is required to qualify a statute initiative. Based on the 1994 vote, this means 433,269 signatures for a statute initiative and 693,230 for a constitutional amendment during the 1995–1998 period. These qualifying numbers will be recalculated in November 1998 in the next governor's election.[1] California and many other Western states have both the statute and constitutional amendment initiative; some initiative states offer one or the other.

The basic steps in the California initiative process are: (1) Interested citizens, interest groups, or politicians draft a proposed measure. (2) The measure (along with a payment of $200, which is refunded if the initiative qualifies) is submitted to the attorney general for titling and summary, sent to the Department of Finance and Joint Budget Committee for determination of fiscal impact, and then forwarded to the secretary of state for the official summary date and calendar of deadlines. (3) Petitions are circulated among voters, and backers have 150 days to qualify their petition. (4) The secretary of state's office determines whether the proper number of valid signatures has been collected within the time frame; if so, it automatically goes on the next state election ballot.[2] (5) If the initiative receives more yes than no votes, it becomes law immediately. However, if provisions of two or more propositions approved at the same election conflict, the measure receiving the higher affirmative vote prevails.[3]

To further protect this citizen weapon from "politicians," Progressives made it difficult for the legislature to amend an approved initiative. Amending a statutory initiative law requires a majority vote of the legislature and approval by the electorate, unless the initiative specifically permits amendment without voter approval (few do). A constitutional amendment can be amended only by passage of a new constitutional initiative or by the legislature passing a new constitutional amendment and submitting it to voters for approval.

Finally, initiatives are subject to review by state and federal courts if challenged. For example, Proposition 21, the anti–school-busing initiative of 1972, and Proposition 105, the consumers' right-to-know initiative of November 1988, were ruled unconstitutional by the California Supreme Court. In other instances, portions of initiatives have been struck down by the courts. Proposition 9, the

Political Reform Act of 1974, underwent a series of challenges in the courts with some portions being declared unconstitutional. Much of Proposition 73 was gutted by the federal court, except the section dealing with special elections. An injunction was issued one day after Proposition 187, the illegal immigrant initiative, was approved by voters, barring implementation until various legal issues had been resolved. Proposition 184, the three strikes initiative, appears to be headed to the courts as well. And, not infrequently, initiatives stand up to court challenge: Proposition 13, the property-tax relief measure of June 1978, was appealed to the California Supreme Court, which upheld the initiative. It went on to the U.S. Supreme Court, which refused to reverse the state court ruling. Proposition 140, term limits of November 1990, was immediately challenged in the courts. It was upheld by the state Supreme Court and appealed on to the U.S. Supreme Court, which allowed the state court decision to stand.

In these litigious days and perhaps because initiative law is drafted sometimes by amateurs, legal challenges of voter-approved initiatives are frequent. Proposition 103, the car-insurance-rate reduction initiative, is a good example. It was adopted by voters in November 1988, but in the ensuing years car-insurance companies brought many legal challenges. For the most part, it's been upheld, but not until 1993 did a few car-insurance companies provide 103-mandated rebates to their customers.

The state constitution stipulates that initiatives must be single-subject, but this is sometimes hard to define. Thus, Proposition 9, the Political Reform Act of 1974, Paul Gann's Proposition 8, the Victims' Bill of Rights initiative of June 1982, and Pete Wilson's Proposition 165 budget and welfare initiative were challenged in court on the grounds that they encompassed more than one subject. The Court said they did not. However, in February 1990, a state appellate court, perhaps emboldened by growing public dissatisfaction with the initiative process and overly long and complicated initiatives, declared Proposition 105, the consumers' right-to-know initiative of November 1988, unconstitutional because it violated the single-subject criterion. (The initiative dealt with consumer information on matters such as toxic household products, nursing homes, trade with South Africa, and initiative advertising of major funding.)

Finally, Proposition 115, the speedy trial initiative of June 1988, was ruled unconstitutional because the state Supreme Court contended it "revised" the constitution (something only a constitutional revision commission may do) and went beyond simple amending.

The petition *referendum* gives citizens the power to "veto," in effect, bills recently approved by the legislature or governor. The process works as follows: (1) The legislature passes and the governor signs a controversial bill. (2) Certain citizens strongly oppose the new law and decide to attempt to qualify a referendum for the ballot before the law goes into effect. (3) To qualify a referendum, they must collect the required number of valid signatures—5 percent of the total vote cast for governor in the preceding election, or 433,269—within 90 days after the governor has signed the bill. (4) If sufficient signatures are secured, the measure goes on the ballot. However, certain types of bills requiring a two-thirds vote of each house are excluded from referendum: calls for special elections, tax levies, urgency measures, and appropriations measures.

The *recall* gives citizens the right to remove incumbents from office using the petition and election procedure. For a statewide recall, valid signatures of qualified voters equaling 12 percent of the total vote cast for that particular office must be gathered. Thus, the signatures of 1,039,039 voters would have to be collected within 160 days to place a recall of Governor Wilson on the ballot until 1998.[4] For state legislators, the requirement is 20 percent of that particular office at the last election. At the local level, required signatures range from 10 to 30 percent, depending on the population of the local district.[5]

We now consider how the recall and referendum have been used in the state and then will focus most of our attention on the critically important initiative.

RECALL
Statewide and State

No recall effort directed against a statewide officeholder has ever qualified for the California ballot. Indeed, only a handful of statewide officials in the various recall states have ever been removed from office, and, with one exception, these all occurred many decades ago.[6] Some states have awesome signature requirements—for example, Kansas requires 40 percent. The few statewide recall attempts in California (directed primarily against governors) have always fallen short of securing the necessary signatures.[7] Probably the most important reason why such recalls have never qualified for the ballot is the number of signatures needed.

Although it is easy to minimize the importance of statewide recalls in California, since none has ever qualified, given voter anger and professional petitioning to get signatures, a statewide recall is conceivable under the right circumstances. Certainly, former Chief Justice Rose Bird took the various right-wing recall efforts launched against her seriously; many of these same people had been successful in qualifying conservative initiatives for the ballot using direct mail. If nothing else, the three separate recall efforts aimed against her were like an early artillery barrage designed to "soften up" the enemy in preparation for the final assault (the reconfirmation election).

However, several California legislators have been removed from office in recall elections. A recall aimed at then-Pro Tem of the California Senate David Roberti qualified for an April 1994 special election. The effort was mainly promoted by NRA activists in Roberti's district who were angry with him for his successful authorship of a bill to ban semiautomatic rifles. Ironically, Roberti was not eligible to run for reelection in the district after November 1994 because of term limits. Thousands of taxpayer dollars had to be spent to pay for this unneeded election.[8] For the NRA, his defeat would be a lesson to other legislators defying NRA views. Though Roberti won the recall, he had to spend thousands of dollars from his campaign treasury to defend himself, and this money drain contributed to his defeat in the June primary race with Phil Angelides in his quest to get the Democratic nomination for treasurer. After Republican, and later independent, Assemblyman Paul Horcher voted for Democrat Willie Brown for speaker in December 1994, thus depriving Republican Jim Brulte of this office (Brown 40 votes, Brulte 40 votes), GOP officials around the state qualified a recall effort against Horcher and succeeded in tossing him out of office. In addition, a recall election will take place in August 1995 to determine whether Democrat Assemblymember Mike Machado (who originally won election by less than 2,000 votes) will retain his seat. His problem: He voted for Brown for speaker. Horcher's recall, the potential recall of Machado, and the threatened recall of new Republican Speaker Doris Allen have poisoned the atmosphere in the assembly.

Local

The local recall is available in thirty-seven states; California is one of twenty-one that provides for recall of all local elected officials. Some states require proof of malfeasance in office, but not California. The percentage requirement needed to qualify local recalls varies, but Chattanooga, Tennessee, has the toughest standard: Recall proponents must secure 50 percent to recall the mayor. Though the local recall is used sparingly, in a few, mainly Western states—Oregon, Nebraska, Alaska, Idaho, Michigan, Nevada, Washington, and California—the device is a factor.

There appears to have been an upturn in local recall elections since the 1970s that parallels the lack of confidence people have in government. Typical local recall issues are: (1) planned-growth or no-growth advocates versus prodevelopment interests, (2) the firing of a popular local official by a governing council or board, (3) the raising of fees for particular services, or (4) having pay raises or fringe benefits adopted by officeholders. Of course, not all local recalls deal with important issues. Two members of the Paradise city council faced major recall drives in 1981 because they had voted to ban parking on the city's main thoroughfare on the day of that community's annual Gold Nugget Days parade. A few years later, other Paradise councilmembers faced recalls because they favored a bond measure to finance a sewer system.

Local recalls seem most plentiful in smaller rural or retirement communities where local, frequently senior, residents take a keen interest in community politics, and in the suburbs of Los Angeles and the outlying Southern California counties of Riverside, San Bernardino, Orange, and San Diego, where the local recall has deep historical roots. Los Angeles was the first U.S. city to adopt the recall early this century and the first to recall a local official.

Negatives and Positives

Critics of the recall process cite several problems inherent in the device, including intimidation of officeholders by disgruntled minorities, heightened acrimony, added expense for special elections, and partisan hanky-panky. For example, part of the motivation in the drive to recall Ronald Reagan as governor in 1968 was an attempt to discredit his presidential ambitions. Politics and the recall process are inextricably linked.

Recall campaigns tend to be particularly mean-spirited because the recallee's integrity may be at stake. In small communities, recalls are frequently polarizing. For grossly underpaid and overworked local officeholders, being targeted for recall is the ultimate ingratitude. Some officials resign immediately rather than wait to see if the recall petition directed against them qualifies. On the other hand, the recall's availability encourages responsiveness of public officials and discourages incumbent arrogance. Thus, as with other direct-democracy devices, the recall carries distinct trade-offs.

REFERENDUM

Most states providing for the initiative also provide for its alter ego, the petition referendum. However, the pattern in these states is similar: Few petition referendums ever qualify for the ballot.

Compulsory and Advisory Referendums

In addition to the petition referendum, there are two other kinds of referendum: compulsory and advisory. When the legislature passes a constitutional amendment or bond issue, this measure is automatically placed on the next election ballot as a compulsory referendum that voters may approve or reject. An advisory referendum is a nonbinding measure on the ballot, posed by a city council or board of supervisors to assess the mood of a community.

Used in virtually every state of the union, compulsory referendums on bond measures are important but usually receive minimal publicity. Constitutional

PETITION REFERENDUMS QUALIFYING FOR BALLOT BY DECADE	NUMBER OF PETITIONS
1912–1919	11
1920–1929	11
1930–1939	11
1940–1949	1
1950–1959	1
1960–1969	0
1970–1979	0
1980–1989	4
1990–1995	0

TABLE 4.1   PETITION REFERENDUM USE IN CALIFORNIA

amendments submitted to the voters are often technical and legalistic. Should counties be required to have an elective district attorney? Should postsecondary education personnel be under civil service? Should local government employees be required to live in the city where they work?

Advisory referendums are used infrequently by city councils and boards of supervisors to put nonbinding questions on the ballot to get a sense of direction from the community. Unlike reputable surveys, though, questions posed on the ballot can be designed to elicit a specific response from voters. For example, Chico residents were asked the following in November 1986: "Should a large-scale apartment and housing development be built next to Upper Bidwell Park, causing tremendous impacts on our park and causing costly urban sprawl? Yes or No? Not surprisingly, the "no's" won.

Petition Referendums

The petition referendum was used occasionally in the early decades after its adoption, but it has been a rarity ever since (see Table 4.1).

Why have so few petition referendums (as compared to initiatives) qualified for the ballot? The major reason is the time constraints placed on proponents. To qualify a measure for the ballot, referendum proponents have only ninety days to collect the needed signatures. Thus, Republicans were furious in 1981 when Democratic Governor Jerry Brown signed the reapportionment bills a few minutes before midnight. This meant that Republicans were robbed of one precious day in their qualifying quest; they had only eighty-nine days to collect signatures. To have any realistic hope of qualifying a referendum, a group has to anticipate action while a measure is moving through the legislature. Initiative proponents, on the other hand, can be organized and ready to roll. In the past, groups as politically adept as the California Real Estate Association have failed to qualify petition referendums for the ballot because of time constraints.

Petition referendums sometimes develop when the legislature and governor go too far out on a limb on an issue. Although the legislature tends to respond to public opinion, occasionally on highly emotional issues—abortion, race relations, sexual practices, death penalty, gun control, or water—legislators may vote their consciences and not their constituencies. This may provide the impetus for a referendum effort. Referendum issues of the 1980s were construction of a Peripheral Canal to transfer "surplus" Northern California water to Southern California and reapportionment (three referenda—congressional, assembly, and senate—that were promoted by Republicans unhappy with the Democratic plan).

Petition referendums on the ballot seem unlikely in the foreseeable future. Nonetheless, for occasional controversial issues, the referendum certainly remains a possibility. And at the local level, referendums have been used by planned-growth advocates to override city council and supervisorial actions.

Negatives and Positives Is the petition referendum worth keeping? Proponents contend that the device keeps government accountable and responsive to the public. Opponents argue that it discourages legislators from taking principled stands against public sentiment. As with other direct-democracy devices, there are good arguments for and against the petition referendum. However, because it's used so rarely, it's not very controversial.

INITIATIVE

Initiative procedures vary widely among the states. California has the second shortest circulation period of the initiative states, 150 days (Oklahoma's is only 90 days), but many states have no circulation period restrictions. Some states have geographical restrictions requiring that petitions be signed in a certain number of counties, but California does not. Most initiative states require 5 to 10 percent of the state's registered voters to qualify petitions, but North Dakota has only a 2 percent requirement and does not even require signers to be registered voters. States have varying requirements on how many months before an election signatures must be turned in to qualify for the ballot. To an extent, initiative procedures, generous or restrictive, encourage or discourage initiative use, but other factors—presence of petition companies or tradition—are more critical. California and Oregon are the lead initiative states, and Arizona, Washington, Colorado, and North Dakota have also averaged a few initiatives on the ballot

UPI / Bettmann

Perhaps the state's most important lawmakers in the 1980s, Howard Jarvis (left) and Paul Gann held no elective positions but were promoters of dozens of successful initiative petitions.

per election. On the other hand, in about half these states, initiatives appear on the ballot infrequently.

Although the number of initiatives circulating and qualifying for the California ballot declined from the 1940s to the 1960s, there has been a remarkable upsurge in the level of initiative politicking ever since (see Table 4.2): About three-fourths of all initiatives filed in this state have been launched between 1970 and 1994.

Reasons for this explosion in initiative activity over the last several decades include: (1) the continued decline in public confidence in governmental leaders and political institutions; (2) the enormous popularity of particular initiatives (e.g., the Jarvis–Gann property-tax relief measure), which encouraged many similar efforts; (3) the inability of the legislature to act on certain issues; (4) the professional petition industry in the state, whose raison d'etre hinges on constant initiative activity; (5) the mushrooming growth of single-issue groups and PACs; and (6) more use of counterinitiatives. Counterinitiatives are measures that are

DECADE	NO. INITIATIVES FILED	NO. AND % QUALIFYING		NO. AND % APPROVED		NO. AND % REJECTED	
1911–1919	44	30	68%	8	27%	22	73%
1920–1929	53	35	66%	10	29%	25	71%
1930–1939	65	37	57%	10	27%	26	73%
1940–1949	42	19	45%	6	32%	13	68%
1950–1959	17	12	41%	2	16%	10	84%
1960–1969	38	9	20%	3	33%	6	66%
1970–1979	138	21	15%	6	29%	15	71%
1980–1989	273	48*	18%	22	48%	24	52%
1990–1994	199	30	15%	11	37%	19	63%
Totals	872	241	28%	78	35%	101	67%

*This figure includes two initiatives that qualified for the ballot but were later removed by the court prior to their being voted upon—the Sebastiani Reapportionment Initiative and the Balance the Budget Initiative.

TABLE 4.2   NUMBER AND PERCENT OF INITIATIVES FILED, QUALIFIED, AND APPROVED BY VOTERS
Source: California Secretary of State's Office. "A History of the California Initiative Process." (March 1992) and "Calendar of Filing, 1911–1994," Sacramento, California. Updated by authors.

promoted because another initiative adverse to one's interests has already qualified for the ballot; opponents decide to qualify their own "more favorable" initiative for the same ballot. Circulating a countermeasure serves several purposes: (1) Proponents do not have to count solely on their "vote no" campaign against the original initiative—they can offer their own more "reasonable" proposal; and (2) they may be able to confuse some voters with similar topic initiatives and perhaps get them to vote against both. There were two campaign reform propositions on the June 1988 ballot; five separate car-insurance and lawyer initiatives in November 1988; and two reapportionment reform measures in June 1990. In November 1990, term limit advocates, pesticide and agriculture forces, and the timber and alcohol industries put countermeasures on the ballot.

What types of issues are brought to voters by the initiative? Clearly, they include some of the most controversial issues of the day: the death penalty, political reform, property taxes, property rights and racial exclusion, marijuana decriminalization, car-insurance rates, school busing and vouchers, farm labor rights, tobacco taxes and smoking regulations, state lottery, tort reform, nuclear energy safety, homosexual teachers, increasing crime penalties (three strikes), and illegal aliens. Although most never qualify for the ballot, their filing provides individuals and groups a chance to begin public discussion of an issue.

The initiative process allows voters an opportunity to express their opinions on a host of controversial issues as an arena for final resolution. Not surprisingly, this critically important process is controversial. Many legislators dislike the initiative because it takes power away from them and undercuts representative government. Knowledgeable observers worry about the public's capacity to vote thoughtfully on complex initiatives. Even initiative supporters are concerned with some aspects of the device. Let's consider the case for and against the initiative as we examine the various phases in the initiative process.

Drafting

Criticisms One major criticism of initiatives is that they are often poorly drafted. Legislative bills move slowly through the bicameral labyrinth. Bills are repeatedly scrutinized, polished, and amended by various committees. But the initiative comes to the voter full-blown, without the give-and-take of polishing and amending. Literally anyone, including cranks and crackpots, can submit an initiative idea and then circulate petitions. In 1974, one individual filed twenty-four separate California initiatives on the same day! Robert W. Wilson has filed initiatives to allow casino gambling in the state twenty-six times (from 1964 to 1994; none have qualified). Initiatives can be vague, bizarre, lengthy, complicated, and potentially unconstitutional. Indeed, a 1989 initiative that circulated but did not qualify would have repealed all state laws adopted since 1926! Among other recent unusual initiative proposals filed is one to require that numbers be tattooed on the faces of violent felons, with repeat offenders getting additional number tattoos. Another proposes that California should secede from the union and become an independent nation.

Rebuttal Direct-democracy supporters argue that if an initiative is patently harebrained, it would never get on the ballot. Voters won't sign just anything thrust in front of them. The relatively few reaching the ballot always have some legitimate rationale, and most of these are rejected by voters (see Table 4.2).

Although some initiatives do have drafting problems, in fairness, the legislature approves legislation hastily at times. This is especially true during the last week or two of a session when there is always a tremendous backlog of bills. Also, a growing number of initiatives are drafted by elected officials or interest group spokespersons (i.e., the "experts") or by skilled attorneys who specialize in political law, such as the Chip Nielsen and the Bagetelos and Fadem law firms. When Fadem drafted the lottery initiative, he used survey data, analysis of other states' lottery laws, and a word-by-word study of the initiative draft—much as committee consultants might do. Of course, groups must have the financial wherewithal to hire these private attorneys. All things considered, legislature-crafted law is usually superior to initiative-drafted law, but the latter type is promoted because the politics of the legislative process can create gridlock.

Finally, although a fair number of initiatives have been declared unconstitutional in whole or in part, so too have measures passed by the state legislature and by Congress. The final word on constitutionality comes from the courts.[9]

Qualifying

Criticisms Critics of the initiative process contend that to amass the requisite number of signatures to qualify a statute or constitutional initiative in the time allotted now requires either a large organization or substantial financial resources to hire a professional petition firm to obtain signatures. Thus, it is argued, the initiative is a tool of narrow special interests—the oil industry, automobile manufacturers and dealers, land developers, tobacco companies, building interests, the liquor industry, and so on—rather than an important citizen weapon.

Under the original provisions of the Political Reform Act initiative of 1974, groups would have been limited in how much they could spend to qualify a measure for the ballot. These limits were struck down by the state Court as unconstitutional because they violated the free-speech provisions of the First Amendment. Several initiative states had laws banning paid signature collecting, but the U.S. Supreme Court ruled in 1989 that such laws were also unconstitutional, again on free-speech grounds.

Large mass-member organizations, such as the California Teachers Association (CTA) or the California State Employees Association, can mail petition forms to their many members, but smaller groups cannot hope to qualify an initiative relying only on their own membership. Financially powerful groups can hire expensive professional petition firms to collect signatures for them.

The two leading "clipboard" petition companies are Kimball Petition Management Company (middle-of-the road causes) and Mike Arno's American Petition Consultants (conservative and business causes). These companies advertise in political journals, send letters to interest groups touting their services, and encourage those unhappy with decisions or nondecisions by the legislature and governor to consider the initiative process. Their very presence on the political scene allows interest group leaders to consider the initiative option without worrying about the grubby work of signature collecting.

After Kimball or Arno are hired to collect a specified number of signatures, many groups agree to collect at least some of their own signatures—usually one-half or so—through volunteers and group members. This reduces the petitioning costs for a group, which can add up to hundreds of thousands of dollars. Kimball and Arno then alert independent subcontractors (mainly in large cities) of a new campaign. Usually, Kimball and Arno prefer to package four or five separate initiatives to energize the efforts of subcontractors and signature headhunters—the more initiatives, the more money that can be made. Subcontractors contact their list of reliable signature collectors and also advertise in the classifieds for help ("Want to make extra cash? Work your own hours? Learn about politics? Be a petition solicitor!"). Solicitors receive about fifty to sixty cents per signature, and subcontractors are paid about five to ten cents per signature. Solicitors are advised to approach people waiting in lines or walking slowly. (According to Kimball, the best single place they found for collecting signatures some years ago was the King Tut exhibit in Los Angeles.) If a voter is wary, petition circulators are taught to emphasize that signing one's name does not necessarily mean agreement.[10] Signing the petition merely helps put the measure on the ballot so that voters can have a chance to express themselves on the issue at the next election. Phillip Morris Tobacco Company hired Arno to qualify its Proposition 188 of November 1994, the statewide smoking restrictions initiative. Phillip Morris had to spend several millions of dollars to qualify the initiative, and there were many complaints that some signers thought the initiative was an antismoking initiative (in reality, it undercut tough local restrictions and would have imposed weak statewide restrictions). Overall, the Kimball and Arno companies have been very successful in delivering the number of valid signatures for which they were contracted. About 75 percent of the initiatives that have qualified in the 1980s and 1990s have been produced by the Kimball and Arno firms.

Finally, while Kimball and Arno are normally cordial adversaries, the school choice (voucher) initiative brought them into direct conflict. Arno was hired by voucher advocates to qualify their petition for the November 1992 ballot, and Kimball was hired by the CTA to run a "don't sign the petition" campaign. Kimball enlisted teachers to hound Arno solicitors and persuade people not to sign. Not surprisingly, this angered signature solicitors by reducing the amount of money they could make. Many invalid signatures were collected; some individuals signed more than once. Arno charged CTA with trying to sabotage the petition campaign, and he and voucher supporters filed a lawsuit against CTA, but the court ruled there was no evidence that either the CTA or Kimball had acted improperly. Because of signature invalidations, the school voucher initiative did not make the 1992 ballot but did qualify as Proposition 174 of November 1993. The CTA was able to contribute mainly to Democratic candidates in 1992 and could wait until later to provide funds to oppose the voucher initiative.

Another option is collecting signatures through computerized direct mailings of petitions. Undoubtedly, the most famous of these petition-by-mail firms is the Butcher-Forde (B-F) Advanced Voter Communications Company of Orange County. B-F first used the mailed petition technique in the successful 1978 drive to qualify the death-penalty initiative. Since then, targeted mass mail has been used occasionally in signature drives, sometimes to supplement signatures collected in the streets. Although the cost per signature in a direct-mail petition campaign is three to four times higher than street solicitation, some mail campaigns have generated enormous return contributions, more than making up for higher postage and printing costs. Clipboard signature companies must start from scratch each petition drive. Direct-mail firms can store names on disk and send new initiative petitions on each successive signature drive. Finally, the validation rate of the signatures of these highly politicized citizens is much higher than that of signers selected at random on the street. However, return contributions of people who have already made contributions has declined lately.

Mass-mail firms such as Below, Tobe, & Associates have become adept in persuading people to open their envelopes, read, and sign the enclosed petitions. The color of the lettering on the envelope, a bold printed warning such as "OFFICIAL DOCUMENT ENCLOSED," and an accompanying letter warning the reader of a looming catastrophe have been used to get readers to respond. Critics of this type of signature gathering complain that only one side is presented to prospective signers, but defenders argue that this procedure is more sensible than urging distracted people walking through shopping centers to sign petitions.

Critics of the initiative process argue that there are many opportunities for deception in gathering signatures. Sometimes petition solicitors do not fairly describe the initiative they are circulating. Ed Koupal, the late founder of the People's Lobby, described the reality of signature collecting as follows (Duscha, 1975, p. 83):

> First, you set up a table with six petitions taped to it, and a sign in front that says, SIGN HERE. One person sits at the table. Another person stands in front. That's all you need—two people.
>
> While one person sits at the table, the other walks up to people and asks two questions. We operate on the old selling maxim that two yeses make a sale. First, we ask them if they are a registered voter. If they say yes, we ask them if they are registered in that county. If they say yes to that, we immediately push them up to the table where the person sitting points to a petition and says, "Sign this." By this time, the person feels, "Oh goodie, I get to play," and signs it. . . . [P]eople don't ask to read the petition and we certainly don't offer. Why try to educate the world when you're trying to get signatures?

Mark Antman / The Image Works

The petition process has been an ingrained feature of the state's political milieu for more than eighty years.

Rebuttal Certainly, the initiative process is popular with voters because it gives average citizens a voice in major policy decisions. Without professional petitioning, few initiatives would be on the ballot and voters would have less opportunity to participate. Although money and large organizations can help in qualifying initiatives, they are not, as has been argued, indispensable. Clearly, over the past several elections, small, less affluent groups have scored impressive victories in signature-gathering campaigns. Among the least expensive initiatives to qualify during the 1980s were two LaRouche AIDS proposals (November 1986 and June 1988), an English voting materials initiative (November 1984), a proposal to ban the inheritance tax (June 1982), and the antismoking initiative (November 1980). Yet even groups with little money to spend on signature campaigns and who rely on volunteer solicitors for most or all of their signatures have to spend money on campaign coordinators, travel costs, meals, and the like. Thus, these nonprofessional signature campaigns can cost proponents hundreds of thousands of dollars too. Moreover, in 1994, all five initiatives that qualified for the November ballot were professional efforts. The average cost to qualify each initiative was $1,097,301. Small, less affluent groups continue to qualify initiatives for the ballot without professional petitioners or large-scale mass organizations. Grassroots appeal and ingenuity can be critical factors.[11]

NO.	INITIATIVE SUBJECT	YES	NO	APPROVED OR DISAPPROVED BY VOTERS	SIDE WITH MOST MONEY
161	Death with dignity	$1,055,000	$3,733,000	Disapproved	Wins
162	State employee retirement	2,455,000	5,800	Approved	Wins
163	End snack tax	2,120,000	85,000	Approved	Wins
164	Congressional term limits	503,000	258,000	Approved	Wins
165	Budget/welfare change	4,943,000	4,085,000	Disapproved	Loses
166	Health care	1,992,000	6,137,000	Disapproved	Wins
167	State taxes	876,000	170,000	Disapproved	Loses
174	Choice (vouchers)	2,962,000	13,775,000	Disapproved	Wins

TABLE 4.3   IMPACT OF SPENDING ON INITIATIVES (1992–1993)
Source: Fair Political Practices Commission. "California's Statewide Ballot Measures: 1992 General Election Campaign Financing." (August 1993) Sacramento, California.

Campaigning

Criticisms One of the most frequently heard criticisms of the initiative process is the role that big money plays in direct-democracy campaigns. Undoubtedly, enormous sums have been spent by proponents and opponents in initiative campaigns. In 1976, nearly $4 million was spent on the nuclear-power initiative; in 1982, $6.7 million was spent on the bottle-deposit initiative and $7.2 million on the handgun-regulation initiative. Even when inflation and population growth are factored in, the amounts spent are monumental. Car insurance interests spent nearly $56 million trying to persuade Californians to vote for "no-fault" Proposition 104. Lawyers spent $16 million in their "Vote Yes on Proposition 100" campaign, and tobacco companies spent more than $22 million to encourage a no vote on the cigarette-tax increase (Proposition 99). In 1994, the vote yes side on Governor Wilson's Proposition 165, the budget powers–welfare reduction initiative, spent $5 million, while opponents spent $4 million; it lost. Million dollar-plus campaigns are commonplace in initiative campaigns (see Table 4.3).

Obviously, the side with more money has an advantage. It can buy more billboards, newspaper ads, TV spots, and the like to help influence the electorate. In some initiative campaigns, the spending disparity between proponents and opponents has reached outlandish proportions. For example, in 1972 opponents of Proposition 20 (the coastline initiative) spent five times as much as the proponents. In November 1988, spending by proponents and opponents on eleven of the twelve initiatives on the ballot was very unbalanced. The most extreme case was Proposition 104, "no-fault" insurance: Proponents spent nearly $56 million, whereas opponents "amassed" $29,098!

Public employee groups spent $2.5 million in 1992 supporting Proposition 162, dealing with modifications in the public employee retirement system, versus opponents' $5,811. And on the voucher initiative of 1993, teachers and other allied groups spent over $14 million defeating Proposition 174, the choice (vouchers) initiative; its promoters spent about $3 million.

Critics emphasize that initiative campaigns are run by slick campaign management firms whose main objectives are making money and winning elections, not informing or educating voters. (Chapter 6 has a more complete discussion of campaign management firms.) Distortions, gimmicks, deceptive slogans, half-truths, and outright lies have characterized many initiative campaigns. Though these campaign pros also manage most statewide and many legislative candidates' races, their impact is greater, it is argued, in initiative campaigns because voters do not have the usual candidate or partisan cues as guides.

Examples of confusing claims and counterclaims are extensive in the history of California initiative campaigns. In 1972, advocates of "tax relief" Proposition 14 argued that a yes vote would reduce taxes; opponents countered that a no vote would reduce taxes. State employee ads in 1972 proclaimed, "It's your money, keep state pay in line, vote yes on 15." In reality, a yes vote would have made it easier for state employees to receive salary increases. Advocates of the measure argued that "keeping state pay in line" referred to having state employees paid at a level commensurate with what they would earn in the private sector! The same year, opponents of Proposition 20 argued that a yes vote would lock up the coast from the people; proponents argued that they were trying to save the coast for the people. Opponents of the 1982 bottle-deposit initiative audaciously portrayed themselves as "concerned environmentalists" worried about the future of recycling centers if Proposition 11 passed.

In 1988, the tobacco industry ("Californians Against Unfair Tax Increases") argued that Proposition 99, the tobacco-tax increase, if approved, would require police to spend so much time trying to stop bootlegged cigarettes from low-tax states being shipped illegally to California that murderers, rapists, and robbers would run rampant. Opponents of the June 1990 primary reapportionment reform, Proposition 119, claimed that a no vote would help save the environment. In November 1990, opponents of the "nickel a drink" alcohol tax, Proposition 134, argued that "not one red cent would go to schools to teach about alcohol abuse"—although millions of dollars would have gone to alcoholism programs and to trauma centers, which deal with the aftermath of drunk drivers. Proponents of the voucher initiative in 1993 contended that it would improve public schools, make them safer from violence, and provide children a better education. Voucher opponents said just the opposite: It would completely undermine public education. And in 1994, Phillip Morris officials said one of their main objectives in promoting Proposition 188, the Statewide Smoking Regulation initiative, was to discourage tobacco sales to youth.

On occasion, because of the populist nature of initiatives, racism and bigotry enter the campaign. For example, several states have adopted laws that stipulate that homosexuals shall receive no civil rights employment benefits. In California, 1994's Proposition 187 (nicknamed Save Our State, or SOS, as a word play on the international distress call), bars public services such as education and health services to illegal immigrants. Although nearly all California elected officeholders in 1994 stated they were concerned about the extent of illegal immigration into California (about 2 million), some of the backers' statements verged on racism. Angered by comments made by Mexican officials about the initiative, one SOS county chair stated, "The Mexican government should shut up about our election." SOS supporters seemed to blame most of California's problems on undocumented workers. In short, opportunities for razzle-dazzle, hocus-pocus politics are considerable in initiative campaigns.

Rebuttal Campaign spending on initiatives has risen steadily, it is true, but so has spending on candidate races. Though the side with more money has a distinct advantage, it is not necessarily insurmountable. Indeed, in several recent initiative campaigns, the side that spent more money lost. Eugene Lee (1978, p. 113) notes that in the sixteen initiative campaigns between 1972 and 1976, the side that spent more money won eight times and lost eight times. In November 1992, twelve initiatives were on the ballot. The side that spent more won in four contests but lost in eight others. Proponents of the insurance industry spent nearly $56 million touting Proposition 104; the other side had virtually no money. Proposition 104 lost. In the same election, the tobacco industry spent more than $21 million fighting the tobacco tax of Proposition 99, while the other side spent $2 million. The tobacco industry lost. In addition, Phillip Morris and other tobacco companies spent millions more than their opponents trying to persuade Californians to vote yes on Proposition 188, the statewide tobacco regulation measure of 1994. This time they lost overwhelmingly, 70–30 percent no. Proponents of the nuclear-freeze initiative of November 1982 spent $3.5 million to persuade voters to support the measure; opponents spent $6,041 to defeat it. The initiative was approved 52 to 48 percent. Similarly, state employees spent $2.5 million trying to persuade voters to support Proposition 162, to opponents' $5,800, yet "yes" received only 51 percent of the vote. Spending figures on the 1992–93 initiatives are shown in Table 4.3. Obviously, an expensive, professional campaign is helpful, but it will fail if it runs counter to substantial public sentiment.

It is easier for those with a lopsided spending advantage to win when they try to persuade voters to vote no. Only occasionally can the underfinanced side persuade voters to vote yes. For example, on the smoking (1978 and 1980), bottle-deposit, and handgun-control initiatives, polls taken at the beginning of the campaign period indicated substantial support for these measures among decided voters. But opponents employed superior financial advantages in expensive campaigns and persuaded undecided voters that these initiatives would be costly to consumers, were confusing, and would mean more governmental red tape and regulation. In such campaigns, the no vote becomes the safe, conservative option for perplexed voters worried about change. However, there are exceptions to the rule. Despite a spending advantage, tobacco companies failed to stop a tobacco-tax increase in 1988, and in 1986 toxic-initiative foes outspent the pro side by a large margin, but citizens voted yes for reform.

Although having superior financial resources is not always the critical factor in initiative campaigns, it does have the potential to distort the results. But there seems little hope in the near future for blunting the impact of money in initiative campaigns. As noted previously, the courts have struck down expenditure limits on initiative campaigns. In addition, efforts to limit the size of individual or group campaign contributions in an initiative campaign have been struck down. In 1980, the Berkeley city council adopted an ordinance limiting individuals and groups to a maximum contribution of $250 in local initiative campaigns. The ordinance was upheld by the state Supreme Court, but the U.S. Supreme Court overturned the California decision (8 to 1) and declared the law unconstitutional. The Court ruled the ordinance violated free-speech rights and that there was inconclusive evidence that "Big Money" was the decisive factor in initiative elections.

One additional factor that used to help narrow the fiscal imbalance in many initiative campaigns was the "fairness doctrine." Instituted in the 1940s, this doctrine required broadcast stations to provide balance in their political programming. In 1974, the Federal Communications Commission (FCC) ruled that when one side in a ballot campaign had no money to buy radio and television spots while the other side had purchased many ad placements, the side without money must be provided free radio and television time by broadcasters (at about a 4-to-1 ratio; every four minutes purchased by one side would be matched by one minute given to the impoverished side). Further FCC rulings during the 1970s required broadcast stations to give the side without money reasonable time allotments— not just between 2 and 6 A.M. or early on Sunday mornings. Of course, to get stations to comply meant many hours of staff contact work in approaching the various stations with free time requests. Fairness advocates argued that voters should be able to hear the arguments of both sides. Stations refusing to give air time to underfinanced sides could be fined or conceivably lose their license. During the 1980s, however, President Reagan, a firm opponent of the fairness doctrine, appointed new FCC commissioners who shared his antifairness viewpoint. Reagan argued that government had gone too far in regulating business, the fairness doctrine limited station owners' free speech, and the addition of cable meant there was sufficient competition.

In 1987, the FCC ruled that the fairness doctrine was no longer valid in candidate campaigns. Left unanswered was whether the doctrine applied to initiative campaigns, although most experts assumed it did. In any case, since the 1988 elections, stations feel under no legal compunction to give free air time to campaigns without money, but some do out of a sense of fair play. President Clinton and Democratic leaders in Congress at one time expressed interest in restoring the doctrine, but action seems doubtful now that Republicans control both houses.

Voting

Criticisms Many initiative critics believe voters are woefully uninformed about the host of complex, lengthy propositions they must confront. The Political Reform Act of 1974 contained more than 22,000 words; it is unlikely that many voters have read all (or any) of its provisions. The November 1990 *Ballot Pamphlet and Supplement* containing the texts and pro and con arguments on propositions was 151 pages long! Other initiatives, such as Governor Reagan's 1973 property-tax proposal, the 1978 Jarvis–Gann property-tax limit, the 1988 "no-fault" auto-insurance initiative, and the park bonds initiative of June 1994 (Proposition 180) were highly technical and complicated.

Voters, it is argued, have a hard enough time knowing something about the candidate races at the top of the ticket; expecting them to have informed views on a host of state and local propositions is not realistic. Reinforcing this view, pollsters have repeatedly found a great deal of ignorance and confusion among voters during initiative campaigns. Most voters only begin to focus on these measures a few days before an election.

Concerns have been voiced by initiative critics that, given the absence of party cues, voters are more likely to follow the lead of newspaper endorsements. Critics of the initiative process also contend that the legislature better represents the unorganized, minorities, the young, and nonvoters in our society, whereas the initiative serves the interests of the voting white middle class.

Rebuttal Few initiative supporters deny that some initiatives are long and complex or that voters are faced with many difficult decisions. Yet most voters expressing a preference at the top of the ballot take the time and feel competent to vote on initiatives at the bottom of the ballot. The more controversial and widely discussed the proposition, the greater the vote cast. On average, voting on the key initiatives drops off only slightly (5%) from the races at the head of the ticket. Indeed, on a few occasions, voting on initiatives has been greater than for candidates. In June 1978, 6.6 million votes were cast on Proposition 13— 750,000 more than were cast in the gubernatorial primary.

Although polls have indicated massive ignorance of some ballot measures in mid-campaign, most potential voters do know something about controversial initiatives long before the election—perhaps 50 to 70 percent of the electorate.

One factor that helps account for low voter awareness of initiatives during the campaign is the typical strategy of campaign managers: "Save your money until the last week or two, and then spend it all in a last-minute blitz." In addition, the public receives its *California Voters Pamphlet* just a few weeks before the election. Some voters probably learn about initiatives by reading through portions of the pamphlet. Some may even decide how they will vote when they read the ballot summaries in their polling place.

Legislative Failure

If the California legislature is unable to reconcile group differences, and interests resort to initiatives, then the legislature, some critics argue, has obviously failed. For example, the inability of the legislature and governor to enact true property-tax relief culminated in the passage of Proposition 13 of 1978, and their failure to deal with spiraling car-insurance rates in the late 1980s led to Proposition 103 in November 1988. The scandals and gridlock of the professional legislature in the 1980s led to the successful adoption of term limits. In all fairness, however, this view of legislative failure seems overly simplistic.

Initiatives usually develop when a group fails to receive satisfactory legislative action. Many of the most critical issues at the capitol pit powerful groups against each other: malpractice (doctors against lawyers against insurance companies) or coastline planning (developers, builders, and labor unions against environmentalists) or workers' compensation (insurance companies and local government against labor unions). The controversies are difficult for the legislature and governor to resolve successfully. Inability to pass satisfactory compromise legislation should not necessarily be construed as failure; it may simply reflect the relatively even balance of power of the various contending groups at the capitol. When there is an impasse, the initiative may offer final resolution.

Dennis Renault / *The Sacramento Bee*

"Ladies and gentlemen, in the late 20th century, when a stubborn
governor had no solutions for the state's problems and
legislators were bought by special interests,
the voters passed an initiative. . . ."

Finally, many experts believe that particular initiatives have made it almost impossible for the legislature and governor to manage the budget because of the fiscal restrictions of Proposition 13 and Proposition 98 (the latter requires that at least 40 percent of the budget go to K–14 spending; see Chapter 10).

Initiative Reform

Overall, one could take several directions in revising the initiative process. One course would be to make it more difficult to launch initiatives. Thus, proposals have been made to increase the qualifying percentages, require signatures to be gathered in public places, or shorten the circulation period.

Although many legislators, journalists, and academics would welcome these sorts of changes in the initiative process—some would abolish the process entirely—the California public strongly supports the initiative process, although less so with each new Field Poll: 83 percent in 1979, 80 percent in 1982, 79 percent in 1985, and 66 percent in 1990. But this remains a sizable majority—only a few thought the process was bad. Public interest lobbies such as Common Cause and the Planning and Conservation League, which have used the initiative successfully, are wary of any attempts to gut the process. They serve as watchdogs against attacks on the initiative.

A second initiative revision would be to make initiative qualification easier, but because so many initiatives have circulated over the last few decades and a fair number have qualified, there is little support for such a proposal.

Finally, a third avenue of initiative revision would be to make the process work more equitably. In this vein, two prime problem areas could be addressed: (1) the amount of information citizens have in making their voting decisions on ballot propositions and (2) the "Big Money" factor. Let's consider proposals on how these might be achieved.

Those who finance an initiative could be required to clearly identify themselves in their ads—for example, Philip Morris on Proposition 188 ads, not Californians for Statewide Smoking Regulations—so voters can make sense of the issue. (In fact, Phillip Morris did identify its participation in the 188 campaign in fine print in its mailers.) The state Supreme Court could be more vigilant in narrowly applying the single-subject rule. A long, tortuous initiative covering many disparate topics is an open invitation to voter cynicism and anger. When voters confront many complex or conflicting sets of initiatives, they have a tendency to vote "no" if they are unsure or wary. Frankly, this is not a bad idea.

The role of big money in initiative campaigns is the second significant problem—particularly because the fairness doctrine is no longer in effect. Attempts to ban paid petitioning, limit initiative campaign expenditures, or restrict the size of contributions to proposition campaigns have all been struck down. There seems little hope for resolution of this in the near future.

In 1992, because of complaints about the process, Assemblyman Jim Costa (now a state senator) authored legislation that was eventually signed by Governor Wilson to establish a Citizens Commission on Ballot Initiatives to consider reforming initiative procedures. The fifteen-member commission consisted of appointees of the senate, assembly, and governor, and designees of the attorney general and secretary of state and was chaired by former Legislative Analyst Alan Post. The commission met periodically in 1993 to evaluate possible reforms. The summary of its recommendations was later introduced in bill form by Costa. The most dramatic proposed change would reinstitute a modified "indirect" initiative system. Qualified initiatives now go on the next ballot automatically; in an indirect system they must first go to the legislature. California used to have an indirect initiative option, but it was rarely used and dropped in 1966. Under the Post Commission's recommendations, the process would work as follows. Proponents would file their initiatives and have 180 days to circulate their petition (30 days more than at present). Once the requisite number of signatures was collected and verified, the measure would go to the legislature, which would hold hearings at which proponents and opponents could testify. Proponents would be allowed to amend their initiative draft so long as they were consistent with the "purposes and intent" of the measure. This allowance for amending would make the initiative process more like the legislative lawmaking process. Within 45 days, the legislature and governor could approve, and there would be no need to place the initiative on the ballot. It would be law. Or if the legislature and governor rejected it, the initiative would go on the next ballot for public vote. The commission also recommended other fine-tuning changes. The Costa initiative reform bill died in 1994 but has been reintroduced in the 1995–96 session.

Of course, the old adage "If it ain't broke, don't fix it" might well apply. Should the initiative process be mightily revamped as the Post Commission recommends or are more modest changes in order? The current initiative process works reasonably well. We're better off with it than without it. Voters do have a voice in major policy decisions. Term limits, illegal immigration, and the "three strikes" initiatives were clearly popular with voters and forced the legislature to confront these issues. And in 1996, citizens may be voting on a much discussed civil rights initiative, which would abolish most state affirmative action programs. If a measure is blatantly racist (as critics of 187 believed), the courts can resolve the constitutional questions. And if voters are overwhelmed or confused, they can vote no. After all, a process that can anger big oil, pesticide interests, the tobacco industry, timber companies, voucher advocates, environmentalists, politicians, and political parties can't be all bad.

SUMMARY

In summary, the initiative provides a last resort to the public to bypass a stymied legislature or governor. A threatened initiative can "encourage" the legislature to act. Initiatives allow for decisive decisions on particularly sensitive, hard-to-resolve issues and give the electorate a chance to affect the key issues of the day. Reforms should be made in the initiative process to make it operate more equitably.

NOTES

1. Strangely enough, even though California gained more than 5 million new citizens between 1982 and 1990, the number of signatures needed to qualify initiatives through 1994 was less than it was in 1982 because of poor turnout!

2. Governors can call special elections wherein qualified initiatives are voted upon. For example, Proposition 174, the school choice voucher initiative of November 1993, was voted on at a special election.

3. As an example (see Chapter 3), Propositions 68 and 73 were approved by voters at the same general election in June 1988, but Proposition 73 took legal precedent because it was approved by a wider margin.

4. At the state level, the petition effort to recall an officeholder theoretically could begin on the first day of the officeholder's term. If the required number of valid signatures is collected, a special election must be called. The ballot for a statewide recall, except for judges, is divided into two parts. The top half lists the charges brought against the incumbent, as well as the incumbent's defense of his or her position. Then the question is posed: Shall be recalled from the office of ———? The bottom half of the ballot lists the various nominees for the office. To be placed on the ballot as a candidate, one would need to secure the signatures of 1 percent of the vote cast for that particular office in the last election. Not surprisingly, the challenged incumbent may not qualify as one of the candidates on the bottom portion of the ballot. If there are more no votes than yes votes, the incumbent remains in office, and votes on the bottom half of the ballot are not counted. Additionally, the state must reimburse the incumbent for the expenses of the campaign. If there are more yes votes than no votes, the officeholder is removed from office, and the candidate with the most votes on the bottom portion of the ballot is elected and serves out the remainder of the recalled officeholder's term.

5. Requirements for local recall qualification in California are as follows:

Number of Voters	Percent to Qualify	Days to Qualify Petition
Less than 1,000	30	40
1,000–5,000	25	60
5,000–10,000	25	90
10,000–50,000	20	120
50,000–100,000	10	160
100,000 or more	10	160

6. Arizona voters nearly recalled former Governor Evan Mecham in 1988. Sufficient signatures had been collected and a special recall election had been scheduled, but the legislature impeached him before the election could be held.

7. Among the leading targets of recalls have been: Governor Culbert Olson, five recall attempts; Governor Jerry Brown, four; Governor Pat Brown, three; Governor Ronald Reagan, three; and Chief Justice Rose Bird, three.

8. Because of the Roberti incident, the legislature passed a constitutional amendment that appeared on the 1994 ballot and was approved by voters in Proposition 183. This measure authorizes recall elections to be held within 180 days (not 60 to 80 days as it was formerly) of certification of signatures to enable consolidation of recall elections with regularly scheduled elections. If this law had been in effect in spring 1994, Roberti's recall could have been conducted with the June primary—no special election would have been required.

9. Perhaps most distressing to direct-democracy advocates is that former Chief Justice Rose Bird argued that the court should declare legal challenges of qualified initiatives constitutional or unconstitutional prior to their being voted upon by the public. She said this would save proponents and opponents millions of dollars in futile campaigns. Moreover, she felt this might deflect some of the hostility directed against the court when it declared an initiative that was overwhelmingly approved by voters, unconstitutional. The defeat of Rose Bird and two other liberals on the court (Justices Reynoso and Grodin) in their reconfirmation elections in November 1986 has curtailed this judicial strategy.

10. In Sacramento in 1986, the rights of petition solicitors and opponents of an initiative became a court issue. Local Sacramento environmentalists launched a petition drive to stop an agricultural area (North Natomas) from being rezoned for business and commercial development rezoning was to accommodate a planned arena for the professional basketball team, the Sacramento Kings. Environmentalists brought suit contending that their petition seekers were harassed by outraged sports fans and others favoring development, and they were unable to collect enough signatures because of the intimidation.

11. After successfully jockeying Proposition 13 (the property-tax relief measure) to victory in June 1978, Paul Gann, People's Advocate founder, had a new government-spending-limit initiative available for June primary voters. Gann placed volunteer signature gatherers at polling places (carefully positioned more than 100 feet from the polls). As people finished voting for 13, they could walk a few paces over to the colorfully marked table of the Gann volunteer and sign the new initiative. It qualified.

REFERENCES

Ainsworth, Bill. "Initiative Wars." *California Journal* 21 (1990), pp. 147–150.

Cronin, Thomas E. *Direct Democracy: The Politics of Initiative, Referendum and Recall.* Cambridge, MA: Harvard University Press, 1989.

Duscha, Carla L. "It Isn't a Lobby—And the People are Few." *California Journal* 6 (1975).

Field Institute. (1983, November). "Initiative Process." *California Opinion Index*. San Francisco.

———. (1990, August). Public Support for the Initiative Process." *California Opinion Index*. San Francisco.

Lee, Eugene. "California." In *Referendums: A Comparative Study of Practice and Theory*, edited by David Butler and Austin Ranney. Washington, DC: American Enterprise Institute, 1978, pp. 87–122.

Older, Fremont. *My Own Story*. New York: Macmillan, 1926.

Price, Charles M. "The Initiative: A Comparative State Analysis of a Western Phenomenon." *Western Political Quarterly* 28 (1975), pp. 243–262.

———. "Recalls at the Local Level: Dimensions and Implications." *National Civic Review* 72 (1983), pp. 199–206.

———. "Experts Explain the Business of Buying Signatures." *California Journal* 16 (1985), pp. 283–286.

———. "Big Money Initiatives." *California Journal* 19 (1988), pp. 481–487.

———. "Lawmakers and Initiatives." *California Journal* 19 (1988), pp. 380–386.

———. "The Fairness Doctrine." *California Journal* 20 (1989), pp. 251–254.

———. "Initiative Reform: Is it Time to Return to the Indirect Initiative?" *California Journal* 25 (April 1995), pp. 33–36.

———. "Citizen Initiators Tilt at the Electoral Windmill." *California Journal* 25 (April 1995), pp. 38–42.

Price, Charles M., and Bob Waste. "Initiatives: Too Much of a Good Thing?" *California Journal* 22 (1991), pp. 116–120.

INTEREST GROUPS AND LOBBYISTS:

YESTERDAY AND TODAY

From the state legislature's first session in December 1849 in its temporary San Jose quarters to the elegant refurbished capitol of contemporary Sacramento, interest groups and "legislative advocates" (a legal euphemism for lobbyists) have been an integral part of the California political scene. In fact, according to former Senate President Pro Tem Hugh Burns, they preceded the legislature:

> Don't forget that the lobbyists were here [in the state capital] even before we got here. The history shows us that at one of the first [legislative] sessions in San Jose, the lobbyists had come to town before the legislative members and had taken up all the rooms in the hotels, and there was no room for the members to stay.
>
> That probably gave rise to the first expression about getting in bed with lobbyists—there was no other place to sleep. (*The Sacramento Bee*, July 14, 1969, p. 5)

Indeed, for much of California's history, lobbyists have been powerful forces within state government. Although interest groups and lobbyists have been active and are influential in all state capitals and Washington, D.C., California has been a particularly strong lobby state. Given the sorts of decisions made by the legislature, governor, commissions, and state bureaucracy, it is not surprising that businesses, trade associations, labor unions, government employees, and literally hundreds of other groups find it necessary to be represented in the state capital.

DEFINITIONS

Interest groups are organizations of people who seek to influence government to make "favorable" decisions on their behalf. Not all groups are "interest" groups, only those that have a desire to get something from government. Thus, the Chico Model Train Club under normal circumstances is not an interest group, but when it attempted to persuade Amtrak to provide train service to Chico, and when it petitioned the Chico city council for funds to refurbish the train station, it acted as an interest group.

People join interest groups for a variety of reasons. For one, Americans tend to be joiners and enjoy socializing with others. Many citizens become involved in group activity to improve their economic situation. However, members of public interest and cause groups are mainly interested in promoting broader, common issues. Members of these groups (e.g., the Sierra Club, League of Women Voters, PTA, NAACP, Common Cause, and pro- and antiabortion groups) do not join to improve their own economic status, but to fight for "worthy" causes. Many groups emphasize the special opportunities members enjoy if they join—medical or dental insurance, group travel, useful publications, programs, and so on. Sierra Club members, in addition to joining an environmentally active group, can participate in various hikes and excursions and are sent a monthly magazine detailing camping news. Farm Bureau members, AMA doctors, American Political Science Association professors, California Bar Association lawyers, and others keep abreast of developments in their respective fields, in part, through group publications. Members of the American Association of Retired Persons receive discounts and advice for the elderly. Finally, some members join labor unions, teacher organizations, or employee groups not because they want to, but as a condition of their employment or through pressure from other workers.

Lobbyists are hired by interest groups to represent the organization's views in Sacramento—an alternative form of representation. Virtually every citizen belongs to at least one group that lobbies at the capitol—business, labor, environmental, racial, seniors, children, women, animal lovers, local governments, employee groups, churches, and many others. Not surprisingly, such well-organized, financially powerful, high-status groups as bankers, insurance interests, real estate brokers, doctors, attorneys, retailers, and petroleum interests have always found ready access there. Disorganized, poor, low-status groups—such as the homeless, motorcycle clubs, and the unemployed—have difficulty gaining a serious hearing. Lobbies representing students in California are more similar to the latter type of lobby: no PAC, no wining-and-dining money, little consensus, and a youthful membership that has a poor voter turnout rate.

Overall, lobbyists perform several critical functions. First, they serve as the "eyes and ears" for groups at the capitol. Because most of the public cannot really follow what goes on at the different levels of national, state, and local government (further complicated by the separation of powers), lobbyists are employed to keep track of what is happening and report these matters back to their groups. Second, they champion their group's interests at the capitol. They attempt to get measures favorable to their group passed and unfavorable measures killed using a variety of techniques. Third, they provide information to legislators and administrators on pending legislation or tell the official what the group members' views are. Remember that the right to lobby is, in effect, guaranteed by the First Amendment in the Bill of Rights—the right of citizens to petition their government for redress of grievance. Moreover, businesses can deduct their lobbying costs as a legitimate business expense for income-tax purposes.

HISTORICAL PERSPECTIVE

As previously noted, Southern Pacific Railroad dominated California government from 1880 to 1910. But in the early 1900s, the Progressive reform movement swept the country. California Progressives fought zealously to eliminate Southern Pacific's corrupt power from state government. They promoted a host of reforms—direct democracy, primaries, and regulatory commissions—as devices to provide the public with power over lobbyists, special interests, and political bosses. But by the 1920s, the third house (i.e., lobbyists and special interests) learned how to adapt and thrive in the post-Progressive period.

From the 1930s through the early 1950s, Artie Samish was the dominant California lobbyist. Physically, Samish was a newspaper cartoonist's dream, the perfect stereotype of how a lobbyist should look: straw hat, large cigar, enormous paunch, and loud tie. After a short stint as a clerk in the state senate, Samish went into lobbying. He was bright, cocky, knowledgeable about the process, and understood the psychology of legislators. He quickly established a reputation as a "fixer." As his reputation grew, more major industries and special interests sought his representation, which only enhanced his power. Before taking on clients, he required them to agree to contribute to his campaign fund treasury. He lavishly wined and dined elected officials and took care of their every need. His dominance was obvious. Former Governor Earl Warren stated, "On matters that affect his clients, Artie unquestionably has more power than the governor" (Velie, August 13, 1949, p. 13).

No single contemporary lobbyist has the dominant power Samish had. However, the 1994 conviction of Clay Jackson, the most powerful lobbyist of the 1980s and 1990s, for extortion and bribery, suggests that old problems linger. From

Southern Pacific to Artie Samish to Clay Jackson, special-interest money and power continue to be a problem at the capitol.

STRONG LOBBIES
Reasons for Their Development

By establishing rules, regulations, and taxing policy, state government strongly affects certain kinds of businesses: banks, insurance companies, mortuaries, dairies, petroleum industries, liquor interests, utilities, horse tracks, agribusiness, real estate, construction, and land development. These and other interests have found it vitally important to be represented in Sacramento. Historically, five factors contributed to the strong lobby focus of California politics: weak political parties, interest group campaign contributions, coterminous development, a nonprofessional legislature, and low public visibility.

Weak Political Parties Progressive reforms, such as the primary and direct democracy, weakened political parties and aided special interests (see Chapters 2 and 6).

Interest Group Campaign Contributions Because political parties were relatively weak and lacked financial resources, interest groups, PACs, and legislative leaders have been the chief dispensers of contributions to candidates. As campaign costs have spiraled, group influence has grown. Many California officeholders feel more indebted to their interest group backers than to their party.

Coterminous Development The industrial revolution and the development of corporate America occurred during the same period that Western territories were attaining statehood. As Harmon Zeigler and Michael Baer (1969, p. 37) note:

> In the Western states . . . political systems and interest groups developed simultaneously. Interest groups did not have to fight existing political institutions; they shared in the development of the political system; lobbyists and politicians "grew up" together. Furthermore, the political traditions of the Western states— nonpartisanship, open primaries, a high rate of participation—invite interest groups (along with everybody else) to compete for the stakes of politics.

Nonprofessional Legislature Special-interest lobbyists attempt to influence all state government institutions—assembly and senate, governor and administration, bureaucracy, commissions, and courts—but the legislature is their central focus. Through 1966, the California legislature was a nonprofessional, part-time institution. Legislators were poorly paid, had no offices, and little staff.

Dennis Renault / *The Sacramento Bee*

Behind the Green Door

Low Pay. The meager legislative salary ($6,000 through 1966) was more a token of civic gratitude than a living wage. The view was that public-spirited citizens who ran for the legislature were, in effect, donating their services in much the same manner that most city council, school board, and planning commission members now do. Some legislators, after serving a few terms, "graduated" into the lobbyist ranks and quadrupled their former legislative salaries. Others returned to their previous occupations to recoup their losses, and some ran for higher office. A few went to Sacramento penniless but learned to play the game and retired wealthy. Some legislators of that era tried to economize by renting rooms in downtrodden Sacramento hotels. One legislator saved money by hitchhiking to and from his Los Angeles constituency. But living off lobbyists' largesse was the normal and accepted means most legislators used to cut costs. Many lobbyists were willing to pay hotel bills, buy meals and drinks, take legislators on expensive travel junkets, provide tickets to sporting events, and give expensive gifts. Rather than return to empty hotel rooms after a long day at the capitol, many legislators found it more appealing to have lobbyists take them out to dinner. Bars and restaurants near the state capitol did a booming lunch and dinner business. The Derby Club, Moose-milk, the Caboose Club, and other regular luncheon meeting spots for lobbyists and legislators were capitol institutions. At the height of his powers, Samish did not even bother to go to the capitol building to testify before committees or buttonhole legislators. Instead, legislators would go to Artie Samish. He would host lavish luncheon buffets in his hotel suite, providing the finest wines, liquor, and gourmet food to his legislator guests. After lunch, there would be card games for interested legislators and lobbyists. A few lobbyists were also known to provide female companionship for some temporary-bachelor legislators.

Shrewd lobbyists could also direct legal business to a lawyer–legislator's law office, buy insurance from an insurance agent–legislator, invest in real estate from a real estate broker–legislator, or do business with a businessman–legislator. A favorite device of banks and savings and loan institutions was to place local legislators on their boards of directors. They provided the banks with increased status and gave legislators extra income with a minimal amount of work.

Skillful lobbyists quickly discovered a particular legislator's interests—sports, dining, hunting, golfing, cards, drinking, and the like—and then tried to capitalize on that knowledge. Well-paid, full-time, savvy lobbyists thrived in this setting.

Inadequate Facilities. In the early years, California legislators did not have private offices. They used their desks on the floor to conduct legislative chores: dictating letters, reading mail, discussing bills with lobbyists, being interviewed by reporters, and chatting with visiting constituents. Experienced lobbyists thrived in this bedlam. Bills could be killed, amended, or lost in this confusion, and few would know the difference.

Lack of Staff. Lobbyists were not only friends and confidants of legislators, but also prime sources of information. Because legislators could not possibly be experts on all the subjects they dealt with, lobbyists provided legislators with much-needed information. Lobbyists helped draft legislation and provided questions that sympathetic legislators might use at committee hearings. Lobbyists were not a neutral source of expertise.

Low Public Visibility Until the last decade or two, California's major metropolitan daily newspapers tended to give short shrift to Sacramento doings. They preferred to concentrate their efforts on national or international news, along with a heavy smattering of local news. Sacramento was viewed as a hot, dusty valley town with few cultural refinements, inhabited primarily by political hacks, local satraps, and faceless bureaucrats. Indeed, in 1994 not one television station covered the capitol regularly, although legislative sessions and committee hearings are now televised several hours per week on cable television.

The closed, secretive nature of the legislative system of the bygone era further played into the hands of the lobbyists. In the senate, committee chairs were able to control their committees and pass or kill bills arbitrarily. Not surprisingly, lobbyists often concentrated their efforts on the upper house because it was smaller, its power more diffuse, its turnover minimal, and its partisanship imperceptible. In both houses, committees frequently met in executive (closed) session or met informally before hearings at a local bistro to decide what should be done. In addition, no official record of committee votes was kept.

In most cases, lobbyists asked a legislator for just a few votes each year. These were usually on technical bills on complicated subjects with little public opinion but that might mean millions to the lobbyist's client.

LOBBY REFORM

Periodic attempts have been made throughout this century to reduce the power of wealthy special interests on the state's political processes, but with only modest progress. In this century, five reform periods stand out: (1) the Progressive era of the early 1900s, (2) the Samish scandal aftermath in the 1950s, (3) the Unruh modernization drive in the 1960s, (4) the post-Watergate period in the 1970s, and (5) the FBI investigations and term limits in the 1980s–1990s.

Early Progressive Efforts

The Progressives made the first concerted attempt early this century to limit special-interest influence. They achieved a constitutional prohibition on any transport company (Southern Pacific was the obvious target) giving public officials free trips. They also established a state railroad commission to set rates charged by Southern Pacific and other public utilities. They promoted direct democracy to bypass a governmental system corrupted by special interests.

As Progressive reform zeal declined in the 1920s, the dominant power of lobbyists and special interests was restored. Indeed, some of the reform weapons designed to thwart the special interests were used by the third house to promote their issues (for example, the initiative process).

The Artie Samish Scandal

In 1949, *Collier's* magazine published "The Secret Boss of California" (Velie, 1949). In the article, Samish described bluntly how he exerted influence over the state legislature and bureaucracy. Accompanying the article was a color photograph of the portly Artie Samish seated in a chair with "Mr. Legislature," a wooden puppet being manipulated by Samish. Said the big man, "And how are you today, Mr. Legislature?"

For the first time, the California public learned about the stranglehold Samish held over state government. A public clamor for lobbying reform ensued. And in 1949, responding to the Samish scandal, the legislature passed the Collier Act, which was patterned after the Federal Regulation of Lobbying Act. The Collier Act required lobbyists to register and file monthly financial reports of contributions and expenditures over $10. In 1951, Samish was convicted and imprisoned for federal income-tax evasion. Although the Collier Act provided modest help in making the lobby process less secretive, in fact, little really changed.

The Unruh Period

Proposition 1A From his first term as state assemblyman in 1955, Jess Unruh (later elected speaker) came to one basic conclusion: The California legislature was hopelessly ineffective and unable to grapple meaningfully with complex state policy issues. From Unruh's perspective, the legislature was a part-time, poorly paid, amateurish institution dominated by special interests and the governor—a horse-and-buggy operation suited to nineteenth-, not twentieth-century, problems. Legislative salaries were locked into the state constitution. Raising them meant passing a constitutional amendment (two-thirds vote in each house) and then submitting it to the electorate. But the public has never been enthusiastic about raising politicians' salaries and has consistently voted them down. A constitutional revision commission proposed in an amendment (what came to be Proposition 1A) that legislators should determine their own salaries and calendar. Unruh led the charge for this proposal. To move the amendment through the legislature and get voter approval required enormous political skill. Unruh secured Republican legislative leader support, lobbied the lobbyists (and received substantial third house campaign contributions), and won the support of many of the state's largest dailies. He argued that poorly paid legislators were fair game for lobbyists, who could influence gratuities-dependent lawmakers. Reasonable legislative salaries would attract better educated and more competent candidates who would be better equipped to resist lobbyists. Higher legislative salaries would free lawmakers from depending on their previous occupations to sustain them, and there would be less need for special interests to hire legislator–lawyers on retainers. Full-time legislators would be able to devote their complete attention to complex policy issues. Proposition 1A was approved by voters in 1966. Beginning in 1967, legislator salaries rose from $6,000 to $16,000 yearly.

The Sacramento Bee

The Cattle Pack, a California cattlemen's lobby, hosts lawmakers at an annual breakfast. Meeting with legislators at mealtime is a traditional lobbying technique.

Adoption of Proposition 1A altered the legislator–lobbyist relationship in several ways. Because the legislature began meeting year-round, some legislators found it more convenient to move their families to Sacramento, which meant fewer lobbyist–legislator dinner outings. As better educated, more politically astute legislators began to get elected, lobbyists had to change their modus operandi to relate to this new breed of legislators. New legislators were somewhat more likely to be influenced by lobbyists with expertise in a subject area rather than simply an unlimited checking account. The development of a professional legislature encouraged the development of a professional lobby corps. Although the practice of lobbyists' picking up tabs continued, the dependency relationship had been altered. Unruh urged his colleagues not to feel obliged to vote the way generous lobbyists wanted them to, but to assert their independence.

Another Unruh innovation that changed the lobbyist–legislator relationship was the creation of a professional cadre of legislative staff (see Chapter 7). By adding professional staff, legislators no longer had to rely solely on lobbyists for expertise; they had a new, more neutral source of information. Although the Unruh reforms put legislators in a stronger position vis-à-vis the third house, special-interest power at the capitol remains a fact of life.

Political Reform Act of 1974

The next reform attempt to grapple with special-interest power came with the Political Reform Act (PRA) initiative of June 1974 (Proposition 9). This initiative was jointly sponsored by then-Democratic gubernatorial candidate Jerry Brown, Common Cause, and People's Lobby. Ever since the 1970s, virtually all significant reform efforts have come through the ballot box, not the legislature or governor. Although opposed by powerful special interests who spent millions to defeat it, the initiative was overwhelmingly approved by voters. The corruption detailed in the federal Watergate scandal was strong incentive.

The PRA has the following key features: (1) All lobbyists are required to register. (A lobbyist is now defined as one who makes at least twenty-five contacts with state public officials and who is paid $2,000 or more during a two-month period.) (2) Lobbyists can spend no more than $10 per month per public official: legislator, staff member, administrator, or commissioner. (3) Detailed reports must be filed periodically with the secretary of state's office and the Fair Political Practices Commission (FPPC), noting who has been lobbied, the subjects discussed, and how much has been spent. (4) The FPPC has overall responsibility for enforcing the act. (See Chapter 3.)

Originally, lobbyists were forbidden to confer with their clients about which public officials should receive campaign contributions (enforcing this feature would have been difficult) and from making campaign contributions. These provisions were later declared unconstitutional.

Overall, the PRA had a positive effect on capitol politics. Lobbyists, public officials, and legislative staffers were concerned about not running afoul of the law and destroying their careers. Elected officials, interest groups, and lobbyists have, for the most part, complied with PRA. Occasionally, fines have been meted out for violations, but, as with other political reforms, those affected quickly learned how to adapt or get around the act.

Criticisms   PRA critics contend that the $10 monthly spending limit per public official imposed on lobbyists is meaningless—or worse, insulting. They argue that only the naive believe that any legislator's vote is exchanged for dinner, drinks, or other gratuities. Legislator–lobbyist lunches or dinners (with no ringing telephones or frequent interruptions) are one of the best places to exchange information, and lobbyist and legislator to get to know each other. The PRA discourages this. Moreover, the $10 limit can be easily outmaneuvered by the less scrupulous—that is, the act limits only the lobbyist, not the lobbyist's employer. Thus, interest group executives can take an elected official out and not worry about the size of the tab. Or the lobbyist can pay with cash, not plastic, for the dinner—how could the FPPC keep track of this? Also, if a legislator's bill is $12.05, the lobbyist can ask the legislator to pay the extra $2.05 and then hand him or her a campaign contribution for $1,000.[1] PRA opponents argue that it fosters a "big brother is watching you" mentality. (In fact, these days the FBI *is* watching.) The FPPC is yet another layer of bureaucracy. Worse, these *appointed* commissioners admonish elected representatives on how they should act.

Rebuttal   Above all, supporters of Proposition 9 contend, the act has improved the tone of lobbying in Sacramento. The extensive entertaining, posh excursions, and gift giving have been reduced. At the very least, on its most innocent level, "wining and dining" buys access and promotes friendships—and access and friendships are the name of the game in Sacramento. As ex–legislator and lobbyist Robert Cline said at the corruption trial of Senator Joe Montoya, "Legislators tend to vote with their friends. One way of showing friendship is to be a contributor." Money spent for entertaining is not expended whimsically by special-interest groups; it is a calculated investment similar to a campaign contribution. Supporters of the act argue that the $10 limit is strict but reasonable. Since California's adoption of the $10 spending limit, other states have adopted similar restrictions. Currently, Iowa has a $3 per month spending limit!

Reformers argue there is no attempt in the act to muzzle lobbyists or reduce legislator–lobbyist interaction, as critics contend. Even if a lobbyist's $10 minimum has been expended for the month on a particular legislator, the lobbyist can still have long discussions at lunch or dinner; the only difference is that each has to pay his or her own check. In any case, whatever initial fears legislators had about being listed on lobbyists' forms seem to have been dispelled. The FPPC reports that hundreds of thousands of dollars are spent each year by lobbyists entertaining legislators, staffers, and administrators.

Over the past several years, the FPPC has sponsored additional reform proposals that have subsequently been adopted by the legislature. These proposals prohibit (1) officeholders from using campaign funds for personal use, (2) state officials from leaving their government posts and then returning to represent clients on matters they had been involved with on the state payroll, and (3) legislators from accepting campaign contributions in the capitol building.

Finally, are interest groups on a more equal footing these days? There is no question that so-called public interest groups such as Common Cause, the Sierra Club, the Planning and Conservation League, and the League of Women Voters have a substantial and growing impact on policy. Historically, "do-gooder" interest groups had difficulty being taken seriously. The PRA has contributed to this new balance. But stemming the flow of special-interest money to elected officials is like trying to dam the Mississippi River—it just keeps rolling along. No one ever suggested that Proposition 9 would be a panacea. The hope was that it would open the political process, reduce the influence of wealthy special interests, and ameliorate the more outrageous practices of the past. It has done this.

FBI Investigations and Term Limits in the 1980s and '90s

Further reform efforts to cope with special-interest influence at the capitol have come in the 1980s and '90s. Two separate FBI "sting" investigations uncovered substantial illegal activity. In 1986, W. Patrick Moriarity, owner of a fireworks company, sought state legislation to preempt local governments from banning his products. His bill was authored by a friendly assemblymember. Using campaign contributions, wining and dining, and gifts, Moriarity was able to push his bill through both houses of the legislature, even though it was opposed by a wide array of organizations, including local government, the Fire Marshals Association, and children's safety groups. Governor Deukmejian eventually vetoed the bill, and Moriarity was convicted of bribery in his lobby effort.

In the second FBI investigation, an agent posed as a shrimp-processing businessman eager to open a facility in the state. Eventually, five legislators, five legislative staff, a coastal commissioner, and Clay Jackson, the most powerful lobbyist at the capitol in the 1980s and '90s, were convicted of extortion, racketeering, and bribery. Responding to this bad publicity, the legislature passed a new ethics amendment, Proposition 112 of June 1990, which was approved by voters and added to the state constitution. The tougher ethical reforms included a ban on honoraria (payments to public officials for delivering speeches to interest groups); limited gift-giving; a mandate that all legislative meetings be open to the public; mandatory biennial ethics classes for legislators, staff, and lobbyists; and a stipulation that legislators had to wait one year after leaving legislative service before they could enter into lobbying. However, one more change was incorporated in Proposition 112 that some voters might not have noticed: the establishment of a Citizens Compensation Commission. Because voters often became upset when the state legislature approved salary increases for themselves, it was decided that an appointive commission setting salaries could better deflect citizen anger. Thus, the legislature was willing to accept long overdue ethics reforms in return for better salaries. The Citizens Compensation Commission (composed of leading corporate executives appointed by the governor) has substantially increased the salaries of state officials. Interestingly, two of the legislators convicted in the FBI investigation, Senators Joe Montoya (Democrat) and Frank Hill (Republican), argued in court that the payments they received were honoraria, not bribes. Instead of honoraria being payments for speeches, Montoya and Hill said that their conversations with lobbyists warranted honoraria payments (the juries did not agree).

Finally, Pete Schabarum (author of Proposition 140, term limits) and others promoted this concept, in part, to attack special interests. During the fall 1990 campaign, Schabarum argued, "Proposition 140 will remove the grip that vested interests have over the legislature. It will put an end to the life-time legislators, who have cozy relationships with special interests" (Price, 1993). Term-limited legislators would be more attuned to the public, not the lobbyists. Of course, only legislators, not lobbyists, have had term limits imposed on them. In the years ahead, experience will be in short supply in the legislature, and lobbyists and staff will be the keepers of institutional memory. And if legislators and lobbyists have a harder time building trust in the term-limited legislature, more emphasis will probably be used by groups to get their memberships to influence legislators.

Certainly, legislators and lobbyists today are warier than ever before about having campaign contributions connected with pending action on bills. Who knows anymore whether the person you're talking to at the capitol is "wired"? Yet the problems remain. The only way the legislature was willing to pass an ethics measure was if it were linked to a pay commission. Fund-raising in the closing weeks of the 1994 session, with many bills up for votes, was as hectic and persistent as ever. So long as campaign contributions from special interests are legal and campaigns expensive, candidates will seek out money to play the game.

THIRD HOUSE POLITICS
Interest Groups

Currently, some 2,100 groups are registered at the capitol to engage in lobbying activities (see Table 5.1, page 134). Well over half of the registered groups are businesses, corporations, or business trade associations. Education, health care, and local government constitute another third of registered organizations. Agricultural organizations, employee groups, trade unions, public interest lobbies, and miscellaneous interests make up the remainder. The Chamber of Commerce, one of the 2,100 groups registered, represents thousands of businesses across California. The League of California Cities represents hundreds of communities in the state. The California Teachers Association represents hundreds of thousands of school teachers. The larger groups represent a broad cross-section of the California population. Each year, another 50 or so businesses or groups decide to have lobby representation at the capitol.

TYPE	NUMBER	PERCENTAGE
Business and trade associations	288	14
Health and social services	239	11
Education	165	8
Local government	139	7
Other/public interest	130	6
Transportation	126	6
Food and agriculture	122	6
Chemicals and energy	119	6
Real estate and construction	102	5
Insurance	97	5
Environment and resources	95	5
Financial institutions	89	4
Recreation, sports, and arts	83	4
Communications and electronics	68	3
Public employees	53	2
Law and justice	51	2
Utilities	34	1
Labor unions	21	1
Total	2,098	100

TABLE 5.1   INTEREST GROUPS REGISTERED IN CALIFORNIA
Source: California Lobbyists/PACs 1993, Directory, California Journal. Sacramento: California 1993.

Lobbyists

More than 1,000 officially registered lobbyists now ply their trade at the capitol (see Figure 5.1). Thus, there are ten times as many lobbyists as legislators, and the lobbyist numbers keep inching up. Many factors contribute to this growth of interest groups, including: (1) the increasing complexity and heterogeneity of California society and economy; (2) the fact that more people have registered as lobbyists since the Political Reform Act's definition of lobbyist; (3) an increase in the number of single-issue lobbies, such as those concerned with the death penalty, abortion, and tax reform; (4) increased efforts by entrepreneurial lobbyists actively seeking new clients; (5) the adoption of Proposition 13 (property-tax relief), curtailing local governments' ability to raise taxes and encouraging them to hire their own lobbyists to fight for funds at the state capital; and (6) the growing specialization of lobbying. (For example, not just doctors, but medical specialties such as radiology and internal medicine, have their own lobbyists.)

146 1993-1994 LOBBYISTS

SPOTTS, RICHARD A.
1228 N Street, Suite 6, Sacramento, CA 95814   (916) 442-6386

Lobbyist Employer
Defenders of Wildlife

SPROUL, KATE
926 J Street, Suite 523, Sacramento, CA 95814   (916) 442-3414

Lobbyist Employer
California NOW, Inc.

STACEY, KENT H.
3605 Marconi Avenue, Sacramento, CA 95821   (916) 483-0426
1124 Vanderbilt Way, Sacramento, CA 95825

Lobbying Firm
Stacey, Kent H.

STEFFES, GEORGE R.
1201 K Street, Suite 850, Sacramento, CA 95814   (916) 444-6034

Lobbying Firm
Steffes, Inc., George R.

STENBAKKEN, DWIGHT R.
1400 K Street, Sacramento, CA 95814   (916) 444-5790

Lobbyist Employer
League of California Cities

STETTNER, JENNIFER C.
1201 K Street, #1930, Sacramento, CA 95814   (916) 447-1698

Lobbyist Employer
Union Oil Company of California dba Unocal

FIGURE 5.1   LOBBYIST REGISTRATION
This is a typical page from the secretary of state's Lobbyist Directory.

   Most contemporary lobbyists did not plan for their careers as undergraduates. There is no prelobby major, graduate-school training, or even state exam to pass for aspiring lobbyists. Most people who become lobbyists do so by happenstance.

And although politicians are viewed suspiciously by the public, lobbyists have an even more notorious reputation. This is unfortunate because most contemporary lobbyists are bright, well educated, honest, and ethical professionals. Of course, much depends on one's perspective as to how lobbyists are perceived. If you're a teacher, the CTA lobbyists are the "good guys" battling the special interests. If you're a Sierra Club member, club lobbyists are heroic figures carrying the good fight against those who would destroy the environment. And if you're a tobacco distributor, Phillip Morris lobbyists are solid citizens trying to hold the line against the health fascists. This is how Rich Kushman, capitol reporter for *The Sacramento Bee* (1988, p. A12), describes lobbyists:

> Loren Smith (a lobbyist) laughs about the reputation of people practicing his trade. "No one I know was ever patted on the head by parents who said, 'I hope you grow up to be a lobbyist,'" Smith said.
>
> To the world outside of politics, lobbyists have an image of lone figures lurking in the shadows of the Capitol with satchels of money waiting for some poor public official to wander past so they can whisper, "Pssst, c'mere, I want to show you something."
>
> In reality, lobbyists are a vital cog in the mechanics of government. They are part ambassador, part lawyer, part psychologist and part Fuller Brush sales representative.

Essentially, people gravitate into lobbying from two prime sources: (1) from within government, or (2) from within the particular interest group or business.

Government Currently, several dozen ex-legislators and an assortment of other ex-officeholders serve as lobbyists for various interests in Sacramento. Some former officeholders become lobbyists not by design but because they have lost elections. Others leave the legislature voluntarily seeking "greener" pastures. A growing number of legislators will be reaching their term limit maximums and may decide to pursue lobbying careers. Although ex-legislators now make up a small portion of the lobby corps, these advocates tend to be contract lobbyists associated with lobby firms who frequently represent many key special interests.

Obviously, ex-legislator lobbyists trade on their friendships with former legislative colleagues and their intimate knowledge of the legislative process. However, under the provisions of Proposition 112 of June 1990, legislators must wait one year after leaving office before launching their lobbying careers. Ex-legislator lobbyists have a special relationship with their former colleagues (it is awkward to keep an "old buddy" waiting for an appointment in the outer office). Better than anyone else, ex-legislators understand the pressures, tensions, and frustrations in the legislator's job. But because of the constant turnover in legislative membership and statewide elective officeholders (even more heightened by term limits), ex-legislator lobbyists cannot simply trade on old friendships for long.

Other lobbyists coming from government include ex-legislative staff, former bureaucrats from different executive departments, and, in some cases, relatives of officeholders or lobbyists. As with former legislators, these individuals know the players, understand the process and informal "rules of the game," and frequently have developed a policy expertise. Some enterprising individuals have persuaded key legislator friends to recommend them to an interest group looking for a lobbyist. A strong recommendation from committee chair X that group Y should hire lobbyist Z is not casually dismissed. Lobbyists coming from within government are a substantial proportion of California lobbyists.

Group Milieu Many lobbyists attain their positions from within the group they represent. Some corporations have public affairs divisions staffed by attorneys who represent them in Sacramento. Many utility lobbyists are attorneys hired by PG&E or Pac Tel, who are then assigned to their government relations offices at the capitol. Employees with skills in public relations, politics, sales, or advertising are obvious possibilities. Some corporations or businesses assign key executives to their Sacramento beat. Individuals going into lobbying from within a corporation, business trade association, or public interest group usually represent that single client. There are ex-teachers who lobby for the CTA and ex-workers who lobby for the AFL-CIO. Generally speaking, the major asset lobbyists in this category offer to legislators and administrators is specialized expertise. Public interest lobbyists, who tend to be the poorest paid in the lobby fraternity, are often longtime members and committed to their groups' agendas. Public interest lobbyists can trade on the fact that they and their group's members support particular bills not for selfish personal reasons but because they believe it will be good for the general public.

The Job: Salaries, Workload, Costs The salaries of lobbyists vary considerably. A few, such as George Steffes, Dennis Carpenter, and Donald Kent Brown, make hundreds of thousands of dollars a year lobbying, whereas a few others (for example, lobbyists for the League of Women Voters or the PTA) receive no salary. Most major, full-time California lobbyists earn about $100,000 yearly, more than California state legislators receive.

To earn their salaries, lobbyists put in long, tiring days, especially when the legislature is in session. They must keep track of countless details. A typical morning might include an early trip to the Bill Room to pick up amended versions of several bills the lobbyist is following; a hurried discussion with a legislator in the hallway about a bill coming before that legislator's committee; a walk over to the office to check the mail, answer telephone calls, or edit the group's imminent newsletter; a conference with group executives on pending legislation; a short coffee break with a fellow lobbyist to discuss testimony for an afternoon committee hearing; a deadly dull Senate Budget Committee hearing; and, finally, lunch with a committee consultant to discuss a bill that the consultant's boss, the committee chair, will soon introduce. Then comes the afternoon. . . .

Most lobbyists enjoy their work. It is financially rewarding, meaningful, and important, and it provides reasonable job security. For the most part, lobbyists have an unwritten rule that once a lobbyist has secured a client, until the contract has expired, other lobbyists are expected not to try to take that client away. The emergence of new, high-powered, professional lobby firms eager to secure new clients, however, has created a far more competitive situation.

Types of Lobbyists   Although some organizations or businesses are represented by a single lobbyist, most groups are represented by several lobbyists. In turn, some contract lobbyists represent many groups. A few major corporations may have several contract firms representing them. The CTA has eight lobbyists, as does the County Supervisors Association, and many major utilities have large lobby corps (Pacific Gas & Electric, five; Southern California Gas, five plus a contract lobby firm; Pacific Telesis, three; and San Diego Gas and Electric, four).

A growing portion of lobby business in Sacramento is conducted by 335 professional advocacy firms. On average, these companies have two to six lobbyists and represent ten to sixty different clients.[2] A contract lobby firm almost always has former government insiders as part of the firm; a few have both former Republican and former Democrat officials. Contract lobbyists often represent groups that have large PACs; they are major power players at the capitol. Much like legislators, contract lobbyists' expertise on some subjects is limited because of the sheer number of interests they represent. But they are mainly hired for their contacts and political savvy, not their issue expertise. Contract lobbyists sometimes serve as "door openers" to allow other experts from a group to get a hearing before a legislator or staff. Many contract lobby firms have expanded their services beyond mere lobbying to include public relations, legal advice, association management, campaign strategy, and affiliate offices in Washington, D.C. These firms constantly hunt for new clients, seeking out businesses or companies not currently represented in Sacramento and watching for clients of other lobbyists who might be interested in changing their affiliation.

Lobbying was once the epitome of a "good old boy" job—drinking, carousing, and so on. This is no longer the case. Lobbying these days requires brains and skill. There has been a dramatic increase in the number of female lobbyists at the capital over the last decade. Women lobbyists began to appear in substantial numbers in the 1960s and '70s, often representing so-called do-gooder groups— the Humane Society, League of Women Voters, PTA, and American Association of University Women. Today women constitute about one-quarter of the lobbyist registrations. Many work for contract lobby firms. And some represent major economic interests in the state. On the other hand, there are relatively few African American or Latino lobbyists.

Many people who engage in lobbying do not fall under the PRA definition. Dozens of unpaid, volunteer lobbyists work for public interest groups but do not have to register. Also, state agency and department personnel (legislative liaisons) assigned to represent those units at the capitol on legislation affecting them (particularly the budget) are not required to register. The governor also has aides who lobby the two houses on his behalf. Finally, some lawyers associated with leading Sacramento law-lobby firms that represent major economic interests also do not register. Although a few of the law partners do register, dozens of lawyer employees working on occasion on political matters do not (Bathen, p. 83).

LOBBY SPENDING
Techniques of Lobbying

Essentially, lobbyists influence legislators in three ways: (1) through financial clout, an obviously critical dimension in the contemporary setting; (2) through the group's political power; and (3) through information, expertise, and member-ship pressure. Some lobbyists can use all three devices; others have to rely on one. Finally, all lobbyists strive to get to know elected and administrative officials and develop friendships and build trust. It is the financial clout aspect of lobbying that is the most controversial.

Financial Clout   Interest groups in California spend millions of dollars yearly to influence policy makers. Organizations that spend substantial sums of money on lobbying view this expense as a prudent and wise investment. A lobbyist operation at the capital (lobbyist salary, office, and staff) costing a few hundred thousand dollars a year could help influence decisions that might mean millions of dollars for the affected group. The most powerful groups make sure they are represented by lobbyists with access and political savvy.

Some groups channel most of their funds into lobbying and provide substan-tially lesser amounts for campaign contributions; others parcel out roughly equal amounts for campaign contributions and lobbying. The top-spending lobbying

GROUP	AMOUNT SPENT
California Teachers Association	$2,826,000
California Medical Association	1,747,000
Pacific Telesis	1,618,585
Western States Petroleum Association	1,357,000
Association of California Insurance Companies	1,327,000
California Association of Hospitals and Health Systems	1,319,000
Chevron Corp.	1,172,000
California Trial Lawyers Association	1,022,000
Atlantic Richfield Co.	978,462
California Manufacturers Association	955,307

TABLE 5.2   TOP TEN LOBBY SPENDING GROUPS, 1993
Source: California Secretary of State, "Lobbying Expenditures and the Top 100 Lobbying Firms, 1993."

groups (not including campaign contributions) in 1993, according to the secretary of state, are shown in Table 5.2.

Although any group has a right to have its say in Sacramento, the reality is that some groups are heard more clearly than others. As an example, consider the battle between the tobacco industry and its health critics at the capitol. Since the late 1930s, a torrent of scientific articles has reported the adverse health consequences of tobacco use—cancer, heart disease, emphysema, and so on. Yet until the early 1990s, the tobacco industry had its way in the state legislature even though tobacco had no local constituency here. (Tobacco is neither grown nor manufactured in California.) However, by playing the money game—campaign contributions, wining and dining, honoraria, friendships with senior legislators, and representation by the most influential lobby firms at the capitol—the tobacco lobby controlled legislation on this subject. They also had strong allies in the business and labor communities. Health groups had to resort to initiatives to bypass the legislature and get things done. Now this has all changed. Momentum on the tobacco issue has clearly shifted, and health groups and the public are demanding tougher restrictions on tobacco use. Today, the tobacco industry has had to bypass the legislature to accomplish its ends by using the initiative. For example, the industry launched the unsuccessful Proposition 188 of November 1994, the statewide smoking restrictions initiative.

Political Power   Lobbyists representing groups such as organized labor's AFL-CIO, the California Teachers Association (CTA), and the California State Employees Association (CSEA) have a further advantage: the vote potential of these large mass-membership organizations. Lobbyists can alert legislators of the consequences their vote will have on the group's membership. Of course, groups vary considerably in their ability to inform their memberships and in helping shape their members' votes. Some groups urge their members to work for political candidates or to run for local office to provide additional leverage.

Information and Group Pressure Lawmakers must be generalists, but lobbyists can concentrate on particular policy issues and play a critical role in providing the specialized information necessary for informed decision making. Because they are in constant touch with group members, lobbyists can also convey to public officials the views of their membership. Moreover, public interest lobbies can compete equally with wealthy special interests in expertise. The point is, lobbyists representing groups with little money and relatively small memberships can be influential. Let's consider how this is done.

Effective Lobbying: Beyond Money and the Power of Numbers

First and foremost, an effective lobbyist has a keen understanding of the complex issues facing his or her client group. A skilled lobbyist must be able to explain clearly and concisely the main facets of an issue to a legislator, administrator, staff member, reporter, or another lobbyist. Advocates impart this information in the lobbies of the capitol (this is how lobbyists originally got their name) as legislators rush to committee hearings or floor sessions, in capitol cafeterias, in nearby coffee shops or cocktail lounges, on golf courses, in memos and reports, and in formal testimony presented at committee hearings. (Most important decisions, however, have been made before committee hearings.) Good lobbyists learn quickly that to be effective they must be brief and succinct. The effective lobbyist knows how to read the legalese of bills, spot flaws, look for key points or problems, and suggest amendments. The effective lobbyist is equally at home at a luncheon meeting at the Sutter Club; in a quiet, informal, frank discussion in a legislator's office; or in a formal presentation of testimony at a committee hearing.

Second, an effective lobbyist understands the legislative process and the formal rules governing that process. Effective lobbyists provide input at all phases of the process: bill origination, bill drafting, assignment to committee, advice to leadership on selection of committee members and chairs, scheduling of bills, floor action, conference committees, the governor, implementation by administrative agencies, court action, and initiatives.

Many effective lobbyists' skills come with experience (something that many lobbyists will have, but most legislators will not because of term limits). How

The Sacramento Bee

"Over the top" at Rancho Seco nuclear power plant. Nuclear power protestors sought to shut down the plant. In a Sacramento County referendum in 1989, citizens voted to close the plant.

many votes are necessary to get a bill out of the assembly Education Committee? Are the votes there or should the bill be held over? How does one avoid a hostile committee? Should one agree to a particular amendment? What are the deadlines?

Third, the effective lobbyist knows not only the formal rules but also the informal, unwritten rules. For example, a cardinal rule in Sacramento is that if a lobbyist determines that he or she will have to oppose a bill, the lobbyist is honor-bound to go to the bill's author and discuss the reasons for opposition with that legislator before committee hearings. The bill's legislative author might suggest amendments in hopes of persuading the lobbyist not to oppose the measure. Indeed, the legislator may not even have a strong commitment to the bill but introduced it on behalf of an interest in his or her district. The legislator might say something like, "Go check with the lobbyist sponsoring the bill and see if you can iron out your differences. Whatever you decide is fine with me."

Randy Pench / *The Sacramento Bee*

Loggers protest environmentalists' attempts to protect the endangered spotted owl and vent their anger near the state capitol.

Among other key unwritten rules is that a good lobbyist never threatens a legislator with defeat. First, he or she probably could not deliver, and second, today's opponent may be needed on another vote the next day. "Don't burn your bridges" is the rule of thumb.

In Sacramento, lobbyists are expected to give "the straight scoop." Obviously, lobbyists present their group's views in the most favorable light, but they must also be able to explain the pros and cons of a bill to a legislator. A lobbyist who knowingly lies to or misleads a legislator not only loses that legislator's support henceforth, but also loses face with other legislators. The Sacramento inner circle of legislators, staff, lobbyists, and reporters is small and intimate. Word of an important transgression spreads rapidly. If a lobbyist should happen to mistakenly give a legislator the wrong information about a bill's effect, the advocate is expected to talk with the legislator and clear up the point as quickly as possible. In short, honesty, discretion, and keeping commitments are essential elements of lobbying in the California state capitol.

Fourth, the effective lobbyist usually tries to become a friend of the legislator and get on a first-name basis with that person. (Under Proposition 140, term limits, it will be harder for lobbyists to cultivate friendships with legislators because of more rapid turnover.) An effective lobbyist makes an effort to know about the legislator's or administrator's special interests, whether they are sports, hunting, or music. Many of the more successful lobbyists of the 1990s trade on the sports interests of the new generation of legislators; tennis, racquetball, and golf are as popular lobbyist–legislator activities today as gin rummy and poker were a few years ago.

Fifth, effective lobbyists work cooperatively with their lobbyist colleagues. They often trade information and help one another. Moreover, on any issue of consequence, coalitions of lobbies work jointly to support or oppose measures.

Sixth, effective lobbyists help to orchestrate the local membership and grass-roots organization with the capitol operation. If a group has a solid middle-class, well-educated, politically savvy, and well-distributed mass membership (e.g., the CTA, CSEA, California Realtors, or Common Cause), it can alert its members to potential problems at the capitol and generate a substantial and effective statewide mail or phone-in campaign. Some groups have become highly adept at finding out whether any of their members are personal friends of particular legislators. Calls from longtime friends to elected officials may have much more effect on an official than a conversation with an anonymous lobbyist. This feature will become even more important with the term-limited legislature. It will be difficult to establish close friendships because of the constant legislative turnover. Obviously, lobbyists work closely with legislators whose districts encompass significant elements of the lobbyist's group.

Teachers, motorcycle-club members, real estate brokers, and the physically handicapped are among the many groups that descend on the capitol yearly in all-out efforts to win policy concessions. Demonstrations and speeches aimed at achieving maximum press and television coverage are held on the steps of the capitol daily. After these gatherings, group members are urged to seek out the legislators and let them know about their problems. Some groups try to intimidate legislators at committee hearings, hoping that angry glares, raucous cheers, or jeers will sway fence-straddling lawmakers. Lobbyists also lobby the print media through press releases, which they hope will be run by newspapers, or by alerting reporters to "good" stories. Having group members write letters to the editor or call radio talk shows helps to increase public awareness of the issue. And elected officials lobby one another on behalf of their issues.

SUMMARY

The many lobby reforms undertaken this century have helped, but not resolved, the issue of special-interest financial clout and influence. If lobbying were exclusively the attempt to get group members politicized and have the group's lobbyist make the most convincing case possible for legislation, there would be no lobby problem. But as the FBI investigations at the capitol showed, bribery and extortion are a part of the contemporary political milieu in California government.

Lobbying is an essential and indispensable part of the American political process—citizens petitioning their government. Lobbyists and special interests have been inextricably linked with California government throughout state history. Interest groups are necessary and vital to democratic government, but some pose a serious threat to democratic institutions through their money influence, entertaining, and "me-first" attitude. Unfortunately, resources are distributed unequally among different groups. The various lobby reforms that have been launched in California have reduced the potential for evil, but further reforms are needed.

NOTES

1. It was obvious at the outset that this feature would have a limited impact considering the group represented by a particular lobbyist, or its PAC, could still provide campaign contributions and thus gain the goodwill of that politician for that lobbyist. Two recent chairs of the FPPC, Tom Houston and Dan Stanford, have stated that they would not attempt to enforce the $10 limit because it was unenforceable. Their view was that you would need a small army of spies posted at various Sacramento bars and restaurants to keep track of lobbyist gratuities.

2. George R. Steffes, Inc., one of the leading contract lobby firms at the capital, has eight lobbyists and dozens of diverse clients, including:

3 M	Carpet Manufacturers Association
Alliance of American Insurers	City of Inglewood
American International Group	Coalition of Apparel Industries
American Express Company	Colonial Life Co.
American Planning Association	Coors Brewing Co.
Association of International Automobile Manufacturers	Copley Press Inc.
Association of Furniture Suppliers	Council of University of California Faculty
Bechtel Inc.	IBM Corp.
Burger King Corp.	IDS Financial Service
Calaveras Cement Co.	Insurance Auto Auctions
California Association of Hospitals	Japan Iron & Steel
California Association of Private Schools	Johnson & Johnson
California Horsemen's Association	Kaiser Cement Co.
California Mining Association	LensCrafters
California Mobilehome Owners	*Los Angeles Times*
California Portland Cement Co.	McClatchy Newspapers
California Thoroughbred Breeders Association	Mitsubishi Cement Corp.
Care CPA	NL Industries
	National Cement Co.

Northern California Golf Association
Orange County Register
Parsons Corp.
Perrier Group
Pillsbury Co.
RMC Lonestar
Riverside Cement Co.

Rohm and Haas Co.
Safe Buildings Alliance
San Diego Metropolitan Transit
San Jose Mercury-News
Sharp HealthCare
Simon & Schuster
Southdown Inc.

REFERENCES

Bathen, Sigrid. "Clay Jackson." *California Journal* 21 (February 1990), pp. 113–114.

———. "Lawyer Lobbyists." *California Journal* 21 (February 1990), pp. 83–86.

Kerr, Jennifer. "Government Spends Tax Dollars to Lobby—Government." *California Journal* 17 (1986), pp. 99–102.

Price, Charles M. "Advocacy in the Age of Term Limits." *California Journal* (October 1993), pp. 31–34.

Rosenthal, Alan. *The Third House: Lobbyists and Lobbying in the American States.* Washington, D.C.: Congressional Quarterly Press, 1993.

Samish, Arthur H., and Bob Thomas. *The Secret Boss of California.* New York: Crown, 1971.

Velie, Lester. "The Secret Boss of California." *Collier's,* August 13 and 20, 1949.

Zeigler, Harmon, and Michael Baer. *Lobbying: Interaction and Influence in American State Legislatures.* Belmont, CA: Wadsworth, 1969.

POLITICAL PARTIES
IN CALIFORNIA:

Reenergized Political Forces?

After a long period of Progressive-induced hibernation lasting for much of this century, political parties are on the verge of becoming more significant forces on the state political scene in the 1990s and beyond.

California political parties were traditionally weak and largely ineffective because of a key historical feature: Progressive reforms of the early 1900s (see Chapter 2). Progressives were concerned about the rise of party bosses and corrupt political machines. San Francisco was under the sway of the Boss Ruef machine, while the parties and institutions of California government were pawns of the Southern Pacific Railroad. Fremont Older, a leading newspaper reporter of the time, later wrote (1926, p. 14): "Southern Pacific Railroad dominated not only the Republican party, but also, to a large extent, the Democratic organization. . . . [I]t was in control—and thus the sole dispenser of political favors." For its efforts, Southern Pacific received huge subsidies from government.

PROGRESSIVE PARTY REFORMS

Progressive reforms made it difficult for political parties to perform their traditional functions: recruiting candidates, endorsing and supporting party office seekers in primaries, taking stands on issues, raising campaign funds, running campaigns, and moderating the demands of conflicting groups. Significantly, most Progressive political reforms remain intact and continue to shape contemporary California politics.

Election Reforms

Primary To remove Southern Pacific's tentacles from political parties and to expand the role of voters, Progressives successfully enacted the direct primary system, which allows party registrants to elect the party nominees, not have them picked by party leaders. If the "open primary" initiative, which has qualified for the March 1996 primary ballot, is approved by voters and survives court challenge, primary voters will be able to vote for their preferred choice for an office—whether Democrat, Republican, or third party (see Chapter 3).

Cross-Filing Under cross-filing, candidates for partisan office were allowed to file not only in their own party's primary but also in the opposition party's primary. Moreover, a Democrat, for example, could not tell from his ballot that particular candidates were cross-filing Republicans (see Chapter 3). Progressives believed that primary voters should be able to vote for the "best" candidate, regardless of party affiliation. Many incumbents captured both parties' nominations and were then listed on the general election ballot as the only candidate, a hyphenated Democratic–Republican, or vice versa. Cross-filing was eliminated in 1959. If approved, the open primary will be a type of cross-filing for voters.

Presidential Primary The presidential primary allows party voters to elect delegates to the national conventions. California was one of the first states to adopt this system and up to 1972 was one of about a dozen states to use it.

California Republicans continue to operate under a "winner-take-all" system: The candidate who receives the most votes in the primary gets to select the California delegation to the Republican convention. Criteria such as party work, candidate loyalty, monetary contributions, and regional balance are frequently used by the winning Republican presidential candidate in selecting delegates.

Since the tumultuous 1968 Democratic National Convention, California Democrats have had two objectives in their delegate selections: (1) achieving ethnic and gender balance in the delegation (national party guidelines mandated this change) and (2) democratizing the delegate-selection process. Under the Democratic format, delegates who have committed themselves to a particular presidential candidate attend delegate-selection caucuses early in the presidential election year. At these caucuses, those interested in becoming delegates give speeches about the candidate and how they would help the ticket. Those at the caucus vote on the merits of the aspiring delegates, and their names and rankings from each congressional district are submitted to the various Democratic presidential candidates' steering committees. These committees have final say in determining how the delegate prospects will be ranked on the presidential primary ballot. Based on Democratic party strength in the fifty-two congressional districts, party voters elect three to eight delegates per district. In addition, some delegate spots are reserved for party leaders and party officeholders and for affirmative-action balancing.

Before 1996, California's traditional June presidential primary came late in the delegate-selection process. Once a presidential candidate had rolled to victory in a few early primaries (e.g., New Hampshire), by mid- to late March the candidate's momentum would have built, and the California presidential primary would be meaningless. In 1996, the state primary *and* presidential primary will be moved ahead on a one-time experimental basis to the fourth Tuesday in March to allow California voters to count in determining a party's presidential nominee. Moving the primary ahead may allow Californians more voice in the nomination process, but many other states have also moved their primaries or caucuses even earlier on the 1996 calendar. Whether the fourth Tuesday in March presidential primary will allow California voters to help shape nominee selection is not clear.

Because of the horrendous defeats suffered by Democrats in the 1994 elections, there could be internal challenges within the party to President Clinton's renomination in 1996. At the same time, several Republicans have declared themselves candidates for the Republican nomination. Leading prospects are U.S. Senators Bob Dole and Phil Gramm, former Tennessee governor Lamar Alexander, and Governor Pete Wilson.

Initiative, Referendum, and Recall These direct-democracy devices allowed voters to propose, enact, and reject legislation, and remove officeholders from office in mid-term (see Chapter 4).

Nonpartisan Elections Progressives also favored nonpartisan local elections and the city manager form of local government in California. They argued that local issues such as road repair, park maintenance, and dog leash laws are not partisan. Voters should make their decisions based on candidate qualifications rather than party designation. On the other hand, as Eugene Lee noted (1960), nonpartisan local elections provide activist business community leaders distinct advantages in running for local office. Conservative members of the business community know one another through service clubs and volunteer community activities and can effectively coordinate political activities. Nonpartisan local elections weakened local party organization.

Party Organization Requirements Progressives placed into the election code a detailed framework within which parties were to operate. It spelled out in detail when the parties could meet, for how long, and how they should be structured.

Endorsements   Political parties were more powerful in some Eastern states than in California in part because they could provide endorsements to trusted party candidates (those who had "paid their dues") at state party conventions or in a primary, if the state had one. In these states, those seeking partisan nominations would vie for the support of the party organization, and party endorsement of a particular candidate meant almost certain nomination. The party could provide campaign advisers, financial assistance, and legions of precinct "foot soldiers" to go door to door for those endorsed. This feature was absent, for the most part, in California. Given their weakened condition, California political parties never really got into the practice of making preprimary endorsements.

Ballots   Progressives championed adoption of the Australian secret ballot to help discourage vote fraud. In addition, Progressives instituted the office block ballot form, forcing voters to vote separately for each office and encouraging ticket-splitting (see Chapter 3).

Civil Service Reforms

Early this century in many Eastern and Midwestern industrial states, party organizations were often composed of state and local government employees. Jobs were dispensed to party activists and relatives as patronage, not on the basis of merit or qualification. Maintaining a job depended on keeping one's party in power. Progressives promoted the concept of civil service reform, insisting that qualifications and test scores should determine who received government jobs.

Today, all states have adopted civil service reforms similar to Progressive reforms in California and other Western states. Some states not influenced by the Progressives, however, still have a substantial number of state and local government jobs not covered by civil service. Workers in these politically appointed positions are usually loyal activists of the party in power. There are very few patronage positions in California. Note, however, that legislative staff are not covered by civil service in California. These staffers serve at the pleasure of the member—that is, they can be hired and fired at will.

Social Setting

Further discouraging effective political organization is the California population's high mobility and the anonymity of urban life. Many California voters refuse to affiliate with either party, and many party registrants do not consider themselves "strong" Democrats or Republicans. Not surprisingly, independent presidential candidate Ross Perot attracted many to his cause in California in the 1992 presidential election. Cynicism about politicians runs deep in California.

POLITICAL PARTY ORGANIZATION
State Central Committee

The state central committee (SCC) is the key party unit for both major parties. Once every two years, the full SCCs convene in Sacramento. At these party conclaves, members thrash out issues, elect party leaders, hear from national and state officeholders and aspirants, and develop strategy for upcoming campaigns.

State central committees marshal their resources to provide assistance to party candidates in marginal districts or to new nominees. (The Republican party traditionally has had more success in raising campaign money and has been a more significant factor for Republican candidates than has the Democratic party for its nominees.) Workshops are conducted to encourage more effective campaign organization. However, the candidate—not the party—has primary responsibility for the campaign.

Throughout this century, incumbent officeholders (governors, state legislators, etc.) have controlled the SCCs of their respective parties. Incumbents knew one another, had more status, and could appoint many additional members to the SCC who generally did what the incumbent wanted. Historically, little was done by the SCC without the elected officeholders' blessings.[1]

The composition of the Republican and Democratic SCCs are similar but have some significant differences. Both parties provide SCC membership to all of their statewide officers, state legislators, board of equalization members, congressmembers, and unelected party nominees. These officeholders and nominees are also able to appoint additional SCC members. Republicans provide their officeholders and nominees more appointments (for example, a Republican statewide elected officer can appoint 12 members to the SCC; a Democrat statewide officeholder can appoint 6). In addition, both parties provide membership to leaders in auxiliary party groups and selected members of the county central committees. Finally, as a democratizing reform and to provide more grassroots input, Democrats elect 12 additional members from each of the 80 assembly districts and offer counties additional membership for every 10,000 registered Democrats. Thus, because Los Angeles County has 1.9 million Democrats, it receives an additional 190 SCC memberships.

Day-to-day party operations are handled by the state chairs, other elected party officials, and executive committees of the state committees. An extensive set of unofficial caucus groups operates within the Democratic party structure—African Americans, Latinos, feminists, gays, youth, unions, and even businesses and professions. This "balkanization" trend has been criticized by some party leaders as being counterproductive.

UPI / Bettmann

Pete Wilson celebrates his hard-fought gubernatorial victory at an election-night party in San Diego in 1990. He was reelected in 1994.

Party Organization Leaders

To an outsider, it might seem strange that candidates for state Democratic or Republican chair may spend thousands of dollars running for an office that is unpaid, has relatively low political visibility (few registered voters in either party know who their state chairs are), and requires a full-time commitment. Not surprisingly, party organization leaders tend to be wealthy, socially prominent individuals who are able to devote time and energy to party work. They usually have strong issue interests and enjoy hobnobbing with elected officeholders. Sometimes prominent attorneys from well-connected Los Angeles or San Francisco law firms seek party posts. Their close ties to incumbents have advantages for their law firms. A growing number of state chairs (particularly in the Democratic party) have used their party position to run for elective office. Among Democrat ex-party chairs: Nancy Pelosi was elected to Congress from San Francisco; Jerry Brown sought the presidential nomination in 1992 but lost to Bill Clinton; and Phil Angelides was the party's 1994 nominee for treasurer (he lost to Republican Matt Fong in the general election). State chairs are top sergeants, not generals. They must not presume too much when speaking for the party. For example, Kathleen Brown, 1994 Democratic gubernatorial candidate, sharply rebuked Democratic chair Bill Press during the campaign after he suggested that Governor Pete Wilson was complicit in 1992's New York World Trade Center bombing. Press had argued that Wilson, while serving as a U.S. senator, had voted for an immigration bill that allowed dangerous foreign nationals to enter the United States.

In both parties, feuds have occurred sporadically between elected officeholders, who view themselves as the major spokespersons of the party, and party chairs and officials, who believe they are the true voices of the party grass roots. A particularly acrimonious dispute arose during Betty Smith's tenure as Democratic state chair in the early 1980s. After gaining the chairmanship, Smith was asked by reporters whether the party would support controversial Chief Justice Rose Bird's reconfirmation to the state Supreme Court. Speaking for the party, Smith expressed reservations about the justice. Speaker Willie Brown reacted:

> Any party leader who utters words of that nature certainly is not as interested in the legislative leaders as she should be. I want to say this directly to the party leadership. You should never, never, never be accepted or tolerated by any Democrat when you in any manner offer any aid or comfort to those who would destroy the independence of the judiciary. (*The Sacramento Bee*, January 27, 1985, p. A-3)

Feuding between volunteer and elected leaders has occurred less often in Republican ranks.[2] Former Democratic governor Jerry Brown's election as Democratic state chair in 1988 was an attempt to placate volunteers while reassuring party professionals. Brown was an ex-officeholder, but he also had the aura of a nonpolitician. The current Democratic chair, Bill Press, is a longtime party activist and former officeseeker. John Herrington, a former member of President Ronald Reagan's cabinet, chairs the Republican party.

County Central Committee

At the bottom rung of the party structure are county central committees. About 10 percent of voters know the names of their assemblymember or county supervisor, but virtually no one knows who makes up their party's county central committee. Individuals run for county committee positions by first securing the names of a few sponsors from within party ranks to qualify for the ballot and then run against other party competitors (if any) in the June primary. Election frequently hinges more on one's ballot position than anything else. If the number filing is the same as or less than the number of openings on the committee, those who file get elected so long as they receive at least one vote in the primary.

The prime duties of county central committees are to assist local party candidates running for office and to maintain the party presence in the area. On rare occasions, county committees can play a critical role in local politics. If an uncontested party nominee should die before the primary or if a selected nominee should die before the fall general election, then the county central committee is given the responsibility of choosing a replacement.

Unpaid, unrewarded, and unnoticed, these party activists are found in virtually every California community. They keep the party presence alive at the local level by doing the necessary grunt work—placing yard signs, working at party head-quarters, holding fund-raisers, and stuffing envelopes. Local party activists are a small, unique subset of the state population.

REVIVAL OF CALIFORNIA POLITICAL PARTIES?

Several important recent changes could lead to a modest revitalization of the state's party organizations. Among these changes are (1) the endorsing rights won by state parties in the courts, (2) the revised selection rules for the Democratic state central committees, and (3) Proposition 140's term limits.

Endorsing

Because of Progressive reforms, parties did not endorse in California. Over the years, some party volunteer leaders (particularly in the Democratic party) con-tended that they had the legal right and moral obligation to make preprimary endorsements for particular party candidates or for candidates in nonpartisan races. Endorsing, it was argued, would help reenergize parties: Activist members of the party organization would have an important role to play, and it would discourage off-the-wall party candidates (for example, a LaRouche Democrat or a Neo-Nazi Republican) from capturing a party nomination because of an uninformed, disinterested voting public.

On a few occasions this century, some county central committees did endorse, but whether they had the legal right to do so was never clear. The endorsing ban extended even more emphatically to nonpartisan races. The state election code stipulated that all judicial, school, city, and county elections were to be *nonparti-san*, which was thought to mean that parties should not get involved in these elections at all. To clarify the matter, a 1963 law prohibited parties from endorsing in partisan contests. Legislative leaders wanted to control who got nominated in particular primaries, not local party activists. Since the 1960s, senate and assem-bly Republican and Democratic leaders have poured vast sums into the primary campaign treasuries of their choices and provided them with campaign staffs.

In 1979, private citizen Sam Unger brought suit against the Marin County Democratic Central Committee because it had endorsed a local school board candidate. Unger argued this was a violation of the law, and he won his lawsuit in court. Three years later, Unger again went to court (dubbed "Unger II" in the press), but this time Republicans were his target. Unger charged that the state Republican party was involved in the "recall Rose Bird" campaign.

While Unger II was pending, a newly formed Committee for Party Renewal, consisting of academics, some Democratic party officials, and a few Republican and Libertarian activists concerned about California's weak parties, brought suit in federal court contending that the endorsing prohibition was an infringement on parties' freedom of speech. A federal judge agreed in 1984 and ruled that (1) parties could endorse in partisan primaries and (2) parties could organize themselves as they saw fit. Left unanswered was whether parties could be barred from endorsing in nonpartisan races. In 1986, voters approved a constitutional amendment barring parties from endorsing in judicial and other nonpartisan races. However, in August 1990, the U.S. Circuit Court struck down this state ban as a violation of First Amendment free speech rights. Democratic and Republican leaders hailed the decision. When the decision was appealed, the U.S. Supreme Court refused to review, allowing the lower court decision to stand. Since then, Democrats have endorsed in some nonpartisan races: In 1993, Democrats endorsed Michael Woo in the Los Angeles City mayoral contest, and in 1994, they backed Delaine Eastin as Superintendent of Instruction.

Although parties now have the legal right to endorse, Republicans and Democrats have gone in separate directions on whether they will.

Republican Nonendorsing At their 1988 SCC convention, Republicans decided not to endorse primary candidates, and this has been their position ever since. Republicans argue that endorsing can lead to (1) rifts in party ranks (unsuccessful endorsement seekers might be angered and fail to support the ticket), (2) friction between local volunteers and state elected leaders, (3) rigged meetings and behind-the-scenes deal making, or (4) fewer choices for Republican voters in the primary because candidates not receiving an endorsement might not file for the race. A few Republican activists have chafed under the endorsing ban, and one county committee went ahead and endorsed a local candidate. But for the most part, GOPers seem to prefer a no-endorsement policy.

However, Republicans do occasionally endorse ballot measures (for example, they endorsed Proposition 174, the choice [voucher] initiative, in 1993 and Proposition 187, the illegal alien initiative of November 1994). In the 1992 Republican presidential nominating race between incumbent President George

Bush and challenger Pat Buchanan, after the latter recorded a reasonably good showing—"a moral victory"—in the New Hampshire primary, Bush wanted to stop any Buchanan momentum. Fortunately, California Republicans were holding their state convention the weekend after the New Hampshire primary, and Bush forces wanted California Republicans to endorse him. After learning of the California Republicans' nonendorsing policy, Bush allies in the California Republican party moved to have the party give Bush a *nonbinding* straw-vote show of support, which they did.

Democratic Endorsing　Democratic leaders enthusiastically embraced endorsing in 1988 and have used it ever since, except for presidential contests. Under their bylaws, caucuses (composed of SCC members resident in the geographic area of the office in question) are held every two years. All party candidates (except those running for county central committees) may request endorsement. To win an endorsement, a candidate must receive 60 percent of the vote in the caucus (assuming a quorum is present), and delegates have the right to vote "no endorsement." The recommendation is then sent to the SCC for approval. It is possible, but highly unlikely, that the SCC could reject a local endorsing caucus choice and endorse another candidate. To win official endorsement, this "other" candidate would have to win at least 75 percent of the SCC vote.

Since 1988, with only one exception, local endorsing groups have endorsed party incumbents running for reelection. The one exception was in 1988, when East Bay Democrats voted not to endorse their State Senator, Dan Boatwright, and instead endorsed a local supervisor. Boatwright did not withdraw, and he won a narrow victory in the primary and an easy victory in the general. Thus, endorsing seems of little consequence when a Democratic incumbent runs for reelection or in districts where Republicans have a substantial registration advantage. The endorsed Democrat will lose to his or her Republican opponent anyway. But, given term limits, many incumbent legislators will have to retire from that particular office, which means more "open" districts and more significance for endorsing. Frequently in these open races, however, several Democratic candidates vie for endorsement, with none being able to reach 60 percent. Moreover, party voters do not blindly follow the dictates of party leaders. For legislative candidates, Democratic endorsing has not been much of a factor yet, although it probably has stirred interest among local party activists.

Endorsing in statewide contests has also not been of critical importance. In 1990, in the two most hotly contested statewide races without incumbents, Democrats endorsed John Van de Kamp over Dianne Feinstein for governor and Bill Press over John Garamendi for insurance commissioner. In both cases, the endorsed candidates lost to their party rivals in the primary. In two open races in 1994—governor and treasurer—no Democrat was endorsed because they could not reach the 60 percent level. In two other open statewide races, endorsed candidates lost: Gwen Moore was the endorsed candidate for secretary of state but lost to Tony Miller in the primary, and Rusty Areias was the endorsed candidate for controller but lost to Kathleen Connell in the primary. Among statewide candidates, only insurance commissioner candidate Art Torres captured the endorsement and won in the primary. If Democrats are not able to elect their endorsees, the importance of endorsing is reduced.

Democratized Democrat State Central Committee

As noted, Democrats have reformed their SCC by increasing substantially the number of delegates elected at the local level and reducing the number appointed by officeholders.

Term Limits for Legislative Leaders: New Opportunities for the Parties

Over the last several decades, assembly and senate majority and minority leaders have been the largest single contributors to their party candidates in close races. Obviously, candidates receiving this transferred fund largesse were expected to support their legislative patrons when they arrived at the capitol. (Of course, none of this is spelled out; it's an unspoken IOU.) Unless they were complete ingrates, legislators usually went along with their benefactors on bills or leadership votes. Because of the growing criticism of this practice, both campaign-reform initiatives of June 1988 (Propositions 68 and 73) prohibited these transfers of funds. Although both were approved by voters, the courts have since struck them down.

The advent of term limits and the inevitable rapid turnover of legislative leaders means that their ability to raise large sums from interest groups and transfer it to their choices will be reduced. Formerly, legislative leaders could pressure large campaign contributions from interests because of their continuity in office. No more. Political party organizations may play a more critical role in dispensing funds to candidates in the future because of this funding vacuum. Indeed, the election of former governor and still politically ambitious Jerry Brown as Democratic state chair in 1988 symbolized the growing potential for the party organization.

California Democrats and Republicans: Issue Differences

What issues separate Democrats from Republicans? On many, there are only minor or subtle differences between the two parties. Republicans endorsed

Proposition 187, which bars education and social services to undocumented aliens, and seem more willing to get tough on illegal immigrants. Most Democrats opposed Proposition 187, but nearly all agreed that illegal immigration was a serious problem. Democrats said the way to deal with illegals was to do a better job stopping them from coming across the border and to fine their employers. Republicans favored the "three strikes" law; Democrats also did, but somewhat belatedly and with less enthusiasm. Elected officeholders in both parties steer clear of meeting budget shortfalls by raising taxes because everyone knows the public's hostility to this strategy. Democrats tend to be more supportive than Republicans of government in general and social programs such as Social Security, Medicare, food stamps, and national health care. Republicans view government as a necessary evil and are unenthusiastic about many social programs, although they're reluctant to dismantle them because of their popularity.

Perhaps the sharpest differences now between the two California parties are on social issues. The Christian right has become an increasingly powerful force in the state GOP in the 1990s. These newly politicized Christians have a wide array of social issues on which they take uncompromising stances; they are antiabortion, anti–gay rights, anti–sex education in public schools, pro–school prayer, anti–affirmative action, antipornography, and provoucher. These issue positions diverge sharply from those of mainstream Democrats.

Dedicated, zealous, and committed "born again" Christians have been encouraged by national figures such as Reverends Pat Robertson and Jerry Falwell to get involved in civic affairs and Republican party organization. Because of their discipline and fervor, they have elected many of their activists to party organization positions. More than half of the Republican county central committees have Christian right majorities, and they are an imposing force on the SCC. Christian right advocates have also been elected to many state school boards to promote their conservative agenda. Republican moderates (for example, Governor Wilson) have come under withering attack when they espouse moderate viewpoints.

POLITICAL PARTY SUBSTITUTES

Because of the traditional weakness of the state's political parties, other organizations have emerged in California to serve traditional party functions.

Extraparty Groups

Republican   In 1934, a group of moderate Republican leaders wanted the state GOP to project a more centrist image. Thus, the California Republican Assembly (CRA) was organized to endorse promising moderates in the party to help them win their primaries and get elected. CRA was an unofficial party group and hence could endorse.

In the 1940s and 1950s, CRA played a significant role in Republican nomination politics, providing financial assistance, campaign expertise, a work force, and the prestige of its endorsement behind its candidates. Those not endorsed were sometimes dissuaded from filing. Former President Richard Nixon got his political start by winning a CRA endorsement in a Southern California congressional district.

Though CRA began as a voice of moderate Republicanism, over the years it has become archly conservative. For example, at its April 1991 convention, the CRA urged Governor Wilson to reregister as a Democrat (members were angry because of the tax increase he had agreed to in order to deal with the massive state deficit). In 1988, CRA endorsed Pat Robertson, not George Bush, for president. Again in 1992, CRA preferred Pat Buchanan to incumbent President George Bush. In 1994, it endorsed political unknown, but conservative Ron Unz rather than Pete Wilson in the Republican gubernatorial primary.

Although other Republican extraparty groups have formed over the years to counter CRA's influence, all have disappeared from the political scene. Today, CRA is no longer the force it once was and its endorsements are of less consequence, but it still plays a modest role in Republican nomination politics through press coverage of its endorsing conventions. Also, CRA remains a factor because the Republican party has decided not to endorse. Currently, CRA is in the vanguard of the militant conservative movement within the state party. CRA leaders care little whether their endorsed conservatives will win against centrists (for example, Wilson). From their perspective, it is important to back the most ideologically compatible candidate. Moderate Republicans generally do not bother to show up at CRA endorsing meetings.

Democratic The California Democratic Council (CDC) was organized in 1953 to play a similar, but liberal role in Democratic ranks. In the 1950s and 1960s, it played a modestly important role in Democratic nomination politics. However, the Vietnam War badly divided the CDC (the issue was whether incumbent Democratic President Lyndon Johnson should be backed or whether the group should speak out against this military engagement). It never recovered.

In 1976, a new group entered the Democratic political scene: Tom Hayden's Campaign for Economic Democracy (CED). Hayden had earlier gained considerable media notoriety for his leadership in the student protest, anti–Vietnam War movement of the 1960s. He became even more famous when he married Jane Fonda, the popular film star and antiwar activist. (They have since divorced.)

Organized initially from volunteers who worked for Hayden in his unsuccessful U.S. Senate bid in 1976, CED was partly Hayden campaign organization, lobby group, caucus within the Democratic party, local grassroots campaign organization, and endorsing group (though it mainly endorsed CED members). CED championed issues such as rent control, solar energy, land-use planning, toxic-waste safeguards, and a nuclear freeze.

In 1980, Hayden ran and was elected to the state assembly from West Los Angeles. Hayden spent more than $2 million in his campaign in reassuring voters that he was not a dangerous radical. Throughout the 1980s, he was reelected from the district.

In the early 1980s, CEDers were elected to local office in several communities (mainly college towns such as Chico, Davis, and Santa Cruz); dedicated, grassroots CED volunteers were instrumental. But in 1985, a well-financed conservative attack against "radicalism" led to the defeat of several CED local officeholders. Hayden's political presence has galvanized GOP conservatives.

In 1986, Hayden announced that CED would be phased out and replaced by a new organization, Campaign California (CC). He contended that too much of CED's time and money had gone into electing local CED candidates. There was also confusion over the meaning of "economic democracy"; Hayden stated that it did not mean governmental solutions for every societal problem. CC would focus on state and national issues and have offices in four prime media centers: Los Angeles, San Francisco, San Jose, and Sacramento.

CC evolved into a liberal, initiative-sponsoring organization. In 1986, CC helped qualify a toxic-waste initiative for the ballot, and members in Sacramento County worked in the successful initiative campaign to shut down the Rancho Seco nuclear energy plant. CC helped qualify and supported the cigarette-tax initiative of November 1988. In 1990, Hayden and other CC officials decided to expend all of the group's financial resources on Big Green, an environmental initiative (Proposition 128). Big Green lost big, and CC ceased operation.

After being reapportioned out of his district in the 1991 Democratic assembly by legislative leaders, Hayden ran for and won election to the state senate. In 1994, he ran for the Democratic nomination for governor but came in third, receiving less than one-tenth of the primary vote, though he continues to hold his seat in the state senate. Throughout his tenure in the legislature, Hayden has faced repeated attacks from Republican conservatives. Conservatives argue that Hayden's anti–Vietnam War activities, particularly his trip to North Vietnam during the military engagement, constitute treason (that is, aiding and abetting the enemy during the time of war) and that he should be removed from the legislature. None of these ouster efforts have succeeded.

Democratic extraparty groups are no longer needed for endorsing purposes because the official party makes endorsements. Of course, still to be reckoned with is Ross Perot's United We Stand (UWS) organization. As a nonprofit group, UWS cannot now endorse candidates, but some of its chapters did invite candidates for interviews and evaluation, and Perot himself endorsed several Republicans and some Democrats in the 1994 general election.

Slate Mailers

Democrats send out slate mailers (when they can afford the costs) to voters in the primary, listing the various endorsed party candidates and propositions. In addition, several campaign firms send out lists of candidates they support—for a fee. The campaign firms ask Democratic candidates if they want to be included on their endorsed list for a fee—say, $50,000 or $100,000. Some candidates, fearful that voters will think this is an official endorsement and not wanting to be excluded from any endorsed list, feel compelled to pay. Companies sponsoring these mailers must stipulate that they are unofficial endorsements. But many voters probably don't pay much attention to this caveat—particularly when the mailing group can call itself anything it wants such as Independent Democratic Voting Guide or Voter Information Guide. Both major parties send out slates in the fall general election campaign.

Kingmakers

On occasion, informal groups of the very wealthy have tried to influence candidate selection, particularly in Republican nomination politics. These "Lords of the Lettuce," as one disgruntled Republican candidate called them, attempt to use their pooled "big bucks" as leverage to encourage or discourage particular Republican statewide prospects. Key "big money" people in the Reagan "kitchen cabinet" strongly influenced Republican nomination politics from the 1960s through the 1980s, but the situation is more fluid in the 1990s. David Packard, of Hewlett-Packard, has always been a generous contributor to moderate Republican candidates. Packard has a circle of well-to-do friends who also are willing to donate. The new conservative fat-cat inner circle for Republicans includes Donald Bren, a billionaire Orange County developer; attorney Karl Samuellian; Alex Spanos, San Diego Chargers owner; Howard Margueleas, former president of the state chamber of commerce; Gordon Luce, San Diego Savings and Loan; and Ken Derr, Chevron CEO. On the Democratic side, statewide aspirants traditionally woo "big labor" and Hollywood tycoons for campaign contributions.

Professional Campaign Managers

California is the birthplace for what is now an international feature of major political campaigns: professional management. The weak party structure, the state's size, the need to use mass media to reach voters, and the many ballot propositions encouraged the development of professional campaign management.

The first campaign management company on the scene was the husband-and-wife public relations firm of Whitaker (former political reporter) and Baxter (former lobbyist). For a fee, they provided expert advice to clients on overall campaign management—raising money, planning, and the wording and placement of ads. Whitaker and Baxter concentrated mainly, but not exclusively, on ballot proposition elections. One key was to select a basic campaign theme and hammer away at it. In working against President Harry Truman's national health care system, the Whitaker and Baxter ads stated, "Stop socialized medicine." (Incidentally, this same message was used by opponents of Proposition 186, the single-payer health plan initiative of 1994.) Whitaker and Baxter also pioneered the radio spot. Their first was an antirailroad union tune, "I've Been Loafing on the Railroad." Whitaker and Baxter encouraged their clients to be aggressive, pore over their opponents' records, and attack. Between 1933 and 1955, Whitaker and Baxter managed seventy-five different campaigns and won seventy.

After World War II, other campaign pros joined the field. Today, hundreds of management firms and campaign consultants advise and run ballot and candidate campaigns. Yet their basic strategy—with modern, technical refinements—is similar to Whitaker and Baxter's. Some firms have expanded their roles beyond campaign work to engage in public opinion formation. Although some consultants work for Republican *and* Democratic candidates, most work with just one party: Stu Spencer, Sal Russo, Ed Rollins, Ken Khachigian, and Baus and Ross work for Republicans; and Joe Cerrell, Bill Carrick, Richie Ross, Clint Reilly, and David Townsend work for Democrats.

Specialization is the order of the day. Although one professional management consultant may be hired for overall campaign supervision, subcontractors may be used to do radio and TV spots, buy media time, compose ads, select billboards, dig up dirt on opponents, advise candidates on handling hostile questions, decide on the coloring and lettering of billboards or yard signs, use direct mail, or get free TV by getting on the evening news. Thus, both Pete Wilson and Kathleen Brown, Republican and Democratic candidates for governor in 1994, held press conferences outside L.A. County, jail where O. J. Simpson was being held. Moreover, the contemporary world of campaign management has gone high-tech—computers, fax machines, satellite links, and audio actualities. If an opponent attacks with a negative hit, the other side should respond with an attack ad on television and radio within twenty-four hours. Opposition research has become a critical dimension of the modern campaign. As Lapin and Doyle (1994) note, "Campaign operatives are paid millions to follow the paper trail: voting records, newspaper clippings, courthouse documents, tax liens, property records, lawsuit filings, campaign disclosure statements, attendance records, published writing, and more." For example, John Nelson Consulting was paid $6,000 monthly by Republican U.S. Senate candidate Michael Huffington to dig up dirt on incumbent Democrat Dianne Feinstein. She, in turn, hired Dan Carol & Co. to delve into Huffington's background.

To the more serious devotees of campaigns—journalists and fat cats—perhaps the most critical decision candidates will make is their choice of campaign consultants. If the consultant is considered one of Sacramento's "high flyers," the campaign achieves instant credibility. When Sonny Bono, one-time recording star and ex-husband of Cher, announced he was running for political office, many experts dismissed him as a political lightweight. But when he hired the respected Bill Lacy to run his campaign, he was soon taken seriously. Bono was elected to Congress in 1994.

At the very least, by hiring a quality campaign firm, a candidate can help attract major contributions from serious investors. Sometimes campaign consultants take themselves too seriously. Thus, Dianne Feinstein's campaign for governor in 1990 suffered a wrenching early blow when her campaign consultant resigned in a squabble over strategy. This is one of the few times in modern campaign politics that the consultant fired the candidate!

From Whitaker and Baxter days to the present, campaign consultants have always been controversial. Some critics complain that issues become unimportant or candidate qualities become irrelevant when one employs the right "hired gun." However, consultants are only one part of the winning equation. Richie Ross was hailed as a genius in 1988 for his campaign for the CTA in winning voter approval of Proposition 98. Two years later, he was the campaign director and chief strategist of John Van de Kamp's losing primary battle with Dianne Feinstein for the Democratic nomination for governor and received much of the blame for the loss. Ross's career in campaign consulting exemplifies the profession's hazards and meteoric ups and downs. Clint Reilly's aura of being a winner was hurt when his candidate, Kathleen Brown, was overwhelmed by Governor Pete Wilson. Campaign consultants can do only so much. It is the quality of the candidate, the issues, turnout, and voting trends, among other items, as well as the skill of the professional consultant, that determine winners and losers.

Among other criticisms of these campaign professionals is that they sell candidates in much the same way that mouthwashes, toothpastes, and underarm

Dennis Renault / *The Sacramento Bee*

Consumer News Item: With the growth of TV shopping, buyers are warned to use caution. Merchandise too frequently looks better than it actually is, impulse buying should always be avoided, and testimonials viewed with skepticism.

deodorants are sold: jingles, endless repetition, thirty-second spots, and attacking competing brands. The political "hired guns" say that this is done is because it works—just ask Excedrin. This is the best and most effective way to reach a bored, alienated electorate. Another criticism concerns the heavy use of attack spots by professionals. The public says in polls that it doesn't like mud-slinging, personal attacks; some citizens get so fed up with them that they decide not to vote. But surveys also reveal that it's the attacks the public remembers when it votes. Consultants know this and feel obliged to offer their candidate the best advice to win. Critics also complain that consultants are too obsessed with winning. Campaign consultant Richie Ross, in justifying a particularly mean campaign he directed, said that the bottom line was "We won." Campaign pro Bill Butcher has said that he would do anything for his candidate that was not strictly illegal. Obviously, campaign consultants are not unique in their penchant for winning. Furthermore, campaign consultants are hired on the basis of their win–loss records, and their fees are largely determined by their previous performances.

What, if anything, should be done about these "hired guns"? Former FPPC Chair Dan Stanford proposed that political consultants be required to register with the state and agree to abide by an ethical code. This suggestion has not been pursued. There is no constitutional way to prevent these professionals from directing campaigns; effective limits on campaign spending, however, would probably reduce their influence. Running a statewide campaign can be very profitable. But too much of the blame for the sleazy quality of campaigns is placed on professional consultants. Candidates have the final responsibility for deciding how they want their campaigns to be structured.

Special Interests and PACs

Special interests and their funding arms, political action committees (PACs), also serve as party substitutes. At the federal and state level, PACs provide more money to candidates than do the parties. In the 1990s, more than half the money raised by California state elected officials comes from PACs.

THIRD PARTIES

Occasionally, third parties have been factors in state politics. In this century, Hiram Johnson's Progressives, at first a Republican party faction and later a separate reform party, have been the most significant third party in state history.

The problems facing third parties in California and other states are little money, overemphasis on a single issue (which may be adopted by one or both major parties), and few "name" candidates. Beyond this, the most significant problem for third parties is getting their message out. The media pay little attention to third parties because they are inconsequential and attract few voters. Third-party leaders say they aren't heard because they receive virtually no media coverage—a vicious circle. Or another example: When Republican Pete Wilson and Democrat Kathleen Brown held their one televised debate in the 1994 governor's contest, no third-party governor candidates were included.

Although some states make it difficult for third parties to qualify for the ballot, not so in California. Under state law, to qualify for a place on the ballot, a new third party must either (1) register at least 1 percent of California voters (about 145,000) into the party or (2) get 10 percent of voters to sign a petition asking that the party be placed on the ballot.[3] Given the enormous number of signatures involved, the second option has never been used. Finally, a 1976 law allows nonqualified third parties to get their presidential and vice-presidential candidates on the ballot if they are able to get 1 percent of voters to sign a petition requesting this. Candidates qualifying under this provision must be listed as "independents."

Staying on the ballot in California is much easier than qualifying. To remain, a party must (1) maintain a registration of at least 1/15 of 1 percent and (2) have one of its candidates for statewide office receive at least 2 percent of the vote. Usually, enough disgruntled voters within the two major parties, independents, and third-party voters guarantee the necessary 2 percent (see Table 6.1).

Peace and Freedom Party

The Peace and Freedom (P&F) party was born from frustration with the Vietnam War. When President Lyndon Johnson sought to maintain the U.S. presence in Vietnam until an "honorable" peace had been achieved, disgruntled California Democrats joined the "Get Out of Vietnam Now" Peace and Freedom party.

Membership in the party has declined sharply since the end of the Vietnam era. Given the conservative trend in California, 1960s radical protest seems ill-suited for contemporary state politics.

American Independent Party

The American Independent party (AIP) espouses a staunch, ultraconservative program. Adherents regularly criticize Republicans for "me-too-ing" Democrats. When the AIP was initially on the national ballot in 1968, its presidential candidate, former Democratic governor of Alabama George Wallace, a leader in the Southern anti-integration effort, took a respectable 12 percent of the presidential vote. Since then, party candidates have attracted only a handful of votes.

Interestingly, though, the AIP has about three times as many registrants as any other third party. The AIP's "success" probably is more an artifact of its name, Independent, than its electoral appeal. Some new voter registrants may be confused and believe they are registering as independents rather than into this archconservative third party.

Libertarian Party

The Libertarian philosophy can perhaps best be summarized in a single word: *against.* Libertarians are opposed to nearly all governmental activity. They argue

	LIBERTARIAN	PEACE AND FREEDOM	AMERICAN INDEPENDENT	GREEN
CONGRESS (45)	31	12	5	3
STATE SENATE (20)	9	4	0	0
STATE ASSEMBLY (80)	31	13	1	3

TABLE 6.1   THIRD-PARTY LEGISLATIVE CANDIDATES, 1994

that those who want a particular service—education, health care, mail delivery, or parks—should pay for it individually. Libertarians favor the dismantling of Social Security, the Occupational Safety and Health Administration (OSHA), regulatory commissions, and nearly every governmental program now in existence. They also adamantly oppose new governmental programs, such as gun-control laws or a national health care system. Libertarians are enthusiastic supporters of virtually all tax-reduction schemes. They favor reduced military spending, getting the United States out of the United Nations, and bringing all American forces stationed abroad back home.

Not surprisingly, the Libertarian emphasis on a strict laissez-faire, profit-motive approach has strong appeal to some ultraconservatives in the corporate community. But Libertarianism also appeals to the other end of the ideological spectrum, the ultraliberal. Libertarians are opposed to all victimless crime laws. They oppose laws that attempt to regulate the sale or use of drugs, they favor legalizing prostitution, and they oppose pornography and antisodomy laws.

Libertarian voting strength has ebbed in California and other states. Party registration has declined. For the foreseeable future, there is virtually no chance a Libertarian could get elected to the state legislature. As an example of the decline in stature of this third party, in 1986 Norma Jean Almodovar, an admitted ex-prostitute, received the party's nomination for lieutenant governor. In the midst of her campaign, Almodovar went to Denmark to attend an international hookers' convention. Another bizarre example is Howard Stern, the notorious sexual libertine and talk-show star who captured the party's 1994 gubernatorial nomination in New York. One week later, he withdrew because he did not want to disclose his income publicly (required of all candidates).

Green Party

The Greens are the "new kid on the third-party block." They began in Europe as an antinuclear and environmental protest party in the 1970s. They were able to elect a few of their members to several different European parliaments and scored some successes within these multiparty frameworks. In the late 1980s, several leaders in the American environmental movement decided to launch a new Green party in the United States. The party was able to qualify for the California ballot (and several other states' ballots) with relative ease. The party takes a militant stance on environmental issues and is similar to the Democrats on social issues. Thus far, the Greens have received only a tiny smattering of votes. Interestingly enough, three Greens fought for this tiny party's gubernatorial nomination in 1994, but Green party voters have another option on their ballot, "none of the above," which received more votes than any of their three candidates.

Third-Party Significance

Obviously, none of the ballot-qualified third parties is a serious threat to the dominant Democrats and Republicans. But third parties have, on a few rare occasions, played an interesting "spoiler" role in legislative races. In close elections, a Peace and Freedom or Green candidate can drain a small but significant percentage of liberal-left votes away from the Democratic candidate, thereby throwing the election to the Republican, or an American Independent or Libertarian candidate can pull votes away from Republican candidates. As an example, in 1994 in the 3rd and 24th congressional districts, voting results were as follows:

Fazio (Democrat)	93,137	Beilenson (Democrat)	84,080
Lefever (Republican)	86,386	Sybert (Republican)	80,879
Crain (Libertarian)	7,808	Koehler (Libertarian)	5,493

Here, Libertarian candidates probably helped Democrats Fazio and Beilenson win reelection.

Thus, the generous provisions in state law allowing nearly moribund third-party corpses to remain in a state of suspended animation on the California ballot can create special problems for Democrats and Republicans in a few marginal districts. It's pretty much the luck of the draw as to whether a Republican candidate has a Libertarian or American Independent opponent on the ballot or whether a Democratic candidate has a Green or Peace and Freedom party opponent.

Even the spoiler's role is diminished if third parties do not field candidates in legislative races. The number of third-party legislative candidates in the November 1994 general elections is summarized in Table 6.1. Finally, the remarkable showing that independent candidate Ross Perot received in California (more than 20 percent of the vote) and other states does suggest there is a potential for third-party or independent candidacies. Many Democrats and Republicans were more than willing to abandon their traditional party allegiances for Perot.

REFORMING POLITICAL PARTIES

The new party reforms, including the right to endorse, the greater number of grassroots activists on the SCCs, and term limits (legislative leaders will no longer be dominant players) should help parties play a more meaningful role in the 1990s. However, the weakness of California's parties will not be easily overcome even with the new changes. The state's Progressive tradition is deeply ingrained.

SUMMARY

Historically, the two major parties were weakened by Progressive reforms. Third parties have not been a significant factor over the past several decades except as potential "spoilers." Elective officeholders are the real leaders of the two major parties, but the state party organizational leaders are attempting to be more assertive. New reforms in political parties may strengthen these organizations.

NOTES

1. The historic weakness of party leaders vis-à-vis elected officeholders was highlighted in a Democratic confrontation in 1982 dealing with the party's official position on key ballot measures. Democratic officeholders planned to send out a slate mailer to Democrats urging them to vote for the party's nominees. Because they were short of funds to finance the project, Democratic Speaker Willie Brown was enlisted to help provide financing. The mailer sent out included not only Democratic candidate endorsements but also ballot proposition recommendations on which the Democratic party had never taken an official stand: yes on textbook loans to private schools (Proposition 9), no on the bottle-deposit initiative (Proposition 11), and no on the water-conservation initiative (Proposition 13). (On the latter two, there was strong sentiment among Democratic activists in support of the measures.)

   Why did the Democratic mailer recommend these aberrant positions? Money. To finance the mailer, Speaker Brown turned to various special interests with an interest in the propositions: Business and labor interests contributed $30,000 for a "No on 11" recommendation, agribusiness forces put up $30,000 for a "No on 13" recommendation, and private-school advocates contributed $15,000 for a "Yes on 9" recommendation. Democratic officials were shocked when these proposition recommendations went out under the party banner, but they could do nothing. In 1984, the Democratic party's mailer neither included nor made any recommendation on the lottery initiative, although the party had officially opposed it.

2. In 1987, William Park, formerly vice-chair of the party, assumed that, following the traditional pattern, he would become chair. However, elected officeholders feared that Park, a toxic-dumpsite operator repeatedly cited by the Environmental Protection Agency for violations, would not be a good symbol for the party. Defeated in his bid to become Republican state chair by Robert Naylor, a former assembly minority leader, Park complained that Republican volunteers were being steamrollered by elected officeholders.

3. Figures based on 1994 voter turnout.

REFERENCES

Hoeber, Thomas R., and Charles M. Price (eds.) "Greens: The New Party" in *California Government and Politics Annual 1993–94*. Sacramento: California Journal Press, pp. 69–70.

Lapin, Lisa, and Michael Doyle. "Foes Master Technology to Hit Political Pay Dirt." *The Sacramento Bee* (August 6, 1994), p. A1.

Lee, Eugene C. *The Politics of Nonpartisanship: A Study of California City Elections*. Berkeley: University of California Press, 1960.

Older, Fremont. *My Own Story*. New York: Macmillan, 1926.

Price, Charles M., Charles G. Bell, and Vic Pollard. "The Party Renewal Movement." *California Journal* 15 (1984), pp. 472–474.

Price, Charles M. "Party Endorsements." *California Journal* 23 (April 1992), pp. 199–208.

THE CALIFORNIA
LEGISLATURE:

Revolving Door Politics

FORMAL STRUCTURE OF THE CALIFORNIA LEGISLATURE

Patterned after the bicameral U.S. Congress, as are forty-eight other state legislatures (Nebraska is the sole exception), the California legislature has two houses: assembly and senate. The upper house, the senate, has forty members (half of them elected every two years to four-year terms). The lower house, the assembly, has eighty members who serve two-year terms. Under Proposition 140 (term limits), which was established in 1990, senators may serve a maximum of two terms (eight years), and assemblymembers may serve a maximum of three terms (six years); these are lifetime bans. Representation in both houses is based on equal population districts. From 1923 until 1965, the legislature operated under the federal plan: Representation in the assembly was based on population; in the senate, on area (counties). Since 1965, however, the U.S. Supreme Court has required both houses of state legislatures to be apportioned on the basis of population. Anyone eligible to vote in California can run for the state legislature.

Although the bicameral structure and basic framework of the California legislature remain basically unchanged from the first legislative session after statehood to the present, much has changed.

THE AMATEUR LEGISLATURE

For much of this century, state legislatures (including California's) were viewed by media and academic experts as outmoded, irrelevant institutions geared to nineteenth-century America. Fettered by antiquated state constitutions, ruled by rural legislators with an antiurban bias, outflanked by the national government's new social programs, confused by bureaucrats, dominated by full-time professional governors, and beholden to lobbyists for meals and sustenance, state legislatures were in a deplorable situation. They were a not very funny joke.

Background to Reform

Through the early 1960s, the California legislature was fairly typical. Legislators were poorly paid, met only a few months every year, and had inadequate offices, haphazard procedures, and few professional staff. The 1965 California legislature's working conditions were set in the state constitution. For example, salaries were $6,000 annually, and the length of session was 120 days for general sessions in odd-numbered years and 30 days for budget sessions in even-numbered years. To change either feature required amending the constitution: It had to be approved by a two-thirds majority vote in each house and then submitted to a suspicious public for final approval. Not surprisingly, raising the salaries of elected officials (politicians!) has always been a difficult notion to sell to the public.

To deal with these constitutional problems and to remove obsolete portions of the document, the legislature established a Constitutional Revision Commission. In February 1966, the commission recommended revisions of articles dealing with the legislative, executive, and judicial branches. These proposed revisions were adopted by each house and submitted to voters as Proposition 1A of November 1966. The legislature also passed a bill that would raise legislators' salaries from $6,000 to $16,000 if voters approved the proposition.

The Campaign for Proposition 1A

The leading proponent of Proposition 1A, and the person most instrumental in getting the constitutional revision approved, was Speaker Jess Unruh, who skillfully jockeyed the proposal through the legislature and helped convince voters of its merit (see Chapter 5).

Unruh argued that improving legislative salaries would help to attract more able, better-educated people as candidates for the legislature. Low pay, he believed, tended to discourage talented citizens from running for office and made it difficult for many African Americans and Latinos to run. Inadequate pay guaranteed that legislators would be dependent on lobbyists for meals, lodging, and other gratuities. Unruh contended that pay should be based on the job's responsibilities. Improved legislative salaries would allow legislators to concentrate their complete attention on their legislative chores.

THE PROFESSIONAL LEGISLATURE

In November 1966, California voters overwhelmingly approved Proposition 1A. A triumphant Speaker Unruh was later invited to address university groups, public forums, and other state legislatures on the topic of legislative reform and the California success story. Delegations of legislators from other states also came to visit the capitol—almost like pilgrims visiting Mecca—to discuss with their California colleagues how this "miracle" might be achieved in their states.

Salary and "Perks"

Proposition 1A gave legislators the power to set their own salaries and legislative calendar. To assuage the public, legislators were to be limited to a 5 percent salary increase per year, and any pay hike approved would not become effective until the next legislative session. Unruh's idea was that the legislature should control its own destiny.

Salaries of California legislators increased slowly and steadily from 1966 to 1990. By the 1989–90 session, legislators' annual salaries had risen to $41,000. But legislative salaries were not keeping pace with inflation. Moreover, every time legislator salaries increased, there was substantial public opposition and anger. Thus, in 1990, legislative leaders decided to change the pay raise process. Because of major scandals and an increasingly bad image, the legislature approved a constitutional ethics amendment. Proposition 112 went on the June 1990 ballot and won solid support from voters. In addition to a series of ethics reforms the legislature imposed on itself, as part of the bargain the measure included the establishment of a new Citizens Compensation Commission. Instead of the legislature having to take fierce criticism for raising public officials' pay, the appointed commission would determine public salaries. State legislators' annual salaries have been raised on three occasions since the establishment of the commission to $75,600. In addition, legislative leaders now receive additional income: The speaker and senate president pro tem receive $90,720 annually, and majority and minority party leaders $79,200. Pollster Mervin Field reported that 82 percent of Californians disapproved of the most recent salary increase.

In addition, California legislators receive $109 a day, seven days a week, for living expenses while the legislature is in session. (New Hampshire legislators receive $100 as their annual salary!) This adds about a $19,000 tax-free supplement to legislators' incomes—a sum greater than the total salary of legislators in about half the states. Among the other perks are (1) $400 a month for car leasing, (2) a gasoline credit card providing free gas and maintenance service on the leased car, (3) money for district office rent, (4) a telephone credit card, (5) office supplies and office furniture, and (6) health insurance.

The Sacramento Bee

Most of the legislature's daily work is done in committees, rather than in general session as here.

Staff Augmentation

Before the 1960s, the California legislature had a small professional staff. The legislative counsel (established in 1913) provides technical bill drafting and amending services to legislators. Auditors in the auditor general's office (1955) conduct postaudits of state agencies to ensure that funds are spent according to law. And consultants in the legislative analyst's office (1957) provide fiscal and budgetary advice to legislators. Under its first director, Alan Post, and successors including current chief analyst Elizabeth Hill, this office has always maintained a solid reputation for fairness and nonpartisanship.

During the 1960s, under Unruh's prodding, the assembly rapidly expanded its legislative staff. The senate, though proceeding more cautiously in adding staff, belatedly followed a similar course.

California State Library

Jess Unruh led the legislative reform movement in California.

Unruh and other legislative reformers argued that professional staff could provide legislators sorely needed policy expertise. Equally significant, these aides would be able to provide legislators a more neutral source of information, freeing them from dependence on lobbyists or bureaucrats. Skilled personal staff would free legislators from having to do the "grunt work" so they could concentrate on important legislative business. Today, some legislative staff receive annual salaries of between $100,000 and $125,000—more than members.

Although 99 percent of state employees are civil service, legislative staff are not. This obviously gives legislators much more flexibility in hiring and firing their staff than other state employers. Some staff are hired because of their connections, family ties, or political work rather than because of their academic preparation. Staff serve "at the pleasure" of members. If a member wants staff to work after hours or on weekends, the latter normally do so. Staff can be dismissed without cause. Overall, the 40 percent budget cut mandated in Proposition 140 has meant substantial reductions in the number of legislative staff employed.

Committee Consultants Before the 1960s, only a few assembly and senate committees had professional consultants. Today, all standing, select, and subcommittees have at least one, and most have three or four. Critically important fiscal committees have dozens of consultants who assist members. Assembly Budget and Senate Finance committees also have a formalized majority–minority staff arrangement, much as in Congress. Committee consultants analyze bills, help to develop legislation, coordinate testimony at committee hearings, and carry out other tasks assigned by the chair.

Because legislators serve on different policy committees and must be knowledgeable in many areas, committee staff provide indispensable expertise to members. In the 1960s and 1970s, assembly committee staff were viewed as professional, nonpartisan experts; some staffers even retained their positions after elections when the committee chair changed. In the 1980s and 1990s, committee staffs have become more political. They owe their allegiance to the committee chair and speaker or pro tem and must be loyal footsoldiers of the majority party.

Research Staff In 1962, the Assembly Legislative Reference Bureau was established; two years later, this office was transformed into the Assembly Office of Research. The office has three prime responsibilities: (1) providing long- and short-range research, (2) lending expertise on a variety of technical subjects to members and other staff, and (3) doing a third-reading analysis of pending bills. Ostensibly nonpartisan, this office has evolved into a mainly extra staff operation for the majority party. To help allay concerns about partisanship, the office today is overseen by a bipartisan Committee on Policy Management. The Senate Office of Research, though smaller, operates similarly.

Personal Staff Assemblymembers and senators are also provided administrative assistants, field representatives at district offices, and clerical help. Because of their larger districts, senators have larger personal staffs. The legislator's personal staff performs a variety of functions: answering constituent mail and phone calls, helping people in the district cope with the bureaucracy, working on legislation, doing research, keeping abreast of newspapers in the district, sending out press releases and newsletters, and attending district functions.

Leadership Staff Assembly and senate party leaders (the speaker, speaker pro tem, senate pro tem, majority floor leaders, minority leaders, caucus leaders, Rules Committee members, etc.) are provided additional staff for their expanded leadership duties and responsibilities.

Party Staff Both houses have dozens of majority and minority party consultants who provide extra assistance to members of "their" party. This staff is primarily concerned with ensuring that their members get reelected. Democrats have recently focused on having district staff respond effectively to constituent problems. Before the Political Reform Act was adopted in 1974, party staff often provided campaign assistance to members while on the state payroll. Today, this practice is illegal and has been sharply reduced. When majority or minority staff go to work on a campaign, they take a leave of absence and go off the state payroll.

Housekeeping Staff Overall administration of the two houses is handled by their respective Rules Committees. Other housekeeping staff include the chief clerks of the two houses, who keep track of floor session details; the sergeants-at-arms, who provide routine ("go-fer") assistance to members; mailroom assistants; secretarial pools; bill-room employees; and messengers.

Interns In addition to regular legislative staff, interns are also helpful to California legislators. The most prestigious of the internship offerings are the Assembly and Executive Fellowship programs and the Senate Associates program under the auspices of the Center for California Studies, California State University, Sacramento. Each year, after rigorous competition, eighteen assembly, eighteen senate, and twelve executive fellows are selected. Those selected work as junior staff, providing research assistance to members and staff. Fellows and associates receive a modest stipend for their efforts. In addition, they are enrolled as graduate students at CSU, Sacramento, and earn credit toward a graduate degree. Several other colleges and universities also have programs allowing students to work in the legislature for academic credit. Interning is one of the very best ways for people to learn about the legislature, gain valuable job experience, and possibly work into staff employment at the capital.

Offices and Procedures

In the "good old days," floor sessions were chaotic. Members had no offices and used their desks on the floor to conduct their activities—studying bills, conferring with lobbyists, greeting visiting constituents, being interviewed by reporters, dictating letters, and talking to colleagues. There was a constant hubbub of noise and distraction, and legislative leaders acting in concert with senior lobbyists could easily sneak items through in all the confusion. Today, in the more professional setting, floor access is strictly limited to members and their secretaries. Each legislator has his or her own microphone, and floor debates usually proceed smoothly, although rancor is still an occasional feature. Unfortunately, in the closing days of sessions when many bills have to be acted upon, there are still opportunities to sneak items through. Indeed, many members see distinct advantages in having their bills voted upon at the last minute, when members are so preoccupied. In the assembly, an electronic voting system is used to record votes, though the senate still uses the more time-consuming oral roll call. As the California legislature became professionalized, impressive progress was made in streamlining, establishing deadlines, and routinizing the legislative process to make it more orderly and less vulnerable to behind-the-scenes maneuvering.

In the old days, committees often met in closed-door, executive session. Indeed, some met informally ahead of scheduled meetings at local restaurants or bars to decide what they would do at the public hearing. Some powerful committee chairs completely controlled the actions of their committees. Because committee votes were taken orally, public interest lobbies or interested citizens had to try to read lips to determine who had voted aye or nay on bills. Today, committee votes are recorded, and committees are not supposed to meet before their scheduled meetings. However, secrecy is still a feature on occasion in contemporary Sacramento. During the last days of a session, some emergency committee hearings are held in back chambers with little or no chance for public input. Moreover, the senate still has an informal "screening group," composed of senate party leaders who meet behind closed doors to decide the fate of major spending bills. On the floor, "ghost" voting (members voting for absent members) was once commonplace; it has become less common with the modern legislature. The two-year session, public hearings, orderly procedures, and the right of anyone so desiring to testify contribute to a relatively open process.

To track the legislative flow, the senate and assembly publish several important documents: The *Daily Journal* contains the official proceedings of each house and the roll calls on all votes taken; the *Files* announces committee hearings and lists bills scheduled for action; and the *Weekly History* indexes legislative subjects and records actions taken on bills. Bills, constitutional amendments, and resolutions are printed and made available to the legislature and the public soon after introduction. The legislature also has computerized its records so that capital and district offices can instantly access the status of pending legislation. Since 1990, the state legislature has also been wired for live coverage by cable television. Assemblymembers are now provided with laptop computers, and a new teleconferencing room has been constructed. Also, members and committees now have private offices off the floor to conduct their work. And with the refurbishing of the old capitol wing in 1986, legislative leaders' offices, committee hearing rooms, and the senate and assembly floors have been restored to Victorian elegance.

EFFECTS OF PROFESSIONALIZATION: GOOD OR BAD?

What effect did professionalization have on the legislature? Proving that more innovative legislation has passed or that public issues have been more successfully resolved since modernization is difficult. At the very least, however, the legislature developed a greater capacity to legislate thoughtfully. Nevertheless, the debate on the merits of professionalization continues: Is the professional legislature more productive? Is the public getting its money's worth? Or did we create a Frankenstein monster? Admittedly, answers to these questions are subjective.

The Case for the Professional Legislature

Those who favor a professional legislature argue that 32 million Californians living in a state confronted by complicated, technical problems, and operating within a multibillion-dollar budget framework need full-time, competent, savvy, and professional elected officials. They contend that monumental problems of contemporary California cannot be addressed effectively or thoughtfully by a part-time amateur legislature. Proponents of legislative professionalization contend that the California legislature has changed markedly, and for the better, over the past thirty years. The legislative reforms enacted have meant substantial improvements in many key areas. Among the various state legislatures, the professional California legislature has been a public policy leader and innovator in several issue areas over the last few decades.

Member Qualities Contemporary California legislators are better informed and better educated than in the nonprofessional era. Nearly every member of the present-day legislature has completed at least some college work, and many have advanced graduate degrees. These members have the ability to deal with the complex problems confronting California. Professional career legislators tend to come from four occupational backgrounds: attorneys, former full-time local politicians, ex-legislative staff, and small-business owners.

Before 1966, when the legislature was part-time and salaries were minimal, legislators were mostly middle-aged, Anglo, male, and well-to-do. Some could afford to be away from their jobs for a few months each year, and they did not have to live on meager legislative salaries. Professionalization has enabled heretofore unrepresented or underrepresented social groups to seek legislative positions (see Table 7.1, page 180). Obviously, many reasons account for the increasing numbers of minority members and women getting elected to the California legislature—reapportionment, growing political awareness in minority communities, and more minority citizens going to law school or working on legislative staff—but the increased pay, status, and career potential in the legislature helped

	IN THE LEGISLATURE*				% STATE POPULATION
	1965		1994		
	NO.	%	NO.	%	
ASIAN	0	0	1	1	9
AFRICAN AMERICANS	2	2	9	8	7
LATINOS	0	0	11	9	29
WOMEN	1	1	25	20	52

*African American and Latino women are double-counted.

TABLE 7.1   MINORITY AND FEMALE MEMBERS IN THE CALIFORNIA LEGISLATURE, 1965–1994

to break down the formerly exclusive, white "gentlemen's club" atmosphere. Term limits have also given women and racial minorities more opportunities to get elected to the legislature.

Turnover   One frequent criticism of nonprofessional state legislatures was the instability created by constant turnover in membership. Although reasons vary for extensive turnover (about one-third of American state legislators are usually freshmen in an average session), the most frequently noted is low pay. "Burdened by low pay, high costs, and the frustrations of the job, members serve a brief tour of office and drop out" (Keefe and Ogul, 1981, p. 137). In the California legislature there are further frustrations: constant campaigning and fund-raising, endless commuting between home and capital, pressures to attend district social functions, and being away from one's family for long periods of time.

In 1966, the average tenure of an assembly member was 7.8 years. In 1989, more than 20 years after professionalization and improved working conditions had been implemented, the average assembly tenure had actually declined to 6.9 years! However, tenure in the senate did increase, from an average of 7.0 years in 1966 to 11.4 years in 1989. Usually, more than half of all senators had served previously in the assembly. Thus, even in the highly professional legislature of 1989–90, a few members in each house had served for many terms (Senator Ralph Dills was first elected to the assembly in 1938 and was reelected to the senate in 1994!), but most served a few terms and then moved on. Given the relatively short tenure of the average member, Proposition 140 may have been misdirected (Speaker Brown, first elected in 1964, appears to have been the prime target).

Implicit in the notion of professionalism was that experienced legislators were generally more effective legislators and could provide more capable leadership.

TEN MOST EFFECTIVE MEMBERS		YEARS OF EXPERIENCE	TEN LEAST EFFECTIVE MEMBERS		YEARS OF EXPERIENCE
1.	W. Brown	30	10.	Haynes	2
2.	Isenberg	12	9.	Knowles	4
3.	Brulte	4	8.	Boland	4
4.	O'Connell	12	7.	Honeycutt	2
5.	Hannigan	16	6.	Mountjoy	16
6.	Speier	8	5.	Martinez	2
7.	Vasconcellos	28	4.	Knight	2
8.	Katz	14	3.	Bronschvag	2
9.	Eastin	8	2.	Murray	6
10.	Costa	16	1.	Ferguson	10
		Average = 14.8			Average = 5.0

TABLE 7.2   MOST AND LEAST EFFECTIVE LEGISLATORS, 1994

In 1994, *California Journal* editor Richard Zeiger (1994, p.12) compiled a ranking of legislators based on a survey of legislators, legislative staff, the capitol press corps, lobbyists, and executive branch staff who deal with the legislature. Table 7.2 shows the results—the ten most and least effective assemblymembers, along with their years of service in the chamber in 1994.

On average, senior legislators seem more effective based on judgments of peers and other capitol observers, but this is not always the case. Several first termers in the 1993–94 session were ranked in the top twenty in effectiveness. Finally, Fiorina (1994) contends that developing a professional legislature had a significant unanticipated consequence in reform: A professional legislature seems to encourage Democrats to seek office. Republicans seem to like to serve in part-time, less time-consuming legislatures.

Legislative–Governor Relations   Professional legislatures are less willing to be doormats for governors. Professional legislators are imbued with the notion that the legislature should be equal with the governor. Gubernatorial appointment rejections are more commonplace with a professional legislature.

The Case Against the Professional Legislature

Thirty years ago, the California legislature embarked on its professionalizing trend. Critics believe that the legislature actually worked better and was more effective before all of the professional reforms had been instituted.

Those unhappy with the contemporary California legislature chastise it for being unresponsive to the public, forcing citizen groups to take issues to the initiative arena; being polarized and paralyzed by excessive partisanship; being wasteful and profligate—too much staff, opulent offices, catered meals for committee members, and so on; having too many prima donnas, not of, but above, the people; allowing too many standing, select, and research committees so more members can be called "chairs"; having an arrogant leadership that condones end-of-the-session last-minute tricks, conference committee hocus-pocus, bill hijacking, and unethical behavior by some; having an overly politicized staff; and allowing special interests and PACs to dominate the legislative agenda.

By the early 1970s, Jess Unruh began to raise warnings about excesses in the reformed legislature. Larry Margolis, former director of the now-defunct Citizens Conference on State Legislatures, which had ranked California as the "best" legislature in the early 1970s, commented in various news columns that the California legislature was no longer the best in the nation.

Although California's legislature remains near the top among state legislatures in terms of member benefits, its success in resolving state problems since the mid-1960s has not seemed very different from less professionalized legislatures. Reformers assumed that if legislators were provided the necessary tools, they would inevitably do the job. This has not happened; gridlock, excessive partisanship, and political scandals have been all too frequent.

Although few critics of the modernized California legislature believe it possible to return to a pre-1965, part-time legislature in a state with more than 32 million people and a multibillion-dollar budget, a growing chorus of critics believe that professional legislatures are frequently counterproductive.

Return to the Amateur Legislature?

In certain respects, the contemporary California legislature appears to be returning to a more amateur status. Although legislative salaries have risen dramatically over the last several years, the Citizens Commission, not the legislature, now determines salaries under the provisions of 1990's Proposition 112. Proposition 140's term limits mean an end to career legislators, another central component of a professional legislature. Rapid turnover will be the rule from now on. Also, the budget cuts instituted under Proposition 140 have reduced the number of professional staff, another integral ingredient of a professional legislature.

POLITICS OF THE
LEGISLATIVE PROCESS: THE ASSEMBLY
The Speaker's Powers

The speaker of the assembly, particularly since the Unruh years in the 1960s, has been second only to the governor in terms of political power within the California government. The speaker (1) selects standing committee chairs and vice-chairs; (2) appoints select and research committee chairs; (3) assigns members to committees (the Rules Committee is the single exception); (4) assigns members to joint and select committees; (5) influences the election of the other majority party leadership positions—majority floor leader, caucus chair, speaker pro tem (presiding officer), and party whips; (6) dominates assembly floor action; (7) acts as chief rule enforcer; and (8) controls, in concert with the assembly Rules Committee chair, how well particular members are treated in the chamber. Those displeasing the speaker may find themselves in an interior office without windows, a back-row desk on the floor, or a less desirable parking place in the capitol garage.

Speakers and Campaign Fund-Raising

Jess Unruh added a major new dimension to speaker powers—transferring campaign contributions to "deserving" party colleagues. Because Unruh controlled the flow of legislation through the lower house, he was able to raise a great deal of special-interest money from those concerned and parcel it out to deserving and loyal Democratic assembly candidates. Democratic recipients felt obligated to Unruh—he helped them get elected—and they, in turn, were expected to follow his lead as part of their unspoken IOU. Unruh's successors have continued to play the fund-dispenser role for majority party members, particularly newcomers in their first races for the assembly. By the 1970s, the minority party leader also felt obliged to raise funds for his or her party flock. Soon those who hoped to move up the leadership ladder felt obliged to have substantial war chests to prove their fund-raising talents. Besides fund-raising, the speaker is responsible for maintaining the majority.

Because of mounting dissatisfaction with the fund-raising role of speaker, pro tem, and minority leaders, and the quid pro quos entailed, reformers sought to end this practice. In June 1988, two separate campaign reform measures qualified for the ballot—Propositions 68 and 73. Although each measure approached campaign finance reform differently, they agreed on one point: Transferring campaign funds should be prohibited. Both measures were approved by voters, but Proposition 73 received more votes and thus had legal precedent, and Proposition 68 was ruled invalid. For a year and a half, transferring was banned.

Courtesy of Speaker Willie Brown   Courtesy of Assembly Republican Leader Jim Brulte

California Assembly Speaker Emeritus Willie Brown (1980–1995) (left), in discussing his vast legislative powers, once kiddingly referred to himself as ayatollah of the lower house. Assemblymember Jim Brulte leads the Republicans.

But several weeks before the November 1990 election, a federal court declared most of Proposition 73 unconstitutional. Attempts to revive Proposition 68 were struck down by the state Supreme Court. Transferring of campaign funds is in vogue once again.

Selection to Chairmanships and Committees

The California speaker's power to name chairs is very different from the mainly seniority system used in the House of Representatives. The congressional chair-selection process is marked by relatively little politicking and an almost ironclad guarantee that the chair will be a veteran with years of policy expertise and experience. Under the leadership of new Republican Speaker Newt Gingrich, all Republican chairs will serve for only six years in this position and then be replaced.

With term limits now in place, all assembly committee chairs beginning in 1996 will have had little legislative experience. Although minority party members were awarded some chairmanships in the preprofessional legislature, since the 1970s with Democrats in ascendancy, there were only one or two token Republican chairs in the assembly. However, in 1994, because of the narrow and controversial reelection of Speaker Willie Brown over Republican leader Jim Brulte, 40–39 with one seat vacant, Democrats agreed to an unprecedented power-sharing arrangement. Of the twenty-six standing committees, thirteen were given Republican chairs. Moreover, Jim Brulte, not Speaker Willie Brown, named the Republican chairs and helped choose which of the twenty-six committees they would lead.

In the new term-limited assembly of the 1990s, the "veterans" will be those serving in their second term, and the grizzled "old timers" will be serving in their third term—ready for pasture. Seniority will still be a factor, but in a much more compacted fashion. In 1992, three Democrats were selected as chairs of standing committees in their second year, and two others were placed on Ways and Means. Speaker Brown was unstinting in his efforts to get the members (particularly Democrats) of the classes of '92 and '94 up to speed as rapidly as possible. Indeed, one Democratic newcomer elected in 1994, Assemblymember Wally Knox, was selected as chair of the Labor and Employment Committee in his first month in office. Although some veteran assemblymembers complained of the naive questions posed by newcomers, the transition of frosh legislators into the complicated world of legislative politics proceeded reasonably smoothly in the 1993–94 session. But this occurred in a chamber where more than half of the members had 10 to 20 years' experience. How the legislators' learning processes will proceed when all are in their first, second, or third terms beginning in 1996 remains unclear.

The speaker's chair-selection criteria generally include (1) loyalty, (2) competence and ability, (3) political philosophy, (4) party affiliation, (5) friendships, and (6) seniority. Speakers constantly face a host of ambitious, upwardly mobile party colleagues eager to wield power as chairs with a finite number of standing committees. Speaker Brown nearly doubled the number of standing committees he inherited in 1980 and also increased the number of select and special committees to placate chair aspirants.[1]

The speaker generally uses similar criteria for committee selections. Obviously, the speaker wants to maintain his or her party's control of the major policy committees. All members are sent forms by the speaker and are asked to rank their committee choices. Selections to committees (except for the Rules Committee, whose members are elected by the two-party caucuses) depend heavily on the interests, background, and district of the legislator. A legislator representing a rural district would want appointment to the Agriculture or Water Committee, a former schoolteacher to the Education Committee, or a former insurance agent to the Finance and Insurance Committee. Speakers can usually accommodate a request or two per member—if they so desire. Speaker Brown over the years expanded the size of a number of major "juice" committees (committees that deal with issues of prime importance to key financial forces) to enable members to raise more campaign contributions.

The Speaker as Rule Enforcer

The style and tone of the assembly have always been set by the speaker. From items as mundane as dress standards to serious breeches of legislative ethics, the speaker has played the central disciplining role. As with any social organization, in addition to formal rules, unwritten rules and customs develop over time to facilitate the legislative process. Among the unwritten rules in the California legislature are honor commitments, keep your word, never attack a colleague personally in public, support committee integrity by not attempting to withdraw a bill from committee, grant a colleague's request for reconsideration of a bill, and never testify in opposition to another member's bill. Clearly, some rules change over time. Dress-code standards have evolved to more informal attire. In the old days, members would not campaign against one another, but many do today. Thus, Republican leader Jim Brulte helped to lead the recall effort against former Republican turned independent Paul Horcher after the latter voted for Willie Brown as speaker in 1994. Lobbyists complain these days that contemporary members no longer can be counted on to honor a commitment. Attempts to pry bills out of committees have become increasingly commonplace, and personal attacks also occur more frequently.

These days members do not socialize with and get to know each other as well as they did in the past. Less time is spent together on the assembly floor, and more time is spent in individual members' offices with their personal staffs. In a typical legislative week, by early Thursday afternoon most of the Southern California legislators will be jetting back home and will not return until mid-Monday of the following week. In the "good old days," most members stayed in Sacramento for a few months until the session was completed. And, under term limits, the old friendship bonds (or enmities) will not be as much of a factor. The clubby, bipartisan tone of the legislature prior to the 1960s is virtually gone.

Although the speaker is powerful and can make a member's life miserable, this officer cannot kick a member out of the chamber. Legislative leaders must put up with the "accidents of democracy" washed upon the legislative shore.

The speaker's disciplining powers encourage those who want to accomplish something to go along with assembly protocol. But some maverick members have refused to knuckle under to the speaker, and they bear the brunt of the speaker's ire—bad offices, reduced staff, and so on. Obviously, a legislature of too many loners would be unproductive. On the other hand, these independents—by refusing to pay homage to the leadership, by challenging stuffy traditions, and by adhering to their own principles—add a breath of fresh air to the sometimes stale legislative atmosphere. Moreover, the new breed of speakers elected after Willie Brown will have far less ability to instill discipline.

Electing the Speaker

Before Jess Unruh's tenure as lower house leader, speakers were elected by a vote of the entire membership every two years after the general election. The candidate receiving 41 votes or more (a majority of the eighty members) became speaker. Those on the winning side were rewarded by the speaker for their good sense. Party affiliation was a relatively minor factor in speakership elections. Usually, Democratic and Republican assemblymembers would vote for one of their own party's colleagues, but not always.

Unruh modified the way in which speakers were elected. In 1964, he got Democrats to agree to a unit rule system (Democrats were required to vote for the winner within the caucus—i.e., Unruh). This meant the minority party members had no role to play in the speakership vote. The full-assembly speakership vote became a formality. In the years since Unruh's speakership, the battle for speaker has usually taken place in the majority party caucus. But on several occasions, majority party speaker candidates have covertly or overtly sought votes from minority party members.

The "Dirty Dozen" Coup Attempt   In 1973, Democratic San Francisco assemblymembers Willie Brown and Leo McCarthy vied to replace departing Speaker Bob Moretti. In June 1974, after Moretti stepped down (he had decided to seek the Democratic gubernatorial nomination and lost), assembly Democrats caucused and voted: McCarthy 26, Brown 23. McCarthy was then elected on the floor by a unified 49 Democratic votes.

Willie Brown, unhappy with McCarthy's leadership, decided to try to unseat Speaker McCarthy after the 1974 general election. In attempting to put together the necessary forty-one votes, he sought support from Democrats who had voted for him in June and new Democrats elected in November. Knowing he did not have the necessary votes from Democrats, Brown sought Republican support by promising chairmanships and other "goodies." In the end, Brown received twenty-five Republican votes but could muster only twelve Democratic votes (dubbed by the press as the "Dirty Dozen") and failed to unseat McCarthy. As punishment for this attempted coup, McCarthy took away the chairmanships of the dissidents, removed them from key committees, reduced their personal staffs, and moved them to less desirable offices.

Willie Brown's Coalition Speakership of 1980   After six years as speaker, in 1979 McCarthy announced that he was considering running for statewide office in 1980. Many assembly Democrats became consumed with the issue of his replacement. Assembly Democrats wanted a good fund-raiser and full-time speaker at the helm as soon as possible. However, McCarthy planned to run for statewide office while serving as speaker and not depart immediately.

Howard Berman, majority floor leader (McCarthy's second in command), was persuaded by Democratic rebels to ask McCarthy to step down immediately so assembly Democrats could elect Berman as speaker, but McCarthy refused. After frenzied vote-seeking by the McCarthy and Berman camps, Democrats caucused in January 1980 to decide the speakership question. Though Berman received two more caucus votes, McCarthy refused to resign. (He contended the unit rule applied only when the speaker was first elected, not in the midst of a term.) Republicans refused to give votes to either side and were happy with the conflict.

Thus, for an entire year, the speaker had no real power. Whenever McCarthy attempted to discipline Bermanites, they threatened to vote with Republicans for a new speaker, and McCarthy had to back down. In the 1980 primary and general election, the two factions spent hundreds of thousands of dollars trying to defeat the other side's Democrats. After the general election, Democrats caucused and Berman again beat McCarthy by several votes. McCarthy resigned as speaker, and the two Democratic factions met to discuss peace terms. The Berman faction was unwilling to assure the McCarthy loyalists that their chairmanships would remain. In the ensuing stalemate, Willie Brown persuaded McCarthy to let him try to round up forty-one votes to become speaker. In the Democratic caucus, Berman and Brown each received twenty-three votes, and on the floor twenty-eight Republicans joined with the twenty-three Democrats to elect Willie Brown as speaker. To get GOP votes, Brown offered chairmanships, reapportionment funds, and extra staff to Republicans. He also agreed to have the assembly Rules Committee, not the speaker, assign bills to committees.

The "Gang of Five"   Over the next several terms, Speaker Brown steadily consolidated power to become, as he described it, the ayatollah of the assembly. Brown honored his promises to Republicans in the 1980–82 session. However, because of increasingly partisan conflict in the 1980s, "goodies" given to Republicans previously were taken back. In 1988, Brown faced a new leadership challenge. Five Democratic assemblymembers—Condit, Calderon, Arieas, Peace, and Eaves—frustrated by one-man rule in the assembly, announced they would pursue an independent course and would no longer be bound by caucus positions; they urged other Democrats to join them. For a time this "Gang of Five," as dubbed by the press, was in the limelight—interviews, media attention, and limitless publicity. Brown attempted to return them to the fold by gradually cutting back on their privileges—removing their chairmanships, moving them to smaller offices, stripping them of committee memberships, and cutting their staffs. But this did not work. Moreover, voting with the thirty-six Republicans, the five could control assembly floor action. On several occasions, bills that Brown wanted left in committee were forced out and sent to the floor. However, the five were unwilling to vote for a Republican as speaker.

After the November 1988 general election, new Republican leader Ross Johnson arranged a deal with the "Five." Republicans would vote for the Gang's speaker candidate, Charles Calderon; in return, GOP members would be given chairmanships and important committee assignments. However, efforts by the Gang to get other Democrats to join them failed. Thus, Willie Brown prevailed on the speakership vote, receiving forty-two Democratic votes. Soon after this vote, the "Five" ended their rebellion and returned to the Democratic caucus; they no longer held the balance of power.

In 1994, Willie Brown faced the ultimate challenge to his longtime tenure as speaker in his final two years in the assembly. (Term limits prevent him from running for reelection in 1996.) For the first time in twenty-four years, Republicans elected a majority in the assembly, 41–39. The court-designed 1991 reapportionment plan, the premature departures of many veteran assembly Democrats because of term limits, plus a strong national conservative tide in 1994 contributed to the Republican victories. Many experts began to write Willie Brown's epitaph as speaker and contemplate the expected election of Republican leader Jim Brulte to the office. They were wrong. Brown had an ace up his sleeve.

Throughout his assembly career, Republican Paul Horcher had often worked cooperatively with the speaker on particular issues and had received plum assignments for his efforts. During the 1993–94 session, Horcher found himself increasingly alienated from the archconservative assembly Republican leaders in the caucus. They, in turn, despised him for his ties to Brown. After the November 1994 election, Horcher privately confided to Brown that he was going to vote for him, not Jim Brulte, as speaker.

Unbeknownst to Brulte, on the day of the speakership vote, Horcher changed his party affiliation to Independent. Stunning his former party colleagues on the floor, Horcher defected from Republican ranks and voted for Brown as speaker. This resulted in a tie vote, 40–40, for speaker and a standoff. However, one Republican, Richard Mountjoy, had been elected in a special election to the state senate as well as to his assembly seat in November 1994. Willie Brown, presiding over the chamber (because there was no speaker, the presiding officer was the most senior member—Brown), moved to oust Mountjoy from the assembly. Brown would then have a majority. Although the chief clerk, acting as parliamentarian of the assembly, initially ruled against the ouster effort, several weeks later Mountjoy was voted out of the assembly. He was then officially sworn in as senator. On a 40–39 vote (one seat vacant), Brown was elected speaker. He immediately agreed to an equal power-sharing arrangement with Republicans on committee chairs, Republican–Democratic ratios on committees, committee assignments, and staffing. Although Republicans grumbled that Speaker Brown and his Rules Committee chair, John Burton, were still providing extra resources to Democrats, for the most part the arrangement has worked.

Furious with Horcher's action, the state Republican party and assembly GOP leader Jim Brulte succeeded in getting Horcher recalled in May 1995. Bowing to the inevitable, Brown stepped down as speaker in June 1995 to run for mayor of San Francisco in November. Next, Brown and the entire Democratic caucus cast their votes for maverick Republican Doris Allen, who defeated Republican leader Jim Brulte, 40 to 38, to become the new speaker. The power-sharing arrangement engineered by Brown for the 1995–96 session will continue under Speaker Allen's direction. Because of term limits, however, she will be unable to run for reelection to the assembly in 1997.

The majority floor leader is second-in-command and responsible for shepherding key bills through the legislature. The caucus chair works to forge unified party stands on major issues. The speaker pro tem is the presiding officer.

The Speaker and the Minority Party

Perhaps the most notable feature of the minority party leader post is its lack of power. Minority leaders must try to build unity in their caucus through campaign contributions to colleagues or through browbeating. If the minority leader is too cooperative with the speaker, he or she may appear to be a sellout to party members. In 1984, assembly Republicans ousted moderate Robert Naylor and elected doctrinaire conservative Pat Nolan, a "Proposition 13 baby" elected in the conservative, antitax tide of 1978. Surprising many, Nolan worked out a unique arrangement with the speaker: Republicans would not be disruptive (for example, try to remove bills from committees) if Nolan were given the power to control Republican committee assignments. Nolan's "powers" were enhanced, while the speaker benefited from a less-confrontational Republican caucus. Unknown to Brown, however, Nolan contacted the FBI to alert it to what he perceived to be bribe-taking by the speaker. Ironically, several years later, Nolan was one of those convicted and jailed in the FBI "sting" investigation. Brown was never implicated and worked out a power-sharing arrangement with Republican leader Jim Brulte.

Speaker Power in the Term Limits Era

Certainly, one main reason voters approved Proposition 140 was their anger at longtime legislative leaders Speaker Brown and Pro Tem David Roberti.

Part of Speaker Brown's power derived from his continuity. Members came and went, but he remained as speaker from 1980 into the mid-1990s. Henceforth, speakers will probably be elected in their second or third terms and will be lame ducks almost as soon as they are elected. When Speaker Brown ran the assembly with a solid majority, bills that he opposed and killed were referred to as being "speakerized." Special interests had to contribute to Brown because he controlled the flow of legislation through the lower house. Brown's successors will have to lead more by persuasion. Speakers from now on will probably not be as effective at fund-raising for party colleagues. So, even if the speakership retains all of its present powers, this officer will be far less consequential. Chaos, confusion, and attempts to overthrow speakers (what's to lose?) could become a prevalent pattern.

Every two years, the assembly will have to deal with a massive influx of thirty to thirty-five new members who will have to be taught quickly the rudiments of the legislative process. Assemblymembers will not be able to develop policy expertise and will have to rely more on staff and the third house for assistance. Advocates of term limits believe waves of new "citizen" legislators elected every two years will be less beholden to lobbyists and will come with fresh ideas and be more attuned to their constituencies. And, as mentioned previously, term limits will provide more opportunities for women and racial minorities to get elected to the assembly because of the many open seats. Rookie assemblymembers will, on average, be older than 1980s frosh and will tend to come from business backgrounds and have local name identification and solid financing.

POLITICS OF THE LEGISLATIVE PROCESS: THE SENATE

Before the U.S. Supreme Court ordered reapportionment in 1966, the state senate was very different from the assembly. The senate tended to be less innovative, more conservative, more northern and rural-oriented, less partisan, and less professional. Differences between the two chambers narrowed after the "one person, one vote" reapportionment decisions, though some persist.

Clearly, the senate is more prestigious. It has sole responsibility for approving governors' appointees. Senators serve four-year terms rather than the two-year terms of assemblymembers, so they don't have to engage in fund-raising as constantly as do assemblymembers. Moreover, senators have an eight-year maximum, not six as in the assembly. Senators get a "free ride" political advantage in the middle of their term: They can run for higher office and still hold their seat. Tom Hayden could run for the Democratic gubernatorial nomination in 1994 knowing that if he lost (he did), he was still a senator and could serve the remainder of his term. This gives senators more courage to gamble on running for other offices. The senate, particularly in the term limits era, will have far more seniority, experience, and impact on policy than the assembly. With half as many senators (forty) as assembly members, the former are better known. Senators also have more power and independence in their chamber than assemblymembers do. Finally, assemblymembers run for the senate when there is an opportunity. Until the onslaught of term limits, senators would never have opted to run for the assembly. It was a step down. However, under term limits it is not inconceivable that a senator finishing his or her two terms might consider running for the assembly (if this person had not previously served there) to prolong one's political career and to add sorely needed political experience to the lower house.

The Pro Tem

The chief leader of the senate, the pro tem, is chair of the Rules Committee. Unlike the assembly, the pro tem is one of just five votes on the Rules Committee. The pro tem's influence rests less on formal authority and more on informal persuasion. An occasional pro tem (for example, Hugh Burns or David Roberti) have been very strong and influential leaders. Roberti was elected in 1980, as was Brown as speaker, for similar reasons. He was a good fund-raiser (his Hollywood constituency was invaluable), he was popular with colleagues, and he promised to maintain and protect his fellow Democratic senate colleagues. (His predecessor was blamed for the loss of several key senate seats.) Roberti sought to make the senate a truly coequal branch with the assembly. Thus, when the old capitol wing was being refurbished, Roberti insisted that his office be equipped with the same number of false fireplaces and chandeliers as the speaker's office. Current Pro Tem Bill Lockyer, a former legislative staffer, is feisty, combative, and highly partisan. In his first test as leader, he was able to maintain the Democratic majority in the Senate in the 1994 election.

In addition to the pro tem, the other four members of the Senate Rules Committee are nominated by the two party caucuses and tend to be veteran members. The pro tem is one of five and cannot control the upper house as the speaker does.

In the "good old days," powerful senior senators tended to serve as chairs and cluster on a few key committees. Seniority was an important criterion for promotion to chairs. Many "old guard" senators believed that new senators ("young Turks") had to be properly trained into senate traditions and customs before they could be given important assignments.

In 1966, Pro Tem Hugh Burns faced an unprecedented situation: Twenty-two of forty senators (a majority) were new to the chamber because of court-enforced redistricting. Fourteen of the twenty-two were former assemblymembers, and all were treated as freshmen by the pro tem. These disgruntled senators and other Burns opponents coalesced to put together the votes needed to oust him as pro tem. Today, power is more diffused in the senate.

The senate has become decidedly more partisan in the 1980s and 1990s. As recently as the 1970s, the minority party always held about one-third of the standing committee chairs. This is no longer the case. There are only a few token Republican committee chairs these days.

Other Senate Leaders

The senate minority leader is in a rather precarious position. In the 1980s and '90s, several Republican senate minority leaders were dumped by their party colleagues, usually because the minority had lost seats to the Democratic majority. However, for the moment, senate minority leader Ken Maddy holds sway. Maddy and Roberti worked cooperatively in promoting legislation, and a similar arrangement with Bill Lockyer has been worked out. However, Senator Rob Hurtt, a wealthy Christian right ideologue and superb fund-raiser, has not been entirely pleased with Maddy's moderate cooperation. Hurtt has a good chance of becoming Republican leader in the senate in the future.

Technically, the presiding officer of the senate, and theoretically one of its leaders, is the lieutenant governor. Because presiding over the senate is a minor, routine duty, most lieutenant governors spend little time wielding the gavel. In case of a 20–20 vote, the lieutenant governor can cast the tie-breaking vote—but tie votes are rare. Clearly, the lieutenant governor is not viewed by senators as an official member of the "club." However, a constitutional amendment designed to remove the lieutenant governor as president of the senate was rejected by voters in 1982 (see Chapter 9).

Term Limits: The Impact on David Roberti and the Senate

David Roberti has the distinction of being the first state legislator in California or the nation to be ineligible to run for reelection because of term limits. After the court-designed reapportionment of 1991, Roberti found himself without a district. To continue his senate career, Roberti moved into an adjoining district in 1992 when its senator, Alan Robbins, was forced to resign from office on federal corruption charges. Roberti ran in the new San Fernando district and was elected in a special election to complete Robbins's term. But he could not run for reelection to the senate in 1994 because of term limit restrictions.

Courtesy of David Roberti   © SIRLIN

David Roberti, former president pro tem of the senate (left), was the first legislator to be forced out by term limits and the first in fifty years to have a recall qualify against him. He won the recall vote. Bill Lockyer is the newly elected president pro tem of the senate.

Roberti was always a staunch policy advocate. He strongly opposed abortion and bitterly attacked Planned Parenthood—a position at odds with his Democratic caucus. He was a strong advocate of latchkey kid programs and led the fight to impose restrictions on laboratories engaged in medical experiments on animals. Roberti was also the lead author of legislation banning certain types of semiautomatic weapons. Because of this, the National Rifle Association (NRA) launched a recall campaign to force Roberti from office. Ironically, though Roberti was forced to defend himself in an April 1994 recall election (at a taxpayers' cost of $100,000 to conduct the election), he had to vacate the office in November 1994 anyway. The NRA's objective, evidently, was to make him an example to other elected officials who dared to defy the organization. Though Roberti defeated the recall, the money he spent reduced the amount he had in his attempt to win the Democratic nomination for treasurer in 1994. In hindsight, perhaps the biggest problem for Roberti was that he viewed his job as defending his Democratic colleagues in reelection efforts no matter what. He fought to save Democratic Senator Alex Garcia, even though the latter missed hundreds of roll calls. And he paved the way for Alan Robbins, Joe Montoya, and Paul Carpenter to become major policy chairs in the senate. All three were later convicted of bribery and extortion in the FBI probe. They were his protégés.

Finally, whereas both the senate and assembly will feel the brunt of term limits, it will change the senate in two distinct ways. First, it has been the chamber where seniority is most evident. The superveterans make the upper house unique. For example, Democrat Ralph Dills was first elected to the legislature in 1938! Milton Marks was first elected in 1959; Nicholas Petris and Al Alquist in 1963; and Newt Russell in 1965. All of the superveterans will be gone by 1998. Second, because most senators are former assemblymembers, the senate will remain the chamber of experience and stability. Given the inevitable weakening of the speaker, the senate is likely to become the dominant legislative branch in the near future.

POLITICS OF THE LEGISLATIVE PROCESS: REAPPORTIONMENT

No single issue has created as much antagonism in the legislature over the decades as reapportionment. Every ten years the census is taken, and state legislatures (in a few states, reapportionment commissions) are required to redraw congressional, upper house, and lower house district lines based on population shifts into and within the state. How these lines are drawn determines legislators' survival; it becomes the paramount issue. But for the public, the issue is of secondary interest at best.

One expert has suggested that allowing the legislature to do its own reapportioning is like putting the "fox into the chicken coop." Although since 1965 the U.S. Supreme Court has required that election districts be virtually equal in population, skilled practitioners can do a lot to give advantages to one party over the other. Strategies such as concentrating the registration strength of the opposing party into a few districts, forcing the other party's incumbents to run against each other, or giving the other party's incumbents substantial new territory to represent have been used. Those in the majority have usually argued that they have the "right" to take advantage of their position in redistricting.

Reapportionments have always been contentious, but the last three (1971, 1981, and 1991) have been epics in frustration. In 1971, though Democrats had majorities in both houses, they had to contend with Republican Governor Ronald Reagan's veto. After several years of impasse, the California Supreme Court had to step in and do the reapportionment.

In 1981, after months of behind-the-scenes maneuvering, the solid Democratic majorities in both houses passed the three reapportionment bills for congress, senate, and assembly without consulting Republicans and then sent them to Democratic Governor Jerry Brown for signature. The strongest Republican objections were aimed at the congressional reapportionment plan (devised by the staunchly partisan former Congressman Phil Burton). Until 1970, the number of Democrat and Republican house members had been nearly equal. With the state gaining two additional house seats (from forty-three to forty-five), Burton's objective was to draw district lines adeptly to give the Democrats at least twenty-seven seats and the Republicans eighteen. Perhaps most outrageous to Republicans was the strangely shaped district Phil Burton drew for his brother John (then also a San Francisco congressman). It included portions of San Francisco, took in part of Marin County, and leapt over the Bay to Vallejo. Reveling in Republican outrage, Congressman Burton called the strangely shaped districts his "contribution to modern art."

After Brown signed the bills, Republicans blocked their enactment by the rarely used referendum. They were able to amass hundreds of thousands of signatures needed on the three referendums, much to the surprise of Democratic leaders, who challenged the referendums in court, contending that reapportionment was a legislative matter not subject to referendum. Democrats also argued that the districts were equal in population, and that the districts devised had to be used or it would create enormous problems (the June primary was looming).

A unanimous California Supreme Court (mainly Jerry Brown appointees) ruled that the reapportionment bills were subject to referendum, which pleased the Republicans. But the Court also stated that the lines drawn by the legislature would have to be used because of the imminence of the election. The Court ruled that if voters rejected the Democratic bills, legislative leaders would have to modify the lines after the November 1982 general election.

Voters in the June 1982 primary election overwhelmingly rejected the Democratic reapportionment plans. In the meantime, Republicans and Common Cause, a public interest lobby, successfully qualified an initiative for the November 1982 ballot to establish a new, independent reapportionment commission. The voters, however, rejected the initiative. Democratic leaders modified the district lines, and Republicans agreed to the changes. However, one disgruntled Republican, former Assemblyman Don Sebastiani of Napa, remained convinced that the reapportionment plans were unfair. He drafted a new reapportionment initiative to undo the "unfairness" of the agreed-upon reapportionment plan. Democrats challenged this initiative in court. In September 1983, the Court ruled that reapportionment may be done only once every ten years, and that the initiative was unconstitutional.

In 1984, Governor Deukmejian qualified a new reapportionment reform initiative to have retired appellate court judges do the reapportioning. A hard-hitting Democratic media campaign led to the initiative's defeat in the November 1984 election. In 1986, the U.S. Supreme Court ruled that partisan gerrymandering was unconstitutional. Exactly how the courts will determine whether gerrymandering has occurred, however, was not addressed. In 1990, two more Republican reapportionment initiatives were rejected by voters.

Republicans as the minority party during the last several reapportionments have generally favored the idea that an independent commission do the redistricting. Democrats, for the most part, have questioned whether there truly is such a thing as an appointed, "independent" commission. They believe that elected representatives should handle the task. To prevent an anti-Republican reapportionment in 1991, Republicans persuaded then U.S. Senator Pete Wilson to resign his senate seat and run for governor because he had the best chance of any Republican of getting elected and could then veto any partisan gerrymandering by Democrats. The Republican strategy worked and Wilson was elected governor in 1990. And, as in 1971, Democratic legislative leaders in 1991 tried to devise districts that would enhance their party's chances for electoral success, which Wilson vetoed. To try to override his vetoes, Democrats provided certain very conservative Republican legislators with exceptionally good districts in the hope that they might defy their governor and vote to override. But Republicans maintained unity, and the override failed. Wilson eventually declared an impasse and requested that the state Supreme Court (mainly Deukmejian appointees) do the redistricting. From a Republican perspective, the plans devised by the Court were fair; however, Democrats complained of bias. In 1991, for the first time ever, all senate districts were divided in population halves into two assembly districts. This potentially pits two assemblymembers in direct confrontation if the local senator retires and they both want to move up.

Finally, the latest reapportionment decision. In June 1995, the U.S. Supreme Court ruled that race can be considered but cannot be the predominant factor in reapportionment. The decision grew from challenges to gerrymandered districts created by state legislatures in North Carolina, Georgia, and Louisiana to promote the election chances of minority candidates. The legislatures had redrawn lines to concentrate African American communities into a few districts. Their plans succeeded, and several black House members were elected, the first since Reconstruction.

POLITICS OF THE LEGISLATIVE PROCESS: MECHANICS

Figure 7.1 (page 198) shows how bills proceed through the California legislature. Although the nuts and bolts of the process are shown, its essence is not.

In a typical two-year session, thousands of bills, resolutions, and constitutional amendments are introduced. Many of them will be killed or held for further study,

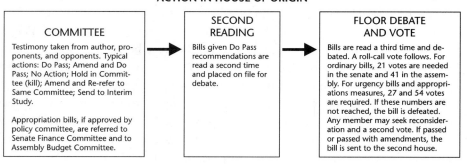

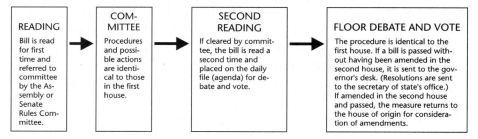

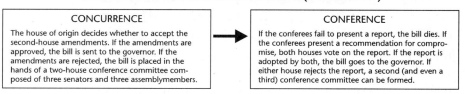

FIGURE 7.1 CALIFORNIA'S LEGISLATIVE PROCESS *Source:* Copyright © 1984 by the California Journal and the California Center.

but about 2,000 will pass both houses and be signed by the governor. Most bill ideas are generated by interest groups, local governments, legislative staff, and executive agencies. Most legislators are receptive or eager to carry bill proposals from different groups so they can establish a record of accomplishment.

Status among one's legislative colleagues hinges, in part, on a member's ability to steer important legislation through the process: being able to explain a measure, knowing when to accept amendments, knowing how to provide leverage, and being able to persuade colleagues on its merits. A legislative lightweight is one who "couldn't even get a Mother's Day resolution through." Some Republicans believe that too many bills are introduced. These conservatives delight in voting "no" and feel no compunction to author legislation.

Each proposed bill is first sent to the legislative counsel's office, which drafts it into proper legal form and indicates the proposed changes in the existing law. The bill is then "placed across the desk" and given a number and dated. After this first "reading," the bill is assigned to a policy committee by the Rules Committee. Most of the time, assignment is routine and bills are sent to the appropriate policy committee (agriculture bills to the Agriculture Committee, etc.). On occasion, however, a bill could logically go to several different committees. In these cases, the Assembly or Senate Rules committees hold hearings with a bill's author to decide which committee should get the bill. Power to assign to a particular committee can be instrumental in a bill's passage or defeat.

Key policy decisions are made in committee. If a committee rejects a bill, it is "dead" for the rest of the legislative session. If a committee unanimously recommends that a bill be passed by the complete house, it almost certainly will be.

On receiving a bill with an author's request for hearing, the committee chair sets the date for a public hearing, usually as soon as possible, and has it published in the *Assembly* or *Senate File*. The legislative process does not allow chairs to refuse to hear a bill or seriously delay scheduling hearings on measures that they oppose. Before the hearing, the author and lobbyist supporting the proposal will work to secure the support of committee members, in some cases by getting members to act as cosponsors. Once a legislator makes a commitment, it is supposed to be honored. Lobbyists opposing the bill are expected to inform the author that they will oppose the measure. Frequently, the bill's author will explore a compromise with lobbyists for and against a measure. Ideally, from the author's point of view, agreeing to certain amendments may head off opposition and guarantee the bill's passage. Nothing is more welcome to a bill author than to have no opposition; this virtually guarantees passage.

Legislators who know that their constituents are solidly opposed to a bill are unlikely to be persuaded by a lobbyist, colleague, or party leader to support the

Randy Pench / *The Sacramento Bee*

Demonstrations on the capitol steps happen frequently when the legislature is in session.

measure. However, most bills generate little public sentiment. These technical bills may be very important to particular interests but are seldom discussed in the press. Thus, legislators have considerable latitude in voting on them.

To the uninitiated, hearings are often anticlimactic and disappointing. Meetings may be delayed for lack of a quorum; observers may travel hundreds of miles for a hearing only to be told that a bill has been held over (put off); expert witnesses may present testimony to empty chairs of absent members. Members who are present sometimes pay little attention to the deliberations. Such unusual behavior by legislators is usually not for lack of interest, but because most members have already made up their minds. Committee members probably have already discussed the bill with experts, lobbyists, and staff; read the reports and bill analyses; held endless hearings on the bill in previous sessions; ascertained the governor's and legislative party leader's stands; and checked for district impact. Thus, hearings usually provide no new information. They tend to be more for the public record and to generate publicity—though on occasion a few legislators on the fence can be swayed one way or the other by expert testimony.

Some groups, in an all-out effort to get committee approval, will pack the committee hearing room with their supporters in hopes of intimidating committee members into supporting a bill. This is sometimes helpful, but it can backfire, too. Virtually every day the legislature is in session, some group (or groups) will schedule a demonstration at the capitol. The aim here is to get as much favorable publicity as possible (see Chapter 5).

After arguments have been presented for and against a bill, committee members can propose amendments that probably, but not necessarily, will be accepted by the bill's author.

After committee action on the bill has been completed, a committee member will move to report the bill out as "do pass" or "do pass as amended." A majority of aye votes is necessary to report a bill out; abstentions or "taking a walk" (to avoid voting) count as no votes. The chair may hold the roll open if members have been called away or have not arrived at the hearing. If sufficient aye votes are not there, a member may move to hold the bill over so the bill's author can have more time to persuade some of his or her colleagues to support it.

If the committee wants to kill a bill gently, or if it deals with a new subject, the committee may recommend it for interim study. Occasionally, bills are reported out of committee without recommendation (a tactic rarely used). Bills with fiscal impact (nearly every important bill) must go to the Assembly Budget and Senate Finance committees after clearing the respective policy committees.

After a bill clears committee, the chair presents a report to the house indicating what the committee recommends, and the bill is read a second time. The committee's proposed amendments are accepted, and then the bill is "engrossed" (checked for accuracy). The next step is the third reading, at which time the bill's author makes a presentation on the floor, as do any opponents. (Noncontroversial measures are placed on the consent calendar for pro forma approval.) Most "do pass" or "do pass as amended" bills are approved on the floor and sent to the other house, though a few will die. On some occasions, a bill's author, seeing formidable opposition to the bill, may ask to send it back to committee for further study.

A clear majority—forty-one votes in the assembly, twenty-one in the senate—is needed to pass a bill. A two-thirds vote—fifty-four votes in the assembly, twenty-seven in the senate—is needed to pass the budget, constitutional amendments, and urgency measures. The bill then goes to the other house for another round of hearings and committee action. Measures passed by both houses, but in substantially different form, will be thrashed out in conference committees.

Finally, the last hurdles in the process are the governor's signature and the bill's administrative implementation.

POLITICS OF THE
LEGISLATIVE PROCESS: PARTISANSHIP

Most bills the legislature votes on are technical, noncontroversial, and nonpolitical. However, a growing number of issues have partisan dimensions, with Democrats and Republicans going in opposite directions. These high-visibility issues tend to be the most critical of the session: reapportionment, election of legislative leaders, gun control, abortion, the budget. Party caucuses are held in both houses before key votes to try to build party unity and solidarity.

REFORMING THE LEGISLATURE

Clearly, no reform issue looms as large as reforming campaign finance. To be competitive in a typical state legislative race, a candidate has to raise about $500,000, and the cost of campaigns continues to escalate. Because few people in the state can raise this much money out of their own pockets, special interests inevitably take up the slack. Of course, one does not have to spend this amount of money to run for office, but to get elected it is a necessity. Term limits have not led to reduced campaign costs. Indeed, given the extensive turnover and many open races, campaign costs have escalated. In any case, the many convictions of legislators, staff, and lobbyists in the FBI investigations of the 1980s and '90s prove conclusively that a problem exists. Meanwhile, the public has become increasingly cynical about the honesty of politicians. A 1989 Field Poll reported that 42 percent of Californians considered state and local officials dishonest and unethical, and a 1990 *Los Angeles Times* survey reported that a majority of Californians considered bribery a relatively common practice at the state capitol. At the very least, sizable campaign contributions buy "access" (which is nine-tenths of the game anyway), and, at the worst, they sometimes buy votes. Perhaps most surprising is how brazen some elected officials have become in seeking money, and this mind-set continues in the 1990s as if the FBI investigations had never happened. As Richard Zeiger (1990, p. 299) notes, the California state legislature is no longer considered the model for other states to imitate.

Finally, two other reform proposals deserve comment. First, instead of requiring a two-thirds vote to approve the budget, many authoritative experts believe it should be a majority vote. The argument is that a small, unified group of legislators can wreak havoc on the budgetary process because of this obstacle (see

Dennis Renault / *The Sacramento Bee*

"Cell inspection is at 0900, followed by visiting hours,
worship services, and the caucus for former
state legislators and lobbyists."

Chapter 10). Second, to save time, money, and duplication and to avoid game-playing, a unicameral, single-house legislature could be adopted. This idea has great merit, but no significant group support. Currently, independent state Senator Lucy Killea is trying to spark interest in the idea and has introduced legislation on the topic. But there seems little likelihood now that a unicameral legislature will be approved. The public and politicians are too used to the bicameral structure. The newly appointed constitutional commission could conceivably propose both reforms in its recommendations to the legislature.

SUMMARY

This chapter has described the tasks, structure, leadership, and procedures of the California legislature. The California legislature was the leader among state legislatures in the trend toward professionalization—full-time, well-salaried, competently staffed, and with quality physical resources. Through the 1970s and early 1980s, this state legislature was considered the reform model for the other forty-nine states. However, over the last decade or so, problems have arisen in this "model" legislature, and voters seem increasingly willing to punish our lawmakers for their unethical behavior, excessive partisanship, and failure to act.

Term limits are having and will continue to have an enormous impact on the California legislature.

NOTE

1. When asked by a student if it was his political philosophy that enabled him to form a coalition with Republicans to win the speakership in 1980, Brown answered:

> Not at all, political philosophy has very little to do with the speakership. My political philosophy is probably light years away from the Republicans. . . . That crop of Proposition 13 babies voted for me across the board in 1980. Some of the liberal Republicans did not vote for me for one reason or another. . . . When people vote on the speakership, they vote for very basic things—sometimes, for things like chairmanships, vice-chairmanships. They vote for parking stalls. They vote for offices [with] windows. They vote for slots [seats] on committees. . . . There are all kinds of reasons, unrelated to philosophy. . . . The speakership is a house management responsibility. (Bud Lemke, December 13, 1985, p. 2)

REFERENCES

Bell, Charles G., and Charles M. Price. *The First Term: A Study of Legislative Socialization.* Beverly Hills, CA: Sage, 1975.

———. "20 Years of a Full-Time Legislature." *California Journal* 18 (1987), pp. 36–40.

Barber, Mary Beth. "Rob Hurtt: New Power on the Right." *California Journal* 24 (February 1994), pp. 7–10.

Fiorina, Morris P. "Divided Government in the American States: A Byproduct of Legislative Professionalism?" *American Political Science Review* 88 (June 1994), pp. 304–316.

Paddock, Richard C. "David Roberti Faces the End: The Mixed Legacy of a Practical Politician." *California Journal* 22 (March 1992), pp. 143–149.

Price, Charles M. "Advocacy in the Age of Term Limits." *California Journal* 24 (October 1993), pp. 31–34.

———. "Class of '92." *California Journal* 24 (April 1993), pp. 34–38.

Scott, Steve. "The Speakership." *California Journal* 26 (February 1995), pp. 8–12.

Zeiger, Richard. "Rating Legislatures." *California Journal* 25 (1994), pp. 8–12.

———. "The Luster Is Off the California Model." *California Journal* 21 (1990), pp. 299–302.

THE CALIFORNIA GOVERNOR:

NUMERO UNO

U nquestionably, executives are the key officers in contemporary governments. In both democratic and authoritarian systems, the executive proposes, implements, and coordinates policy. At all three levels of U.S. government
(national, state, and local), the day-to-day activities of government usually focus
on the executive. Indeed, the very word—*executive* (to execute)—implies action.

HISTORICAL BACKGROUND

In the original thirteen colonies, governors acted as the king's agents and held
most of the power. After the American Revolution and as a reaction to the former
royal governor's authoritarian power, elected governors' powers were reduced
and term limits imposed on them. In early post–Revolutionary War America,
state legislatures were the dominant political institutions.

Over time, the need for continuous program direction and policy coordination
and for someone to "manage the store" while the legislature was not in session
(much of the time) forced states to establish minimal executive authority. The
emergence of full-time professional executives was inevitable. By the latter half
of the nineteenth century, governors had become the dominant figures in state
politics. Those serving in large electoral vote states became automatic presidential prospects. Between 1876 and 1932, eight of fifteen presidents were former
governors. However, the Great Depression of the 1930s—which gave rise to the
New Deal—and the emergence of the United States as a world power following
World War II substantially enlarged the powers of the national government. In
turn, the political status of governors declined in national politics, and fewer were

nominated or elected to national office. Yet over the past several decades, governors have again become major players on the national political scene. Domestic issues have become critical and management skills highly desired. Examples are former Georgia governor and ex-president Jimmy Carter, former California governor and ex-president Ronald Reagan, former Massachusetts governor and 1988 Democratic presidential nominee Michael Dukakis, and former Arkansas governor and current President Bill Clinton. To further emphasize this point, Pete Wilson resigned his U.S. Senate seat to run for governor—further attesting to the position's importance. And now Wilson is a Republican presidential prospect. (Complicating this is the fact that if he leaves the office to run for president, his replacement as governor would be Lieutenant Governor Gray Davis, a Democrat.) Being a presidential prospect enhances a governor's status politically in the state. On the other hand, the lure of the presidency, which requires substantial time and energy to run in various state primaries, can lead to charges of neglect back in the capitol. Thus, Jerry Brown was hurt by his failed presidential quests in 1976 and 1980.

CONSTITUTIONAL FRAMEWORK

California, as other states, has a plural executive system. This is a legacy of the antigovernor feelings rooted in early colonial experience. Dividing executive power into separate elective positions means that no one person exercises all executive authority. In a sense, it is a system of checks and balances within a single branch of government. The California governor is just one of eight elected state executives (see Chapter 9).

To run for California governor, the state constitution stipulates that a person must be a citizen of the United States, a resident of California, and a registered voter. With only two exceptions, Culbert Olson (1938) and Ronald Reagan (1966), those elected as governor since 1934 have previously held some other statewide office. The governor receives an annual salary of $126,000 and has an expense allowance of $45,000 per year.

By custom, most California governors served only one or two four-year terms. However, Earl Warren was elected to a third term and Pat Brown tried unsuccessfully for a third term. But now, under term limits, the governor is constitutionally limited to two terms.

POWERS OF THE GOVERNOR

The California governor is a major force in state and national politics because of the size of the state's population and its economy. As noted, California governors are frequently considered as prime presidential timber. One recent study of state governors ranked California's as the sixth most powerful in the nation. The most powerful weapons in the California governor's arsenal are the budget, veto, appointments, and special sessions and elections powers.

Budget

In theory, the legislature has the "power of the purse," but, in fact, the governor dominates the process (see Chapter 10). He has the critical task of putting the annual budget together initially, shaping it through Department of Finance consultants at legislative hearings, determining which items should be reduced (governors are almost never overridden), and deciding whether it should be signed. Because the budget is at the top of the legislative agenda, the executive has enormous leverage. Executive policies and programs come first; individual legislator's ideas are considered later and must conform to the budget's limits.

Veto

One of the governor's most important legislative powers is the veto—or the threat of its use. The California governor has two kinds of veto: general and item. To override either requires a two-thirds vote in both houses, which rarely happens.

The general veto applies to any bill passed by the legislature. The governor can reject any legislation within twelve days of passage by sending it back to the legislature. Normally, the governor makes a short statement of his reasons for vetoing the bill.

The item veto applies only to an appropriation bill—typically, the annual budget. Instead of having to reject or accept the entire budget (as the president must), governors using the item veto can reduce or eliminate items they do not like and approve the rest. Governor Wilson has used this power extensively.

Governors Reagan, Brown, Deukmejian, and now Wilson after his first term, vetoed an average of 10 percent of the bills sent to them—approximately 300 per year. However, there are variations year-to-year in the number of vetoes issued by the last four governors, depending on the partisan composition of the legislature and governor's office and the level of mutual animosity. Thus, in the contentious election year of 1994, Governor Wilson vetoed nearly 19 percent of the bills that came across his desk. In addition, the promised threat of a governor's veto can sometimes discourage legislators from bothering to pass a particular bill.

Appointments

Further enhancing the influence of the governor is his power of appointment to (1) key administrative posts, (2) commissions and boards, (3) the judiciary, and

(4) executive and political posts. In addition to stressing competence in their nominees, more recent governors have tried to find qualified women and minority candidates to fill these positions.

Key Administrative Positions The governor nominates about 2,400 civil service exempt positions including agency secretaries, deputy secretaries, and agency directors—and other key positions on important boards and commissions. Annual salaries for these positions range from $75,000 to $100,000.

Most of these positions are subject to confirmation by a majority vote of the state senate. Traditionally, senators acquiesce to a governor's nominations to key administrative positions; after all, these people are supposed to reflect the governor's policies, not the senate's. However, more recent governors—Ronald Reagan, Jerry Brown, George Deukmejian, and Pete Wilson—have had a small, but not insignificant, number of their nominations rejected by the senate. At the very least, senate confirmation is no longer pro forma.

For example, in the early months of his first term, Deukmejian nominated Michael Franchetti, a longtime aide and confidant, as his finance director, the key appointee in the administration. The senate (Deukmejian's former colleagues) rejected the nomination. Wilson has also battled legislators over some of his nominees; both nominees he named to replace departing Superintendent of Instruction Bill Honig were rejected by the legislature. The position remained vacant for several years until Delaine Eastin was elected to the office in 1994.

Not surprisingly, governors usually nominate individuals who not only are competent but also share the executive's political philosophy. Because many commissioners are nominated to terms of office that overlap or exceed the governor's own four-year term, it may take a governor several years to gain a majority on a particular board or commission. A one- or even two-term governor may never gain control of some commissions and boards—for example, the University of California Board of Regents have twelve-year terms.

Commissions and Councils Nearly 4,000 people serve part-time on more than 400 state commissions and boards. They are usually paid a flat, daily fee per meeting ($50 to $100) and are often reimbursed for expenses. These bodies review state policy and make recommendations for change (see Chapter 9).

Judiciary Whenever vacancies occur, the governor appoints judges to the various California courts (see Chapter 11). Many judges serve long after the governor who initially appointed them has left office. For example, Justice Stanley Mosk was originally appointed by Governor Pat Brown in 1964 to the state Supreme Court; he remains on the Court today.

Executive and Political Appointments   If a statewide elected official or county supervisor resigns or dies, the governor nominates someone to fill the vacancy. When Treasurer Jess Unruh died and when Superintendent of Instruction Bill Honig was forced to resign, Republican governors Deukmejian and Wilson sought to fill the vacancies. In both instances, the Democratic-controlled legislature rejected their nominees. Democrats were unenthusiastic about the nominees and, more important, did not want them to run for election as incumbents.

Governors can use appointments to secure support from legislators or key interest groups. For example, the hundreds of appointments to the District Agricultural Association are largely patronage positions. Appointments to many minor commissions, councils, and boards are often used to reward the party faithful and the governor's supporters or to gain support from various organizations or groups or legislators.

Appointments can sometimes exacerbate tension in executive–legislative relations. Legislators expect to be consulted about appointments that relate to their district or ethnic ties. On the first day he was sworn in, Governor Jerry Brown was criticized by two Latino legislators because they had not been consulted about Brown's appointment of Mario Obledo as Health and Welfare secretary. Of course, for every pleased nominee, there are probably a dozen other disgruntled hopefuls who were not selected.

As part of the "team," appointees often help the governor win political support. Governor Wilson in his first term was praised by Republicans and Democrats alike when he nominated the highly respected Thomas Hayes to be his director of finance. Hayes resigned in 1994.

Just as the governor can appoint, so too can he remove someone whose actions or judgments run counter to the administration's policy or needs. The removal power is weaker, however, than the appointive power. About two-thirds of gubernatorial appointees serve for fixed terms. Persons appointed to fixed-term positions cannot be removed before the end of the term without good reason, such as illegal activities or gross incompetence.

Special Sessions and Special Elections

The governor has the power to call the legislature into special session at any time. During special sessions, legislators may consider only those issues presented by the governor. Before 1967, governors would call special sessions for one of two basic reasons: (1) The legislature was not in session and the governor thought an issue important enough to require immediate action, or (2) the governor wanted the legislature to consider an issue that it had ignored while in regular session.

And, in the old days, when the legislature met for only a few months a year, being called back into special session could be very inconvenient.

Since 1967, the legislature has been meeting nearly year-round, thus the governor has fewer opportunities to discipline legislators by calling them into special session. Today, the only real reason for a governor to call a special session is to force legislators to consider an issue on which the governor wants action or publicity. For example, Governor Wilson called the legislature into special session in October 1992 just a few weeks before the general election to pressure legislators into acting on the workers' compensation crisis. By doing this, he pulled them away from their reelection campaigns and forced them to address the issue. Modest reforms were achieved, but Wilson's hope to hurt Democrats in the elections didn't work. Democrats retained sizable majorities in the two houses after the 1992 election.

Legislation passed in a special session becomes law in ninety days. Legislation passed in a regular session does not become law until January 1 of the following year, unless passed by a two-thirds vote in both houses. Because it is difficult to get a two-thirds vote (called an "urgency measure"), the governor can use a special session to accelerate the effective date when only a simple majority is available.

In January 1978, Governor Jerry Brown called a special session to consider property-tax relief. That special session ran concurrently with the regular session and was designed to focus the legislature's attention on what had become a hot political issue. Had the legislature been able to reach agreement on some reform, it would have gone into effect immediately and might have eliminated much of the support for Proposition 13 in June 1978. In 1986, Governor Deukmejian called the legislature into special session in a failed attempt at resolving a prison-siting conflict in Los Angeles.

The governor also has the power to call special state elections at any time. Wilson exercised this power to call a statewide special election in November 1993 to have the electorate vote on various constitutional amendments referred by the legislature and on Proposition 174, the choice (voucher) initiative. Generally, Democrats are mistrustful of special elections because they fear they will have more difficulty turning out "their" voters than will Republicans. Indeed, Governor Deukmejian called a special election to vote on the Sebastiani reapportionment initiative in December 1983. (The state Supreme Court ruled the measure unconstitutional and removed the initiative from the ballot.)

Minor Powers

Clemency The governor has the power to pardon criminals, commute sentences, and issue stays of execution. In doing this, he considers the advice of the

California Adult Authority and his clemency secretary—but the final decision is his. This has sometimes produced critical problems. The most publicized occurs with the death penalty. Governor Pat Brown and his son, Governor Jerry Brown, and daughter, Kathleen Brown, Democratic gubernatorial candidate in 1994, opposed the penalty on moral grounds. State voters, on the other hand, clearly supported it. The Browns were all politically damaged by their opposition to execution. Although Kathleen Brown said she would abide by the law and enforce it if elected, voters mistrusted her on the issue. This issue contributed to her defeat in 1994. Given the tenor of the times, contemporary governors are leery of pardoning a criminal or commuting a sentence.

Extradition   The governor can extradite persons who live in California but have been charged with a crime in another state. Normally, California's governors approve extradition automatically, but on rare occasions a governor will not do so. Thus, Jerry Brown refused to extradite Indian activist Dennis Banks to South Dakota because he believed that Banks would not get a fair trial in that state.

Military   The governor is commander-in-chief of the state National Guard. In times of emergency, such as earthquakes, floods, or riots, the governor can call out the guard to help provide transport, deliver food and medical aid, or keep order. Governor Wilson ordered guard units to the Mexican border to back up the Border Patrol and try to stop illegal aliens from crossing into California.

Ceremonial   As head of state, the governor is the personal representative of California. For example, Governor Deukmejian helped to host Soviet President Mikhail Gorbachev on his visit to California in 1990. Jerry Brown took advantage of the national press coverage surrounding the first landing of the experimental space shuttle *Columbia* by awarding the pilots the Order of California when they landed in the state. Whenever there is a major natural disaster, governors are there. This reassures the public and gives the governors plenty of free publicity. Governors particularly enjoy announcing good news. For example, Wilson was ebullient when he officially announced that the drought was over. He renamed the state's "drought office" the "water conservation office."

OTHER LEADERSHIP FACTORS

In addition to a governor's formal, constitutional powers, there are a host of informal ingredients to leadership, including the ability to unite and lead his political party, popularity with the electorate, personal relationships with legislators, and leadership style.

Party Leader

Automatically, the governor is the chief spokesperson for his party. However, not all governors have enjoyed the role of party leader, and some have not been successful at it. Many governors have paid relatively little attention to their party's organization (see Chapter 6). Governor Warren, for example, preferred going to University of California at Berkeley football games rather than attending state central committee meetings. And throughout his tenure as governor, Jerry Brown was aloof from the Democratic state party organization. Thus, many observers were mildly surprised when he ran for election to be state chair several years after he completed two terms as governor. (Brown hoped to use his party chair election to jumpstart his political career.) And governors must, to an extent, be above crass partisan politics. They are, after all, the leaders of all Californians—Republicans, Democrats, independents, third-party members, and nonvoters. Many of the most popular governors, such as Earl Warren and Goodwin Knight, have been relatively nonpartisan. Governors Ronald Reagan and Jerry Brown were perceived by many voters as "nonpoliticians," which helped their political careers.

Governor Pete Wilson has had a long-standing, love–hate relationship with the state's Republican party leadership. Wilson—pro-choice, pro-environment, supporter of gay rights, and a political moderate—has frequently been at odds with GOP conservatives. While serving as U.S. Senator, Wilson was nearly booed off the stage at the 1985 Republican state convention.

However, conservative party leaders collectively "bit their tongues" and persuaded Wilson to resign from his safe U.S. Senate seat to run for governor in 1989. Wilson, they believed, had the best chance of any Republican of defeating the 1990 Democratic gubernatorial nominee. He then would be able to serve as a veto backstop for Democrat reapportionment bills. After being elected governor, Wilson's relationship with conservative elements in the party soured further. Conservatives were angered when he agreed to compromise with Democrats in dealing with the massive $14 billion deficit in 1991 by raising taxes. Thus, some Republican right-wingers urged various conservative Republican officeholders to challenge Wilson for the party's gubernatorial nomination in 1994. None did. However, political unknown Ron Unz, a conservative computer-industry tycoon, did file against Wilson in the 1994 Republican gubernatorial primary. Unz captured about one-third of the GOP vote. That a political unknown would receive this much Republican support is indicative of Wilson's problems with the conservative wing of his party. To placate this conservative opposition, Wilson has taken increasingly conservative stances as governor. However, this has not entirely assuaged party conservatives.

Dennis Renault / *The Sacramento Bee*

"Prove you're not illegal!"

Popularity with the Public

A governor's popularity with the public affects his power. If a popular governor is able to persuade citizens to write or call their legislators and let them know that the public supports a particular program, then the legislature is likely to respond.

Governors also serve as lightning rods for the state. If the economy is doing reasonably well, there are no major scandals in the administration, and times are good, then the governor's popularity will build. Governor Wilson has not had such luck. Floods, mudslides, fires, earthquakes, a drought, riots, defense cutbacks, and a lackluster economy—all mainly out of his control—combined to

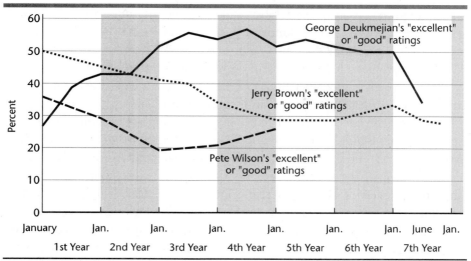

FIGURE 8.1 BROWN'S, DEUKMEJIAN'S, AND WILSON'S JOB RATINGS AS GOVERNOR
Source: Field Polls.

send his popularity plummeting to all-time lows in his first term (see Figure 8.1). Yet he was able to win reelection handily in 1994. Voters viewed his Democratic opponent, Kathleen Brown, the first woman to be nominated by a major party for the California governorship, even more unfavorably. Wilson, in effect, was viewed as "the lesser of two evils." With term limits now in place, Wilson begins his second term as a lame duck (i.e., he cannot run for reelection as governor), and although a *Los Angeles Times* poll reported in March 1995 that his popularity had risen (47 percent said he was doing a good job, 44 percent a poor job), Californians had little enthusiasm for his potential candidacy for national office.

Legislative Relations

Much, perhaps most, of the governor's time and energy is devoted to legislative relations. Getting the budget passed, desired legislation approved, unwanted legislation rejected, and nominees on board are the core tasks of the governor's workload.

Every governor takes office having made campaign promises and having a personal set of policy and political objectives. Some goals, such as reduced governmental regulation or more "friendly" interpretation of laws by state agencies, can be accomplished without legislative approval by a governor's appointees to various agencies. But many other goals—welfare reform, increased public-school funding, prison construction, new energy or environmental policy—require legislative cooperation in the form of more money or expanded governmental activity. These kinds of goals require legislation or support for budget expenditures; the governor cannot do it alone.

A governor's personal relationship with legislators is important. When the governor strongly supports a bill, it is easier to get a legislator's vote if the legislator and governor are friends and trust one another.

Ronald Reagan had star appeal and charisma to many in the public, but he was remote from rank-and-file Democratic legislators. On the other hand, Governor Jerry Brown was seen as "Pat's boy," an elected official who had attained the office mainly because of the family name. Brown was not a close confidant of many legislators. Governor George Deukmejian had close friendships with certain Republican legislators but was frequently at odds with Democratic leaders.

No governor in California history has ever had such an extensive elective career background as Wilson did before becoming governor. He had previously served as assemblymember, mayor of San Diego, and U.S. senator. He obviously understood the political process at the local, state, and federal levels.

Wilson, however, has never been trusted by conservative Republican legislators, although they have never been willing to cooperate with Democrats in an override of a Wilson veto. Democratic legislators expected that the former assemblymember and political moderate would be more than willing to bargain and compromise with Democrats to achieve mutual goals. This belief was reinforced when Wilson, in his first State of the State message, proposed a state preventive program of prenatal care for mothers and said he wanted to keep children in school and out of prison.

Pete Wilson's first-term working relationship with Democrats was not particularly good. He was a champion of Proposition 140 (the term limits and legislative budget reduction initiative), which many legislators (mainly Democrats) despised. Wilson's enthusiastic support for the measure was seen by many Democrats as the critical factor in the initiative's narrow (52 to 48 percent) victory. Wilson was also unyielding on the Democratic reapportionment bills. The impasse meant that the state Supreme Court, not the legislature, did the redistricting. Democratic legislators also strongly opposed Wilson's Proposition 165, the welfare reduction and budget-power enhancement initiative of 1992. In that same year, Wilson and the legislature set a new record for budget delays (sixty-four days). From a Democratic perspective, Wilson was consistently tacking to the conservative right and away from his centrist roots. In 1991, he vetoed a bill forbidding job discrimination against homosexuals, further angering liberal Democrats. After proposing a tax increase in 1991, Wilson has since become an ardent no-new-taxes crusader. He became an enthusiastic proponent of the "three strikes" bill and initiative in 1994, which further alienated him from liberal Democratic legislative leaders. Finally, his staunch support of Proposition 187, the illegal immigrant initiative of 1994, and his endorsement of a proposed civil rights initiative to abolish affirmative-action programs in the state (slated for the 1996 ballot) further strained relations with Democrats. However, the massive Republican victories in the 1994 elections, culminating in the approval of the three strikes and illegal immigrants initiatives, a nearly even Republican–Democratic balance in the two houses (formerly Democratic strongholds), and statewide GOP victories greatly strengthen Wilson's hand in his second term.

Finally, Wilson's successors as governor will have one key advantage: Legislative term limits mean the assembly in particular will have constant waves of newcomers elected every two years with little expertise and weakened legislative leadership. A resourceful governor could thrive in this legislative chaos.

Campaign Support   One of the most effective ways for a governor to build good personal relations with legislators of his party is by providing them campaign support. This applies, of course, only to candidates of the same party. Governors are expected to hit the "rubber chicken" circuit—appearing at fundraising dinners and praising local party candidates' fine qualities. Legislative candidates (incumbents or aspirants) like to be seen rubbing elbows with the governor; it makes them look important to the home folks. Helping the incumbent legislator raise money at a dinner featuring the governor as guest speaker puts the legislator in political debt to the chief executive. Both understand that the governor may collect that unspoken IOU later.

Partisan Balance   From 1959 to 1994, Democrats controlled both houses of the legislature (with the exception of two years in the assembly). As a result, Democratic governors had a "built-in" majority with which to work. Republican governors had to build a majority vote for each of their programs. Wilson's hand is strengthened by Republican control of the assembly, but the Democratically led state senate will probably become even feistier in Wilson's second term.

Leadership Style   Leadership style is another critical ingredient of effective leadership. California's last four governors (Reagan, Brown, Deukmejian, and Wilson) have all had unique political styles[1]: the charming and affable Ronald Reagan; the mercurial Jerry Brown (dubbed by the media as Governor Moonbeam); the less exciting but honest George Deukmejian; and the dour, nononsense, professionalism of Pete Wilson.[2] Wilson wanted to be a proactive governor, but the troubled economy and the refusal of the federal government to properly compensate California for federally mandated services to illegals—

education, health, and incarceration costs—meant that he could not pursue his activist agenda in his first term.

OFFICE OF THE GOVERNOR

The governor is more than a single individual. In meeting the many responsibilities of office, governors must delegate authority to others. To this end, California governors have hundreds of aides, including administrative staff and cabinet members.

Staff

Because the basic tasks of the governorship remain largely the same over time, regardless of the office's occupant, the major staff positions are essentially the same in every administration. These positions are:

Executive secretary—acts as chief of staff, coordinating the governor's staff

Legal affairs secretary—concerned with the problems of clemency, pardons, and extradition

Press secretary—the link between the governor and the print and broadcast media, and hence the public

Legislative secretary—in charge of liaison with the legislature

Appointments secretary—in charge of screening applicants for the many appointments the governor makes

Cabinet

The governor's cabinet is composed of seven superagency secretaries, directors of several departments, and the governor's executive secretary (see Chapter 9). The cabinet facilitates policy development and program coordination. Each of the seven secretaries represents the many departments, commissions, and boards that make up his or her agency. Because no governor can hope to deal with each of the several hundred agencies, departments, commissions, and boards in California government, the cabinet serves as a way of delegating responsibility.

SUMMARY

The governor dominates the executive branch and is the most important officeholder in the state. The legal–formal powers of budget, veto, appointments, authority to call special sessions and elections, and a host of minor powers provide the state's chief executive with a formidable political arsenal. The less tangible factors of popularity and party leadership further enhance gubernatorial power, particularly in California because of the national stature of its governor.

Yet the governor is also a person—a personality—about whom each of us can have personal feelings and attitudes. This personality dimension is seldom a major consideration for other state political figures, such as legislators, administrators, or judges, because they are identified with a larger group. A legislator is one of 120 lawmakers; a judge is one of 1,500 judges. But the governor is the governor—there is only one.

NOTES

1. Perhaps no event better symbolized the Jerry Brown legacy as his official governor's portrait. All former governors' photograph-like portraits are on display on the first floor of the capitol building. These paintings show serious and somber former officials standing stiffly beside the capitol building or working in their offices. Jerry Brown's portrait is only of his face. Unlike the other lifelike portraits, his appears to be in an expressionist style. It stands alone in splendid isolation, hidden away from the other governors' portraits on the third floor of the capitol building. It has become a favorite "in" spot for capitol guides to show to the waves of tourists coming to the building.

2. As U.S. Senator, Wilson, on a close budget vote, was brought into the Senate chambers in a hospital wheelchair (he had had an emergency appendectomy the previous day) so he could cast the deciding vote in favor. Republican Senate leader Bob Dole kidded later that Wilson does "better under sedation."

REFERENCES

Decker, Cathleen. "Survey: Wilson Shouldn't Run." *The Sacramento Bee* (March 12, 1995), p. A1.

Melendy, H. Brett, and Benjamin F. Gilbert. *The Governors of California*. Georgetown, CA: Talisman Press, 1965.

Sabato, Larry. *Goodbye to Good-time Charlie: The American Governorship Transformed.* Washington, DC: Congressional Quarterly, 1983.

Zeiger, Richard. "Pete Wilson: Steering Through a Sea of Woes." In Tom R. Hoeber and Charles M. Price, eds., *1994–1995 Annual: California Government and Politics*. Sacramento: California Journal Press, 1994, pp. 18–21.

ADMINISTRATION:

EXECUTIVES, CIVIL SERVANTS, AND CITIZENS

A lthough the political spotlight focuses most often on the governor, hundreds of other, less visible executives are busy in the daily administration of government. Voters elect a lieutenant governor, six department heads, and four members of the five-member state Board of Equalization (the controller is the fifth member). The governor appoints several hundred other top administrators. According to the Little Hoover Commission, more than 400 boards, agencies, and commissions operate with some autonomy: 53 advisory, 182 administrative, 56 regulatory, and 34 marketing. In addition, more than 268,500 state employees hold jobs ranging from scientific laboratory positions to highway patrol officers, construction engineers, college professors, and construction workers.

Few Californians have much direct contact with elected public officials; fewer even know their names. But all Californians have frequent direct contact with state employees. They are important in the daily lives of California residents.

PLURAL EXECUTIVE

Like other states, California has an independently elected plural executive. The positions and salaries, as set by the Citizens Compensation Commission, are: governor, $126,000; lieutenant governor, $94,500; attorney general, $107,100; treasurer, $94,500; secretary of state, $94,500; controller, $94,500; insurance commissioner, $95,052; the four elective members of the Board of Equalization, $95,052 each; and the superintendent of public instruction, $107,000. Only the last position, the superintendent, is elected as a nonpartisan; the others are all elected on a partisan basis. In some states, several of these positions are appoint-

FIGURE 9.1 CALIFORNIA'S PLURAL EXECUTIVE

ive; in California, with the exception of the state auditor, these are all elective (see Figure 9.1 and Table 9.1, page 222). Proposition 140 limits all constitutional officers to two terms. The governor and the two U.S. senators are the most sought after elective positions in California. The other members of the plural executive, excluding the low-profile Board of Equalization members, are in the best positions to move up the political ladder and run for governor or U.S. senator. In 1992, Democratic Lieutenant Governor Leo McCarthy ran for a U.S. Senate seat but lost in the primary to Barbara Boxer. In 1994, Treasurer Kathleen Brown and Insurance Commissioner John Garamendi each sought the Democratic gubernatorial nomination. Brown won the nomination but lost to Wilson in the 1994 general election. Also, Controller Gray Davis, in a more lateral move, decided to shift positions (perhaps to buy himself more time under term limits) and was elected to the office of lieutenant governor.

Lieutenant Governor

The lieutenant governor becomes governor when a vacancy occurs in the office of governor because of disability, impeachment, retirement, recall, or death. This function is similar to the vice president at the federal level succeeding to the presidency. However, in California, the lieutenant governor also becomes acting

OFFICE	CALIFORNIA ELECTS	A MAJORITY OF OTHER STATES ELECT
Lieutenant Governor	Yes	Yes
Attorney General	Yes	Yes
State Treasurer	Yes	Yes
Secretary of State	Yes	Yes
Superintendent of Public Instruction	Yes	No
State Auditor	No	Yes
Insurance Commissioner	Yes	No
Controller	Yes	No
State Board of Equalization (four members)	Yes	No

TABLE 9.1 COMPARING CALIFORNIA'S PLURAL EXECUTIVE WITH THOSE OF OTHER STATES
Source: The Book of the States, 1989–90.

governor whenever the governor leaves the state. Because California governors travel out of state frequently (particularly if they are campaigning for the presidency), the lieutenant governor occasionally serves as acting governor. Thus, Democrat Lieutenant Governor Gray Davis served as acting governor frequently in 1995 as Wilson began his bid for the presidency. In addition, like the vice president, the lieutenant governor is the president of the senate and theoretically its presiding officer. In fact, the lieutenant governor and vice president rarely preside over their respective senates. Normally, the lieutenant governor presides for only a few minutes a year at most. The only time that McCarthy presided over the senate in his third term was when senators held a session to honor him. When lieutenant governors and vice presidents preside, it is mainly a ceremonial event or photo opportunity. Senators do not consider these officers real members of the "club." Moreover, the lieutenant governor and vice president cannot introduce legislation or serve on committees as senators can. And they cannot vote in the senate except to break a tie. This rarely occurs. Lieutenant Governor McCarthy never had the opportunity to cast a tie-breaking vote during his twelve-year stint in office. Vice President Al Gore did cast a tie-breaking vote to adopt the 1994 budget.

Unlike the vice president, the lieutenant governor is not chosen by the governor to be the running mate. At the federal level, it's a team effort: Clinton–Gore or Bush–Quayle. In California, the lieutenant governor's race is completely separate from the governor's contest. Occasionally, the Republican (or Democratic) candidates for governor and lieutenant governor will run cooperatively as a team in the general election, but they usually maintain a distance from each other, focusing mainly on their own individual campaigns. Over the last few decades several vice-presidents have become president— Republicans Richard Nixon, Gerald Ford, and George Bush and Democrat Lyndon Johnson, for example. Others have been their party's presidential nominees, such as Democrats Hubert Humphrey and Walter Mondale. Thus, the office of vice president, although at times the butt of jokes, has become a significant position; the office of lieutenant governor, however, has not undergone a similar transformation. Although several California lieutenant governors did manage to move up and win election as governor in the past, this has not happened since the 1950s. Our two most recent former lieutenant governors, Mike Curb and Leo McCarthy, tried desperately to move up the political ladder to higher office but failed. Current Democratic Lieutenant Governor Gray Davis clearly has higher political ambitions and would replace Wilson as governor if the latter won the presidency. To forestall this eventuality, Republican leaders want to change the succession process. They have discussed placing an initiative on the 1996 ballot that would require a special election for a new governor if the incumbent vacates office midterm.

In 1978, for the first time this century, voters elected a governor and lieutenant governor of different parties, and this pattern has continued ever since—a governor of one party, a lieutenant governor of the other. Substantial tension developed between liberal Democratic Governor Jerry Brown and conservative Republican Lieutenant Governor Mike Curb. Curb was anxious to establish a record of accomplishment, but he occupied a job that did not allow for this. In the spring of 1980, when Jerry Brown left the state to campaign in the New Hampshire presidential primary, Mike Curb took advantage of this opportunity to embarrass the governor politically. Traditionally, when lieutenant governors serve as acting governors, they perform routine administrative duties and act within the guidelines set by the governor. Curb instead nominated an archconservative judge to a vacancy on the appeals court. When Brown returned to the state, he angrily withdrew this nomination (then pending before the Commission on Judicial Appointments) and nominated his own choice. Curb objected, asserting that once a judicial nominee had been submitted, the governor could not withdraw it. (Under pressure from Curb, Brown hastily made more than thirty additional justice nominations in less than a week and then left the state again!) Brown contended that so long as he could communicate with his office— whether in New Hampshire or Paris, France—he was still the governor. Curb filed suit to settle the matter, and it was quickly appealed to the California Supreme Court (mainly Jerry Brown appointees then). At issue: (1) When the governor leaves the state does the lieutenant governor automatically become acting governor or is the governor still in command? (2) Does the lieutenant governor serving as acting governor have the full power and authority of the office? In December 1979, the Court upheld the lieutenant governor's powers and authority to act as governor when the governor is out of the state. (The state constitution states that the lieutenant governor shall act as governor during the latter's "absence from the state.") However, the Court also ruled that the governor could withdraw a judicial nomination presented to the Commission on Judicial Appointments before it had acted on the matter. Thus, technically, a lieutenant governor serving as acting governor can make appointments to vacant positions and sign or veto bills. But, in practical terms, this officer must follow the governor's instructions. On a later occasion when Mike Curb was acting governor, he wanted to veto a bill that was awaiting Governor Brown's signature. However, when Curb requested the bill from Brown's staff, they said they were unable to "find" it. Ironically, current Lieutenant Governor Gray Davis was then Governor Jerry Brown's chief of staff.

In 1982, Mike Curb decided to run for the Republican gubernatorial nomination. However, he lost to George Deukmejian in the primary, and Leo McCarthy was elected as lieutenant governor. McCarthy promised that he would not play a disruptive role—whether the governor was Republican or Democrat. He kept this pledge throughout his tenure as lieutenant governor. His relationship with Governors Deukmejian and Wilson was cordial and correct but remote. On occasion, McCarthy signed bills for Governor Deukmejian and later Governor Wilson when they were out of state, but the lieutenant governor did not exercise independent judgment. Neither of the two governors was a close confidant of McCarthy. Governor Wilson and Lieutenant Governor McCarthy had a luncheon meeting once a year and met briefly a few other times in Wilson's first term. Neither of the two Republican governors was anxious to enhance McCarthy's status by assigning him additional responsibilities. Current Lieutenant Governor Gray Davis complains that Governor Wilson usually refers to him as a "problem" because of the succession process. Davis also was ordered to vacate his suite of capitol offices, and he lost funding for the Economic Development Commission, which he chairs.

After leaving office in 1982, Curb publicly disavowed the position of lieutenant governor. He said the office should be abolished; it was a waste of taxpayer dollars. Ironically, in 1986, Curb again sought election as lieutenant governor in order to allow Governor Deukmejian "to explore a national ticket option" and be replaced by a Republican. However, cynics interpreted Curb's candidacy as a way to get back on the political ladder. In any case, he lost.

Although the media and capital insiders treat the lieutenant governor's position mainly as a joke, polls indicate there is little public interest in abolishing the office or in having the governor and lieutenant governor elected together as a team.

Finally, the lieutenant governor also serves as a member of the State Lands Commission, the University of California Regents, and the California State University and College Board of Trustees. If the governor and lieutenant governor were of the same party and simpático, the governor could give the latter some important responsibilities. For the most part, being lieutenant governor puts one in a holding pattern to run for a "real" office afterward.

Attorney General

Second in importance to the governor, the attorney general is a major force in California government. As head of the Department of Justice, the attorney general has overall responsibility for enforcing all state and local laws. However, because of the strong tradition of home rule in California, the attorney general seldom enters into local law-enforcement matters except in emergencies. The attorney general's duties cover a wide range of activities, including civil and criminal law, investigation, and legal advice.

The attorney general is also responsible for representing dozens of state agencies in court. However, on a few politically sensitive issues, the attorney general may not always choose to defend the state. For example, in court cases involving state-funded abortions, environmental-protection regulations, and public-employee collective-bargaining rights, then–Attorney General Deukmejian either refused to defend the state's policies or, in a few instances, actually joined with the other side in challenging the state's positions. Current Attorney General Republican Dan Lungren has vigorously fought for executions for those on death row. Robert Alton Harris, a double murderer, was executed in 1992 through his efforts. This was the first execution in California in twenty-five years.

In recent years, attorneys general have frequently sought election as governor. Earl Warren (1942), Pat Brown (1958), and George Deukmejian (1982) went directly from attorney general to governor. However, two recent attorney generals, Evelle Younger and John Van de Kamp, failed in their bids. Attorney General Dan Lungren has made no secret that he is considering running for governor in 1998.

Controller

The controller is chief fiscal officer of the state. The main duties of this officer are to pay state bills and keep track of state accounts. The controller is responsible for four major programs: fiscal control, tax administration, local government fiscal affairs, and administration. The controller is also a member of the State Lands Commission, the Franchise Tax Board, and the Board of Equalization.

Perhaps because fiscal policy is not very exciting, controllers traditionally have tended to have only modest political ambition. However, two former controllers were able to get elected to the U.S. Senate, and Democrat Gray Davis went from controller to lieutenant governor in 1994. In the same election, Democrat Kathleen Connell, a Southern California businesswoman, was elected to the post.

Secretary of State

The secretary of state is guardian of documents and records for California. The secretary also serves as the state's chief elections officer. Until the 1970s, this office generated little interest. Two incumbents, Frank C. and Frank M. Jordan (father and son), held the office from 1911 to 1970 (except for three years).

When Jerry Brown was elected secretary of state in 1970, he used the office to promote campaign reform and his own gubernatorial quest in 1974. He was the first secretary to go on to higher office. His successor, March Fong Eu, the second woman and first Asian elected to statewide office, served from 1974 to 1994. In 1994, President Bill Clinton named Eu as ambassador to Micronesia, and she resigned as secretary of state. Given the lengthy tenure of various secretaries of state, Proposition 140's two-term limit will have a major impact on this office. In the 1994 Republican election landslide, former GOP assemblymember Bill Jones narrowly beat Democrat Tony Miller to win the office.

Treasurer

The treasurer is state banker and investment counselor. The treasurer's most important duty is to prepare, sell, and redeem state bonds. These bonds, which are sold to large financial institutions, provide the money to pay for major state construction projects (such as the California State Water Project) and to support programs such as the California Housing Finance Agency's low- and moderate-income housing projects.

Entrusted with selling billions of dollars in bonds, it is important that the treasurer secure the lowest possible interest rate. A difference of half a percentage point is equal to hundreds of millions per year! In addition, by carefully managing the state debt, the treasurer plays an important role in maintaining state credit. Governor Wilson was incensed when Treasurer Kathleen Brown, a Democrat and gubernatorial candidate, criticized Wilson's handling of the state budget crisis. Wilson complained that Brown's "bad-mouthing" of the state's fiscal situation helped to lower Wall Street confidence in California's economy and its bond ratings.

Until recently, the treasurer's second most important task was to invest surplus state funds. Since 1981, treasurers have not had to "worry" about fulfilling this responsibility.

With the election of Jess Unruh as treasurer in 1974, the office took on new importance. During his tenure, the legislature appointed the treasurer to more than thirty commissions dealing with fiscal matters, in many cases as chair. Unruh put together and led the Council of Institutional Investors, a national coalition of twenty-six separate state employee and union pension funds groups with combined assets of more than $100 billion.

Because Unruh made the office of treasurer into a powerful position and great base for Wall Street campaign contributions, Democratic and Republican party leaders have since been keenly interested in which party holds the office. Kathleen Brown was able to use her position as treasurer (as well as the name identification of her father, Governor Pat Brown, and brother, Governor Jerry Brown) to get the gubernatorial nomination of the Democratic party in 1994. The current controller is Republican Matt Fong, the son of former Democratic Secretary of State March Fong Eu.

Insurance Commissioner

Much as spiraling property-tax rates spawned Proposition 13 of June 1978, rapidly escalating auto-insurance rates encouraged California consumer activist Harvey Rosenfield to author Proposition 103 of November 1988. This insurance initiative stipulated that (1) car insurance rates were to be sharply reduced and regulated by the state, and (2) the state insurance commissioner would become an elective position rather than be appointed by the governor.

After Proposition 103 was approved, various insurance companies brought legal suits challenging the constitutionality of particular sections of the new law, effectively delaying their implementation while the suits were pending. After years of turmoil, the Court ruled in 1994 that Proposition 103 was constitutional and that the 10 percent profit margin settled on in the proposition was reasonable. After successfully winning the battle to become insurance commissioner, Democrat John Garamendi took a proconsumer stance. He battled the auto-insurance industry, stopped an insolvent state earthquake-insurance program and formulated tough new regulations. He attempted to use the positive publicity he had garnered as commissioner to run for governor in 1994 but lost to Kathleen Brown in the June Democratic primary; he stepped down as insurance commissioner after the November 1994 general election. Chuck Quackenbush, former Republican assemblymember, was elected as insurance commissioner in the 1994 election over Democrat Art Torres. The major issue of the campaign was which special interests were donating to which campaigns: Insurance companies donated to Quackenbush, and lawyers contributed to Torres.

Obviously, there are trade-offs in having an elected insurance commissioner. Elected commissioners are likely to be more mindful of the electorate and less influenced by the insurance industry. But having an elected commissioner adds one more voting decision to an already crowded ballot. As car insurance wanes as an issue, will voters be able to evaluate satisfactorily the performance of the commissioner? Will campaign contributions from the insurance industry have negative effects on future elections?

Superintendent of Public Instruction

The superintendent is an unusual executive. Elected to office on a nonpartisan ballot, this official not only heads the state's public school system but also is responsible to a ten-person Board of Education appointed by the governor. As the administrative head of the Department of Education, the superintendent is expected to implement board policy. Yet this officer is elected and so ultimately responsible to the voters rather than to the board. Further complicating the situation is that most of California's education is delivered at the local level.

State and local education programs cover a wide range of activities in addition to the three R's, including child-care centers, migrant child care, preschool and early childhood education programs, programs for the disadvantaged, and programs for the physically handicapped.

An important and often controversial area for the Department of Education is its text-adoption authority for kindergarten through eighth grade. Local districts may use only texts on the approved list. Controversies over "God and science," sex education, and "fundamentals or frills" often end up on the superintendent's desk.

With more than one-third of the state budget flowing through the Department of Education, the superintendent is clearly a major figure in California government. Since the state Supreme Court in *Serrano v. Priest* (1971) ruled that local property taxes were not providing equal funding opportunities for every child, state government has been forced to increase substantially its support to local school districts. In addition, voter approval of Proposition 13 in 1978 cut local school district revenues by about one-third. The state replaced most of the lost funds out of its budget surplus. In 1988, voters approved Proposition 98, which guarantees that at least 40 percent of the state budget goes to K–12 public education. Increased pressure for more state money for public schools makes the superintendent's position more powerful and more political than in the past.

In 1990, Bill Honig was elected to his third straight term as superintendent. Honig throughout his tenure was a tireless advocate for improving California schools and raising the test scores of public school students. To accomplish this, he fought zealously for increased funding for schools, and this not infrequently brought him into confrontations with economy-minded Republican governors. Unfortunately for Honig, he was indicted and convicted of steering state government educational funds to his wife's nonprofit foundation in a conflict-of-interest violation. Honig had to resign his position, and from 1992 to 1994 an interim superintendent was nominally in charge. Governor Wilson twice nominated successors for Honig (Republican State Senator Marian Bergeson and businessman Sanford Sigoloff), but both lost their senate confirmation fights. In 1994, Democrat Delaine Eastin, a former assemblymember, won election to the nonpartisan position with the strong and enthusiastic support of the California Teachers Association. Thus far, Eastin has worked hard to develop a cooperative rather than adversarial relationship with Governor Wilson.

Board of Equalization

The Board of Equalization has five members—four are elected in partisan contests from districts comprising one-fourth of the state's population, and the fifth is the state controller (Democrat Kathleen Connell). The board's most important function is to administer and collect state and local sales and use taxes. It is also responsible for collecting excise taxes, including those on alcoholic beverages, cigarettes, and gasoline. The board's other major function is to review each county's tax assessments and procedures.

Board members have a low political profile. Once elected, they are usually reelected easily, often facing only token opposition. Thus, former board member William Bennett was reelected, even though he was widely criticized for misuse of public funds, as was another former member, Paul Carpenter, who had recently been convicted of extortion. Proposition 140's term limits will mean much swifter member turnover. Two former legislators (Democrat Johann Klehs and Republican Dean Andal) were elected to the board in 1994 along with incumbents Democrat Brad Sherman and Republican Ernest J. Droneburg.

Figure 9.2 (page 230) shows the partisan affiliations of executive offices since 1935.

THE ADMINISTRATION

Government programs approved by the legislature and governor must be implemented. The state bureaucracy is charged with doing this. Three superdepartments and seven superagencies make up the governor's cabinet.

	1935-38	1939-42	1943-46	1947-50	1951-54	1955-58	1959-62	1963-66	1967-70	1971-74	1975-78	1979-82	1983-86	1987-90	1991-94	1995-98
Governor	R	D	R	R	R	R	D	D	R	R	D	D	R	R	R	R
Lt. Governor	R	D	R	R	R	R	D	D	R	R	D	R	D	D	D	D
Secretary of State	R	R	R	R	R	R	R	R	R	D	D	D	D	D	D	R
Attorney General	R	R	D	R	D	D	D	D	D	R	R	R	D	D	R	R
Controller	R	R	R	R	R	R	D	D	R	R	D	D	D	D	D	D
Treasurer	R	R	R	R	R	R	D	D	R	R	D	D	D	D	D	R
Insurance Commissioner	—	—	—	—	—	—	—	—	—	—	—	—	—	—	D	R

R	Office held by Republican	D	Office held by Democrat

FIGURE 9.2 PARTISAN CONTROL OF EXECUTIVE OFFICES, 1935–1998

The Superdepartments

Department of Finance The Department of Finance is the governor's budget and fiscal control agency. Its director, appointed by the governor, is normally the second-ranking member of the administration. The department is responsible for preparing and administering the annual budget, analyzing program effectiveness and efficiency, monitoring all legislation that has fiscal implications, and providing economic and demographic research. Although this department has a smaller staff and budget than other state agencies, it remains the single most important and powerful department in California government (see Chapter 10).

Department of Food and Agriculture The Department of Agriculture is responsible for regulating and protecting California's food supply. The department deals with issues such as pesticide regulation, insect infestations, meat and poultry inspections, farmworker regulations, and raw milk standards.

Department of Industrial Relations The Department of Industrial Relations enforces California's occupational and safety laws, negotiates threatened strikes, and administers workers' compensation claims.

The Superagencies

Much of California's administrative system is organized into seven superagencies, each housing several departments, boards, and commissions. The governor appoints each agency head, or secretary, as well as the department heads and most members of the many boards and commissions, subject to confirmation by the state senate.

State and Consumer Services The State and Consumer Services agency serves the state's public employees and consumers. Among its more important units are the Franchise Tax Board, which administers the collection of personal income taxes, bank and corporate taxes, and senior citizens' property taxes; the Department of Consumer Affairs, which oversees departments such as Auto Repair and the Medical Board along with regulating various professions (doctors, dentists, barbers, morticians, cosmetologists, veterinarians, nurses, accountants, architects); the Department of Fair Employment and Housing; and the state Fire Marshall.

Business, Transportation, and Housing Three departments are combined in the Business, Transportation, and Housing agency. One is concerned with transportation—the California Highway Patrol, Caltrans, and the Department of Motor Vehicles, for example. The second covers business activities—the Department of Banking and the Department of Corporations are examples. The third deals with housing such as the Departments of Real Estate and Housing and Community Development.

Resources The Resources agency oversees the preservation of water, air, land, natural life, and recreational resources. One major subunit is the California Coastal Commission, which was created by initiative in 1972. In 1981, six coastal conservation commissions were merged with the statewide commission. Charged with regulating land use and development along California's coastline, the commission has been involved in numerous conflicts with coastal cities, counties, and developers. Another key unit is the California Conservation Corps, a workforce of California youth who perform services such as park maintenance, trail building, stream cleaning, tree planting, and so on.

Health and Welfare The Health and Welfare agency supervises a variety of health and welfare programs. Its units serve the poor, mentally ill, developmentally disabled, elderly, and unemployed. Given the rapid increase in the costs of health and welfare, the controversial nature of abortions and drug-treatment programs, the middle-class reaction to welfare programs, and the budget squeeze imposed by Proposition 13, the agency's programs and departments are under intense political pressures.

Environmental Protection Environmental Protection is one of the smaller agencies. It includes the Air Resources Board, State Water Resources Control

Board, and the California Waste Management Board. Governor Wilson has proposed an expansion of this agency's duties and responsibilities.

Youth and Adult Corrections The Youth and Adult Corrections agency has two departments and three boards, all concerned with prisons, prison terms, youth corrections, and parole. Undoubtedly, in terms of numbers of state employees and budget, this agency has exhibited the most rapid expansion over the last decade because of Californians' fears about crime. Since 1984, 16 new prisons have been constructed. Experts have estimated that, under the "three strikes" sentencing law, another 41 prisons will need to be constructed by 2003 to house about 350,000 prisoners (three times the current prison population). Thousands of new prison guards will have to be hired; their numbers already have increased 37 percent in the last five years.[1]

Child Development and Education The new cabinet-level Child Development and Education agency launched by Governor Pete Wilson is responsible for delivering social, medical, and mental health services to children. No other units are assigned to this agency.

Regulatory Commissions and Boards

Several boards and commissions share executive power with the governor. A commission or board comprises several people (typically five or seven), with each having an equal vote in policy making. The governor nominates potential members, and the senate decides whether or not to approve these nominations. When members' terms of office extend beyond the governor's, holdovers may find themselves in sharp disagreement with a new governor's appointees. Members of the Agricultural Labor Relations Board appointed by Jerry Brown, for example, had entirely different philosophies from those subsequently appointed by Governor Deukmejian. On some boards and commissions, appointments are made by different public officials. On others, such as the Consumer Advisory Council and the Commission on the Status of Women, legislators serve as members. Membership on some executive boards and commissions is predetermined. For example, most members of the State Lands Commission and the Franchise Tax Board become members automatically because they hold some other elective office. Some boards, such as the Wildlife Commission Board and the State Board of Control, have both predetermined and appointed members. The more important commissions and boards follow.

State Lands Commission The State Lands Commission's members are the lieutenant governor, controller, and director of finance. The commission controls the management of all state lands (some 4 million acres). Increasingly important is the commission's authority to administer state land leases, permits, and sales of state oil, gas, and minerals.

Public Utilities Commission (PUC) With five members nominated by the governor to six-year terms, the PUC is a very important regulatory agency. The commission is theoretically independent, but it usually reflects the governor's position on utility issues. The commission is charged with regulating utility rates (natural gas, water, and electricity) and transportation rates within the state. Rates are supposed to provide utilities a reasonable return on their investment. At the same time, the commission must also protect consumers against unreasonable rates by seeing that utilities provide adequate facilities and services.

Energy Resources Commission Legislative concern over the PUC's inability to fulfill its responsibilities, its apparent bias in favor of utilities, and the energy crisis led to the establishment of the Energy Resources Conservation and Development Commission in 1975. This commission has authority over locating new power-plant sites in the state. It also promotes the development of alternative energy resources, including solar and geothermal energy. It is a perennial candidate for elimination in government cost-cutting efforts.

Agricultural Labor Relations Board (ALRB) After years of turmoil, including strikes, violence, and consumer boycotts, California finally established the ALRB—an idea championed by Governor Jerry Brown—in 1978. In its early years, bitterness between growers and the United Farm Workers (UFW) and attempts by the Teamsters Union to organize farmworkers led to constant conflict.

Brown appointed commissioners who were sympathetic to the farmworkers' plight. Governors Deukmejian and Wilson later counterbalanced the board with commissioners concerned with farmers' problems. Although the ALRB has had rocky moments, overall it has helped to reduce the tension between farmer and farmworker by formalizing a process for labor-conflict resolution.

Public Employee Relations Board Created in 1975 to oversee collective bargaining activities involving school employees, the Public Employee Relations Board's powers have been enlarged to include collective bargaining of state employees.

Fair Political Practices Commission (FPPC) Created by initiative in 1974, the FPPC has control over implementation of the Fair Political Practices Act (see Chapters 3 and 5).

World Trade Commission The World Trade Commission promotes California's products in overseas markets. The growing interdependence of the world economy heightens this commission's importance.

"Little Hoover Commission" Formally titled the Commission on California State Government Organization and Economy, the "Little Hoover Commission" encourages governmental efficiency and issues reports delineating how government can operate more effectively and frugally.

Lottery Commission Established by initiative in 1984, the Lottery Commission has become a major player in the California economy virtually overnight—ticket sales run into the billions of dollars. Some 34 percent of revenues generated go to public education (nearly $1 billion a year). Although its critics complain that the lottery's main participants are those on the bottom of the economic ladder who can least afford to play, the lottery has become deeply ingrained in California society. Revenues, however, have declined in the 1990s.

Citizens Compensation Commission Established by Proposition 112 (ethics) of June 1990, the Citizens Compensation Commission sets the salaries of state elected officials.

Constitutional Revision Commission In 1993, the twenty-three-member Constitutional Revision Commission was established by the legislature and governor to suggest revisions to the state's constitution dealing with the budget process, the state–local relationship, and the structure of state governance.

Public Education

Public education—kindergarten through high school (K–12) and higher education—provides a good example of the many boards and commissions involved in delivering a particular service to the people of the state, and it reflects the diversity of needs involved.

State Board of Education Ten State Board of Education members are nominated by the governor to staggered four-year terms. The board sets policy and oversees the Department of Education, although the latter is headed by the independently elected superintendent of public instruction. Theoretically, the board sets policy and goals for the state's elementary and secondary schools (K–12).

State Department of Education The independently elected superintendent of instruction heads the State Department of Education. This officer oversees a host of education programs, approves instructional materials, and distributes funds to local school districts.

Commission for Teacher Preparation and Licensing With fifteen members appointed by the governor, the twenty-member Commission for Teacher Preparation and Licensing reviews teacher-training programs, gives licensing examinations, and enforces teacher standards.

Community Colleges In theory, the state's 107 community colleges are financed and funded by local community college districts with locally elected boards of trustees. Each district covers all or part of a county. Since Proposition 13, however, these local colleges have become increasingly dependent on the state for funding.

Community colleges are designed for (1) high school graduates whose grades are too low to win admission to a four-year college immediately (some of these students eventually go on to state universities or colleges), (2) students interested in two-year associate degree programs (often vocational), (3) students interested in pursuing personal interests in noncredit courses, and (4) older students, retired people, or those considering a midcareer change.

State University System The various campuses of the state university system offer many different Bachelor's and Master's degrees. Graduating high school students in the top third of their class with requisite test scores are eligible for admission. These institutions stress instruction rather than research; most of their funding (about 95 percent) comes directly from the state. This gives the governor and legislature great power over the system.

The California State University (CSU) system is governed by a twenty-three-member board of trustees (most nominated by the governor). They direct the nation's largest system of higher education, enrolling more than one-half million full-and part-time students.

The University of California Recognized as one of the premier academic institutions in the world, the University of California (UC) accepts students from the top one-eighth of the state's graduating high school seniors. Approximately one-third of its students are in graduate or professional programs.

As a major research university, the UC relies on the state for about 40 percent of its annual income and the federal government for about 20 percent. The remainder comes from student fees, private sources, and income generated by the university.

The UC system is governed by a twenty-six-member Board of Regents, which is vested by the state constitution with full powers of organization and management.

YEAR	STATE POPULATION (1,000s)	NO. OF STATE EMPLOYEES	EMPLOYEES PER 1,000 POPULATION
1955–56	13,004	77,676	6.0
1960–61	15,863	115,737	7.3
1965–66	18,464	151,199	8.2
1970–71	20,039	181,151	9.1
1975–76	21,537	206,361	9.6
1980–81	23,780	225,567	9.5
1985–86	26,365	227,209	8.6
1989–90	29,063	254,589	8.8
1992–94	31,961	268,419	8.4

TABLE 9.2   STATE EMPLOYEES AND STATE POPULATION BY DECADE
Source: Governor's Budget Summary, 1993–94.

Civil Service

State employees (see Table 9.2) are responsible for delivering the goods and services that California government provides—patrolling freeways, distributing tax forms, checking the accuracy of gas station pumps, helping campers at state beaches, collecting and distributing money. The nearly 270,00 state employees and 250,000 county employees account for about 2 percent of California's population.

The standards by which state employees are hired, promoted, or fired are important in determining the quality of service provided to California citizens. In the "good old days," public employees were hired on a political patronage basis, with little regard for their ability to do the job. One major reform of the Hiram Johnson Progressive administration was to establish a civil service system; virtually all state employees except legislative staff are members.

Under civil service, state employees are hired and promoted on the basis of job skills, education, and experience, not as a political payoff. Civil service regulations protect state employees from pressure to participate in the "correct" political party or to support a particular candidate for office. At the same time, California law states that, except for some reasonable limits, "no restriction shall be placed on the political activities of any officer or employee of a state or local agency." Critics argue, however, that civil service has produced mediocrity, cumbersome procedures, and stifled innovation.

Although the state's civil service, or bureaucracy, appears to be ponderous and rigid, it has changed and is under substantial pressure for more change. Among the changes recently instituted are (1) collective bargaining, (2) affirmative action, (3) changes in personnel practices (hiring, firing, and discipline), and (4) some preliminary steps toward contracting for services.

Collective Bargaining   In a major departure from tradition, state employees (in both civil service and higher education) have borrowed from the private sector and entered into collective-bargaining elections, selecting an organization to represent them in negotiations with their employing government agency. These negotiations cover wages and salaries, fringe benefits, and working conditions.

Affirmative Action   Affirmative action—a program that encourages the hiring of African Americans, Latinos, Asians, women, and other historically disadvantaged groups into state employment, all other factors being equal—has posed a serious challenge to the fundamental philosophy of civil service. Although civil service exams, according to critics, have a built-in bias toward white, middle-class males, since the latter half of the 1970s there has been substantial growth in state hiring from historically underrepresented groups and in promoting some of these individuals into key policy-making positions.

Cuts in state employment have threatened these new minority jobs. Under traditional civil service practice, seniority determines layoffs. Thus, those most recently hired (minorities and women) are the first to be laid off. Moreover, a much discussed civil rights initiative slated for the 1996 ballot could abolish affirmative action programs if approved by voters and upheld in the courts.

Contracting for Services   Can private business do the same job at less cost than the civil service? Court interpretations of the state constitution restrict the performance of routine jobs to state employees. Such jobs as freeway maintenance, janitorial work, and clerical tasks may not be contracted to private firms. Prisoners also are allowed to produce manufactured goods for use by state government.

Duplication   Some critics complain that too many state programs are duplicative and thus wasteful. Bernstein (1995) reports that twenty-three separate job-training programs cost taxpayers $3.8 billion yearly.

PROBLEMS AND REFORM

California's plural executive has been the subject of considerable debate. The duties of the secretary of state, controller, treasurer, insurance commissioner, and Board of Equalization are largely administrative, and some critics suggest that they should be gubernatorial appointments. Electing executives who have little or no policy-making function, it is argued, makes the offices unnecessarily political. Reducing the number of elected executives would shorten the ballot and make voting less onerous to Californians. The plural executive also obscures responsibility.

This proposed change should not be made for at least two good reasons. First, making these positions appointive would increase the governor's power substantially. Second, by electing these officers, voters have some control over them.

Another suggested reform is to have the lieutenant governor run on the same ticket as the governor, as in half the states and in presidential and vice presidential elections. Because the lieutenant governor is often the acting governor, the argument goes, the occupant of that office should be someone who is in general agreement with the governor on the major issues.

Finally, the idea of having an elected nonpartisan superintendent of public instruction operating under the authority of a board appointed by a partisan governor has also evoked criticism.

How responsive is California's bureaucracy to the public? Being immune from political pressure, is the bureaucracy so independent that it pursues its own goals and ignores the public's? In theory, the constitution and statutes establish two kinds of executives: those who make policy, and those who administer it. Those who make policy are either elected by the public or appointed by elected officials to positions exempt from civil service. Those who administer policy—deliver services—are required to secure their positions by passing tests. Elected officials and exempt appointed officials are subject to election results; civil service personnel are not. In theory and in law, it appears that policy makers are subject to public will. But reality and theory are not always the same.

Until recently, boards and commissions were usually dominated by the very people they were supposed to regulate. Attorneys were appointed to the California Bar, dentists to the Board of Dental Examiners, doctors to the Board of Medical Quality Assurance, real estate brokers to the Real Estate Commission, and termite exterminators to the Structural Pest Control Board. The few public members on these bodies were heavily outnumbered. But more recently, many of these boards and commissions have been given many more public members and, thus, more accountability to the public.

SUMMARY

Clearly, in a democracy, there can be conflict between a professional civil service and the public. The pressures for affirmative action and for patronage appointments are good examples of that conflict. The plural executive obscures policy responsibility. And citizen executives are sometimes in conflict-of-interest positions. Yet in comparison to many other states, California has a reasonably efficient and responsible executive–administrative–bureaucratic system.

Whether the administrative system needs a major overhaul or a tune-up is debatable. Nevertheless, pressures for change will continue.

NOTE

1. According to Chance and Bernstein (1995), some correctional officials double their salaries by working many overtime hours.

REFERENCES

Bernstein, Dan. "State Agencies Are Drowning in Duplication." *The Sacramento Bee* (April 24, 1995), pp. A1, A 10.

Chance, Amy, and Dan Bernstein. "State's Spending Resists the Knife." *The Sacramento Bee* (April 23, 1995), pp. A1, A14.

Green, Steven (ed.). *Political Almanac, 1993–1994*. Sacramento: California Journal Press, 1993.

THE BUDGET PROCESS:

THE ANNUAL ORDEAL

Without question, the budget is the most important bill the legislature and governor must deal with each year. More time is spent on the budget in endless committee hearings than any other single piece of legislation. Putting together the budget and getting it approved is a year-long process of state agency deliberations; legislative hearings with input from the legislative analyst, Department of Finance, and Commission on State Finance; May revisions by the governor based on the most current economic considerations available; final approval by the required two-thirds vote of each house; and submission to the governor, who can sign or veto the entire budget (rarely done) or cut or reduce specific budget items. Finally, the governor can be overridden (which rarely happens) by a two-thirds vote of each house. And, as soon as one budget is signed, the next inevitably is beginning to be prepared.

The constitution mandates that the budget be: presented to the legislature by the governor within the first thirty days of the session, sent back to the governor by June 15th of each year, and signed and ready to go into effect by July 1. But these constitutional deadlines are seldom met these days. Increasingly, the most partisan and acrimonious issue of the year is the budget.

The budget is the dollars-and-cents statement of state policy and priorities. And since 1978, when voters approved Proposition 13's property-tax cuts, state budget decisions have become even more important because they directly affect local government, too.

The state budget is also closely linked to the federal budget and several thousand local budgets within California. Although we will focus on the state budget, we will also take into account local and federal budgets (revenues and expenditures) as they affect the state budget. As we will see, the state is quite often a "middleman," collecting and distributing more money than it controls.

Budget size and complexity have grown markedly. More and more groups are getting involved in the budget process besides the legislature and governor: interest groups, lobbyists, media, local governments, and state government agencies are also key players.

The state budget changes dramatically over relatively short time spans. During the Deukmejian–Wilson years, the state went from budget deficits in 1983 and 1984 to substantial surpluses in 1985 and 1986 to austerity in the 1988 budget, to a deficit of nearly $14 billion in 1991 and $3–4 billion deficits ever since. Of course, no budget stands alone; each is strongly influenced by the preceding one.

Because supermajorities (two-thirds in each house) are required to approve the budget in the legislature or override the governor, an unyielding one-third of members in either house can bring the process to a halt. Partisan stalemate has been a constant feature of the budget process in the 1980s and 1990s.

THE BUDGET PROCESS
Administrative

The governor, the director of the Department of Finance, and key personnel in this department are the major actors in budget formulation.

First, the Department of Finance sends a letter to departments in July explaining the governor's priorities and what their budget expectations should be. Field offices and specific units of larger departments are requested to assess their budget needs. How many new file cabinets will the San Bernardino Highway Patrol office need? Does the Oroville office of the Water Resource Agency need a new pickup truck? How many faculty positions are needed in the political science department at California State University, Chico?

Budget requests are based on three major considerations: (1) previous budget levels, (2) estimated changes in workload for the coming budget year, and (3) plans for new programs and modification or abandonment of old ones. If, for example, the political science department expects more students in the budget year under consideration, it must estimate how many more faculty will be needed to teach the increased number of students. How many more secretaries, how much more copy paper, and so forth will also have to be estimated.

As the local agency and field office requests move up the bureaucratic ladder, they are combined and modified. By July, each department is working on its total budget, made up of all the "local" requests. By late August, each department submits its budget request to the Department of Finance, which represents the governor. In September, the Department of Finance meets with each department's budget officer(s) to review their budget requests. In October, the finance department prepares the governor's budget. And in November, each department head has the opportunity to meet with the governor to appeal Department of Finance decisions. Up to this halfway point, the process is closed. After any final adjustments, the governor submits his budget to the legislature in early January in the State of the State message, and then public scrutiny begins.

Legislative

The Legislative Analyst's Office (LAO) begins its fiscal assessment in the fall, and various staff members work on specific program areas—health, welfare, or public education. The LAO is the fiscal expert for the legislature. It plays a major role in shaping the legislature's response to the governor's budget. In December, the Department of Finance provides the LAO galleys of what the governor will propose in his new budget. Reciprocating, the LAO in February provides the Department of Finance the galleys of its *Analysis of the Budget Bill* and *Perspectives and Issues* so that Finance can be thoroughly prepared for the issues raised in the legislature's budget committees.

The governor's budget bill is technically introduced by the chairs of the Assembly Budget (formerly Ways and Means) and Senate Budget and Fiscal Review committees. (This is a formality; they do not necessarily agree with the budget proposals.) This is the one bill where legislators have no pride of authorship. In reviewing the governor's budget, legislators rely heavily on the LAO's evaluation. Budget hearings are held by the appropriate committees in both houses in March, April, and early May to give the public (represented by interest group lobbyists, state agencies, local governments, and legislators) an opportunity to support or oppose programs, suggest changes, or defend pet projects.[1] The fiscal committees and subcommittees have majority and minority staff who also help frame the budget debate and look for partisan advantage.

During this process, each house amends the governor's budget, so that by late May there are, in fact, three budget documents: (1) the governor's original budget, (2) the assembly version, and (3) the senate version. The three documents reflect different goals and values and must be compromised to produce a final budget.

The first compromises occur within the legislature. The assembly and senate budget versions are sent to a conference committee, which prepares a single legislative budget. After the required two-thirds vote by both houses, the budget is sent to the governor—supposedly, by constitutional mandate, by June 15 of each year. But in recent years, the legislature has often failed to meet this deadline.

Dennis Renault / *The Sacramento Bee*

After receiving the budget, the governor meets with legislators, staff, and others to decide which sections are acceptable and which are not. California's constitution, as we have seen, gives the governor item-veto power, which means that governors can eliminate or reduce budget items they do not like.

After signing the budget, the governor sends it back to the legislature. (The legislature has the constitutional authority to override the governor's vetoes by a two-thirds vote in each house.)

Thus, the governor has the first and last word on the budget. He prepares and submits it to the legislature. And after the legislature sends it back to him, he has the item veto. As a result, a budget signed into law usually looks very much like the budget originally submitted by the governor some six months earlier.

Trailer Bill

While the legislature hears the budget, a trailer bill is prepared that amends state law to accommodate required budgetary changes. Much of the state's spending policy is set by statute—perhaps as much as 80 percent of general-fund expenditures. Because the budget bill does not have legal authority to change (amend) a law already on the books, the legislature must pass and the governor must sign a separate bill to make the needed amendments. Today's budget is a policy plan for state government, and the trailer bill contains dozens of policy changes.

A prime example of the trailer bill's function is in changing cost-of-living-adjustment (COLA) statutes. By law, welfare recipients and state employees are to receive annual cost-of-living adjustments in their benefits and salaries. But the tight budgets of the 1990s often do not allow these statutory requirements. A trailer bill, reducing COLAs to the amounts provided in the budget, is required.

POLITICS OF THE BUDGET

Throughout Deukmejian's two terms (1983–1990) and Wilson's first term (1991–1994), budget conflict pitted the two fiscally conservative governors and their Republican, antitax, legislative allies against liberal and socially committed Democratic legislative leaders. While Democrats had solid majorities in the two houses until 1995, they did not have the necessary two-thirds vote needed to override the two Republican governors. In 1983, in Deukmejian's first year as governor, the budget stalemate broke all existing records, lasting nineteen days, but in his last year as governor, the 1990 budget crisis set a new delay record of twenty-eight days. However, in Wilson's second year, the impasse stretched to sixty-four days. The item veto (the blue pencil) is a powerful tool, particularly when the governor has a solid one-third in either house to back him up. However, he cannot increase appropriations for favored departments. Getting two-thirds of each house to finally approve the budget is often difficult, and attempts by Democrats to delay action to force governors to compromise have not succeeded.

Not surprisingly, those most seriously and immediately affected by budget deadlock are among California's most vulnerable: (1) several million Aid to Families with Dependent Children (AFDC) recipients and (2) the aged and the physically and mentally disabled. Later, state workers and Medi-Cal providers begin to suffer if no budget is in place.

The Governor's Goals and Priorities

Like his Republican predecessors Reagan and Deukmejian, Governor Wilson has been able to get nearly all of what he wanted in budget deliberations with Democratic legislative leaders. Through blue-pencil cuts, governors can shape their social priorities. For example, Deukmejian reduced the budget of the Coastal Commission and Family Planning Services. Wilson has added more correctional officers. These decisions have more than fiscal ramifications.

A further advantage for Deukmejian and Wilson is that they proposed to reduce funding for particular departments, eliminate regulations, and reduce the number of state employees, and the item veto put them in the driver's seat.[2] Launching new programs in the difficult economic times of contemporary California is extremely difficult, but if the governor supports one that requires legislation, then he needs at least a majority vote in both houses before he can sign the bill. Getting these votes may be difficult, particularly if the governor has vetoed some legislators' pet projects. But the governor has a lot to give: a signature on a bill, an appointment of a legislator's friend to some board or commission, and for lawmakers in the governor's own party, the promise of campaign support.

The Legislature's Goals and Priorities

Although the governor's spending goals and priorities are usually clear, identifying the legislature's is harder. Initially, there are 120 individual legislators' goals and priorities. But each legislator quickly learns to compromise. Some have more power than others and get more of what they want—in particular, the assembly speaker, senate pro tem, chairs of the fiscal committees, minority leaders in the assembly and senate, and other legislators who are "close" to the leadership.

On Member's Day (an annual event), individual legislators troop before the Assembly–Senate Budget Conference Committee to advocate for statewide or local pet projects near and dear to their constituents. In past years, some members would fight strenuously for "their" projects and get them placed in the budget, then bitterly criticize the "big spenders" responsible for the size of the budget.

Traditionally, the legislature maintains a "hands-off" policy toward the funding of the governor's non–civil service political administrative appointments, while the governor reciprocates by not touching the legislature's own budget. Wilson's championing of Proposition 140's term limits and 38 percent legislative budget reductions prompted Democratic legislative leaders to propose 38 percent cuts in the number of his administrative positions, but this was not approved.

The Voice of the People

In addition to the governor and the legislature, there is another increasingly important element in the California budget process: the public. The public must give final approval to bond measures and fiscal constitutional amendments submitted by the legislature, and to initiatives that have budget implications such as Proposition 13, the property-tax relief initiative of 1978. In the late 1970s, as property taxes were skyrocketing and the state budget had a $5 billion surplus, 65 percent of voters agreed with Howard Jarvis and Paul Gann, Proposition 13's authors, that enough was enough. Property-tax revenue dropped by 57 percent. Since 1978, Proposition 13 has reduced governmental tax revenues by $200 billion and made it almost impossible to raise taxes. The surplus that was used to bail out local government for a few years is gone. Local governments are impoverished, and some teeter on the brink of bankruptcy.

A "Balanced" Budget

Although the public's tax-cut revolt fever of the late 1970s may have subsided a bit in the 1990s, polls suggest that the public remains wary, if not hostile, to new taxes. Bond measures have been big losers in the 1990s. In his first year in office in 1991, Wilson decided to close a massive budget deficit of nearly $14 billion by proposing a $9 billion tax increase; in turn, Democrats agreed to $3 billion in program cuts. Republican conservatives bitterly attacked their governor for the compromise, and Wilson has refused ever since to raise taxes any further. Of course, many in the antitax movement remain convinced that much fat can still be cut in the public sector. Those in the public sector contend that the decade's squeezing and trimming have led to declines in quality, and all elected officials have become gun-shy about raising taxes.

Compounding the budget dilemma are:

1. a growing public concern about crime and violence, which has meant more public money shifted to police, jails, and correctional officers and away from public services such as higher education, libraries, and welfare;
2. a sputtering economy with high unemployment fueled by a sizable defense cutback, which means more spent on unemployment compensation and reduced revenues;
3. a constant partisan budget impasse fostered by the two-thirds requirement;
4. a prodigious population growth mainly of new foreign immigrants and a high birthrate, which means heightened demands for public services;
5. a voting electorate that overrepresents seniors, Anglos, and the well-to-do; and
6. constraints on the budget process imposed by "ballot box budgeting."

Proposition 13 was followed closely by government spending limits (Proposition 4 of 1979), the elimination of gift and inheritance taxes (Proposition 5 of 1982), the indexing of income tax (Proposition 7 of 1982), Jarvis's limits on local government's ability to levy taxes (Proposition 62 of 1986), Bill Honig's guaranteed minimum funding level for K–12 public education (Proposition 98 of 1988), and the tobacco tax initiative's (Proposition 99 of 1988) earmarking of tax funds for antitobacco programs. All reduced the government's budgetary flexibility.[3]

The net effect is that California has gone from a high-tax, high-service state to a decidedly reduced status. Tuition and fees have increased dramatically at public universities and colleges, while state support has declined. Faculty have been encouraged to retire early. Those leaving have not been replaced, and hundreds of classes have been cancelled. The state had been one of the top five in achievement of its K–12 students; today it ranks among the bottom ten. California ranks 50th in student–teacher faculty ratio among the states. California students rank near the bottom among states in reading achievement. California ranks 41st in per capita spending for public school students, while spending on prisons and correctional officers rises inexorably.

Attempting to "balance the budget" is fraught with peril. As Krolak (1990, p. 4) notes, "the Constitution states that the Legislature shall not create 'any debt or debts, liability or liabilities, which exceed the sum of three hundred thousand dollars' . . . and that the governor, '. . . shall recommend the sources from which the additional revenues shall be provided.'" But, this language has enough wiggle room to allow elected officials to do what they want without raising taxes. The prime ways are to have overly optimistic revenue projections (Governor Wilson based his 1994 budget on receiving $3.1 billion from the federal government for the costs of illegal immigrants—few expected a reimbursement of more than $1 billion); extensive use of bond measures (this puts off paying until another day and weighs heavily on the next generation); and rolling over the debt until the next year in hopes the economy will pick up. In addition, the 1994–95 Wilson budget has a trigger. To get a $7 billion loan from Wall Street bankers, the state had to agree to make cuts in all unprotected spending if projected revenues fell short of projected expenditures after the November 1994 election. The state university and UC higher education systems (unprotected, unlike K–12) are most vulnerable. Lastly, the state budget can reduce the amount of money allocated to local government. To pay for the state's constitutional priority to K–12 public schools and federally mandated programs, the state shifted nearly $4 billion to schools from local government in 1993 and 1994.

ECONOMIC POLICY

We are often reminded that death and taxes are inevitable. But unlike death, which falls evenly on all, some pay more in taxes than others, and some receive more services than others. In this section, we will consider how the state raises the money needed (revenues) and spends the money it collects (expenditures).

Revenues

Long ago, people paid their taxes "in kind" with grain or livestock. In today's complex economy, most wealth is not in property or goods, and money comes in the form of credit, checks, plastic cards, and computerized accounts.

Although the state has many revenue sources, most of its money comes from three taxes: the personal income tax, the sales tax, and bank and corporation taxes. The remainder comes from a wide variety of other sources (see Figure 10.1).

Personal Income Tax　California's largest revenue source is the personal income tax. The tax rate is progressive; that is, the rate increases as personal income increases. A 1 percent income tax increase will yield about $2 billion.

Since 1971, California has used payroll withholding to collect income tax in order to improve compliance. In 1982, voters approved a constitutional income-tax indexing proposal; tax brackets move up with inflation.

Sales Tax　The sales tax is another major revenue source in California (currently six cents on each dollar of taxable purchases). Some basic necessities, such as food, prescription drugs, and utilities, are not taxed. A one-cent increase in the sales tax produces almost $2 billion more in tax revenues each year. The major advantage of the sales tax is that it is easy and inexpensive to collect and generates large amounts of revenue. But the sales tax is regressive in its effect; that is, it imposes a heavier burden on the poor, who spend a larger proportion of their income on sales-tax items than do the rich.

Bank and Corporate Franchise and Income Taxes　The state also levies taxes on business income and collects a fee for conducting business in California.

Other Taxes　Several other taxes and fees generate significant additional state general revenues, including taxes on insurance companies, horse tracks, cigarettes, and alcoholic beverages.

The Lottery　The lottery generates millions of dollars a year for public education (about $173 per K–12 student). But ticket buyers tend to be low-income individuals, so the lottery becomes, in effect, a regressive tax.

As the novelty of the lottery has worn off, ticket sales in the 1990s have declined. Whether new games, rolling over more money in jackpots, or increased advertising will increase sales is unknown. However, many fiscally pressed school districts no longer think of lottery funds as an extra fringe, but as a needed budget

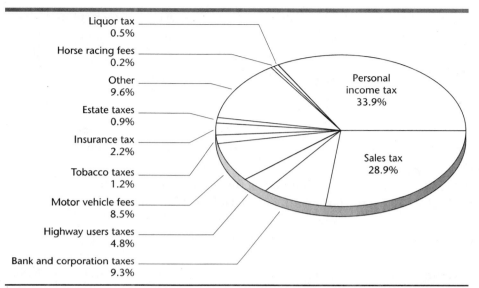

Liquor tax
0.5%

Horse racing fees
0.2%

Other
9.6%

Estate taxes
0.9%

Insurance tax
2.2%

Tobacco taxes
1.2%

Motor vehicle fees
8.5%

Highway users taxes
4.8%

Bank and corporation taxes
9.3%

Personal
income tax
33.9%

Sales tax
28.9%

FIGURE 10.1   GENERAL FUND REVENUES AND TRANSFERS, 1994–1995 *Source:* Governor's Budget Summary 1994–1995.

supplement for teacher salaries or supplies. These districts will be hit hard if lottery ticket sales go down appreciably.

Federal Funds   The federal government is a critical part of the state revenue picture. Billions of federal dollars pour into California each year in defense spending, military bases, grants to local government, and payments to individuals (for example, Social Security). As noted in Chapter 1, California's economy has been hurt by defense cutbacks and base closures because the state has been the leading military state. Governor Wilson, angered because the Clinton administration has not provided sufficient funds to compensate the federally mandated costs for illegal aliens, has filed three lawsuits against the federal government seeking compensation for costs incurred by the state since 1988: $2 billion for prison costs, $0.5 billion for health costs, and $10.5 billion for educational costs. In his most recent lawsuit, Wilson argues that, "The massive and unlawful migration of foreign nationals . . . constitutes an invasion of California against which the United States is obligated to protect California, pursuant to Article 4, Section 4 of the Constitution of the United States." Wilson's opponents say the founders were talking about an armed invasion, not foreign immigrants, coming here illegally. And critics of Wilson argue that undocumented workers, overall, make a strong contribution to the California economy: They pay taxes, work for low wages, and take jobs that Californians refuse—particularly agricultural labor. Even Wilson now concedes that undocumented aliens generate about $1 billion in state and local taxes to California. Of course, California also provides the federal government billions of dollars in taxes.

Tax Burden

The issue of tax burden entails several questions: (1) How much does the average citizen pay in taxes and fees? (2) Is the burden the same for everyone? (3) To ease the pain, do those with more wealth pay more in taxes? Because of factors such as number of dependent children, whether one is a renter or homeowner, and medical expenses, the tax burden unavoidably is different for different people.

Tax equality can be considered in two ways. The first is horizontal—the idea that people in the same circumstances should pay the same amount in taxes. If you and your neighbor own the same type of tract home and receive the same government services (police, fire, trash removal, etc.), both of you should pay the same property tax. In fact, as a result of Proposition 13, if you recently bought your house but your neighbor lived there before 1978, you will pay far more property taxes than will your neighbor (the tax is based on what was paid for the property, not its worth).

The other dimension of tax equality is vertical. Presumably, it is harder for someone with a $10,000 income to pay an 11 percent tax than it is for someone earning $1,000,000. The idea is that people with higher incomes should pay a greater percentage of that income in tax (a progressive tax) than people with low incomes. The idea of tax equality is reasonable but difficult to apply.

In addition to trying to make taxes fair while producing revenue for the state, California (like the federal government and other states) tries to use tax laws to promote certain social and economic goals. One can deduct charitable contributions, health costs, and mortgage-interest payments from state income taxes. Each dependent child is "worth" a tax reduction. These deductions and tax credits are designed to encourage home buying, promote contributions to charity, and recognize the cost of children. Also, tobacco and alcohol are "sin" products, and making them more expensive through taxes is an attempt to discourage use.

Contributing to the tax burden of Californians, according to the Franchise Tax Board, is the state's approximately $4 billion annual loss from underpaid and unpaid taxes. The main culprits are self-employment income, unreported capital gains, overstated deductions, unreported interest and dividends, drugs, prostitution, and nonfilers.

Also, there are tax loopholes—devices by which taxes can be avoided or reduced. Once written into law, they tend to remain, and the lost tax revenue

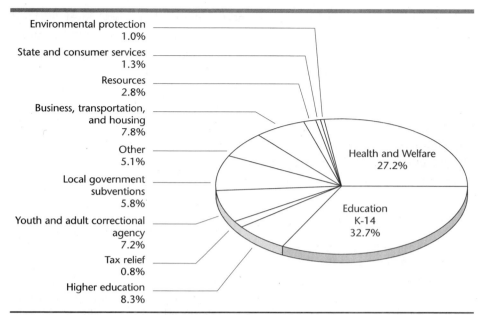

Environmental protection
1.0%

State and consumer services
1.3%

Resources
2.8%

Business, transportation,
and housing
7.8%

Other
5.1%

Local government
subventions
5.8%

Youth and adult correctional
agency
7.2%

Tax relief
0.8%

Higher education
8.3%

Health and Welfare
27.2%

Education
K-14
32.7%

FIGURE 10.2   GENERAL FUND EXPENDITURES, 1994–1995 *Source:* Governor's Budget Summary 1994–1995.

tends to be forgotten. The legislative analyst reports that tax loopholes total many billions of dollars. The largest single loophole is the deductibility of mortgage-interest expenses. Few loopholes ever get closed because of powerful interest group pressure, and new loopholes tend to be added each year.

Some types of income are taxed, while others are not. Social Security benefits, scholarships, food stamps, and welfare benefits—and a wide range of other programs designed to help the poor—are not considered income for tax purposes. At the other end of the economic ladder, high-income individuals have real estate depreciation, interest deductions, income deferrals, and capital gains to reduce their tax burden.

Expenditures

Approximately one-half of the state budget goes to assist local governments, primarily school districts. Another large portion goes to aid individuals at the local level. Of the total general fund budget, the state spends only about a quarter directly at the state level. As Figure 10.2 shows, Governor Wilson's proposed 1994 budget anticipates spending the most on K–12 education, health and welfare, and higher education.

Most state money (about 70 percent) is spent at the local level by local government agencies. The state collects the money, but the counties, school districts, special districts, and cities spend it. Since Proposition 13 went into effect, local governments have become ever more fiscally dependent on state government.

The size of the California budget has grown steadily over this century. Several factors contribute to budget growth. Some are beyond the state's control—population growth, inflation, the nation's economic health, and natural disasters. Other factors—the decision to add or expand programs or to cut or add taxes—are within the political control of the legislature, governor, courts, and voters.

SUMMARY

When state government rescued local government after Proposition 13, local governments lost substantial control over their revenues (see Chapter 12). Yet citizens expect their local governments (city, county, or school district, for example) to make program decisions, determine policy, and decide how to spend the money. But local governments often cannot make those decisions because state control comes along with state money.

In the state legislature, a minority of legislators frequently take advantage of the two-thirds vote requirement for approval of the budget and thereby deny majority rule. As noted, California government has been doing a better job of spending money than it has in raising it lately. Budget policy is never fixed, and pressures to reform the process will continue.

NOTES

1. The Budget and Fiscal Review Committee has jurisdiction over the budget and amendments to it; the Appropriations Committee has authority over all other fiscal bills. The main reason the senate has two committees involved in budget politics, rather than one as it did before 1985 with a Finance Committee, is to parcel out the workload more broadly. (Cynics suggest it's because leadership wants to keep members happy, and with two committees, more members have an input in budget deliberations.) Because of the relative parity between assembly Democrats and Republicans in 1995, the Budget and Appropriations committees deal with fiscal matters formerly handled exclusively by Ways and Means.

2. Governor Wilson attempted to expand the already considerable budget powers of the state's chief executive with Proposition 165 of 1992, the Budget Process and Welfare initiative. Wilson wanted to gain new emergency budget powers for himself. To win support for his plan, he incorporated welfare cuts of 25 percent in AFDC payments (popular with voters) as part of the package. Wilson's Proposition 165 lost.

3. One important stumbling block in the 1990 budget controversy was a loophole provision in Proposition 98 that stipulated that the measure (which guarantees about 40 percent of the state budget to K–12 schools) could be suspended in an "emergency." In the fall of 1989, with the concurrence of the education community, the legislature suspended implementation of Proposition 98 to provide financial assistance (a quarter-cent sales-tax increase) for Bay Area earthquake relief. In June 1990, Governor Deukmejian argued that the budget deficit of $3.6 billion was a fiscal "emergency"; he wanted to suspend Proposition 98 once again. This time educators disagreed that there was an emergency, and they successfully fought against the suspension.

REFERENCES

Krolak, Richard. *California's Budget Dance: Issues and Process.* Sacramento: California Journal (1990).

Schmidt, Robert. "Is the Gann Limit Unbearable?" *California Journal* 18 (1987), pp. 154–157.

Walters, Dan. "Closing Tax Loopholes." *California Journal* 14 (1983), pp. 255–256.

THE CALIFORNIA JUDICIAL SYSTEM

For most Californians, the state's system of justice is represented by the traffic officer, "bail by mail," a jury summons, or lurid headlines detailing some aspect of the O. J. Simpson murder trial. Yet the system is much more than this.

Rendering justice remains one of the few government activities that is still mainly a state function. Nine of ten court cases in the United States are argued in state courts, attorneys are licensed to practice by states, and corrections—jail, prison, parole, and probation—are largely state activities. For most of us, state laws have the most frequent and immediate impact. As former U.S. Supreme Court Justice William Brennan once observed, it is state courts that deal with the day-to-day issues of life, liberty, and property: marriage, divorce, annulment, juveniles, will probate, contracts, and consumer protection, among other subjects. Fifteen million cases were filed in 1993; one-third were parking violations.

The California judicial system has 194 courts and 1,554 judgeships, although the system is more than just courts and judges. Equally vital are police officers, district attorneys, public defenders, private attorneys, witnesses, trial and grand juries, prison guards and administrators, and probation and parole officers. Each plays an important part in adjudicating conflict, allocating rewards, imposing punishment, and attempting to rehabilitate.

FUNCTIONS OF THE JUDICIAL SYSTEM

Lawsuits filed can be divided into two categories: criminal and civil. In a criminal case, the state prosecutes an individual charged with violating a criminal statute. In a civil suit, the dispute is usually only between two private parties.

Criminal Cases

There are three types of criminal cases: felonies, the most serious; misdemeanors, less serious; and infractions, minor violations. Felonies are crimes such as murder, rape, and armed robbery. Felony convictions may carry a penalty of one or more years in prison, a heavy fine, or both. In felony and serious misdemeanor cases, the defendant must appear before the court and enter a plea (guilty or not guilty). Misdemeanors are crimes such as assault and drunk driving. If found guilty, the defendant may be imprisoned in county jail, fined, or placed on probation. For less serious misdemeanors—an illegal U-turn, for example—the accused may post bail (often by mail) and, failing to appear, automatically plead guilty and forfeit bail as a fine. The least serious crimes are infractions—jaywalking, driving a motor vehicle with a faulty headlight, and illegal parking. Because of the thousands of infractions and backlogged courts, there is no right to a jury trial. Punishment is limited to fines.

Civil Cases

California courts handle more than one million civil cases each year. There are two kinds of civil cases: law and equity. In law cases, the plaintiff sues the defendant for damages—usually a certain amount of money. Such suits may arise from property damage, personal injury, medical malpractice, and failure to meet a contractual obligation. In equity cases, action is requested to prevent harm or irreparable damage—for example, the plaintiff asks the court to issue an injunction to prohibit a defendant from doing something. Equity cases also include probate of wills, administration of trusts, and divorce.

THE HIERARCHY OF CALIFORNIA COURTS

The California court system has four levels: (1) municipal courts, (2) superior courts, (3) district courts of appeal, and (4) the state Supreme Court (see Figure 11.1, page 256). For the most part, municipal and superior courts are trial courts in which cases are first heard. District courts of appeal and the Supreme Court are appeals courts; they mainly hear appeals from trial courts. The California Judicial Council oversees the entire operation of the state's court system.

Municipal Courts

Municipal courts handle the vast majority of court cases in California: about 90 percent, 14 million. These are the courts most of us know well. They process millions of parking citations and traffic violations each year. (Most traffic cases don't go to trial; they're are settled at the bail clerk's window.)

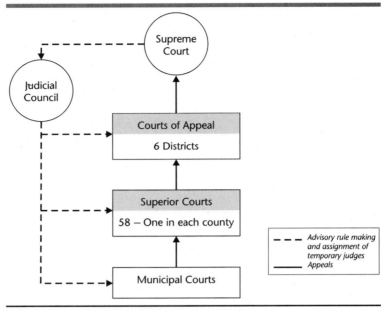

FIGURE 11.1   THE CALIFORNIA COURT SYSTEM

Jurisdiction   Municipal courts hear civil suits of less than $25,000, minor traffic violations, and lesser crimes. Before 1995, rural areas were served by justice courts, but under Proposition 191 (approved by voters in November 1994), these courts were merged into municipal courts. Municipal courts also serve as small claims courts (the so-called people's courts) in cases involving amounts of $5,000 or less. No attorneys are allowed in small claims. The disputes brought by individual citizens or businesses deal with issues such as unpaid bills, defective refrigerators, and improperly serviced cars. Unlike other courts, most small claims do go to trial. Disputants argue their own cases before a judge (there is no jury).

Superior Courts

California has 630 superior court judges. Each county, even sparsely populated ones, has at least one superior court, and large counties are divided into several departments, with judges specializing in various kinds of law (family, juvenile, probate, or criminal). For example, Los Angeles County has more than 200 superior court judges.

Jurisdiction   Superior courts have original jurisdiction over: (1) civil cases involving $15,000 or more; (2) divorce and dissolution of marriage, regardless of amounts involved; (3) probate; (4) major crimes that carry a penalty of one year or more in state prison; and (5) cases involving juveniles. Superior courts also act as courts of appeal for municipal courts, with three-judge panels reviewing misdemeanor or infraction cases.

Of the hundreds of thousands of cases that superior courts hear each year, most involve family law; many others deal with probate and guardianship and civil suits. Many are settled either before trial or after an uncontested trial.

A probation department is part of each county superior court. Probation departments provide background information to the court about criminal defendants, and they take custody of juvenile wards of the court.

Courts of Appeal

California has six district courts of appeal. About 60 percent of their cases are brought on appeals from lower courts and 40 percent start at the court of appeal. Few cases are appealed further. Cases usually concern an interpretation of law, and arguments are presented in written form to three judges (there is no jury).

Supreme Court

The California Supreme Court stands at the top of the state's judicial structure. Only 3,000 to 4,000 cases reach the Court each year. If four of the Court's seven members concur that a case appealed to them has important enough legal or constitutional ramifications to be heard, it is accepted for review. Almost all of the cases heard by the Supreme Court come on appeal. The Court also automatically reviews all death-penalty cases from superior courts. Its written opinions—about 160 per year—are based on interpretations of the state constitution and statutes. The Court's decisions are final, except for appeal to the U.S. Supreme Court (which rarely happens). The chief justice receives $127,104 yearly, and each of the six associate judges receives $121,207 per year. Their offices are in chilly San Francisco, far from the hot political winds of the capitol in Sacramento. However, regular court sessions are also conducted in Sacramento and Los Angeles for a few weeks each year.

Judicial Council

The Judicial Council oversees the state court system. The chief justice of the California Supreme Court chairs the council and appoints fourteen judges to it, the state bar appoints four members, and each house of the legislature appoints one. The council's major responsibility is to study the state's court system and recommend needed constitutional or statutory changes to the legislature.

Courtesy of the California Supreme Court

THE CALIFORNIA SUPREME COURT

SELECTION OF JUDGES

All California judges must be members of the state bar when selected. In addition, they must meet separate standards for different levels of the court system (see Table 11.1).

Judicial Appointments

The governor nominates all judges to the appellate courts (supreme and appeals) and to the trial courts (superior and municipal).

Before designating his judicial choices, the governor is required to consult the Commission on Judicial Nominee Evaluation. This twenty-five-member commission (nineteen elected by the bar and six public members selected by the governor) is charged with determining the fitness of prospective candidates and has ninety days to make its assessment. In evaluating judicial candidates, the commission considers factors such as industry, temperament, honesty, objectivity, community respect, health, and legal experience. Each potential appointee is rated on a four-point scale: exceptionally well qualified, well-qualified, qualified, or unqualified. If the governor should go ahead and nominate a judicial candidate deemed unqualified by the commission, the latter body could make this ranking public. (This would be embarrassing to the governor and the candidate.)

COURT	TERM	QUALIFICATIONS*
Municipal court	6 years	Member of state bar for five years immediately preceding election or appointment
Superior court	6 years	Must be attorney admitted to California bar or have served as a judge of a court of record for 10 years immediately preceding appointment
District court of appeals	12 years	Same as superior court
State Supreme Court	12 years	Same as superior court

*Judges must also be registered voters in order to run for reelection. They are ineligible to practice law or hold other public employment while serving as judges.

TABLE 11.1   QUALIFICATIONS AND TERMS OF CALIFORNIA JUDGES

After the governor nominates candidates to the court of appeals and the Supreme Court, they must be approved by the three-member Commission on Judicial Appointments, which is composed of the chief justice, the attorney general, and the senior presiding justice on the court of appeals. Most nominations create little controversy; the appointments commission almost always approves the governor's judicial choices (only twice in its half-century history has this commission rejected a governor's choice). As noted, the governor also fills vacancies on superior and municipal courts, but these do not require approval by the appointments commission.

California trial court judges serve six-year terms, and appellate judges serve for twelve years. (Judges are not encumbered by term limits.) To serve another term, a judge must run for reelection: statewide for Supreme Court, by district for appeals courts, by county for superior court, and locally for municipal court. Supreme Court judges must stand for confirmation at the next regularly scheduled election after their appointment. If the appointee is filling a vacancy of an appellate judge who has retired or died after, say, five years in office, the replacement would serve the remaining seven years (assuming he or she won confirmation in the first regularly scheduled election after appointment) and could then run for reconfirmation.

Appellate court judges have usually served on a lower court. Sometimes, however, a governor will nominate a candidate to an appellate court who has had little or no prior judicial experience. Governors usually justify such "inexperienced" appointments on the basis that the appointees' social philosophy and personal values are of greater importance than judicial experience.

Before the 1970s, nominations to the Supreme Court and the appeals courts usually emphasized judicial experience, independence, and competence. As partisanship has increased over the past few decades, governors increasingly have nominated judges who share their own values and belong to the same political party. Recent governors have been more sensitive to nominating women and minorities to the judiciary.

Undoubtedly, politics and social circumstances have become an inseparable part of the California judicial process.

Judicial Elections

Once appointed, federal judges remain on the court until they die, resign, or on rare occasions are impeached. They never have to stand for election, and therefore can be more independent. Judges in California must run for reconfirmation to hold their position; they can also be recalled. This makes California judges more accountable to the public than their federal counterparts; by the same token, this helps politicize our courts. Long ago, in an effort to deemphasize partisanship, Progressives established nonpartisan judicial elections. But today parties have the legal right to endorse and are likely to become increasingly enmeshed in confirmation-election politics.

Trial Court Judges As a general rule, most trial court judges seeking reconfirmation are not challenged. More than 95 percent, on the average, face no opposition and are automatically reelected in the general election. In the few contested races, if one candidate receives 50 percent plus one vote in the primary, then that person is elected. Thus, out of hundreds of trial court elections every two years, in only a handful are judge candidates forced into a general election runoff. Except for the few races with challengers, little or no campaign money is spent in the races.

In the few contested races, most voters have little knowledge of the record of their local judge (unless they have had to spend time in court as defendants). Judicial incumbents invariably prevail. They are better known; can list their profession as, for example, superior court judge; can engage in local community charitable activities; can perform marriages for what may be potential voters; and can usually raise more campaign money, if needed, than their opponents. (Most judicial race campaign money comes from local attorneys vitally concerned about the election outcome.) It takes an unusual set of circumstances to defeat an incumbent judge. Over the last several decades, however, in a few instances district attorneys stressing that they would be "tougher on law and order" issues than the incumbent judge have prevailed.

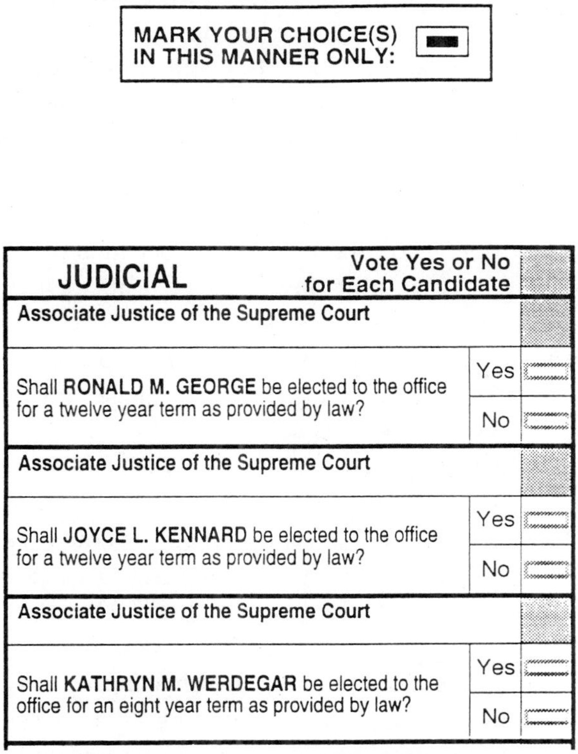

```
┌─────────────────────────────────────────┐
│ MARK YOUR CHOICE(S)   [ ▬ ]              │
│ IN THIS MANNER ONLY:                     │
└─────────────────────────────────────────┘
```

JUDICIAL	Vote Yes or No for Each Candidate	
Associate Justice of the Supreme Court		
Shall **RONALD M. GEORGE** be elected to the office for a twelve year term as provided by law?	Yes	
	No	
Associate Justice of the Supreme Court		
Shall **JOYCE L. KENNARD** be elected to the office for a twelve year term as provided by law?	Yes	
	No	
Associate Justice of the Supreme Court		
Shall **KATHRYN M. WERDEGAR** be elected to the office for an eight year term as provided by law?	Yes	
	No	

FIGURE 11.2 CONFIRMATION ELECTIONS OF CALIFOR-
NIA SUPREME COURT JUDGES, 1994

Appellate Court Judges Supreme and appeals court judges running for reconfirmation do not face actual opponents. Voters are asked in the general election
to vote yes or no to confirm a particular judge (see Figure 11.2).

Before the 1960s, appellate court elections were pro forma: The percentage
of the public voting yes usually ranged from 90 to 95 percent. The California
Supreme Court had a well-deserved national reputation. In the 1960s, however,
the public attitude toward the Court began to change. The civil rights struggle,
mandatory busing, criminals' procedural rights, and reapportionment were issues
that sorely divided Californians, and decisions made by the then-liberal Court
were inevitably unpopular with conservatives. Through the 1960s and 1970s, the
percentage of the public voting no on Supreme Court justices steadily increased.

When Governor Jerry Brown nominated Rose Bird as chief justice of the
California Supreme Court, conservatives were quick to denounce the appointment. Bird's critics argued that she had no previous judicial experience and that

her appointment was designed to appease women's groups. Not unexpectedly, several incumbent justices on the Court were upset that they had not been selected for the post. After her appointment, Bird became a consistent member of the majority liberal bloc at a time when crime was rapidly becoming the number-one state issue. While the public and state legislature were clamoring for tougher penalties—in particular, the death penalty—Bird and the liberal majority tended to emphasize defendants' legal rights, police abuse problems, and search-and-seizure violations. Liberals on the Court also upheld abortion rights and affirmative action while overturning lower court death-penalty recommendations.

In 1978, in Chief Justice Bird's first confirmation election, only 52 percent of voters voted yes; 48 percent voted no. Several other liberal judges up for confirmation in 1978 received only 55 to 60 percent yes votes.

After narrowly winning their confirmation elections, the Court's liberal members were immediately confronted with a host of new controversial issues. In December 1978, a charge was leveled at Bird that she and the court majority had delayed issuing a decision ("use a gun—go to jail") until after the election because it would have been unpopular with voters. The Commission on Judicial Performance (discussed later) investigated the allegation. Although charges of delay were never proved, the Court's once lofty reputation was badly tarnished in the public hearings. In the early 1980s, unhappy Republican legislators and other conservative activists launched a steady stream of initiatives, many of which came under legal challenge and eventually reached the Supreme Court. When Chief Justice Bird and the liberal judges supported Democratic positions, they were attacked for being too partisan. On several occasions, conservative activists began recall drives against Bird, though none ever qualified.

Six of the seven Supreme Court judges were up for reconfirmation in 1986. Three judges—Chief Justice Rose Bird and Justices Cruz Reynoso and Joseph Grodin—were the focal point of right-wing anger. The liberal court trio was blamed for the Court's failure to order executions under the state's death-penalty law, while state public opinion polls showed overwhelming public support for the imposition of this penalty. After Bird's narrow reconfirmation, from 1978 to 1986, not one of 213 convicts on death row was executed, and in only 8 percent of the death-penalty recommendations sent to it from lower courts did the Court affirm this penalty. Frequently, the state Supreme Court reversed lower court death-penalty sentences based on procedural grounds or on the vagueness of the death-penalty initiative law.

The 1986 state election was unprecedented because Supreme Court confirmations were the central issue. Bird's notoriety and fears that her coattails might drag other liberals down to defeat presented Democratic officeholders with a sensitive dilemma. Should they support Bird and the other Court liberals, remain silent, or oppose them? Most Democrats chose the second option, although a few leaders such as Speaker Willie Brown staunchly supported the chief justice.

The campaign waged against Justices Bird, Reynoso, and Grodin resembled partisan officeholder campaigns: professional campaign consultants, fund-raising, television spots, and negative hit pieces—not the more typical genteel judicial contest. Millions of dollars were raised by the campaign committees working against the three liberal judges, and they, in turn, raised lesser but substantial amounts in their own behalf. Chief Justice Bird noted that her efforts to win reelection were complicated by the fact that judicial rules forbade justices from commenting on pending court cases and making promises to voters. Justice Grodin worried that judges had to rely on contributions from lawyers who might, in the future, be appearing before the Court.

For the first time in state history, three justices on the Supreme Court lost their reconfirmation bids. Only 33.8 percent of California voters voted yes on Bird; the margins against Reynoso and Grodin, though not as one-sided, were also decisive.

The defeat of the three liberal judges gave Governor Deukmejian the opportunity to nominate (some might say "pack") the Supreme Court with three new "common sense" conservative judges, while Justice Malcolm Lucas was elevated to chief justice.

After serving only a few years on the Supreme Court, the three replacement judges retired at the end of Governor Deukmejian's second term. This allowed him the opportunity to nominate their replacements: current Justices Joyce Kennard, Armand Arabian, and Melvin Baxter, his former appointments secretary. Governor Wilson has since appointed Justices Ronald George and Kathryn Werdegar. Only one of the seven current Supreme Court judges, Judge Stanley Mosk, is not a Deukmejian or Wilson appointee.

Many legal experts were disappointed that the three judges named to replace the liberal threesome retired from the bench so quickly. Such rapid turnover detracts from the Court's reputation, stability, and prestige. The main reasons for their departure were evidently financial: the relatively "low" salary (as compared to top lawyers in the state), the generous retirement benefits for judges with twenty years' experience, the workload strain, the desire to spend more time with their families, and the opportunities to make top salaries with corporate law firms after leaving state service.

The Lucas court has veered away from several Bird court tendencies. It has affirmed nearly all death sentences (from 1987 to 1993, 84 percent), dismissed "minor" procedural matters in death-penalty cases, and deferred more to the legislature. The Lucas court, however, has not issued as many opinions as its predecessor. The Court has reviewed far fewer cases—80 cases annually compared to about 268 cases annually under Bird—in part, because of the increase in the number of death-penalty affirmances. Interestingly, on one occasion the mainly Deukmejian-appointed Court rejected Deukmejian's legal argument that Dan Lungren, now attorney general, should be confirmed for state treasurer because he had won approval in at least one house of the state legislature. The Court contended the constitution required both houses' approval. The current Court tends to be sympathetic to popularly approved initiatives—for example, the conservative Proposition 140 for term limits and the liberal Proposition 103 for auto-insurance rates. Initially, it appeared that the Court would be tougher in enforcing the single-subject rule for initiatives. Proposition 105 of November 1988 dealt with a variety of consumer-information subjects. Although voters approved it, the Court upheld a court of appeals ruling striking it down as a violation of the single-subject rule. But a short time later, the Court upheld Wilson's Proposition 165, the budget powers and welfare reduction initiative, as being single-subject.

Liberal critics of the Lucas court argue that it is as biased toward the Republican position as the Bird court was to the Democratic point of view. Upholding Wilson's controversial Proposition 165 as single-subject is one example; refusing to reinstate the campaign spending limits of Proposition 68 after federal courts had declared Proposition 73 unconstitutional is another. The vitriol in the majority's opinion on term limits could not be missed: "Proposition 140 will free the legislative process from the control of entrenched, apathetic veteran incumbents and will allow fresh, creative energies to flourish free of vested, self-serving interests and dynastic legislative bureaucracy." Half-hearted efforts by the legislature to reduce the judiciary's budget by 38 percent (as Proposition 140 had done to the legislature) failed.

In the 1990 general election, five Supreme Court judges were up for confirmation. Unlike 1986, no campaigns were waged for or against any of the judges. Yet in the anti-incumbent, negative mood of the 1990 election, about one-third of the electorate voted against Judges Lucas, Baxter, Kennard, and Panelli, and 44 percent voted against Judge Arabian. One can only assume Arabian's high negative vote was caused by his name: Voters were reacting to Arab terrorism or the invasion of Kuwait (ironically, Judge Arabian's ancestry is not Arab, but Armenian). In 1994, three conservative judges were up for confirmation—Ronald George, Joyce Kennard, and Kathryn Werdegar. There was virtually no controversy in these three low-key confirmation contests, yet approximately 40 percent of the electorate voted no on each judge. According to the authors of *Justice in the Balance, 2020* (p. 83), more than half of all Californians believe state courts are "poor" or only "fair"; 70 percent of African Americans hold this opinion.

Commission on Judicial Performance

The Commission on Judicial Performance reviews the quality and performance of judges after they have been appointed. The commission receives, investigates, and evaluates all complaints (about a thousand a year) against California judges—who have been investigated for making racial slurs, being senile, making obscene phone calls, soliciting prostitutes, and violating conflict-of-interest laws, among other inappropriate actions. Under the terms of recently approved Proposition 190 of November 1994, the commission will be required to open all hearings to the public. Previously, a judge could resign or retire quietly while facing misconduct charges, but no longer. In addition, the commission no longer will recommend disciplinary action to the Supreme Court. The commission will have the power to admonish, censure, or even remove a judge from the bench, but its actions will be reviewed by a tribunal of seven court of appeal judges. Under Proposition 190, the commission has been broadened to eleven members: three judges (one each from the appeals, superior, and municipal courts) appointed by the Supreme Court, two lawyers appointed by the state bar, and six citizens (two appointed by the governor, two by the Senate Rules Committee, and two by the speaker). Commission members may serve a maximum of two four-year terms.

ATTORNEYS

No one may practice law in California without being admitted to the state bar. The bar derives its authority from the state constitution, which gives it the power to set ethical standards and to admit to practice, discipline, and expel attorneys. Being admitted to practice entails passing a bar-administered examination.

Clearly, there is a growing antilawyer sentiment among the public, and lawyer jokes abound. In the campaigns surrounding the 1986 "deep pockets" initiative (Proposition 51) and the 1988 lawyer and car-insurance initiatives (Propositions 100, 101, 103, 104, and 106), attorneys bore the brunt of numerous sharp attacks in the broadcast media. Indeed, in certain parts of rural California, some nonlawyer candidates for the state legislature have been known to boast that they were not attorneys in their campaign appeals to voters. Although the legislature passed legislation to revamp and improve the way the bar disciplines its members in 1989, most observers of the legal scene believe little has changed, saying the bar cannot really do an effective job of policing its own ranks. Most complaints against lawyers by their clients are dismissed.

District Attorneys

The district attorney (D.A.) is the government's prosecuting attorney at the county level. After an arrest is made, this official decides whether to prosecute, change the charge, or drop the case. Given statutory time limits, limited staff, and the backlog of pending cases, the D.A. has to limit the number of cases pursued. In some counties, the D.A. may drop as many as half of all felony cases and prosecute the rest.

Few cases actually go to trial. Usually, the district attorney will reduce the charge in exchange for a guilty plea—commonly called plea bargaining or "copping a plea." The negotiated plea of guilty to a reduced charge is then formally presented to the judge.

Indeed, plea bargaining has increased steadily over the last several decades. According to California Judicial Council data, about 80 percent of criminal cases were plea bargained in the 1970s, 88 percent in the 1980s, and 95 percent in the 1990s.

Defense Attorneys

The California constitution guarantees the accused in a criminal case the right "to appear and defend in person and with counsel." In fact, prosecution may not begin until the defendant has legal counsel. In a few instances, the court may allow individuals to defend themselves without legal counsel, but there is no absolute right to do so. Those with money will hire a private attorney (for example, O. J. Simpson hired a battery of attorneys and other legal experts for his defense team), but the great majority of criminal defendants have limited financial resources and must depend on the public defender or assigned counsel.

The public defender, like the district attorney, is a county employee. The job of the defender is to defend the accused in a criminal case when the defendant cannot afford to hire a private attorney. Because the district attorney usually prosecutes only cases having a good chance of conviction, the public defender, given staff limits, usually tries for reduced charges through plea bargaining. In small counties without a public defender, the court appoints an attorney in private practice to defend the accused. Legal service clinics, such as California Rural Legal Assistance and the Western Center on Law and Poverty, also provide legal representation to the indigent.

Cartoon by Robert Minter

"Would you like to write out the ticket?"

POLICE

The police officer is another important figure in the criminal justice system. Besides law enforcement, today's police officers are involved in a broad range of social and personal problems, including family fights, runaway children, neighborhood disputes, enforcement of racial integration, crowd control at demonstrations and marches, and keeping the peace at athletic events. But more time is consumed by automobile-related activities, including traffic control, parking, and accident investigation, than any other item.

Under the California constitution, law enforcement is a local function. Each California county has an elected sheriff responsible for law enforcement within unincorporated areas.

The California Highway Patrol patrols our state freeways, and unincorporated areas are protected by the county sheriff's office. However, the bulk of police work is done by city departments, because most Californians live in cities. City departments are headed by chiefs who are usually appointed by the city manager. Problems facing city police departments vary widely. Police departments in major cities such as Los Angeles and San Francisco often deal with serious crimes, including murder, arson, and armed robbery. These days small cities also face these same crimes, just less frequently. In 1992, the Los Angeles Police Department was hit with a major scandal: A private citizen videotaped a brutal police beating of African American suspect Rodney King, who was stopped on suspicion of drunk driving. After an all-white suburban Los Angeles jury acquitted the white police officers of any wrongdoing in May 1992, the worst urban riot in U.S. history engulfed Los Angeles. King later was awarded millions of dollars from Los Angeles in a lawsuit he filed against the city.

CITIZEN PARTICIPATION

Private citizens also play a role in the state's judicial system—as witnesses and as members of trial or grand juries.

Trial Juries

Juries are used only in the trial courts. As noted, most cases do not go to trial but are settled by plea bargaining.

All California citizens are required to serve on a trial jury if called. Only a few individuals are automatically excused from serving: police officers, ex-felons, and some government employees. Even a governor is required to serve if called. This happened to Governor Jerry Brown. (But only some 20 percent of adult Californians have ever served on a jury or acted as witnesses in a trial, according to the authors of *Justice in the Balance, 2020* [p. 84].)

Most counties use lists of registered voters to draw names of potential jurors, but counties are increasingly using lists of licensed drivers. This is designed to produce juries that are more representative of the people living in a community (and to avoid discouraging people from registering to vote). Under new legislation signed in 1994 by Governor Wilson, it is a misdemeanor (punishable by six months in jail and a $1,000 fine) for jurors or witnesses to sell their stories to media before a trial has ended. This new law was rushed through in the wake of money-making by jurors and witnesses in the Menendez brothers and O. J. Simpson trials. Some potential jurors in the O. J. Simpson trial seemed eager to serve and were willing to be sequestered for six months or longer in order to have a front-row seat at this highly publicized trial. In highly publicized trials, civic duty for some potential jurors may be a form of voyeurism and instant fame.

Grand Juries

Every county has a grand jury, which usually consists of nineteen citizens selected by the county's superior court judges. Grand jurors serve one-year terms, and only rarely are they appointed to a second consecutive term. Grand jurors are the county's "watchdogs." They spend much of their time investigating the conduct and operation of local government agencies, issuing reports, and proposing recommendations for reform. Only occasionally do grand juries indict.

Witnesses

All parties to a trial—plaintiffs and defendants—have a constitutional right to present witnesses in their behalf. In fact, the court has the authority to compel people to testify (except against themselves).

RIGHTS OF THE ACCUSED

Once a person has been charged with a crime, his or her first contact with the legal system is usually arrest by a police officer. At the time of arrest, police are required to inform the suspect that he or she has the right to remain silent and the right to an attorney. Suspects also have the right to know the charges under which they are arrested. After booking, the suspect is allowed one phone call to an attorney, friend, relative, or bail bondsman.

Before trial, the suspect is brought before the court—usually a municipal judge—and arraigned. At arraignment, the judge formally notifies the suspect of the charge and his or her legal rights, sets a date for a preliminary hearing, and establishes bail. (Bail is not allowed for those charged with capital offenses, violent felonies, and felony sexual assaults.) At the preliminary hearing, the prosecution presents what it hopes will be a sufficient case to have the judge order the defendant to be tried, but they usually save much for the trial. At the trial a judge or jury determines guilt or innocence.

Those under 18 are treated differently than adults in our legal system under the concept that juveniles are not responsible for themselves. Typically, the juvenile's case is heard in juvenile court. The juvenile criminal becomes a ward of the court, which attempts to isolate him or her from the conditions that contributed to the problem. Juveniles are not punished by terms in jail or prison. They may be housed in a detention facility (separate from adult prisoners), placed under probation, or put into some form of counseling program. The difference is that in criminal cases involving an adult, the court acts to protect society, whereas in cases involving a juvenile, the court acts to protect the juvenile as well as society. However, given the number of violent crimes committed by very young defendants, there is growing sentiment to try these youngsters as adults.

PENALTIES, CORRECTIONS, REHABILITATION, AND DAMAGES

Courts are involved in determining guilt (criminal cases) or liability (civil cases). Following a criminal trial, the court begins the penalty phase of proceedings. In a civil suit, the court determines the dollar amount of the settlement damages.

Determining Penalty

Criminal Following conviction, the court requests that the county probation department recommend a suitable sentence. The district attorney and defense attorney also make recommendations. In imposing sentence, the judge weighs several factors: What are the statutory penalties? How severe was the crime? What are the circumstances surrounding the crime? Does the defendant have a prior record? The defendant's age, mental competence, and community status are also considered. Increasingly, victims, families, and loved ones of victims are demanding to be part of the legal equation. The 1982 Victims' Bill of Rights Initiative and the 1990 Crime Victims Justice Reform Act are examples.

Up to 1977, California operated under an "indeterminate sentence" provision. The judge would remand the convicted defendant to the California Adult Authority for an indeterminate period of time (one to ten years, for example). Felons were to be incarcerated until, in the judgment of the parole board, they were rehabilitated and ready to rejoin society. While the goal of the indeterminate sentence was rehabilitation, few prisoners were rehabilitated.

Since 1977, California has operated under a Uniform Determinate Sentencing Act, which provides that three specific periods of time may be imposed in sentencing for a specific crime. For example, a person convicted of robbery may receive a minimum sentence (three years), a medium sentence (four years), or the maximum sentence (five years). The circumstances of the crime must be considered in adding to the basic sentence imposed. However, even under the Uniform Act, judicial discretion remains important in fine-tuning sentences to fit individual circumstances. Judicial discretion will be even more circumscribed if a defendant is convicted of a third felony. Recently, several judges have refused to impose the "three strikes" penalty for lawbreakers facing 25 years to life for committing a minor felony such as shoplifting for their third offense. These judges argue the law violates the constitutional prohibition on cruel and unusual punishment. This issue is likely to be appealed soon to the state Supreme Court.

Civil After determination of liability in a civil suit, the court (or jury) may award damages. The amount may simply be that needed to repair an automobile or for doctors' fees. Such an amount is easy to calculate. But if the award is for loss of a leg, an eye, or a life, what is the correct amount? How much should be awarded for pain and suffering? Most civil suits, in fact, are settled out of court.

Imposing Penalty

Probation Rather than fill prisons, judges sometimes place a convicted person on probation (particularly first-time offenders). Often an individual will be given a sentence of time to be served in jail, with two-thirds of it on probation. Failure to meet the requirements of probation can lead to a return to jail.

Incarceration Each county jail is run by a sheriff. County jails hold two types of prisoners: (1) persons held for trial who have been denied bail, cannot make bail, or do not qualify for release on their own recognizance; and (2) persons convicted of lesser crimes.

State institutions hold prisoners convicted of more serious crimes—homicide, assault, rape, and robbery. More than 60 percent of the prison population has committed a violent crime. Most of these prisoners are male (94 percent), young, and have minimal education, and many are minority ethnic group members. Today, the state prison population is largely made up of "repeaters"; only 18 percent have never been in a prison or jail before. By 2003, under the new "three strikes" and other sentence-lengthening laws, there will be an estimated 360,000 prisoners locked up in California (each prisoner costs the state about $20,525 a year) in the dozens of new prisons that will have to be constructed. Superintendent of Instruction candidate Delaine Eastin in 1994 complained bitterly that money that should go for schools was being siphoned into prisons in what she referred to as, "Cadillac prisons and jalopy schools." Drug convictions account for much of the crime increase in the state in the 1980s and 1990s.

Parole Under law, after serving two-thirds of a sentence, a prisoner is eligible for parole. Parole for each eligible inmate is considered once a year by the California Adult Authority, and it can be granted on the basis of the inmate's behavior and prior record.

Juveniles After a hearing, juveniles may be placed on probation, placed in custody of the county, or sent to the California Youth Authority (away from adult prisoners).

Rehabilitation Recidivism rates remain high in California. Unfortunately, prisons and jails are fine places for young criminals to hone their skills.

COURTS AND POLICY MAKING

Theoretically, courts are not supposed to make policy. Within the American government framework, the argument goes, legislatures make policy, executives administer policy, and courts ensure that everything is done according to the laws and constitution, but this latter function inevitably leads to the court's role as policy maker.

Judicial policy making occurs when judges are asked to resolve a conflict between two laws or between a law and a constitutional provision. Policy is also made when courts interpret a law or constitutional provision. Frequently, legislators will enact a law in general terms, doing little more than stating their legislative intent. Thus, courts become involved inevitably in making policy.

In fact, appellate courts and the state Supreme Court were established to resolve conflicts between laws and the constitution. A state Supreme Court has the constitutional authority to significantly interpret or modify U.S. Supreme Court decisions. For example, the state Supreme Court in 1975 significantly restricted police searches of suspects. The U.S. Supreme Court had earlier ruled that full-body searches by police officers of persons arrested for minor offenses did not violate the U.S. Constitution. But the California Supreme Court, citing the California constitution, substantially restricted police searches in the state.

Courts sometimes review the constitutionality of referendums and initiatives. Those who lose in an election may feel that some provisions violate constitutional rights and challenge those features in court (see Chapter 4).

Finally, the courts interpret and make law on occasion. The California Supreme Court ordered the state legislature to equalize public school financing in *Serrano v. Priest*. This decision required the addition of $1 billion to the state's budget in 1972. The court in the 1970s and 1990s had to devise the reapportionment maps for legislative districts after the governor and legislators deadlocked. In July 1990, after weeks of impasse on the budget, a federal judge issued a temporary restraining order to force the governor and other state officials to deliver millions of dollars in welfare payments to recipients of Aid to Families with Dependent Children, even if the budget had not been signed.

Society's controversial issues—abortion, the death penalty, illegal immigrants, and the right to die, for example—reach the courts because those who lose the struggle in other political arenas hope for success there.

REFORMING THE LEGAL SYSTEM

Should California judges have lifetime tenure as do federal judges? Would this make our judges more independent? In a democracy, shouldn't judges be held responsible to the electorate through confirmation elections? Independence and accountability—both laudable objectives of a democratic judicial system—are perhaps irreconcilable. The merits of electing judges continue to be controversial, although unlikely to be changed in the foreseeable future. Another frequently proposed reform would be to have nominees to the appeals court and the Supreme Court approved by the senate, rather than by the Commission on Judicial Appointments. But this would probably lead to further politicizing of the court by a partisan branch of the legislature.

Sometimes the press reveals facts that a judge believes damages the judicial process. Judges have sometimes demanded that reporters reveal their sources. Newspapers traditionally refuse to reveal them, and reporters at times have been jailed for their refusal to do so. The media argue that the public is best served by providing more, not less, information and that being forced to reveal sources would dry up the information and deprive the public. In 1980, California voters approved a "press shield" constitutional amendment designed to protect confidential sources from judicial inquiry. At the same time, defense attorneys in well-publicized cases are increasingly requesting changes of venue because of the difficulty of empaneling an impartial jury after pretrial media coverage in the community.

Another major problem plaguing courts is the civil and criminal case backlog. Delay in hearing cases has been steadily increasing. The wait to have a civil case tried is more than five years in some counties.

In 1990, voters approved the "speedy trial" initiative, Proposition 115, jointly authored by prosecutors around the state and strongly backed by Governor Wilson. Among the reforms: (1) Allow police officers to testify at preliminary hearings about statements given by witnesses and victims; (2) permit judges, rather than lawyers, to pick juries; and (3) force court-appointed defense lawyers to prepare their cases for trial within sixty days. However, a unanimous state Supreme Court ruled major sections of the initiative unconstitutional. In its ruling, the Court declared that Proposition 115 was such a massive change of constitutional law that it amounted to constitutional revision rather than amendment. Such revision, the Court argued, can only come through a constitutional convention.

Another critical issue: As noted, California has a racially diverse population, but these dimensions are not reflected in the state's judiciary. According to the authors of *Justice in the Balance, 2020* (p. 75), only 5 percent of judges are African American, 5 percent are Latino, and 3 percent are Asian; a single judge is Native American. Yet young male Latinos and African Americans constitute a sizable part of the prison population. For example, African Americans account for 7 percent of the state population but 34 percent of the state's prison population.

Concerns have also been raised about the length of trials because of various court delays. For example, the trial of staff members of the Virginia McMartin Manhattan Beach Nursery School for allegedly sexually abusing their students took nearly three years to complete, and one staff member faced an additional two years of trial.

Because California criminal defendants have a constitutional right to a trial within sixty days, civil cases tend to be pushed further back on the court calendar.

One promising way out of civil case impasse is a new rent-a-judge option. Thus, in 1989, when actress Valerie Harper sued Lorimar Productions for replacing her on an NBC sitcom, both sides jointly agreed to hire and pay (at $500 an hour) a retired judge to hear the case. Critics complain that under this format only the wealthy will be able to obtain speedy justice.

Given the current number of courtrooms, judges, and clerks, plea bargaining is a necessity. If every criminal case went to trial, the state would need more than twice as many judges, courtrooms, and so on. Few people are willing to support such a costly expansion of the court system. At the same time, however, many feel that the accused should be tried for the crime committed and not be allowed to plead guilty to a lesser charge.

Several major reforms offer potential for improvement of the justice system. The use of videotaped testimony by witnesses unable to appear in court physically, or for young children who might be intimidated as witnesses, has sometimes been used. A much larger issue is the admissibility of evidence obtained illegally in violation of "the right of the people to be secure in their persons, houses . . . against unreasonable seizures and searches." California courts lean toward strict enforcement of the exclusionary rule, which makes evidence so obtained inadmissible in court. And now DNA evidence is becoming increasingly critical.

Californians seem increasingly inclined to settle disputes in court. It may be that the mobile, impersonal, urban lifestyle in California has eroded the influence of community, family, and church. Lacking the traditional informal methods of settling differences, people turn to the formal methods: civil suits.

Finally, over the last several decades, the state's prison population has grown dramatically, and new tougher sentencing laws further exacerbate this situation. Many billions of dollars will be spent on prisons, new prison construction, and correctional officers' salaries in the foreseeable future, further draining state budget resources.

SUMMARY

In this chapter, we have looked at the various elements of the California judicial system. First, it is not so much a system as it is many governmental agencies functioning in the same area. Second, there is continuing debate and controversy over how judges are selected, elected, and kept accountable. Third, other links in the justice system—the police, lawyers, prosecutors—are targets for new reforms. And, fourth, because of new sentencing laws, more people will be going to jail for longer periods of time. Costs of implementing these new "get tough on crime" sentencing laws are staggering.

REFERENCES

Bell, Charles G., and Charles M. Price. "Running for Judge in California . . ." *California Data Brief.* Berkeley: University of California Institute of Governmental Studies, 1983.

Cochran, Dana. "Paying for Judicial Races." *California Journal* 12 (1981), pp. 219–220.

Culver, John H. "What's Happened Since the Coup: The Post-Bird Supreme Court in California." Paper presented at the 1993 Annual Meeting of the Western Political Science Association Meeting in Pasadena, California (March 18–20).

Cuno, Alice. "The Expanding Role of the Judicial Performance Commission." *California Journal* 14 (1983), pp. 237– 239.

Egelko, Robert. "The Revolving Door." *California Journal* 21 (1990), pp. 347–354.

———. "The Low-Profile Court." *California Journal* 25 (1994), pp. 35–38.

Hall, Michael J., and Jean Guccione. "Bar Discipline for Attorneys Is Still Erratic." *The Sacramento Bee* (August 14, 1994), p. Forum 1.

Jacobs, John. "Prisons, A California Growth Industry." *San Diego Union-Tribune* (August 12, 1994), p.1.

Justice in the Balance, 2020. Report of the Commission on the Future of the California Courts. Sacramento, 1993.

Supreme Court of California: Practices and Procedures. Report of the Judicial Council of California. Sacramento, 1990.

TWELVE

LOCAL GOVERNMENT IN CALIFORNIA:

FISCAL WOES AND ECONOMIC CONSTRAINTS

Local governments provide more services to Californians than any other branch of government—buying a house, paying a parking ticket, riding a city bus, checking out a library book, picnicking in the park, or flushing a toilet, among many other services, are contingent on local government. Much of the money raised by state government is spent at the local level (about 70 percent). Because of the importance of local government and the easy access to local officials, more citizens are involved with it than with state or federal government.

Yet local governments have no inherent constitutional existence; they are creatures of the state. In theory, much of our local government could be abolished, consolidated, or sharply reduced by legislative action. In fact, political pressure from citizens, local elected officials, and many interest groups make it difficult for legislators to directly change the power and scope of local government.

California has four basic types of local government: county, city, school, and special district. These local units provide the day-to-day services for the public.

COUNTY GOVERNMENT

When California entered the Union, it was divided into twenty-seven counties. As population grew, more counties were created, and by 1907 the current fifty-eight had been established (see Figure 12.1).[1] Uniquely, San Francisco is both a city and county. A county is a geographically defined administrative unit

FIGURE 12.1   CALIFORNIA COUNTIES

established by the state to provide services such as police, fire, justice, and land-use planning to citizens living in unincorporated areas and state-mandated services such as welfare, health, and mental health to all county residents. In rural counties, county government provides most essential services; in urban counties, cities provide most of these services to local residents.

County governments thus serve two masters: the state, which established them, and local voters, who elect county officials. The result is powerful political tension; county officials are torn between providing state-mandated programs (sometimes without enough state funding) and serving their local constituents. Finger-pointing is common among California state and local elected officials: Locals blame the state for mandates and insufficient funding, and state officials blame the federal government for not properly compensating California for federal mandates.

Boards of Supervisors

The county board of supervisors combines legislative and executive functions, governing the county as a collective executive. Board members are elected to four-year terms on a nonpartisan basis; some counties have adopted term limits for their supervisors. In the past, most boards were dominated by men with business and law backgrounds; more recently, substantial numbers of women have been elected. Several counties, in fact, have a majority of women on their boards. Smaller rural counties such as Modoc and Alpine pay their supervisors $9,000 to $10,000 annually; larger counties pay much more: Los Angeles County supervisors receive $99,297, and Orange County supervisors $82,056 yearly.

County Administrators

The chief administrative officer is the top appointed official in county governments. In some counties, this official is known as the county executive, and in others as the chief administrative officer. Whatever the title, more than forty counties have someone who manages the day-to-day administration of county services, oversees county operations, and controls expenditures. Those few counties that do not have such an official are generally sparsely populated.

General Law Counties County government in California takes two forms: general law and charter. Forty-six general law counties operate under structures and powers enacted by state government. All general law counties have an elected five-member board of supervisors, a sheriff, district attorney, and assessor. Other county officials can be elected or appointed: tax collector, superintendent of schools, coroner, treasurer, surveyor, and several other minor officials. The supervisors appoint several administrators, including the county's chief administrative officer, director of social services, head of public health, director of the planning department, chief probation officer, and head of public works.

These counties are divided into five geographic districts of equal population, each of which elects a member of the board of supervisors. The board enacts county ordinances (laws), adopts the annual budget, raises local revenue, and is responsible for running county government.

Charter Counties   Twelve counties have adopted their own individual charters (constitutions). With the approval of local voters, charter (or home rule) counties can control their own internal structures. Los Angeles was the first county to adopt a charter (1912). Since then, eleven others have joined the list: Alameda, Butte, Fresno, Placer, Sacramento, San Bernardino, San Diego, San Francisco, San Mateo, Santa Clara, and Tehama.

Charter counties permit more organizational flexibility, have more control over their employees, have more leeway in deciding which local officials should be elected or appointed, and can contract for services more readily than general law counties. Thus, San Francisco has an eleven-member board of supervisors and a mayor. San Francisco and Tehama Counties elect their supervisors "at large" rather than by district.[2] In fact, California's charter counties are not very different from general law counties.

County Programs and Services

Welfare   Regardless of county size, welfare programs are the largest part of the budget—about 40 percent of the total. Aid to Families with Dependent Children (AFDC) is the largest single item, but other forms of public assistance also are important, including aid to the blind and infirm, hospital care for the poor, and general relief for the needy. In recent years, the federal government has provided a significant part of the funding for welfare. And since the passage of Proposition 13, which put limits on property-tax assessments and rates, the state has picked up more of the costs. Nonetheless, counties continue to administer the programs.

Public Safety   The sheriff, courts, jails, flood control, and fire protection combine to form the second largest part of the typical county's budget—about 27 percent. The sheriff, an independently elected public official frequently well known and powerful, heads the county's police department, although the supervisors control the sheriff's budget. The district attorney, public defender, and probation department are also important to public safety (see Chapter 11).

Environmental Protection   Environmental management, including pollution control and land-use planning, are significant county activities. Much of California's population growth has taken place in the suburbs—often in unincorporated areas. County zoning and land-use plans are crucial in preventing the destruction of natural resources, open spaces, and agricultural lands.

Public Health Sanitation, drug- and alcohol-abuse programs, mental health, and restaurant inspection are important county jobs. Vector control—keeping the community safe from rats and rabid animals—is another important duty.

Recreation Parks and recreation are another county responsibility. These are particularly important in urban counties, where crowded living conditions place a premium on open space.

Roads Road construction and maintenance are other important county activities.

Selected Problems

In recent years, California counties have had increasing difficulty in meeting citizens' needs. The reasons are many. First, many problems that counties face originate outside their boundaries and cannot be solved by individual counties. For example, counties have little influence over air and water pollution, poverty, immigration, and unemployment.

Second, state–county fiscal relations were fundamentally altered by Proposition 13 in 1978. Before Proposition 13 was approved, counties derived much of their operating budget from property taxes. Since 1979, the average county's revenues have been reduced by about 20 percent, and the state has become the major dispenser of funds to local government. State bailout funds cushioned the drop in revenues in the early years, but these funds were used up long ago. Along with increased state aid has come increased state control. Counties have been hit far harder by Proposition 13 than have cities, because cities have revenue sources other than property taxes.

Counties' fiscal problems became worse in the early 1990s when the state's own budget problems persuaded Governor Wilson and the legislature to shift property-tax revenues away from local governments to schools. Counties suffered the biggest losses. This additional pressure squeezed county budgets, leading supervisors in Butte and Lassen Counties to threaten bankruptcy. To avoid catastrophe, the Wilson administration resorted to special relief measures, particularly for rural counties. Indicative of this northern rural anger, there was overwhelming voter support to split the state in the various referendums conducted in northern rural counties in 1992. County officials and voters in these northern rural counties believe that California government is tilted to meeting urban needs. Currently, Orange County, once one of the wealthiest and still most staunchly conservative counties in the nation, is in dire economic straits. Risky investment practices by county Treasurer Robert Citron in the derivatives market led to a loss of some $2.02 billion in county funds. County securities were used as short-term collateral on the assumption that interest rates would go down. Unfortunately for the county, interest rates went up. Citron has resigned, and new officials have been brought in to deal with the largest financial disaster that any county in the nation has ever faced.

Third, there are so many elected county officials (on the average seven or eight) that responsibility and authority become scattered. Voters seldom know who is in charge.

Fourth, in the larger counties, supervisorial districts have too many citizens to permit meaningful representation. In Los Angeles County, the average district has 1.8 million residents (about three times as large as a congressional district). In Orange County, the average is 519,000.

Fifth, no county executive is comparable to a governor or mayor, and no one has a veto. Thus, there are fewer checks and balances in county government.

Sixth, in many counties, expanding cities eager to annex a shopping mall or urban areas wanting to incorporate into a new city have battled with county governments over their attempt to change their status. As cities annex shopping malls or car dealerships and as areas incorporate, the amount of revenues flowing into county coffers declines. Counties and cities have fought bitter jurisdictional battles in many parts of the state.

Seventh, as California's population mushrooms, counties struggle with more waste, crowded schools, traffic congestion, crime and drugs, and air and water pollution. Some counties have adopted measures to try to manage growth and preserve agricultural land. Sometimes, when local leaders fail to provide leadership on this subject, citizen groups have promoted local initiatives to slow growth—winning in some localities and losing in others.

Eighth, county boundaries are based on nineteenth-century politics and have little meaning in the contemporary setting. Los Angeles County has more than 8 million residents; Alpine, 1,100. San Bernardino County comprises 20,000 square miles; San Francisco, 49. Counties have different problems; it's difficult for the County Supervisors Association to reflect the views of all of the counties in their lobbying effort at the capitol.

CITY GOVERNMENT

California's oldest cities were established during the Spanish era—San Diego in 1769, Monterey in 1770, San Francisco in 1776, and Los Angeles in 1781. Today, some 470 cities, ranging from Vernon (population 80) to Los Angeles (population 3.6 million), provide a wide variety of services to their residents. Approximately 90 percent of Californians live in cities.

Unlike counties, cities are not automatically created by the state. Any group of residents that decides county services do not meet their needs can (with a few restrictions) form a city. As California has grown, so has the number of cities.

Most new cities incorporate for two reasons: to control land-use decisions and to capture local revenue. Unincorporated areas become cities to avoid county supervisors' development choices. This desire for land use is linked to residents' interest in keeping local revenue in their community and for their local priorities. Sometimes citizens living in unincorporated areas of counties become dissatisfied with county sheriff's officials or the slow response times of fire personnel in responding to emergencies and decide to become a city. Some cities incorporate to provide tax shelters to local businesses and to protect them from regulations that would have been imposed if neighboring cities had annexed them—Vernon, Commerce, Industry, Sand City, and Emeryville, for example. Bradbury and Del Rey Oaks incorporated to protect exclusive residential neighborhoods.

Sometimes cities are formed to ensure greater local political control to protect residents from being "swallowed up" by larger neighboring cities. And sometimes cities are formed as a matter of local pride and identity. West Hollywood has a large homosexual population and a gay majority on its city council. And Latino activists have repeatedly tried to form a city in East Los Angeles that would be more responsive to their social and cultural needs.

Many cities have been formed as a result of suburban migration—people moving from major cities to the suburbs surrounding them. Those leaving often complain about the dirt, noise, racial tension, and crime rates of central cities; many are looking for more room and privacy. New cities also have been springing up in rural and low-density urban fringe areas, and some cities have experienced incredible rates of growth in the 1990s (see Table 12.1).

Proposition 13 seems to have accelerated the formation of new cities. Cities have greater tax resources than counties. By incorporating, residents of a particular area can gain access to more tax revenues and thereby provide more governmental services for local residents.

City Councils

Every city has a city council (usually numbering five to seven members) elected on a nonpartisan basis. The mayor, the city's top executive, is elected in most cities by councilmembers to a one-year term, primarily as a presiding officer. However, in some of the largest cities, this officer is elected directly and is not a member of the council. Any citizen 18 years of age or older and registered to vote in the city may run. Usually, the business community is well represented on city councils—they know one another and contribute to the campaigns of business-

CITIES UNDER 50,000 POPULATION		CITIES OVER 50,000 POPULATION	
CITY	% GROWTH 1993–94	CITY	% GROWTH 1993–94
1. Adelanto	18.8	1. Palmdale	9.5
2. Maricopa	16.5	2. Clovis	5.9
3. Lathrop	13.1	3. Victorville	5.9
4. Coronado	12.6	4. Roseville	4.6
5. Twenty-Nine Palms	12.5	5. Santa Clarita	4.0
6. Imperial	11.9	6. Salinas	3.7
7. Murrieta	9.0	7. California City	3.4
8. San Jacinto	8.6	8. Laguna Niguel	2.9
9. Brentwood	8.3	9. Irvine	2.8
10. Temecula	8.2	10. Mission Viejo	2.5

TABLE 12.1   FASTEST-GROWING SMALL AND LARGE CITIES IN CALIFORNIA, 1993–1994
Source: California Department of Finance, Population Research Unit, Report 94-E-1, 1994.

oriented candidates. In most cities, councilmembers receive only a modest stipend, but most spend many hours per week on council and committee work and community activity. This is a high-burnout position.

To increase turnout for low-profile local elections, cities and counties now time their elections to coincide with state elections in June and November. Although turnout is enhanced, it does add to the number of voting decisions a voter must make.

Most cities elect councilmembers from "at large" districts (i.e., candidates seek votes throughout the entire city). This tends to favor candidates from the local elite. A few large cities elect by district. Los Angeles, Sacramento, and San Jose are examples. Their legislative bodies tend to be more representative of all people in their city. At-large elections are an advantage for the business community and the white middle class, but they favor any group that is organized and politically motivated. Thus, public employees tend to have strong voices in local government. Gays have considerable power in San Francisco, and students wield influence in some university towns.

Local party organizations can endorse candidates, and some office seekers place their literature at particular party headquarters. While candidates do not hide their political orientations, most voters are usually unaware of them.

Interest groups operate at the local level just as they do at the state and national levels. Not surprisingly, lobbying is more casual—a few homeowners meeting with a member of the city council to discuss a traffic problem, for example. Public employee and property-owner groups—such as real estate brokers, developers, construction businesses, labor unions, the Chamber of Commerce, PTA, Rotary, and Kiwanis—are often involved in local issues.

City Managers

Many California cities have a city manager who is hired and can be fired by the council. The manager is a professional who carries out the council's policies, including preparing the budget. The manager also hires most city department heads. The city manager concept was promoted by Progressives early this century to have local government be less political, more professional, and more business-like. Given that city council turnover is fairly rapid, a long-serving manager can exert great influence over the council. Some smaller cities appoint a city administrator who tends to the municipal business but has fewer powers than a manager.

General Law Cities   About four-fifths of California cities operate under the state's general laws. Once incorporated, they have authority to provide a wide range of services. Currently, state law requires a minimum of 500 residents to form a city or a resolution to the board of supervisors requesting such an action. After the proposal has been approved by the Local Agency Formation Commission (LAFCO), elections are held in the area to determine whether local residents want to incorporate.

Charter Cities   California has nearly ninety charter cities. Almost all of the state's major cities, and many others with more than 100,000 population, operate under charters.

Charter cities are formed in much the same way as general law cities—by petition and election. Charters can be amended by the city's voters. One of the strongest arguments for charters is that they allow for more flexibility. For example, Los Angeles has a city council of fifteen members elected by district and a mayor elected at large. Santa Ana, a medium-sized city in Orange County, has a city council of seven members, nominated by wards but elected at large.

Although most charter cities retain the council–manager form, some have established a strong mayor form. As a rule, larger cities elect councilmembers by district and their mayors at large. Thus, in these cities, the mayor is not a member of the council. Independently elected mayors have substantially more administrative and budgetary authority than the more "ceremonial" mayors of general law cities. Governor Pete Wilson, former mayor of San Diego, and U.S. Senator Dianne Feinstein, former mayor of San Francisco, used these local offices to their advantage in promoting their statewide political ambitions.

City Programs and Services

Public Safety   Typically, public safety is the largest single item in a city budget (about 25 percent is for police and fire services). Police are expected to maintain a community's law and order.

In some large cities, demands for some form of civilian police-review process have been raised. Police departments are often reluctant to investigate or punish officers charged with illegal or unprofessional acts committed in the line of duty. Increased recruitment of minorities, more community policing, and educating police on racial issues and prejudices may provide for a more effective police force. Fire fighting and fire protection also add to public safety costs.

Streets   A not insignificant portion—about one-tenth—of a typical city budget is spent on street construction, maintenance and repair, parking, lighting, and storm drains.

Parks and Recreation   Parks and recreation are another important city service. Because of California's rapid population growth, large communities of tract homes frequently have few parks or community recreation facilities. Inner-city parks are often small and poorly maintained. Culture and leisure services take up nearly 10 percent of cities' budgets.

Redevelopment   Redevelopment has literally changed the way the state looks. By annually diverting more than $1.5 billion in property-tax revenues, community agencies have cleared slums, built new public works, and financed thousands of housing units. City councils run most of the 385 redevelopment agencies, but a growing number of counties have started their own.

Utilities and Transportation   Many California cities provide water and electricity to their residents. San Francisco brings water from the Sierras through the Hetch Hetchy Aqueduct. Most major cities also provide airport facilities. A bus or streetcar system is often provided either by a city or jointly with other cities in regional transportation districts.

Land Use, Planning, and Development   One of the most controversial functions of cities is the control of land use, planning, and development. Though not a significant budget item, it is important to a city's quality of life.

One major feature of a land-use and planning policy in cities is growth management. Limiting growth has become a major policy issue in many communities—usually affluent communities. Although growth brings new jobs and a larger tax base, it also brings increased demands for tax-supported services.

Proposition 13's reduction of property-tax revenues has made land development more expensive and less useful for many cities.

Another set of planning questions involves building and zoning policy. How large should residential lots be? What is the best mix of single-unit dwellings and apartment houses? How wide should streets be, and how should the city control traffic flow? Where should shopping centers and commercial and industrial facilities be located?

Another set of land-use and planning problems emerges as a city ages and begins to decline. How can a city, with limited financial resources, attract investment capital into its inner core to restore blighted areas? How can the city facilitate construction of affordable housing? Often, these questions are closely related to problems of job opportunities, new industry, and public transportation.

Cities have considerable power over land use. Under California law, each city (and county) is required to have a long-range use plan. Zoning must conform to the plan according to type of use—single- or multiple-unit housing, commercial, industrial, light or heavy manufacturing, and so on. But as population patterns change and people's needs change, zoning patterns may also have to change.

Selected Problems

Like counties, California cities seem to be increasingly burdened with formidable problems. Typically, many of these problems originate beyond the city's geographic boundaries. Smog, transportation, land use, and crime are not localized within cities. A whole range of economic problems—inflation, unemployment, housing, and tax resources—are national problems.

Proposition 13 complicated the problems of counties and cities. Proposition 62, the 1986 Jarvis initiative designed to close "loopholes" opened through court interpretation of Proposition 13, further compounds these problems because tax increases must be approved by two-thirds of voters. Many cities have become adept at raising various fees to survive financially in the post–Proposition 13 era.

SCHOOL DISTRICTS

Public education in California has historically been a local activity. More than 1,000 local school districts, 58 county offices of education, 71 community college districts, and 107 community colleges serve 5 million young Californians (to age 18) and 3 million adults, at an annual cost to taxpayers of about $30 billion. Public education is clearly a major part of local governmental activity in the Golden State.

School Boards

Most public school districts are governed by a school board, its five members elected at large on a nonpartisan basis. School board members are part-time officials. They usually meet once or twice a month.

Board members are not professional educators but interested members of the community. School boards set policy but do not attempt to become involved in the day-to-day management of district business. School boards hire a district superintendent to manage the district. This official prepares the annual budget, hires and fires school personnel, and prepares policy proposals.

California schools employ thousands of teachers, administrators, teacher aides, pupil service employees, clerks, secretaries, cafeteria workers, bus drivers, gardeners, janitors, maintenance personnel, and others. School districts have more employees than any other type of local government in the state.

The course of instruction offered in the state's schools varies. Each school is required by the state to offer 180 days (36 weeks) of instruction each year. Every child over 6 and under 18 years of age is required to attend. However, a certificate of proficiency is available to those who pass the exam, and they need not continue in school. The certificate is not equivalent to a high school diploma, however.

Public (K–12) schools in California—elementary, junior high, and secondary—select their texts from an approved list evaluated by the Board of Education. The State Board of Education, appointed by the governor, establishes instructional guidelines and requirements for graduation.

California also provides funds for education of the physically handicapped, gifted and talented education (GATE), and driver education in the high schools.

Selected Problems

Educational Reform   From the Sputnik era in the late 1950s, when the United States' supremacy and leadership in scientific research was challenged by the Soviet Union's orbiting of the world's first satellite, through the 1990s, there has been a growing chorus of criticism of public education in California and elsewhere in the nation. Many citizens were convinced that our scientific preeminence had been lost, and they believed that the public school system was the chief culprit.

In 1982, Bill Honig, a wealthy Marin County lawyer turned elementary school teacher, beat incumbent Wilson Riles to become superintendent of instruction of California's public schools. Honig contended that the California public education system confronted a massive crisis: too many students lacking basic skills, too little discipline, too many uninspired instructors, a scandalously high dropout rate, too many teachers trained in teaching skills rather than subject content, low student scores on standardized tests, and inadequate graduation standards. Honig noted that academic courses such as English, algebra, chemistry, French, Western civilization, and U.S. government faced declining student enrollments, while students were opting for less rigorous courses in subjects such as food and cooking, driver education, marriage and adulthood, and health and physical education. Honig was concerned that quality teachers were being lured away from teaching because of the poor pay, while many new teachers had mediocre grades and lacked subject-matter knowledge. Reforms to right these deficiencies were launched in 1983 and seemed to revitalize the system for a time. But in 1992, Superintendent Honig was forced to resign when a grand jury convicted him of steering government business to a foundation run by his wife. His departure, and the inability of the governor and the legislature to agree on a successor, left the position vacant for several years until 1994, when Delaine Eastin was elected. Currently, some Eastern states such as New York and New Jersey spend nearly twice as much per capita on public school children as California does, and the state's public schools now have the highest student-to-teacher ratio in the nation. School libraries, computer equipment, and laboratories in many districts are in woeful condition. Guns on campus, immigrants with English-language deficiencies, discipline problems, racial tensions, and the nation's highest teenage pregnancy rate also afflict the state's public schools.

In 1993, public schools faced a new challenge: the voucher initiative. The measure would have provided cash subsidies to parents so they could choose the school—public or private—their children would attend. Though the measure was defeated, the one-third vote it received indicates deep dissatisfaction with public schools as they are. Clearly, more and more parents are placing their children in private schools or are acting as teachers for their own children in home schooling because of the various problems of the public school system. And this trend could accelerate. A new 1995 National Assessment of Educational Programs report compared public school students in grades 4, 8, and 10 in 39 states. Overall, California students did poorly when compared with students in other states. California 4th graders tied with 4th graders in Louisiana for last place in reading competency (Cohen, p. 1). In one of her first actions, Superintendent Eastin established two task forces to examine how reading and math are being taught and to propose reforms because California students' test scores on these subjects indicate serious problems.

Financing Education Proposition 13 altered the way public school funding was handled. Before 1978, public school funding was mainly accomplished through

Dennis Renault / *The Sacramento Bee*

The Golden State

local property taxes. When Proposition 13 went into effect, however, the amount of money local school officials could generate from property taxes was sharply reduced. To make up for lost local revenues, public schools have had to look to state government for financial help. To ensure the schools' funding, Proposition 98 was placed on the ballot by the education community in 1988. This initiative amended the state constitution to establish a minimum level of financing for school and community college districts, diverting to them a portion of any state revenue in excess of the current constitutional limit on state spending. Nearly 65 percent of funding for K–14 now comes from the state budget (see Figures 12.2 and 12.3, pages 290 and 291). In addition, in its 1971 *Serrano v. Priest* decision, the state Supreme Court ruled unconstitutional the wide disparities between local districts in per-student spending and ordered the state to devise a means to equalize funding.

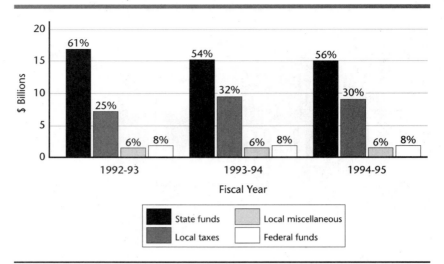

FIGURE 12.2 REVENUE FOR CALIFORNIA'S K–12 PUBLIC SCHOOLS *Source:* Governor's Budget Summary, 1994–1995.

Population Growth and Diversity A rapidly growing student population, needs for new schools and properly maintaining old ones, and demands for higher teacher salaries put public schools under enormous financial pressure. Besides population growth, California schools also face a diverse clientele. Because of continuing legal and illegal immigration, as well as high birthrates among Latinos and Asians, a sizable portion of California youth do not speak English as their native language (23 percent) or have limited English proficiency. This complicates public schools' ability to educate ethnically diverse students. Bilingual instruction is offered in some schools, but the overwhelming support given to Proposition 63 (1984), making English the state's official language, indicates an impatience among some citizens with immigrants who do not speak English. And frequently, because of language difficulties, ethnic minority students are more likely to be dropouts. According to Catlin (1986), 25 percent of Anglo students drop out between the 9th and 12th grades, but 43 percent of Latino students do so. Asians have the lowest dropout rate: 15 percent. In addition, drugs, violence, and gangs further complicate California's educational process. The Proposition 187 (Save Our Schools) initiative of 1994 was aimed partly at the estimated 307,000 children of undocumented workers attending California public schools at a cost of $1.5 billion. Governor Wilson argued that public schools were strapped because of the diversion of funds to illegal residents' children. Proposition 187 passed easily but is now under court challenge.

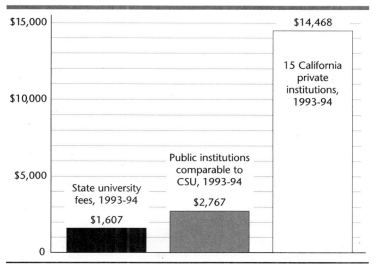

FIGURE 12.3   A COMPARISON OF RESIDENT FEES AND TUITION LEVELS
Source: Governor's Budget Summary, 1994–1995.

School desegregation, a significant concern in the 1960s and 1970s, has been replaced by issues of school quality and finance. Yet the basic housing patterns that led to segregated schools remain, and Proposition 1 of 1979 prohibits mandatory busing as a solution to segregated schools. School hiring practices have been modified more recently by affirmative action regulations that require schools to make an extra effort to hire African Americans and Latinos (see Figure 12.4, page 292). However, the strong likelihood that the civil rights initiative will be on the 1996 ballot and will be approved by voters means that affirmative action could be curtailed in the near future.

Labor Relations   Finally, labor relations are also critical to public schools. Collective bargaining is now available to California public school teachers, and the Public Employment Relations Board attempts to mediate conflict.

SPECIAL DISTRICTS

A special district is a local public agency that provides services within a defined boundary. Less is known about special district government and functions than any other form of local government, yet these special districts provide a wide array of vital services to their residents. Most—84 percent—provide one service; others can provide multiple services. Many are independent districts governed by a board of directors elected by voters of the district; the others (one-third)

Students
5,267,777 children attend California public schools

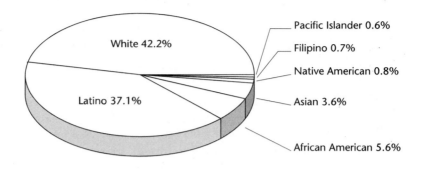

White 42.2%

Latino 37.1%

Pacific Islander 0.6%

Filipino 0.7%

Native American 0.8%

Asian 3.6%

African American 5.6%

Teachers
211,409 teachers work full-time in California schools

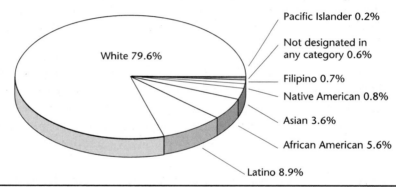

White 79.6%

Pacific Islander 0.2%

Not designated in any category 0.6%

Filipino 0.7%

Native American 0.8%

Asian 3.6%

African American 5.6%

Latino 8.9%

FIGURE 12.4   WHO'S IN CALIFORNIA'S PUBLIC SCHOOLS?   *Source:* California Department of Education.

have governing boards made up of local officials—a city council or board of supervisors, for example.

The 3,400 special districts provide a multitude of services from airports to zoos. The most common are (1) county service areas, (2) fire protection, and (3) community service. The range of services includes highway lighting, cemeteries, libraries, garbage disposal, citrus pest control, hospitals, irrigation, and mosquito abatement. The total cost of special districts in 1993 was $24 billion. To pay for these services, citizens are assessed fees in some districts, or they pay through property-tax assessments. Funding for special districts from state government has steadily declined because of the budget shortfalls. The Special District Augmentation Fund was abolished in the 1993–1994 state budget.

Forming a Special District

The first special district, irrigation, was created in 1887 by San Joaquin farmers seeking a publicly owned water supply that would give them economic independence from private water-supply companies and unpredictable water rates. Local residents and landowners form special districts because they want more services than existing local governments provide; to do so, they file an application with the county's Local Agency Formation Commission (LAFCO). Local governments also can adopt a resolution to establish a special district. The LAFCO then reviews the application and can reject or approve it. If approved, a public hearing is called to discuss the proposal. If public sentiment supports the district, then an election is held, and voters are asked whether they want the district.

Special District Governance

About 66 percent of special districts are independent; they elect boards of directors who are voted on by district residents in very low-profile elections. These boards usually have five to seven members, and incumbents are rarely challenged for reelection. Dependent special districts are governed by a county's board of supervisors or a city council.

Selected Problems   Although they are the most numerous type of local government, special districts face several challenges. First, critics say that the districts' invisibility blocks accountability and may lead to political domination by groups that want to promote their own economic self-interest. They point to the Santa Margarita Water District in Orange County, which allowed district officials to spend public money without permission. Some firefighters' unions heavily influence the directors of the district that employ them. Second, the sheer number of districts, particularly in suburban communities, makes it hard to coordinate public programs. Counties and cities make land-use decisions but special districts can ignore them. Third, the property-tax shifts of the early 1990s distorted districts' budgets. Some districts had to drastically cut programs after the state shifted revenue away from them and to public schools. Pressure is increasing to consolidate or dissolve smaller, inefficient special districts.[3]

Other Forms

LAFCOs are a unique form of governing agency with both planning and regulatory power. They were established by the legislature in 1963 in response to the explosive growth of cities and special districts following World War II (each county has one except San Francisco). LAFCOs discourage urban sprawl, encourage the orderly formation of local government agencies, and promote the creation of efficient urban development patterns. LAFCOs have boards of five to seven members—two from county supervisors, two from local city councils, two from special districts, and one public member chosen by board members.

Municipal Advisory Councils An interesting new form of local government is the Municipal Advisory Council (MAC). Typically, MACs are found in rapidly growing unincorporated suburbs. They are formally established by a county board of supervisors in response to petitions by area residents. They have no independent authority or tax base, but are essentially advisory groups.

Regional Government

Most of California's population lives in urban counties. It is a highly mobile population; people often live in one city and work in another. Many of our social and governmental problems crisscross city and county lines. Smog ignores political boundaries, the need for urban area transportation transcends city and county lines, a metropolitan area's need for water cannot be met by local supplies, and the plight of the homeless extends beyond a particular city's or county's boundaries. Thus, the ability of a single city or county to solve its problems is limited.

For example, when the city–county of San Francisco was first formed in 1853, it was the Bay Area's dominant economic and political center. Today, it is only a small fraction of the area's population, economy, and government. The San Francisco Bay Area includes nine counties, one hundred cities, and hundreds of other local government jurisdictions. Similarly, the number of governmental units in the Los Angeles–Orange–San Bernardino–Riverside area is staggering.

Functions To solve some of their common problems, the legislature has created several regional agencies. Others have been formed by local governments. But any attempt at regional government inevitably means reducing the power of local governments, something they often resist. As a result, regional government has been typically limited to a few functions. Some regional governments serve a research, advisory, or communication function. These are Councils of Governments (COGs). Prime examples are the Association of Bay Area Governments (ABAG), the Southern California Association of Governments (SCAG), and the San Diego Association of Governments (SANDAG).

Another function of regional government is to deliver a specific service or material that individual governments within the region cannot provide. Water and mass rapid transportation are prime examples of such single-service regional governments. The Metropolitan Water District of Southern California (Los Angeles, Orange, Riverside, San Bernardino, and San Diego counties and most of their cities and water districts) constructed a delivery system from the Colorado River, including dams, tunnels, pump stations, artificial lakes, and all of the other components of a complex water-delivery system.

Perhaps the most famous of California's regional governments is the Bay Area Rapid Transit District (BART). This rail transit system has reduced commuter and traffic problems in the Bay Area counties it serves. Los Angeles is now developing its own rail transit system.

A final function of regional government is regulation. Air-quality control is an example. Los Angeles, which has long had a smog problem, could not control the air emissions of industrial plants outside county limits. Thus, the legislature responded by forming the South Coast Air Quality Management District, which comprises Los Angeles, Orange, Riverside, and San Bernardino counties. Similarly, the legislature created the Bay Area Air Pollution Control District to serve the nine Bay Area counties.

Management Regional government in California is usually managed by an appointed board of directors. Appointment is usually by the constituent units—cities, counties, or special districts—of the region served. Each member government gets at least one representative on the board.

LOCAL GOVERNMENT FINANCES
Sources of Revenue

Two features characterize local government revenues: (1) multiple revenue sources and (2) heavy dependence on other governments (state and federal) for a substantial part of their revenues.

Property Taxes What was once local control is now local dependence under Proposition 13's provisions. Moreover, attempts by local governments to impose special taxes must be approved by two-thirds of the electorate. Property-tax revenues were effectively reduced by 57 percent after Proposition 13 took effect. Although the legislature provided bailout funds to local governments in the late 1970s and 1980s, state budget deficits in the 1990s have curtailed this practice. Governor Wilson and the legislature shifted nearly $4 billion from counties, cities, and special districts to K–14 public schools (because of the Proposition 98 requirement).

Shared Revenues Some of the revenues collected by the state, such as sales and fuel taxes, are shared with local government. For example, the state sends more than $3 million yearly in vehicle-license fees to cities and counties.

Dennis Renault / *The Sacramento Bee*

Federal Funds   The federal government provides local governments with funding grants for specific programs. In addition, under block-grant programs, it provides funds that cities and counties may use as they wish. Federal funding has been a significant source for counties, cities, and special districts. Welfare, flood control, highway construction, municipal airports, and harbors are all recipients of federal funding.

Other Sources   Other revenue sources include the fees that cities may charge for permits, fines, and licenses.

Public Employment

Because most public employment is at the local level, the problems and issues of public employment are usually local government problems. These include "contracting out," public employee collective bargaining, and various forms of "agency shop" public-employment contracts. Contracting out—the use of private firms to provide services—has, not unexpectedly, been opposed by public-employee unions throughout the state. Public-employee unions have been successful in securing the right to engage in collective bargaining and agency shop contracts and, in effect, the right to strike.

SUMMARY

California government is largely urban government. More than 5,000 local governments provide services to Californians. Our major social problems—education, welfare, housing, crime, pollution, transportation, and racial and ethnic equality—have to be dealt with on the frontlines by local governments. But local governments are increasingly feeling the pain of Proposition 13 and state cutbacks in funding.

Local government is a jungle of jurisdictions with overlapping authority, complex boundary lines, divided responsibilities, and conflicting powers that are part of the local government scene in the state.

The average urban resident pays taxes to the county, city, unified school district, community college district, and other special districts.

It is not surprising that many citizens are confused. Faced with a problem, where does the citizen go? The problem may overlap from one jurisdiction (e.g., city) to another (e.g., county, planning commission). Because there is no single urban government, local governments can only tackle citizens' problems on a piecemeal basis. But even with the public's skepticism about governmental programs, voters still feel closer to their local governments than they do to Sacramento or Washington, D.C. No matter what the fiscal and political pressures, there will always be a need for local government.

NOTES

1. There have been several abortive attempts to form additional counties during this century.

2. Tehama County elects supervisors at large, and San Francisco County alternated several times in the late 1970s and early 1980s between district and at-large elections.

3. But should the various cities in the Helix Water District (San Diego County) pull out to form their own individual water systems, or should Orinda, Moraga, and Lafayette be required to have their own separate fire departments? No way! Perhaps the problem is the growth of so many new cities.

REFERENCES

Assembly Office of Research. *California 2000: Getting Ahead of the Growth Curve, the Future of Local Government in California.* Sacramento: 1989.

Catlin, Sally. "New Kids in the Classroom." *California Journal* 17 (1986), pp. 189–191.

Christensen, Terry. *Local Politics: Governing at the Crossroads.* Belmont, CA: Wadsworth, 1995.

Cohen, Richard Lee. "Reading Skills Lagging in State and Across the Nation." *Los Angeles Times*, April 28, 1995, p. 1.

Davis, Gray. *Financial Transactions Annual Reports: Cities, Counties, Community Redevelopment Agencies, Special Districts.* Sacramento: State Controller's Office, 1994.

Fourkas, Ted. *Open & Public II: A User's Guide to the Ralph M. Brown Act.* Sacramento: League of California Cities et al., 1994.

Fulton, William. *Guide to California Planning.* Point Arena, CA: Solano Press, 1991.

Manatt, April. *What's So Special About Special Districts?* 2nd ed. Sacramento: Senate Local Government Committee, 1993.

Martis, Nancy H. "The Local Government Lament." *California Journal* 25 (1994), pp. 39–40.

———. "Orange County's Fiasco." *California Journal* 26 (1995), pp. 17–21.

Senate Local Government Committee. *What's So Special About Special Districts?* Monograph, 1993.

Schilling, Elizabeth. "Brown Act Reform." *California Journal* 25 (1994), pp. 41–43.

Scott, Steve. "Pay As You Go: Privatizing California's Public Higher Education System." *California Journal* 25 (1994), pp. 25–29.

Taub, J. S. "COGS." *California Journal* 17 (1986), pp. 551–554.

Waldman, Tom. "Super Government." *California Journal* 21 (1990), pp. 287–290.

INDEX

"This book is a must-read for every pastor and ministry leader who wants their church to exhibit the heart of Jesus. Infused with the grace of the gospel, it brings healing and hope to the hearts of Christ-followers and those we are called to love."

Shayne Wheeler, senior pastor, All Souls Fellowship, author of *The Briarpatch Gospel*

"I have been hoping for a book like *The Recovery-Minded Church*—one that could find the wisdom of recovery and its necessary revelation to all people, and also articulate the hurt of those in recovery addiction as its own particular malady. Jonathan Benz's book provides the roadmap through the wound of addiction into recovery and healing while also making the journey accessible and relatable to all of us.

We all hurt and are wounded. In this book Jonathan bridges the gap between 'addicts' and the rest of us in a way that calls us to the sacred mission of including all God's people in the ministry of the church and finding the golden nuggets of strengths specific to those in addiction recovery. He weaves together his understanding as both provider in recovery and human who clearly understands hurt and healing, along with biblical references to illuminate the sacred path.

This is a guide for professionals in the helping fields and pastoral contexts to understand addiction, understand those who suffer from this wound and connect back with the biblical contexts that call all of us—providers, sufferers, humans—into dynamic relationship with the 'first shall be last and the last shall be first' credo of ministry to all who suffer from addiction."

Teresa B. Pasquale, licensed clinical social worker

"*The Recovery-Minded Church* might be the most timely and important book I will ever recommend. Many of us who struggle with an addiction turn first to our faith communities for help and hope—and too often fail to find it. The powerful insights and gentle truths of this message, if implemented, can transform our churches, save lives and ripple outward to change the world. Bravo!"

Heather Kopp, author of *Sober Mercies*

"*The Recovery-Minded Church* is an invaluable resource for communities seeking to be transformed by the prodigal love of God."

Bryan Dunagan, senior pastor, Highland Park Presbyterian Church

"*The Recovery-Minded Church* is essential reading for every leader who wants their church, ministry or spiritual community to be on the front lines of cultural relevancy and spiritual usefulness. Marked by sound theology, biblical wisdom and practical application, this is a good and necessary book for our time. Please read it, use it and share it with others."
T. C. Ryan, author of *Ashamed No More*

"This is a resource every church needs because no church is exempt from responsibility toward people with addictions. This very practical book will help churches take their rightful places as centers for support, unconditional love and redemption. It's best to approach this resource with humble Christian theology firmly in place, ready to be equipped not just to respond but to engage with people who are just like the rest of us—unrighteous beneficiaries of God's lavish love and grace, ripe for transformation."
Amy Simpson, author of *Troubled Minds*

"If you are a pastor, chances are your formal training did not prepare you to serve those with addictions you meet in your church and your community on a daily basis. Nor did it foster the kind of vulnerability and rigorous honesty that your own ongoing transformation demands. Jonathan Benz and Kristina Robb-Dover offer a challenging, inspiring and eminently practical guide for becoming a 'prodigal church'—a hope-full community where the grace of God brings healing to those of us willing to tell the truth about our addictions, brokenness and sin, as well as a place to celebrate the freedom we have found."
Sean Gladding, author of *The Story of God, the Story of Us* and *Ten*

The
Recovery-Minded
Church

Loving and Ministering to
People with Addiction

JONATHAN BENZ
with KRISTINA ROBB-DOVER

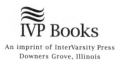

An imprint of InterVarsity Press
Downers Grove, Illinois

InterVarsity Press
P.O. Box 1400, Downers Grove, IL 60515-1426
ivpress.com
email@ivpress.com

InterVarsity Press® is the book-publishing division of InterVarsity Christian Fellowship/USA®, a movement of students and faculty active on campus at hundreds of universities, colleges and schools of nursing in the United States of America, and a member movement of the International Fellowship of Evangelical Students. For information about local and regional activities, visit intervarsity.org.

Scripture quotations, unless otherwise noted, are from the New Revised Standard Version of the Bible, copyright 1989 by the Division of Christian Education of the National Council of the Churches of Christ in the USA. Used by permission. All rights reserved.

While any stories in this book are true, some names and identifying information may have been changed to protect the privacy of individuals.

Cover design: Cindy Kiple
Interior design: Beth McGill
Images: church interior: ©Sean824/iStockphoto
    bronze cross: ©lauchenauer/iStockphoto
    back of man's head: ©DRB Images, LLC/iStockphoto

ISBN 978-0-8308-4125-7 (print)
ISBN 978-0-8308-9939-5 (digital)

Printed in the United States of America ∞

Library of Congress Cataloging-in-Publication Data
Names: Benz, Jonathan, 1970-
Title: The recovery-minded church : loving and ministering to people with
  addiction / Jonathan Benz, with Kristina Robb-Dover.
Description: Downers Grove : InterVarsity Press, 2015. | Includes
  bibliographical references.
Identifiers: LCCN 2015036043 | ISBN 9780830841257 (pbk. : alk. paper)
Subjects: LCSH: Church work with drug addicts. | Church work with alcoholics.
  | Church work with recovering addicts. | Substance abuse--Religious
  aspects--Christianity.
Classification: LCC BV4460.5 .B46 2015 | DDC 259/.429--dc23
LC record available at http://lccn.loc.gov/2015036043

P	20	19	18	17	16	15	14	13	12	11	10	9	8	7	6	5	4	3	2	1
Y	33	32	31	30	29	28	27	26	25	24	23	22	21	20	19	18	17	16		

For every prodigal child headed in the direction of home

*But when he came to himself he said, "How many of my
father's hired hands have bread enough and to spare, but here
I am dying of hunger! I will get up and go to my father, and I will
say to him, 'Father, I have sinned against heaven and before you; I
am no longer worthy to be called your son; treat me like one of
your hired hands.'" So he set off and went to his father.*

LUKE 15:17-20

*To go forth now from all the entanglement that is ours
and yet not ours, that, like the water in an old well,
reflects us in fragments, distorts what we are.*

RAINER MARIA RILKE
"THE DEPARTURE OF THE PRODIGAL SON"

Contents

Introduction

So he set off and went to his father. But while he was still far off, his father saw him and was filled with compassion; he ran and put his arms around him and kissed him. Then the son said to him, "Father, I have sinned against heaven and before you; I am no longer worthy to be called your son." But the father said to his slaves, "Quickly, bring out a robe—the best one—and put it on him; put a ring on his finger and sandals on his feet. And get the fatted calf and kill it, and let us eat and celebrate; for this son of mine was dead and is alive again; he was lost and is found!" And they began to celebrate.

LUKE 15:20-24

THIS BOOK IS MEANT FOR THOSE WHO DREAM of a prodigal future for their church.

But what, you may wonder, is a "prodigal future"?

The story that Jesus tells in the fifteenth chapter of Luke helps to answer this question. The story, best known as "the parable of the prodigal son," is about a younger son who disgraces his father by running away from home and recklessly squandering his whole inheritance on booze and sex.

But the story is also about an older son, who despite fulfilling his duties as the elder child and going through the motions of a morally upright, responsible life, is equally lost and in need of being found by the life-giving grace of an extravagantly generous God.

And the story is most essentially about a prodigal God—a God who will spend all he has to recover lost children and expects nothing in return. This truth is at the heart of the gospel and is central to what Christians call "grace." In his book *The Prodigal God: Recovering the Heart of the Christian Faith*, New York Times best-selling author Tim Keller puts it this way: "If the teaching of Jesus is likened to a lake, this famous Parable of the Prodigal Son would be one of the clearest spots where we can see all the way to the bottom." At the bottom of that lake is a "God of Great Expenditures."[1] A God who greets long-lost children with great big bear hugs and throws lavish parties to welcome them home. A God who is uninhibited in dispensing grace.

As it turns out, both the shiftless younger son who wanders back, tail between the legs, and the responsible older son, who wallows in self-righteousness, depend on that grace. Both of the brothers have taken wrong turns down dead-end streets, and both need their father's gracious redirecting back to where the party is. But the older son doesn't know it quite yet.

The recovery-minded church, in contrast, knows where the party is—and wants to host the party: receiving those on the path to recovery and celebrating their homecomings, giving them a place to call home where they can discover—and recover—their true identity as beloved children of God. Recovery-minded churches are *prodigal* churches (I will use these two terms interchangeably at times): they celebrate God's mission of healing and restoration in this world, because that's what the prodigal God is all about—and because that's where the joy, laughter and life are. So recovery-minded churches are those busy hanging "Welcome Home" signs and stringing up balloons, or manning the grill while picking out dance tunes. They're the communities that wayward children know they can go to and be received with open arms, regardless of where they've been.

So this book is for those who dream of a prodigal future for their church and seek the tools for their own spiritual transformation in the form of vibrant, radically loving relationships with the addicts in their pews and just outside their doors.

In giving you tools for doing this, I want to say what this book will *not* do. It will not give you directions about how to set up an addiction recovery program in your church. The concluding appendix will connect you with helpful resources that can jumpstart you in this endeavor; but the approach here is not programmatically prescriptive or a one-size-fits-all model for doing addiction recovery work. Instead, the insights in this book are meant to jumpstart discernment about what being in relational outreach to addicts might look like in your unique church context; the questions answered here are a way of easing, if not entirely dismantling, the obstacles that rank-and-file churches face in approaching the task of loving and encouraging addicts on the road to recovery. In other words, if you're looking to be in grace-filled, transformational relationships with a greatly overlooked but huge segment of the American population, this book is your toolkit.

The Distant Country of Addiction

Few things better encapsulate the parable of the prodigal son and the general condition of human lostness to which it speaks than the blight of addiction today. In his book *The Return of the Prodigal Son*, author Henri Nouwen writes:

> "Addiction" might be the best word to explain the lostness that
> so deeply permeates society. Our addictions make us cling to

what the world proclaims as the keys to self-fulfillment: accumulation of wealth and power; attainment of status and admiration; lavish consumption of food and drink, and sexual gratification without distinguishing between lust and love. These addictions create expectations that can't but fail to satisfy our deepest needs. As long as we live within the world's delusions, our addictions condemn us to futile quests in "the distant country," leaving us to face an endless series of disillusionments while our sense of self remains unfulfilled. In these days of increasing addictions, we have wandered far away from our Father's home. The addicted life can aptly be designated a life lived in "a distant country." It is from there that our cry for deliverance rises up.[2]

If addiction is that distant country in which many addicts find themselves, then what might "home" be? What if home were *your* church—or if addicts showed up on Sunday morning thinking it was? Would you be ready to receive addicts in your pews? Are you equipped for the task of loving addicts into recovery and throughout that journey? Do you have the necessary tools to help your congregation become a prodigal community that, like the God it worships, will be extravagant in loving children God seeks to restore?

Addiction recovery is more than a referral to the closest AA group. It is a one-of-a-kind opportunity for a whole community of wayward children to be transformed by the grace of a wildly-in-love-with-you God.

> Addiction recovery is more than a referral to the closest AA group. It is a one-of-a-kind opportunity for a whole community of wayward children to be transformed by the grace of a wildly-in-love-with-you God.

I have designed this book as a toolkit to help you encourage, plan for and celebrate the homecomings of recovering addicts, which in this country means finding ways to be in relational outreach to an estimated 30 percent of the population who struggle with some form of addiction. Here is how this staggering estimate was calculated:

- At least 6 percent of Americans struggle with some form of sexual addiction.

- Approximately 10 percent have drug or alcohol addictions.

- Around 7.5 percent exhibit some form of an eating disorder.

- Some 5 percent are compulsive shoppers.

- At least 1 percent are pathological gamblers.

Add these numbers together, and you're in the whereabouts of 30 percent.[3] The estimate is conservative, because many of those struggling with addiction will never report their struggles out of fear or shame, or they will become casualties of their addiction before they can get the help they need.

Social scientist, therapist and founder of *The Daring Way*, Brené Brown, whose TED talks on shame and the power of vulnerability have reached millions of online viewers, describes our plight this way: "We are the most in-debt, obese, addicted and medicated adult cohort in US history."[4]

So the distant country of addiction is vast and maybe not so distant as your church may be inclined to think: it may be as close as your own nose.

What Sets This Book Apart: Your Toolkit

If the story of the prodigal son is ultimately a story about a prodigal God who lavishly forgives detours and wrong turns—a God for whom "recovery" isn't just about getting clean but about finding wholeness, restored relationships and the joy of being truly alive—then churches seeking to know and love this prodigal God need to love and learn from people with addiction and to be part of the beautiful work of restoration that God is doing through faith-based recovery.

This book is the fruit of the conviction that when more and more churches have the information and tools they need to understand addiction and the recovery process, and when more and more churches embrace addicts and families in recovery, and when they peel back the layers of their own hidden addictions, churches will encounter the prodigal God they serve in powerful, transformative ways. And maybe, in the process, God will begin to fill the addiction treatment gap in this country—one addict, one family, one church at a time—and, as those in recovery have come to know, one day at a time. (For more on the nature of the addiction treatment gap, see chapter five.)

This book belongs to that vision and to that prayer, as a go-to manual on faith-based addiction recovery for church leaders and their congregations. In the chapters to come, you'll see answers to some of the questions you yourself have probably asked about addiction and addiction recovery. That's because the questions answered here are ones real church leaders are asking.

I surveyed an ecumenical focus group of one hundred church leaders (both lay and ordained) to discover the biggest obstacles they face in loving and ministering to people with addictions. The results of that survey, shared in the course of this book, may surprise you. Each chapter addresses the very real questions, quandaries and gaps in education or experience among today's church leaders, with biblically grounded insights and practically accessible tips for making your congregation a recovery-friendly community for addicts. The questions at the end of each chapter are intended for small groups, Bible studies, local church book clubs and governing bodies—as a way to live into your shared future as a prodigal church.

The Recovery-Minded Church also presents a challenge—and an invitation. Until now, addiction recovery has remained largely uncharted territory for far too many churches across this country, as results from my survey confirm. Congregations may host Alcoholics Anonymous (AA) and other twelve-step recovery groups in their basements, but beyond that, far too many ministers and laypeople are ill-equipped to know what to do if the same addicts in those basement meetings show up in church on Sunday morning or join a Sunday school class, asking for help in the recovery process. Similarly, seminaries provide limited training, if any, in addiction counseling and recovery. Yet many people struggling with addiction are looking to the church for answers. This book will equip you and your congregation for meeting addicts and their families where they are and journeying with them in their homecomings.

The chapters that follow will lay out a clinically informed, biblical and theological framework for loving the addicts in your midst, along with practical tools and strategies to help you in this endeavor. The chapters in section 1 will outfit you with practical tools for loving the people with addiction in your midst. The chapters in section 2 will equip you with tips and practices for building a recovery-friendly church. The appendix will inform you on various addiction-related offerings, such as Christian treatment programs, recovery groups, websites and suggested readings. The appendix also includes detailed information on the various addictions you may encounter.

My Own Journey with Addicts and Addiction

Growing up in a recovery-friendly home and following in a long line of ministers on both sides of my family, I was probably destined for the work I now do directing faith-based clinical programming in the areas of addiction recovery and mental health.

The story of how I landed in recovery ministry begins with the influence of my father. In the 1980s, my dad, a minister, became friends with a parishioner named Bill. Bill was an old-timer in AA, having remained sober years after his plane was shot down in World War II. Bill took my dad, a nonalcoholic, to his first AA meeting. Soon after, my dad began regularly attending meetings and working the program. He even found a sponsor. My dad realized that AA and twelve-step programs taught lessons applicable to all of us, whether or not we struggle with addiction.

My dad and Bill were soon hosting faith-based AA meetings in our church. As a young teenager, I would go to some of those meetings and hang out with the smokers outside. I distinctly remember that anyone and everyone was welcome and that it was not out of the norm to see more than a hundred people from the community gathering regularly to talk about their recovery from addiction.

Within this context, addicts and alcoholics were not "bad" people or "less than" others; they were my teachers, mentors, friends and family who just happened to suffer from a disease for which they were seeking help. These same relationships not only helped to keep me away from drugs as a teenager and young adult, they also introduced me to a gentler form of Christian ministry birthed out of humility, compassion, historic Christian spirituality and unconditional love.

Following college and a brief stint in teaching, I entered ministry. After completing a master's degree in counseling psychology, I took a job with my church's counseling center. The heavy recovery emphasis and twelve-step approach there shaped my counseling of addicts and people with mental illness from a variety of religious backgrounds.

Since 2008, I have been working again in the behavioral health and substance abuse field, first as a chaplain, then as a certified addictions professional and now as a director of faith-based clinical programming. As program director, I am charged with overseeing the clinical treatment of clients, who are usually struggling with drug or alcohol addictions.

Through my extensive work in the field of faith-based recovery, I have come to believe there is no one-size-fits-all approach for churches seeking to be in relational outreach to people with addictions. For example, choosing the right recovery program to partner with or to send struggling addicts to can depend on your congregational context and the demographics of the people and community you serve. This book stops short of prescribing any one approach or program in Christian recovery over another. (If you're looking for treatment programs and recovery meeting resources in your area, as well as other helpful resources, see the comprehensive list in the appendix.) But my experience in the world of addiction recovery has convinced me of the lifesaving importance both of connecting addicts with supportive faith communities that can provide a spiritual home and of connecting faith communities with the addicts in their midst.

Your Invitation to the Party

Today the God we read about in parables is still running out to greet prodigal children with big bear hugs and a wide-eyed grin. Finding lost people, restoring broken lives, celebrating homecomings—this is what God wants for addicts; these are God's plans for them. And God's ways, in addition to being higher than ours, are often surprising. They might not be safe, predictable or comfortable.

The disease of addiction, for all the pain and damage it causes, is an invitation to see this prodigal God in action. The question is, *will* we? Will we as the church step out of our comfort zones into uncharted territory that will at times be unpredictable and even scary for us? Or will we, like the older son, gloat, sulk and stomp off in

> The disease of addiction, for all the pain and damage it causes, is an invitation to see this prodigal God in action. The question is, *will* we?

resentment? Would we rather be party poopers or partygoers, estranged children or reconciled ones?

The recovering addicts are at the party. They are enjoying a raucous hoopla with their long-lost dad (the prodigal God). They know that nobody sets out to become an addict, which is why grace is an even bigger deal for those who once were lost but now are found (in the words of the old, familiar hymn).

So they're getting down with gusto and moving to the liberating rhythms of God's new life.

They're living in the space of recovery—the now of the celebration, the exhilaration of a resurrected life.

They're experiencing God's grace, and it's better than any cheap thrill or fleeting high.

Want to join them? Then read on.

Discussion Questions

1. Read the parable of the prodigal son in Luke 15. Where do you see yourself and/or your church in the story? Are you the prodigal son or the older brother? Or can you identify more with the father? What new thing might the parable be saying to you personally or to your church in relation to where the life of the party is?

2. Does the term "prodigal church" resonate for you? Why or why not? Does it scare you? Why or why not?

3. What do you make of Brené Brown's conclusion that Americans are "the most in-debt, obese, addicted and medicated adult cohort in US history"? How have you experienced this to be true in your own life? In the lives of those around you? What might it look like for your church to minister more effectively to this population?

Section 1

Tools for Loving
People with Addiction

one

Responding to Addiction

The breaking of so great a thing
should make a greater crack.

William Shakespeare
Antony and Cleopatra

THE FUTURE CAN TIPTOE IN ANY DAY: One morning you're leading worship, and in he walks, clearly high on something. Or you are in the office of the suburban church that you pastor, preparing for Sunday's sermon, and she knocks on your door, asking for advice about her husband's compulsive use of porn. Or your worship leader begins showing up to practice with the smell of liquor on his breath.

Any number of real-life scenarios can propel your congregation into its prodigal future. The question is not whether you will encounter addicted people, but how you will respond when you encounter them. Will you encounter addicts with an effective pastoral response that points them in the direction of recovery—or not?

Chances are that when one of these situations or a variation of them occurs, your first and most pressing question will be "How can I get this person into recovery?" And if you are asking this question, you are not alone. My survey of one hundred church leaders found this question to be the one that most plagues church leaders—next to its corollary, "How do I help an addict stay in recovery?" This chapter offers some answers.

The Essential Prep Work First

Far too often, even the most experienced pastoral caregivers with all the right recovery resources at their fingertips view their main task at this juncture as one of providing one or more referrals, such as to the local AA/NA group or a therapist. And knowing whom to refer to, so that addicts can connect with the right providers who can help, *is* a very important part of the answer.

But too often church leaders' care for addicts *ends* with this referral step. Sometimes the referral can serve as a convenient way to hand off a thorny pastoral problem to the "real pros." Busy pastors already have a multitude of other pressing concerns on their plates, and pastoral dealings with addicts can be messy and inconvenient. Beyond this, a church leader often feels less equipped than a trained clinician to deal with all the issues that might arise, so there is a certain level of comfort in knowing that the matter is now in the hands of a specialist. This feeling is not just understandable but even commendable to a degree. Pastors should not have to be, or expect to be, the experts on every issue that walks through their door, addiction included. Connections with trusted Christian recovery programs in your area, AA groups and therapists are essential, and you may find some in your own congregation.

Still, I want to correct the knee-jerk assumption that loving the addicts in your midst *ends* with a referral to the pros or a twelve-step group. When the homeless stranger on crack sits down in your pew or when a spouse unburdens the secret she has kept hidden all these years or when your worship leader shows up late to practice for the umpteenth time with liquor on his breath, that is actually just the beginning, not the end, of an opportunity to encounter the prodigal

God who loves you beyond your wildest imagination. This critical first encounter with the problem of addiction in your midst can be the start of a life-giving transformation that happens not just in the life of the addict seeking your help but also in the very DNA of your congregation.

Such transformation is not essentially about learning to minister to an at-risk population. At its heart, this process of growing in God's grace is ultimately about tapping into your community's potential to be transformed into prodigal people by the grace of a prodigal God. And this ongoing journey can't be reduced to a quick fix (pun intended) in the form of a referral.

Transformation happens when we see our own crippling brokenness and need for God's grace in the face and story of the addict in front of us. When addicts are not just the heroin pushers or prescription pill junkies "out there," but are in our pews and among us, we are in the right position to begin helping addicts step into recovery. And this identification can't be emphasized enough: my own secret cravings, patterns of self-destructive behavior and unchecked forms of consumption (of money, power, approval—you name it) may not manifest themselves in quite the same way as those of the crack addict in front of me, but they fall within the same realm of human bondage. So getting addicts into recovery means first standing in solidarity with addicts, recognizing that their plight and their stories are hitched to our own and in many ways are similar.

> When addicts are not just the heroin pushers or prescription pill junkies "out there," but are in our pews and among us, we are in the right position to begin helping addicts step into recovery.

Few characters better embody the nature of addiction than the slimy underworld creature, Gollum, in J. R. R. Tolkien's fantasy series *The Lord of the Rings*. Gollum was once a man, but an obsession with a ring that makes him invisible has turned him into a sniveling, grasping, enslaved wretch, part man, part animal. Gollum's pathetic, groveling submission to this one thing, the ring, and his willingness to do anything to have "My Precious," causes repulsion even as it can strike a chord of recognition: at least a little bit of Gollum is in each of us.

A similar dynamic can play out in how we relate to people with addictions. If we are preparing to help an addict into recovery and find ourselves dealing with intense feelings of revulsion and disgust toward his compulsive behaviors, we have not done the hard work of looking at our own inner Gollum and sizing it up for what it is: a dehumanizing compulsion to choose our own enslavement over the Spirit's life-giving freedom. Chances are, too, that the greater the repulsion, the greater the externalizing of that inner Gollum.

Philosopher Francis Seeburger at the University of Denver describes the dynamic this way:

> At least part of what makes us react with such abhorrence to images of the depths of addiction, refusing to admit any community with addicts who have plumbed those depths, is our hidden fear that we are like them, or might become so, if we relax our vigilance. Perhaps we can, in fact, all too easily imagine ourselves in their places. Perhaps that is really what frightens us so.[1]

Effectiveness at getting an addict into recovery thus first requires some rigorous interior work done either alone with God or, preferably, with a close friend or accountability partner, before all else. The following components can belong to this spiritually formative process:

Make a moral inventory. A good place to start, if you are not already doing this daily work in your personal devotional life, is to "make a searching and fearless *written* moral inventory of yourself," to paraphrase step four of AA's twelve steps.[2] Here you are examining the messes in your own life and the areas where your soul needs a bit of housekeeping work. You may have issues with anger or fear or the use of your sexuality. In recovery groups like AA, step 4 usually takes place in the context of working with a sponsor, someone who's further along in the working of the twelve steps; so, in the spirit of the twelve-step model, this work should be done with at least one other person, like a close accountability partner or spiritual mentor or director.

If this exercise in introspection seems daunting at first, some resources can jump-start and guide the process. The eighteenth-century theologian John Wesley's "22 Questions," developed for the sake of private daily devotional use by members of Wesley's Holy Clubs—small groups committed to encouraging one another in the pursuit of a sanctified life—are one helpful tool; they are also easily accessible online. The Alcohol Addiction Foundation has also made a handy worksheet with a checklist for approaching step 4.[3]

An exercise in ruthless inspection before even approaching the task of getting other addicts into recovery is also in keeping with the advice of Jesus himself: to take the plank out of our own eye before taking the speck out of our neighbor's (see Matthew 7:5). We all have at least one plank to assess and unload in the light of God's tender love for us. Writing out a list of these things can help us to look them squarely in the eye. So ask yourself whom you resent. Do you find yourself harboring anger toward something or someone, and if so, why? What groups of people do you resent? Who has wronged you? Who do you need to forgive? What have you "done and left undone" (a phrase from *The Book of Common Prayer*)?

Review fears. Now review your fears. What keeps you awake at night, and what is the source of that fear? Where do you most seek to control outcomes in your life, and how? Do you worry about finances, a relationship or your reputation? If so, these things may be, metaphorically, idols that you need to let go of and let God replace. If addiction is in fact "a disorder of worship," as some contemporary Christian scholars have called it—or if addiction is a matter of "disordered loves," to borrow St. Augustine's language—then unveiling these misplaced objects of love will help *re*order priorities, so that God is at the center rather than at the outskirts. These blockages to real connection (with God and, in turn, with neighbor and self) may be feeding unhealthy patterns of behavior. Again, write these things down.

Identify false gods. Identifying the false gods that dictate how we live our lives is, as psychologist Ed Welch and pastor Gary Steven Shogren suggest, to fill in the blank in the following statement: "If only I had _____, I'd be happy."[4] Alternatively, ask yourself what in your life, if you lost it, would cause you the greatest grief.

Look at intimate relationships. Finally, take a look at your intimate relationships (both past and present), and ask yourself where you have been hurt or caused hurt to others. Many addicts have experienced childhood trauma like physical, verbal, emotional, spiritual or sexual abuse. Such things need to be addressed (if they have not been already), ideally with the help of a good therapist. In this step, you will also need to scrutinize the places where you have been inconsiderate or disingenuous toward others. How have you used your sexuality to harm others?

This is not the time for moralizing, but for gentle, honest and rigorous introspection. Because twelve-step programs like AA seek to create a nonjudgmental environment and because they view problems with sex as on par with other problems, AA will not make your sexual choices and behaviors a litmus test for membership by ranking it above other issues.[5] A review of your most intimate relationships within the context of step 4 is really about uncovering another dimension of your recovery by shedding light on your addictive thoughts and behaviors.

Following the above steps will allow you to assess what one thing, or two or three, you have pursued over and above a connection with God. We need to be brutally honest about these things. Do you find yourself constantly obsessing about a particular thing—like that bonus at work or a new car? Maybe you catch yourself paying more attention to your iPhone than to the person in front of you.

If a personal inventory unearths certain unhealthy behavioral patterns, that's because nobody is invulnerable to addictive tendencies, regardless of where they fall on the continuum. So continue to ask God on a daily basis to reveal the fault lines in your soul that keep you from finding real freedom in the Spirit and deeper relationship with the One who most wants you to be happy, joyous and free. God will show you the areas where you, too, display addictive tendencies or compulsions, a clear measure of which will be the humble recognition that addicts are not "over there" but right here in our midst, among us, and even in the mirror.

In this way, our own homecomings are inextricably bound with those of the addicts we hope to help recover. And the adventure, messiness, joy and heartache—both the risks and the possibilities of a shared journey together—really begin with the question "How do I help this person get into recovery?" As is the case with most journeys, there are some ways you can prepare while surrendering the rest to the guidance of the Holy Spirit. Soulful, meditative preparation is just the first of a number of things you will need for your journey home to the heart of God—but it is arguably the most important.

> Our own homecomings are inextricably bound with those of the addicts we hope to help recover. And the adventure, messiness, joy and heartache really begin with the question "How do I help this person get into recovery?"

Recognizing and Identifying Addiction

Once you have inventoried your own issues, you are ready to begin the next step of helping addicts get into recovery. This step entails becoming familiar with the signs of addiction and the forms addiction can take. The summary that appears in the appendix can help, with the disclaimer that it is meant to be an introduction for laypeople and is by no means clinically exhaustive. Some recovery centers also offer free assessments for people who are unsure whether they or a loved one has an addiction, so you might consider connecting with one or two such treatment programs in your area.

The main thing to look for when identifying whether an addiction is at play is a repetitive behavior (be it drug use, sex or exercise) linked to a cycle of cravings and withdrawal that causes negative life consequences. Over time, as addicts build tolerance to a particular drug or behavior, they start craving more of it to get the same high, doing whatever they can to have their "drug" of choice, despite the consequences. And their cravings and withdrawal can manifest as a loss of control and responsibility.

A more recently studied phenomenon is our capacity to become addicted to certain human activities that generate pleasure. Process addictions can involve eating, work, sex, falling in love, exercise, gambling, shopping and technology. Such activities can become our taskmasters, unleashing similar dynamics to those of a chemical dependency, such as highs, lows, tolerance, craving and withdrawal. As the sex addiction expert Patrick Carnes writes in his book *Out of the Shadows*, "Addiction taps into the most fundamental human processes. Whether the need to be high, to be sexual, to eat, or even to work—the addictive process can turn creative, life-giving energy into a destructive, demoralizing compulsivity."[6]

The seductive power of process addictions lies in the fact that so many of these activities are necessary to our survival in the modern world. Eating, shopping, technology—such things are the stuff of contemporary life. We need to eat in order to survive. If our ancestors' hunting-and-gathering rhythms are no longer a necessity, we still need to shop in order to provide for material needs. Most of us have to work, unless we are independently wealthy, and the great majority of us now have to communicate by email and depend on smartphones. All of us depend on love and intimacy with other human beings for psychosocial health and happiness.

As a church leader, you may not be qualified to make a clinical diagnosis, but you can be mindful of when these ordinary, often necessary and life-giving activities have gained an unhealthy stranglehold in your church members' lives. For example, you do not have to be a behavioral therapist to ascertain that one of your parishioners does not just like to shop but may actually be enslaved to those weekly sales at Nordstrom and Neiman Marcus. And, for that matter, anyone can reasonably conclude that an unhealthy attachment (an addiction) to collecting things may be at play when they read real headlines like this: "Mummified body found inside hoarder's San Francisco home."[7]

Similarly, you do not have to know all of the latest drug slang to be aware that the street person who stumbles into your Sunday morning worship is high on something and may be struggling with an addiction. You *do* need to know how to respond wisely and effectively with the love of Jesus, which first involves helping that addict get into recovery, if at all possible. And you need to be aware of your limitations in helping as well as the professional resources available to you in the process.

Intervention, Referral and Follow-Up

Helping a person with addiction get into recovery will look different depending on her circumstances. In many cases, intervention is the first step in getting an addict into recovery. (Chapter 2 is about that process.) Other times a typical intervention may not be at all appropriate—ever. In cases of sex addiction, for example, I have found from experience that the principles of group intervention that might usually work with other addictions are not applicable, because of the greater stigma and sensitivity unique to sex addiction. The better part of discretion is to keep the matter completely confidential between you, the addict and only those directly affected by the addiction, such as a spouse. Refer out to the professionals (sex therapists, marriage counselors or addiction specialists), and provide ongoing informal check-ins. In these cases, one-on-one intervention may have a better chance of getting an addict into recovery than a group intervention process that may only feed the addict's humiliation.

So, in cases like sex addiction, there will be times when your first line of action will be to refer out to a therapist, and then be available for informal conversation, prayer and encouragement. At other times, you may decide that you are able to provide some limited pastoral counseling to the person in need. Your decision will depend on discerning a number of things within an initial encounter: the nature of the addiction and your own familiarity with it; the presence of a mental disorder requiring professional treatment (like clinical depression, for example); the nature of the addicted person's existing support network; and your own comfort level in ministering to the person.

Some pastors place a strict limit on the number of times they will meet to discuss a particular pastoral concern; honor such boundaries. Your main role in these conversations is not a clinical or therapeutic one. It is to minister the love of Jesus in word and deed through a relationship of trust and care that brings glory to God. This way you will be doing your job while leaving the clinical complexities of an addiction to professionals like me. When in doubt, you can refer out and then follow up with the person to see how he is doing.

Every pastor should therefore have an addiction recovery referral list on hand. Take time to prepare it and make it available to your Stephen Ministers (pastorally trained lay leaders), pastoral care team and those who come to you seeking help with addiction-related concerns. You might even keep the checklist on hand in a visible place, be it at your front reception desk or in the foyer of your sanctuary. (Of course, be sure that the resources you list are accredited and have been vetted by one or more clinical professionals in your church.)

Here are some suggestions for what to include on your referral checklist:

- Twelve-step groups with personal contacts for each of these groups

- Clergy and churches in your area with thriving support-group ministries and recovery expertise (if your church does not have these)

- Physicians and psychiatrists with addiction and dual-diagnosis specialties

- Hospital facilities and detox centers providing services to alcoholics and addicts

- Outpatient and inpatient treatment programs with good reputations

- Halfway houses and other follow-up programs for addicts coming out of treatment programs

- Mental health professionals with addiction expertise, as well as therapists trained in stress management

- Treatment programs for homeless addicts, such as the Salvation Army

Have a Policy Regarding Financial Assistance

In some situations, you may find yourself asking whether it is appropriate to use church funds to help people with addictions get into recovery. Maybe a transient person with a drug addiction wanders into your building asking for gas money, or a poor, uninsured family from your congregation wonders aloud how they will afford the next few days of detox for Dad. Having a financial policy in place can help you navigate these situations better.

If you do not have a policy, consult your denomination's benevolence ministry guidelines; or, in the absence of an existing strategy on which to model yours, consider undertaking a discernment process with your leadership team in order to create a policy for your church. (For resources that will help you create a benevolence strategy, consult the appendix.)

Your policy can list the specific types of financial requests that your congregation will and will not grant. For example, if your church has agreed to meet people's "basic needs," your policy can include examples of what you mean by basic needs. Will your church provide food, lodging or medical treatment? Will your church cover transportation to a job or funeral expenses? The more specific you can make the list of needs you are committed to providing, the better. Similarly, your policy can list the types of handouts that your church does *not* believe fall within the category of basic needs and thus will not grant. These might include legal fees, private school tuition or business investments.

Another consideration as you create your policy will be what forms of assistance your congregation may or may not be prepared to provide. If, for example, your church is committed to helping transient people get a warm meal or a coat on their back, your policy should explicitly list "transient assistance" and examples of it among the various forms of aid you provide. In such instances, your church can determine whether to hand out monetary gifts or in-kind donations and the necessary protocol for distributing those handouts.

To visitors who come through our doors asking for money, my church often gives meal gift cards (for use at grocery stores or fast-food joints). Other churches hand out bus or subway cards. If you are worried about feeding an existing addiction or are unsure about whether someone is telling the truth, erring on the side of caution when it comes to what you give is perfectly appropriate.

There is also another line of reasoning in favor of giving money handouts to whoever is in the unenviable position of having to ask for money from strangers. In River Falls, Wisconsin, Servant of the Shepherd Church has been featured in local newspapers for its work among addicts. Some 90 percent of its four hundred to five hundred members are in recovery from one addiction or another. Pastor Frank Lukasiewicz says he often hands out cash to those who come to him in trouble. In cases involving homeless people with addictions, he advises praying for discretion before giving any sort of handout.

He cites as one example a young family who was on the verge of homelessness when they asked him for money. They had no food for themselves or formula for their baby. Lukasiewicz chuckles, recalling that, no sooner had he given this young couple fifty dollars from his own pocket than he heard a friendly holler from across the street. This person, having not seen or heard the preceding interaction, approached Lukasiewicz with a wad of cash that she wanted him to have, for no other reason than she had felt God wanted her to give it to her pastor; it was forty dollars.

By not withholding financial support to underresourced people with addictions, Lukasiewicz believes he has a better chance at building long-term relationships with people who, in addition to often being itinerant, might not otherwise trust someone in a clerical collar. While he recognizes there is a risk involved in this approach—a generous church member may inadvertently be fueling an addiction and the manipulations that go along with it— Lukasiewicz believes that financial giving prayerfully entrusted to the will of God ultimately can't go wrong.

Why? Because the act of giving changes the heart of the giver, freeing him to be more like Jesus, and because the ultimate recipient of our giving, when all is said and done, is Jesus. Here Lukasiewicz quotes Jesus' words in Matthew 25:40 as a plea to remember that anything we do for "the least of these" we do for Jesus himself. How we love people with addictions, then, is ultimately about the One at the center of all things and his invitation to become more like him.

> How we love people with addictions, then, is ultimately about the One at the center of all things and his invitation to become more like him.

Back to the Future

Let's return for a moment to the three scenarios that opened this chapter, with a view to answering the question "How do I help this person enter recovery?"

A new high in worship. Disheveled-looking street types grace the Sunday morning worship at your inner-city church, but this visit is a first; you can't think of a time when someone walked in behaving *this* way. With his slurred speech, a glazed, clouded expression and occasionally strange outbursts, there is no telling what he is on. He looks out of control, and for all you know could be dangerous—but he also seems to *want* to be there, in your midst. As a ministry leader, what do you do?

Here are some pointers for how to proceed:

- *Assess the level of disruption or danger this person may pose to those in your congregation—and act accordingly.* For example, if the man is having loud outbursts during the service, a previously deputized team of two or three members (ideally those who are in recovery themselves) can escort the man respectfully to a private place and engage him there. If the man is violent, is making aggressive gestures or appears to be a danger to himself or those around him, call 911. If the man is strung out but poses no real disruption or danger during the worship service, wait until worship is finished to reach out to him with one or more members.

- *Stay calm, and get as much factual information as possible from your visitor.* You can ask him if he knows where he is and what the date is. You can ask him what drug he is on and when he last took it. (The answer may reveal whether he is likely to have withdrawal symptoms, for example, that may be life threatening and require the attention of a doctor.) Try to get to know as much as you can about your visitor: Where is he from? Does he have family members who live nearby? Here again, include the help of anyone from your congregation whom you know to be in recovery or medical professionals in your midst.

- *Treat the person with as much respect as you would any other first-time visitor in your congregation, speaking gently, calmly and clearly, with attentiveness to what he is telling you.* This is not a time for small talk, but it is also not a time for lecturing or patronizing someone with a problem. One way you can assess whether you are talking down to your visitor is by your own body language: Are you sitting across from him and conversing at the same eye level, or standing above him? The first option is a better one. Your default mode is a listening stance with short, calm and kind directives when necessary, such as, "Please sit down here" and "Tell me more."

- *In consultation with the medical and clinical professionals in your church and those whom you know to be in recovery, discuss your referral checklist and identify resources that will best support*

your visitor's unique circumstances. Together, encourage your
visitor to telephone his family (if he has any in the area) and, with
his family, to initiate a first step into treatment via at least one of
the resources on your list.

- *If your visitor is asking for a handout, consult your church's policy
  regarding financial assistance to those in need, and strive to be
  prayerfully generous, asking that God's will be done.* In many
  cases, your visitor will be homeless and requesting a handout.
  Having a policy in place for these situations can help, as long as
  it doesn't hamper your attentiveness to the leading of the Holy
  Spirit. Sometimes the "letter of the law" must be broken for the
  sake of lovingly attending to the unique needs of the person in
  front of you. At other times, your policy will be a helpful
  boundary to which you can appeal.

- *Set clear boundaries and be clear with yourself and your visitor
  (if necessary) about what you can and can't do in the situation.*
  You and your team can point him in the direction of some helpful
  recovery resources. You may be able to help put him in touch
  with family or connect him with people in your congregation
  who are already in recovery. You can invite him back to church
  the next Sunday, and if he is unruly or belligerent when high, you
  can gently insist that he be sober the next time he shows up (or
  at least less disruptive). You can tell him how glad you are he is
  there and that you are committed to helping him get on the path
  to recovery. But avoid making commitments that could endanger
  you or others, or extending promises you can't fulfill.

Desperate housewife. You are as shocked as she is to learn of
her husband's secret porn addiction. He has been a faithful member
of your church: he regularly tithes, serves on your vestry and even
taught the sixth-grade Sunday school class last year. Together this
couple parented three children who are now grown. They are

respected in your church and community. As a pastoral caregiver, what do you do?

The following tips will help:

- *Listen calmly and attentively without expressions of shock or revulsion.* This woman needs to be listened to compassionately without judgment. Validate her feelings, and avoid contributing to the shame and trauma she already is experiencing. Even if your jaw is on the verge of dropping, assure this woman that what she is going through is not uncommon, as painful as it is, and that the problem is pervasive within the ranks of the church. Letting her know that sex addiction is a disease that can be treated may also be helpful.

- *Encourage the wife to focus on her own self-care, and refer her to a therapist (if she is open to this) and to a recovery group for family members of addicts, such as Co-Dependents Anonymous.* Consult your referral checklist here. Encourage her to protect herself physically, which may include getting tested for sexually transmitted diseases. You can also invite her to lean on her existing inner resources and network of relationships in the church as supports during this time.

- *Help the wife articulate some clear boundaries in relation to her husband's behavior, and encourage her to uphold them.* One such boundary may be issuing a zero-tolerance rule with respect to porn in the house as well as installing monitoring technology. It may also require asking for access to the husband's email and computer passwords and that he submit to a lie detector test or tests for sexually transmitted diseases (depending on the seriousness of his addiction). But emphasize *your* boundaries here, too: as her pastor, your job is to love her through this crisis; a therapist will be better positioned to provide her with the ongoing clinical care she will need to uphold the boundaries.

- *Avoid potential triangulation or attempts to help that may actually dissuade the wife's husband from getting help.* For example, the wife may ask you to meet with her husband in hopes that you might persuade him to get help. Taking this initiative before any show of interest from the husband himself is not your role. Let the wife know that you are happy to talk in confidence with her husband and refer him to the right professionals but that he needs to reach out to you first, by his own volition and on his own initiative. In the meantime, be present to the wife as a sounding board and a prayer support.

- *Pray together, asking God to help the husband recognize his problem and take the first step into recovery.* There is only so much we can do to help others find recovery; they must take responsibility for their own recovery. But we can pray for them and pray incessantly.

- *If the husband does seek your help, either on his own or with his wife there, refer him to a certified treatment center or to a certified sex therapist.* Also connect him with a recovery group like Sex Addicts Anonymous. Be prepared for some resistance. The following are possible reactions and objections (in italics) with suggested ways to respond in quotation marks:

  - Denial: *I have no idea what you're talking about.* "Your wife found the porn on your computer. She couldn't believe it either." *If I have a problem, I'm not hurting anybody but myself.* "Your compulsive behaviors are hurting your wife and your kids."

  - Anger: *This is none of your business.* "As your pastor, I'm charged with caring for you. And your challenges, in addition to having negative consequences in your life, affect this church, too."

- Self-pity and victimhood: *You don't care about me.* "If that were true, I'd just keep my mouth shut and let you ruin your life. I'm here because I care and want to help you get into recovery."

- Self-reliance: *I can handle this problem on my own.* "You're facing a chronic and progressive disease that, if untreated, could have tragic consequences for you and your family. Like anyone who has walked this path, you need help, and we are here to walk with you in finding recovery."

Poor harmony: a case of hitting the low notes. Your worship leader, Harmony, has fallen on tough times lately, with her recent divorce and a sick mother to care for. She has begun showing up late for staff meetings and choir practice, often blaming her lateness on one issue or another. One Sunday morning, she called in sick at the very last minute. Members of her worship team say they often smell liquor on her breath. As a pastoral caregiver and as her boss, what do you do to help her into recovery?

The following suggestions will set you on your way:

- *Approach her with prayer and in a spirit of humility.* Dealing with substance abuse or dependence issues is tricky, whether the addict in question is a volunteer or a paid staff member. If she is salaried personnel, the chances are greater that if you challenge her, she will deny having a problem. (Naturally, she doesn't want to lose her position or paycheck.) The biblical approach is one of restoring the individual. Ask yourself how to help your worship leader while maintaining her integrity in ministry and keeping in mind the spiritual care of your congregation. You can come to her in a spirit of genuine concern and seek to understand, while assuring her that if she is struggling with alcoholism, you will help her do what she needs to do in recovery. But she also needs to know that the other option—continuing to show up late to work with liquor on her breath—is not working. Lay out as matter-of-factly as possible what behaviors are being brought to your attention as her boss.

• *Be honest about your concerns and observations—and about your own discomfort in having to wear two hats, both as her employer and as her brother or sister in Christ.* As the employer, you must set and enforce your boundaries, which apply in the same way to this employee as they do to every member of your staff; your expectations are that she perform her job responsibilities. You are also concerned that her alcohol use may be out of hand if it is causing her to show up late and is affecting her job performance. Be gentle but direct in stating that you and others (not naming names) have regularly noticed the smell of liquor on her breath. Give her an out if she needs it, at least initially, by letting her know that you are aware that in some cases individuals on medication experience the effects of just one drink more dramatically. (Also be prepared to suggest an intervention to her family if she rebuffs your efforts to address the behavior and continues to show up late to work with liquor on her breath.)

• *Listen to her with respect and attentiveness.* Ask her if she is using alcohol to cope with life stressors, and validate her feelings of stress. Let her know that you understand that when life becomes tough, we all look for ways to cope and get by—and that some ways are healthier than others. Ask her if she has given thought to her alcohol intake and whether she thinks it is resulting in some of the behaviors you and others have noticed.

• *Ask her if the issue is something she is dealing with already or if she needs some help—and let her know that both as her employer and a pastoral caregiver, you are committed to helping her get into recovery.* You might ask her what she needs to rectify the problem(s), and let her know that, where you can support her in meeting these needs, you will. (For example, if she needs an hour once a week to see a therapist, you will honor that need and find ways to support it.) This way you can also gauge to what degree she is already aware of and dealing with the root issue, and you can gently prod her further in the direction of seeking help.

* *Honor privacy and confidentiality.* Let her know that, as her employer, you are bound by rules of confidentiality when it comes to her health issues. With the exception of suspected risks of suicide, you should *never* share anything she divulges to you without first asking for her permission. Here, too, proceed very carefully with great discretion. For example, if you are obliged to justify her leave of absence with your vestry, session or leadership team, invite her to write out a one-sentence explanation for why she needs a leave of absence. That way you are in agreement about the boundaries of confidentiality. You also have a written record; the last thing you need as her employer is a lawsuit for violating strict HIPAA guidelines for health confidentiality. Equally important, you do not want to undermine your pastoral integrity and betray her trust in you as a pastoral leader.

Get Up and Start for Home

The question "How do I help an addict into recovery?" is rife with all sorts of contextual considerations that depend on the circumstances. But one assumption can underlie every interaction with an addict you seek to help into recovery—namely, that your point of contact and referral is just the beginning of a journey home; it is when the prodigal son comes to his senses and "arises" or "gets up," as the biblical language says.

Ultimately, addicts must make the decision for themselves to arise. They must consider their circumstances under the sometimes-painful glare of God's grace-filled light and choose whether to get on their feet and turn toward home or to continue in the same destructive patterns. But churches can challenge addicts to arise and can be there to lend a helping hand. Churches can extend the invitation to come home.

The catch is this: lending a hand to someone on the ground requires that the one who extends the hand is standing. Only a church that is itself arising from its own addictive tendencies will be able to lend that helping hand. Standing in an upright position has little to do with moral or spiritual perfection and instead has everything to do with the recognition that one is a long way from home and wants to get back there. In this sense, getting an addict into recovery is as much about getting recovery into the church. When recovery is in the church and churches are in recovery, they are able to offer that helping hand.

Discussion Questions

1. Have you ever had to ask the question "How do I help an addict get into recovery?" If so, how was it answered? What might you do differently next time, based on reading this chapter?

2. What unhealthy attachments and behaviors leave you in the same state of bondage as other addicts? What will it take for you to arise?

two

The Intervention

The redemptive way goes through pain,
not around it.

PHILIP YANCEY
THE QUESTION THAT NEVER GOES AWAY

CHUCK ROBINSON KNOWS A THING OR TWO about getting addicts into recovery. His home congregation, Henderson Hills Baptist Church, is on the frontlines of ministering to people with addictions. The frontlines are where Robinson, who is thankful for more than thirty years of sobriety from alcohol and drugs, spends most of his time in ministry these days: participating in twelve-step meetings and working the program; driving to and from detox facilities, treatment programs and jail cells to be in prayer and conversation with addicts; and comforting the families of those lost to addiction. Robinson has also facilitated many an intervention (an orchestrated attempt by a small group of family and friends to try to convince an addict to seek professional treatment).

When I asked Robinson to share one story (among many) of a family he helped via an intervention, he remembered sixteen-year-old Rose and her parents. Rose was hooked on drugs and alcohol, and like a tornado, her life was spinning out of control, sweeping the lives of those around her into its destructive vortex and leaving only wreckage in its path.

When Rose's parents came to Robinson and asked for his help, they were at the end of their rope, having already taken desperate measures—going so far as to appear on a national talk show to seek advice. Their daughter had spent days in rehab only to relapse, during which time she had gotten pregnant out of wedlock with a boyfriend who was abusive and himself an alcoholic. Even after the birth of her daughter, Rose could not sober up, no matter how hard she tried—even after losing custody of her child.

In the meantime, Rose's parents had been working a Christian twelve-step program, which is where they first met Robinson. He encouraged the couple to share their story and, in the process, to undertake a "searching and fearless moral inventory" of their own behavioral patterns, insofar as these issues may have contributed to Rose's addiction. By way of an intervention, Robinson encouraged them to write their daughter "love letters," in which they described for her the daughter they once knew, before addiction stole her from them. And with Robinson's support, these heartbroken parents pressed their daughter to give treatment one more try—this time in a different rehab center.

The intervention was successful in getting Rose to "arise": to enter recovery and begin a long journey home. During her time in a treatment center, she began to rediscover herself apart from her addiction and developed a new set of friendships and a network of support. But her breakthrough, coming on the heels of a successful intervention, was soon to meet the tragic consequences of addiction.

While in treatment, Rose learned the news that her daughter had been killed at the hands of her own father (Rose's alcoholic ex-boyfriend). In a drunken state, he had pushed their young child down some stairs to her death. The tragedy threw Rose into a deep depression, out of which she was able to emerge only gradually with the help of a competent therapist and a few close female friends also in recovery. Their love, support and compassion helped Rose stay in treatment, so that today she is now several years clean and active in her church recovery program, carrying the message of recovery to those who suffer from addiction.

Demystifying the Intervention

Rose's story illustrates an important truth about extending care to people with addiction: in many cases, your heart will be enlarged and broken, captivated and crushed. The same can be said about the intervention process itself, which may be one reason why so many of us are intimidated if not terrified by it. If it's true that *intervention* is the most immediate and familiar one-word answer that comes to mind in response to the question of how to get an addict into recovery, it is also true that the mere mention of the word can send blood pressures soaring and cause the most experienced pastors among us to tremble or shudder at least a bit.

Consider *Intervention*, an Emmy Award–winning, reality TV show that once aired on the A&E channel with a foreboding soundtrack, jaw-dropping statistics about the morbidity of the addiction in question, and tense, tearful revelations by family. All this was interspersed with scenes from their loved one's descent into hell—leading up to a final, climactic encounter: the intervention.

The riveting suspense of these real-life stories of people whose lives literally hung in the balance because of a spiraling heroin addiction, eating disorder or other habit captivated viewers. And invariably the show's heroes were the interventionists, whose no-baloney straight-talk won the day. Their winsome one-liners seem to stick: "Everyone here loves you like crazy," says a favorite interventionist, Jeff Vanvonderen. Or "we are here to fight for your life, and we're asking you to join that fight!"

Most of us find the prospect of staging an intervention daunting at the very least. And this is understandable. When two or more of an addict's closest family or friends present that addict with the reality and consequences of his disease, along with a concrete plan for getting their loved one into recovery, their most desperate hopes for his healing can indeed be met with some of the deepest heartbreak (if he rejects their overtures).

> Success has far more to do with the sheer presence of love—a love that is genuine, relentless and on display when two or more are gathered in Jesus' name.

The fact is that intervention can be an uncertain and stressful enterprise marked by both setbacks and encouragements, hurdles and healing. Hope and despair rarely share such close proximity in one relatively short encounter as they do in this context, and tragedy can follow on the heels of the most encouraging of breakthroughs. But as Rose's story conveys, love can and often does prevail—maybe not magically or overnight, but miraculously and in the darkest of circumstances.

If the clearest measure of an intervention's success is whether it helps an addict get into recovery, the freeing takeaway from Robinson's story is this: the biggest chances for success have much less to do with an impeccable intervention format or a perfect performance on the part of those involved; success has far more to do with the sheer presence of love—a love that is genuine, relentless and on display when two or more are gathered in Jesus' name.

And if love can surround and comfort a young woman in a treatment center who has just heard the news that her young child has died, that same love can surely help you to encourage grieving parents to write a love letter to a daughter in need of coming home, or to sit with an anxious, grieving family as they initiate a hard but necessary conversation. Such love can help hope triumph in the worst of circumstances.

Writing "love letters" to the one we want to see enter treatment may not square with the preconceptions that have been drummed into our heads about what a typical intervention should look like. We may imagine a barren, fluorescent-lit room with a somber circle of people seated around a belligerent kid in the hot seat. The whole affair can sound like the spiritual equivalent of having one's molars removed, and it probably does not top the average church leader's ministry bucket list.

Common Challenges

To be sure, when it comes to a more traditional intervention, certain challenges are inevitable. When I asked a group of pastoral care-givers to share their biggest challenges when intervening in cases of addiction, a majority said their biggest hurdle is denial on the part of the addict or the addict's family. Denial—or an unwill-ingness to "surrender," in the words of one caregiver—can present a formidable roadblock to helping those with addictions. The same obstacle can present itself in the intervention itself.

A predominant question among this group, according to one respondent, Christine, was "how to actually get [the addict] to accept they have a problem and physically get them into a program." Christine shared from her experience that "there was always a lot of talk or promises" but no real show of commitment. "In the meantime, more damage is done, and it snowballs." Like denial, empty promises on the part of the person you are trying to help can also surface in the course of an intervention.

Another hurdle in helping addicts into recovery is the shame, em-barrassment and sense of failure that afflicts so many people with addictions and their families. Brad Bosworth, who coordinates a program for recovering addicts and their families at Smyrna First United Methodist Church in a suburb of Atlanta, shared how these emotions are one inspiration for the name of the program he runs.

Peter's Promise embraces the example of the disciple Peter, who, in spite of his fear, shame and faltering denial of Jesus, went on to become a foundational pillar of the church—all because of the resurrection.

Bosworth invokes Peter as a way to tap into the intensity of emotion that addicts and their families experience at the beginning of recovery. On the eve of Jesus' death, Peter's shame, fear and sense of failure would have been overwhelming. Yet in the light of the resurrection, these stumbling blocks were not the final story, and in fact helped to shape "the Rock" on which Jesus built his church.

The intervention may very well become the venue in which you and others there must address shame head-on. (For tips on how to do this, see chapter five.) But this encounter, when undertaken in a spirit of genuine and relentless love, will at the very least be one building block, however small, in the making of a story that, when prayerfully surrendered to the will of God, can end up like Peter's. It can be a story of turnaround—a story that makes God God and the church God's turnaround children, turning and returning on a path toward home.

What You Can Do

When preparing for an intervention as a pastor or church leader, you can benefit from knowing your role, which will primarily be one of providing pastoral presence and support to the addict and family as well as connecting them with the resources they need to undertake an intervention.

Most of the time—unless you lead interventions regularly in a recovery group like AA, you are a certified interventionist or you direct a recovery ministry—you will not need to *lead* the intervention yourself. That role can be outsourced to the pros that do this sort of thing regularly. A certified interventionist, for example, will require a fee, which the family of an addict will usually need to cover. Your role may be to connect with the intervention pros in your congregation and community and to support their work with the family.

Your role may also be to identify others in your congregation who will have the greatest chance of influencing a decision in favor of recovery. Ideally, these folks are themselves in recovery and well established in their sobriety. Most of the time, they will be your biggest cheerleaders and delighted to serve in this way.

Lukasiewicz, who sometimes leads interventions himself and other times calls in professionals to facilitate in his place, says he finds the most success when he taps the right people to participate. He recommends identifying as many as four or five people who, in addition to being in a twelve-step group, are of the addict's age and gender and are willing to intervene with key family members.

One question to consider as you provide support to the addict and her family in this tense time is whether to tell the addict in advance that the intervention will be taking place. Generally, upfront honesty with the addict is the best policy here. Surprise interventions have the potential to stoke an addict's anger and to dissuade her from even sitting down to hear what you have to say.

But each case is different, which means there may be times when you really should *not* tell the addict what is going to happen, because he simply will not come (a scenario that misleadingly is the norm in the show *Intervention*). If ever in doubt about how to proceed, always consult the pros in your congregation (those in recovery with a long record of sobriety) or contact a certified interventionist in your area. (To find interventionists, see the appendix of this book.)

When you have a basic familiarity with addiction and have done the hard work of prayerfully scrutinizing your own unhealthy attachments and coping mechanisms (see chapter 1), you are ready to provide a supportive pastoral presence to the family and the addict in the course of the intervention. And a few tools for participating in an intervention will help you in this endeavor. But before proceeding, I want to make something very clear: to be a healing interaction and to be the primary vehicle of getting an addict into treatment, an intervention must not be understood in terms of a few healthy people trying to cure the one "sick person" in the room. I have seen how this far-too-frequent mindset on the part of well-meaning church people can cause deep spiritual and emotional damage to the very people churches honestly but misguidedly are trying to help. Avoid this snare—even if it means saying to an overactive savior complex, "Get behind me, Satan."

> An intervention grounded in love will put a bunch of equally flawed human beings in a room together and require them to tell the truth about what is going on, their part in it and their responsibility for one another.

An intervention grounded in love will put a bunch of equally flawed human beings in a room together and require them to tell the truth about what is going on, their part in it and their responsibility for one another. The assumption, in other words, is that this sickness of addiction took more than one dysfunctional person to develop and will need more than one person (the addict) to be conquered. Yes, ultimately the addict must take responsibility for his own recovery, but this initiative usually comes only after deep-seated, family-related issues of abuse, trauma and past hurts have been dealt with from within the painful but hope-filled crucible of an intervention.

Often, just the words "I love you" from a long-distant father can be just what a person needs to choose treatment. (Many addicts say they never felt loved growing up.) Similarly, a mother's heartfelt plea for forgiveness for the times she failed to be present or to protect her daughter from molestation can be a hopeful turning point: it can be just enough for that daughter to "get up" and, like the prodigal son of the parable, see brighter possibilities for her future than a needle in a dark basement. The intervention is where humbled, desperate, heartbroken people cut to the chase in addressing their shared pain and move through that pain toward the possibility of resurrection, trusting and praying for this new beginning with every fiber of their soul.

If pastors are privileged to share in these moments, they can bear witness in word and deed to both the achingly real pain and the bold hope of resurrection that coexist in the room. Listening attentively and prayerfully; dispensing plenty of hugs and tissues—and sharing in the tears; inviting forgiveness to happen in your midst; praying silently for those present from start to finish; *being there*—these are the most important things that pastors and ministry leaders can do.

Tools for Participating in an Intervention

Admittedly, interventions look different based on who is leading them, but there are some usual features involved in any traditional intervention. Participants—those most influential in an addict's life and those with the most at stake in seeing an addict recover—must be prepared for the encounter, and usually must prepare their remarks in advance.

The guiding principle for any intervention is to remember the goal of getting an addict into recovery. This objective must govern how participants conduct themselves in the course of the intervention. The following guidelines are worth remembering here.

Challenge, don't confront. Intervention has sometimes been described in terms of confrontation, with the idea being that a few close family and friends confront an addict about his behavior. *Confrontation*, however, connotes negative associations that from the get-go can influence the mindsets of the stakeholders in this process (both the addict and those who intervene). To confront is to oppose forcefully. And for those of us who have been on the receiving end of opposition, especially when it is clothed in spiritual language, the likely response is to duck and dodge the flying bullets rather than to listen carefully and give thoughtful consideration to what is being said. Most of us don't like being confronted and, instead of feeling helped, will feel attacked or diminished in worth.

One biblical illustration of confrontation occurs in Matthew 18:15-17, where Jesus sets out some guidelines for resolving conflicts between brothers and sisters in the church:

> If another member of the church sins against you, go and point out the fault when the two of you are alone. If the member listens to you, you have regained that one. But if you are not listened to, take one or two others along with you, so that every word may be confirmed by the evidence of two or three witnesses. If the member refuses to listen to them, tell it to the church; and if the offender refuses to listen even to the church, let such a one be to you as a Gentile and a tax collector.

Confrontation thus implies an existing conflict and suggests that the one initiating the confrontation is finding fault with the person being confronted. And indeed, family members or dear friends who have been hurt or violated by an addict's actions may benefit from confronting the wrongdoer. But for pastoral caregivers, a more helpful, less intimidating language with which to frame this stage of getting addicts into recovery is that of *challenge*. Challenging the addict's behaviors still requires the directness that Jesus commands in Matthew 18, but it is usually more effective in its gentleness. It also embodies what, I believe, is at the heart of Jesus' words in Matthew 18—namely, a restorative approach that seeks to build up the person being challenged.

In my own clinical work, I have found that challenging behaviors or attitudes of the heart is very helpful. Asking the individual, for example, "How is that resentment working for you?" is usually far more effective than saying point-blank, "You need to get rid of your resentment." The latter statement can inadvertently unlatch an addict's deep reservoirs of shame. She then shuts down, so paralyzed that she can't lift herself out of the shame enough to see beyond it.

But when we challenge the unhealthy behavior, we enable addicts to see how their addiction is not working for them and is, in fact, wreaking havoc. Our challenge thus empowers the addict to evaluate his behavior for himself, as opposed to reinforcing his sense of powerlessness. If an addict becomes defensive when challenged, church leaders can understate the case rather than avoiding head-on confrontations, and they can encourage addicts to answer the questions posed by their habit for themselves.[1]

Avoid labels. I have learned through years of walking with addicts through their recovery processes that labeling people with addiction is counterproductive. The labeling is something addicts must do for themselves when they are ready, having accepted that they have a diagnosable addiction. And when addicts are ready to adopt a terminology of addiction, they may have different language preferences: some people prefer to be called addicts, while others like to consider themselves people recovering from an addiction. Each individual can choose to give expression to her condition in a way that best helps her embrace and own her recovery process. We do not need to do this for her, and the same holds true during an intervention.

If an addiction has led to sinful behaviors, labeling these behaviors as sin (even if they are) is also not helpful to the addict. Addicts need to apprehend for themselves, with the help of the Holy Spirit, what their sins are—and in some instances may need some straight talk from family members or an interventionist about how their behavior has hurt those around them. But church leaders usually need not assume this role. Instead, pastors can encourage people with addictions to unweave the various strands of experience that are keeping them in bondage.

Pastors can also approach this process of disentangling unhealthy thoughts, emotions and behaviors from the knot that has become addiction, one strand at a time (as opposed to trying to "fix" the problem all at once). There will be times when the forceful, quick-fix directive will be necessary—when, for example, an addict has already overdosed and his life is literally hanging in the balance. But more often than not, pastors have the opportunity to listen attentively without leaping to rash prescriptions for a cure (which often involves dispensing unhelpful labels).

During the intervention, pastors can also demonstrate sensitivity to the disease nature of addiction without labeling the person in front of them as sick. By referring to addiction as a disease, pastors give addicts the grace they need to seek treatment—rather than guilt and yet another reason to drown negative feelings. This truth bears out in a study that found that clergy who understand addiction mainly in terms of disease, as opposed to sin, are *three times* more likely in the course of one week to be approached for help by a person with an addiction.[2]

Identify, don't compare. Your own ongoing spiritual inventory will come in handy at this juncture. Hopefully, you have become intimately aware of your own weaknesses and shortcomings, and with this awareness, you are cultivating humility in your relationships. This prep work makes it harder to approach the addict in your midst with an off-putting sense of moral superiority or self-righteousness; you are coming to the aid of a fellow addict rather than as a savior from on high.

When you identify, compassion comes more naturally. Whereas you might have been inclined to contrast yourself to the drug addict—much like the Pharisee who thanks God that he is not a sinner like the tax collector—now you are positioned to recognize that the addict using heroin is suffering, and that the needle in her arm is not unlike your own misguided ways of dealing with pain.[3] You are ready to identify, not compare; you will be relationally more open to understanding the emotions underlying such destructive behavior. This identification is the pathway to loving well. If all you do is compare, you limit your ability to find connection with the humanity of another person in need, and you hamstring your capacity to share in the beauty of her healing process.

As the philosopher Francis Seeburger writes in his book *Addiction and Responsibility*,

> Instead of comparing our own lives negatively with those of [addicts], attentive to all the ways in which we are not like them (a ploy at which addicts themselves are masters), we need to develop an eye for the ways in which we are all too like them. We need to let the light of the depiction of their experiences illuminate our own lives, permitting us to see the addictions and addictiveness present, to one degree or another, in ourselves.[4]

Comparison is a cruel taskmaster. It always wins; we always lose. But identification is the avenue to finding connection with God and with one another. It is the means by which we ourselves enter into God's very best for us, being renewed more and more in the image of God.

If you are unsure what you have in common with an addict, here are some ideas to jump-start your identification process:

- *Impulsivity.* "I want it, and I want it now."
- *Perfectionism.* "Failure is not an option—and anything less than perfection is failure."
- *Grandiosity.* "The world revolves around me."
- *Self-reliance.* "I don't need anyone."
- *Power and control.* "I call the shots."
- *Difficulty managing emotions.* "Feelings are so painful that I'd rather feel nothing."[5]

It takes a group. If the following guideline for interventions has not been made clear, I want to enunciate it clearly: never do an intervention on your own; always have the right others there. The power of two or more is essential in the recovery process from start to finish. Consider the image of three strands or cords of rope woven together. The reference is to Ecclesiastes 4:12: "And though one might prevail against another, two will withstand one. A threefold cord is not quickly broken." Jesus may be saying something similar when he promises that whenever two or more are gathered in his name, there he is also (see Matthew 18:20).

There are a number of reasons pastors need never approach an intervention on their own. For one thing, family members and close friends are crucial in this process. In the vast majority of situations, addiction occurs within a dysfunctional family system in which residual patterns of relating to one another reinforce addictions rather than undermine them. Therefore, participation of the family is essential in the recovery process.

A group presence also lends a stronger sense of accountability to all participants, especially when they begin with a time of corporate prayer. Opening your conversation with a prayer of repentance helps to level the playing field, so to speak, between those challenging and the one being challenged, with the implication that the gap between you is not that great after all.[6] Also, Jesus' promise that he is there when two or three gather is more palpable in the room when you open your time in prayer.

Then there is the fact that a team intervening (as opposed to one individual) ensures that statements made from a place of loving concern meet their mark. The person with the addiction will have a chance to hear the same bottom line from different people; sometimes what an addict isn't able to hear from me, she will be able to hear from someone else. The more stakeholders present, the greater the chance that the message is heard and received.

Finally, a group's presence ensures that you have the support you need, should an addict turn violent (a highly unlikely possibility) or issue threats—or if any sort of conflict occurs.

Have a plan of action for treatment. A follow-up plan must include referrals to appropriate resources, such as local counselors, AA groups, detox programs and other support groups (provided in the appendix). The plan will have been determined beforehand in a joint effort usually involving the family in consultation with the one or more professionals who will facilitate the intervention and who will present the plan to the addict during the course of the intervention.

If the addict refuses to enter any form of treatment, do not despair or give up. Consider this intervention a dress rehearsal, and then try again. You can't force someone into recovery against his will. Even in cases where self-harm or harm to others is a real possibility, your ability to make decisions for an addict is next to null. But your persistence sends the message that you are with the addict for the long haul and that your commitment to his recovery is genuine.

If the next step involves detoxification from an addictive substance, your group will have consulted a medical doctor in advance, before recommending detoxification in a detox facility or hospital, or within the confines of home. In many cases, a short detox is the preferable route, since it means less disruption of job and family commitments; but a longer-term rehab program can also be a viable option.

There is no magic number of days in rehab that works for everyone. Depending on factors such as the nature of their addiction and co-occurring mental disorders, insurance coverage and the advice of clinicians, some people spend a couple weeks in a recovery program. Others need as long as six months.

Encourage family members to consider the following criteria in deciding on a program that is right for their loved one:

- Length of program
- Total cost, including insurance coverage
- Length of waiting list
- Demographic of those in the program and whether they are a good fit
- Staff qualifications
- Accreditation of the program
- History and reputation of the program
- Familiarity with and treatment of co-occurring disorders

Follow-up with family. Follow-up with family after making the appropriate referral is essential. If the addict agrees to enter treatment, your main pastoral focus in the immediate future will be how to support this family still very much in crisis. Communicate that you are in this journey for the long haul by staying in touch with the family and being available for prayer, a listening ear and as a referral resource in instances where family members could benefit from working with a therapist or attending twelve-step meetings for co-dependency issues. Having a basic familiarity with codependency and enabling issues can ensure that you are encouraging family members in the right direction in their own much-needed recovery.

Family members of addicts often become so emotionally enmeshed in their loved one's struggle that they assign more worth to the addict than to themselves, spend exorbitant time obsessing about their loved one's condition or frantically try to change their loved one's behavior.[7] Or they turn to alienating patterns of communicating with the addict that fuel the addict's behavior.

In these instances, getting an addict into recovery should coincide with getting the addict's family into recovery, through twelve-step groups like Al-Anon, Alateen and Co-Dependents Anonymous (CODA). Sometimes an addict is more amenable to entering recovery once an immediate family member has been able to detach from and release the addict—a necessary step toward healing.[8]

A pastor need not be a professional clinician to encourage a family to do the following, suggested by the late pastoral-care professor Howard Clinebell in his helpful textbook *Understanding and Counseling Persons with Alcohol, Drug and Behavioral Addictions*:

- Let go of feeling responsible for the loved one's addiction, and stop trying to control the addict's behavior.
- Let go of tendencies to punish the addict overreactively or to shield him from the consequences of his behavior.
- Let go of waiting around for the addict to find sobriety in order to make improvements in your own personal and family life.[9]

Encouraging family in this direction of detachment and release may precede getting an addict into recovery, or this work can begin once an addict has entered recovery—but its importance can't be overstated. In a vast majority of interventions, family are present and therefore should be invited into a long-term process of healing and recovery that pertains as much to them as to the addict. In this way, loving the addicts in your midst can have an enormous impact on families and in turn your whole community.

When Love Is Enough

In the fourth episode of season 13 of *Intervention*, the camera pans in on a dialogue between Gina, a hardened and hopeless heroin addict, and her mother. Gina's mother is a hard-driving, tough-talking, self-made woman. A first-generation immigrant from Korea, she made her way to the United States via an unhappy marriage to an American GI. When Gina was six, her mother decided to leave Gina's father and strike out on her own as a single mother to two girls. When she spoke on camera about Gina's addiction, her face was contorted in uncensored disbelief, shame and disgust at the fact that her daughter was providing sexual favors for strangers on the street in order to sustain five daily heroin injections.

Gina is six years into her addiction, the words that scroll across the screen tell us. She makes $5,000 a week renting out her body—and she has at least one STD and a host of other health issues to show for it.

Until then, Gina had explained her addiction in terms of an unhappy childhood marked by her mother's beatings, shunning and disapproval. This childhood abruptly ended one night in a tent on a camping trip, when a male friend of her mother reportedly slipped into Gina's tent and raped her. After the incident, Gina's mother did not believe her story, blaming the crime on Gina and insisting that the sex could only have been consensual. In a clip just minutes before the intervention, Gina's mother insisted on her version of the events in question: the perpetrator was handsome, and Gina would have been looking for some action in her tent that night.

After the rape, heroin became Gina's "best friend," she said. It provided an escape from the painful feelings of her mother's rejection and the trauma of being violated as a young teenager by a man who should have been held accountable for his crime. Heroin let Gina check out and stop caring; it made it possible for her to cope.

But then, in a room with her closest family, who had been preparing with the help of a professional interventionist, Gina tuned in to her mother's prepared statement, which was read to her in broken English with pleading expressions, prompting Gina's intermittent tears. "Gina, I've done so much things hurting you. . . . You carry inside your heart until this day. I am here to say sorry. How I ask can you forgive me? And to take me inside your heart? I don't know how to show you my heart. I want you to forgive me. I want to be your mother. Truly, it's all my fault, baby. I love you—I always do, Gina. I will be there anytime you need me."

It was an appeal for forgiveness, a profession of love, a promise to be there—a love letter to a prodigal child that this time was convincing. Gina went to a treatment center, but not without first crumpling in her mother's arms with a hug and a word of consolation that it was not all her mother's fault.

It was the first healing glimmer of reconciliation, an outward sign of an invisible grace, a sacrament not crowned by church steeples or flanked by pews, but a sign that God was in the house and Jesus was present.

And where Jesus is, there the church can be also.

Discussion Questions

1. What most scares you about the prospect of taking part in an intervention? Why?

2. Watch an episode of *Intervention*. How do you see Jesus at work in the lives of those taking part?

three

Myths About Addiction

There was a lot of praying over me: prayers for an instant and permanent cessation of my drug use; for a miraculous recovery in which I'd never have even a flicker of desire to use drugs ever again—like faith healing for the drug addict; the laying on of hands, with the occasional really loud "in Jesus' name!" where there was that awkward psychological pressure to fall backward, even though I didn't feel the need to, or want to—but it was always seen as an indication that something had "happened." Overall, they were highly emotional events, and I remember crying and shaking a lot, which I was told was the Holy Spirit.

MARY

MARY GREW UP IN CHURCH. Her addictions to various drugs prompted many a prayer, the laying on of hands and even a number of attempted exorcisms, all with the goal of ridding her once and for all of her affliction. Fortunately, Mary found recovery—but not in the church and not even with the help of the church. Disappointingly, the church failed to provide that safe, sacred space of unconditional love and acceptance that Mary says she needed in moving toward recovery.

Mary's journey to recovery was a jagged, nonlinear one. Along the way, there were multiple relapses, extended stays at the local county jail and many a disingenuous prayer for healing. The instances when the church failed Mary can serve as teaching moments, insofar as they help illustrate various myths about addiction and recovery that can hamper churches' efforts to be of greater service to people like Mary.

Rats on Crack, and Other Insights from Neuroscience

In 1953, two neuroscientists, Peter Milner and James Olds, stumbled upon a surprising discovery after implanting electrodes in the brains of rats, whose brain circuitry is similar to that of humans.[1] They wanted to see what would happen when electrodes delivered electrical currents to a part of the brain known as the midbrain reticular system. Rats in a box with corners labeled A, B, C and D received an electrical jolt every time they traveled to corner A. In no time, those rats were spending a whole lot of time in that corner, looking for the same stimulus. When Milner and Olds introduced a lever in the box that the rats could press to generate the same electrifying rush, those poor rats were pressing the lever as many as seven thousand times per hour, ignoring food or drink just to get their high.

Another study, this one by researchers at Texas A&M University, took Milner and Olds's rats-in-a-box-with-a-lever scenario and added one variation: cocaine. Gone was the electrical current. This time, rats pressing the lever received a tiny intravenous injection of the drug best known on the streets as crack. In no time, the rats had quickly learned to press the lever at a furious pace to get their high.

In a similar way, the phenomenon of addiction happens when our brain comes to associate a particular substance or action with a whole set of pleasurable sensations, so that we keep compulsively coming back to "the lever" (alcohol, drugs, food, sex, whatever), even when this compulsive behavior has become self-destructive.

In other words, we human beings are hardwired to seek pleasure, and that search can quickly go haywire. The findings of Milner, Olds and others more recently have thus strengthened a claim now largely accepted by today's medical and scientific communities: addiction is a disease.[2]

Myths That Get in the Way

In the area of addiction, I believe the church in many quarters is still very much grappling with the implications of science. For example, whereas the prevailing consensus in the medical and scientific communities is that addiction is a disease, many people of faith still use the term *sin* to describe the affliction—or, if they have adopted the disease definition, they are hard-pressed to explain how it fits within a Judeo-Christian worldview and are looking for a scripturally faithful understanding.

> A majority of church leaders can accept that addiction is a disease but have not yet contextualized this understanding within a biblical and theological framework.

Results from my survey of one hundred church leaders indicate something similar. An overwhelming majority of respondents agreed with the statement "Addiction is a disease," and very few disagreed (5 percent) or were unsure (3 percent), which would suggest that, at least among church leaders, the scientific consensus is largely accepted. Nevertheless, 56 percent of the respondents said they could use a biblical and theological framework for understanding addiction. In other words, a majority of church leaders can accept that addiction is a disease but have not yet contextualized this understanding within a biblical and theological framework—hence this chapter.

Next to shame in importance is the language we use in addressing addiction: how we talk about this modern-day epidemic is critically important to how we love the addicts in our midst. In my work connecting recovering addicts with faith communities, I have found that this task first involves dispelling various misconceptions—myths, in essence—that get in the way of loving addicts well. Dispelling these myths means providing a more faithful interpretation of Scripture and the Christian faith, one that accommodates the latest insights from science. In this chapter, I will call attention to the various misunderstandings that in many churches can wrap addiction in a shroud of fear and isolation, and I will call attention to some biblically sound, pastorally effective ways to talk to addicts as people of faith.

"Addiction is a sin." Naturally, if addiction is a medically diagnosable and treatable disease, to characterize it as a sin is at best unhelpful and at worst harmful for people in its grips. In the church, we are usually careful to distinguish medical diagnoses from sin, so that, for example, we would never equate cancer or Parkinson's disease with a person's bad behavior. Even in cases when it is very clear that a person's behavior contributed to her illness, we do not then label her disease a sin; so the lifelong smoker with lung cancer can rest assured that we won't call her diagnosis a sin. We might infer (sometimes erroneously) that she has lung cancer because she smoked; and, in the case that she did or does smoke, we might understandably draw a link between her behavior (smoking) and her diagnosis. But we are careful to parse the term sin *out* of such interpretations, just as we are with other illnesses, like high blood pressure or diabetes. Most of the time, then, we do okay maintaining a careful separation between illness and individual sin.

However, with addiction, this separation seems harder to maintain. A person can't become addicted without first choosing to take that pain pill or light up a joint. Was that initial decision (or two or three) to pop those pills or inhale that joint a sin or the sign of moral failing? Possibly, but to speculate here is, for one thing, a useless exercise in splitting hairs. The woman with disabling hip pain who takes Oxycontin and becomes hooked as well as the loner kid who begins lighting up joints in the school parking lot in order to feel accepted are sinners like the rest of us. And approximately half of people who abuse drugs or alcohol are attempting to medicate an underlying mental health issue.[3] To equate their resulting chemical dependency with sin or to seek to localize that sin somewhere along the path of its development into a full-blown disorder is senseless, cruel and pharisaical.

Certain process addictions, such as food or sex addictions, are arguably easier to label as sin: we are probably quicker to conclude that a person's obesity reflects gluttony or that an adulterous affair is an indication of lust and covetousness. But regardless of their credibility, these snap judgments blunt our capacity to love addicts in real time: the person in front of us may have made those choices, but often her current problem is now of a different nature; it's a medically diagnosable illness that requires treatment.

By defining addiction as a disease (as opposed to a personal sin or moral failing), I am not suggesting that addiction bears *no* relation to sin, insofar as sin according to a Christian worldview is fundamentally a universal human condition, one into which we all are born. On the contrary, addiction, like any other sickness, takes its place within a whole pantheon of ills that beset human beings as a result of the pervasive brokenness Christians call "sin." The apostle Paul observes in Romans 8 that all creation has been groaning in labor pangs, longing for a day when it will be set free from bondage to sin and suffering.

The issue is not that addiction somehow falls outside the overarching category of what Augustine in the fourth century called "original sin" (and which Christians who subscribe to this doctrine would describe as a genetically inherited state of sinfulness). Yes, addiction, like all illnesses, exists because our world is a sinful mess and needs the Redeemer, Jesus. But addiction is not the same thing as the particular sins of a person who has the illness, nor should it be equated as such. The problem with this myth, then, is that it presents a false, misleading reductionism about addiction *and* sin. Put another way, it is not a sin to be an addict: having the disease of addiction may result in sinful consequences, but a simple equation between addiction and sin fails to account for the tragic complexities of the illness and its development and impact on addicts' lives.

The heartbreaking story that the late author Brennan Manning liked to tell of a peer in AA, "Max," who eventually found recovery from alcoholism, helps to illustrate this point. Manning recalled a group intervention with Max, who needed to be confronted with the consequences of behavior resulting from choices he made while drinking compulsively. The man had ended up in a rehab center after leaving his little girl in the car in freezing temperatures in order to go drink with his buddies.

Manning writes that Max's "daughter's ears and fingers were badly frostbitten, resulting in the need for amputation of a thumb and permanent hearing loss." Confronted in the rehab center with the truth of his actions while under the influence, Max "collapsed on all fours and began to sob."[4]

Max needed to know the consequences of his misdeeds. The disease of alcoholism itself was not the sin in question; the abuse and mistreatment of his daughter were. Max needed to face the consequences of his actions in order to see how letting his disease progress untreated was hurting not just himself but also those he most loved and cherished.

"Addiction is God's punishment or a sign of God's judgment." The biggest problem with this myth is that it makes human beings mouthpieces of God's judgment—and Jesus explicitly commands us not to do this. "Do not judge," he tells us in Matthew 7:1. But, like the misguided witnesses to Jesus' healing of the man born blind

(John 9:1-3), who attribute the man's condition to either his sin or the sin of his parents, we can make arbitrary inferences about why someone struggles with an addiction. Concluding that someone's addiction is a sign of God's judgment is arguably the worst of these. And often we can so subtly cast judgment that we are not even aware that we are doing it, at the expense of the person in front of us.

This dynamic can also play out in how we treat the loved ones of addicts. Parents of children in recovery can be especially prone to self-condemnation, and the last thing they need is another finger-pointing voice in the mix to echo their own. A friend whose daughter was the epitome of the all-American girl before discovering meth asked, "How did I fail so much as a mother that this would happen?" These sorts of questions plague family members of addicts all the time and offer no easy answers.

Yes, actions have consequences: a particular form of upbringing or set of choices or traumatic event may contribute to a developing addiction—but not always. Studies have shown that at least half the risk of developing an addiction is genetic and that children who grow up in very troubled homes may not become addicts, whereas children from loving, happy homes can become addicts. Layering on the suggestion that a person's addiction is a sign of divine judgment (which we are not qualified to declare in the first place) is like pouring salt in a festering wound. Even if there is some truth to be found in the particular claim, there is nothing compassionate or biblically faithful about drawing this connection for those suffering from the effects of addiction.

On the contrary, if we genuinely believe that God's mercies are "new every morning" (Lamentations 3:23), we will also recognize in those lines a God for whom mercy trumps judgment over and over again. As the writer of the book of James puts it, "Mercy triumphs over judgment," and those who fail to show mercy will themselves be judged (James 2:13). Mercy, not condemnation, should be the guiding principle behind what we say to people with addiction. In response to the question "Is God judging me?" we can answer with the promise that "God's mercy endures forever" and that "great is God's faithfulness."

"Addiction is demon possession." One church leader in our survey said addiction is "a demon." This answer squares with findings from a larger survey of Christian leaders undertaken by Amy Simpson in her book *Troubled Minds.* There Simpson reports that 19.7 percent of leaders (almost one in five) say their congregations believe mental illness is "indicative of demon possession/demonic influence."[5] Admittedly, Simpson's survey addressed mental illness more generally (rather than just addiction), so deciphering whether this misconception is as pervasive when the mental illness is specifically addiction is hard to say; a reliable conclusion would probably depend on surveying a much broader demographic than my focus group permitted. Still, one leader's conviction that addiction is a demon would suggest that at least in certain pockets of the church, the belief that evil spirits lurk behind addiction's door is alive and well.

Mary's story strengthens this inference. Mary, who grew up in charismatic circles, reports having been the object of multiple attempts to cast out her demons:

> I distinctly remember one woman claiming she could "see the demon behind my eyes." When I expressed disbelief, I was told this was the demon talking through me, because the demon didn't want to leave. It liked living inside of me, and it was very strong and very high up in the demon hierarchy. I was told it had taken over my ability to think or judge accurately, so I couldn't trust myself. I realize now how incredibly disempowering this was.

For Mary, addiction was already disabling enough. She didn't need yet another way to externalize her problem (in the form of evil spirits wreaking havoc), so that her inner resources seemed even less sufficient in the face of that problem. Accusations of demon possession further dispossessed Mary of a sense of accountability for her actions, ownership in the recovery process and a capacity for loving self-connectedness. Instead, what she most needed was to discover and then tap into her own unique and God-given inner resources for overcoming addiction. In Mary's words, "I needed to be able to use my God-given brain, and to have a little faith in myself." She recalls,

> I needed some control, a sense of power, and it needed to come from *within* me, not from outside of me—not good versus evil forces battling for my soul while I sat on my hands and tried to believe hard enough, and not repetitive, redundant meetings with regurgitated catch phrases, where people tell you how they stay sober.

In addition to posing obstacles to loving the addicts in our midst, the notion that addiction is demon possession is also more often than not a fallacy. Matthew Stanford, in *Grace for the Afflicted*, notes that even in Scripture, demon possession in general is relatively rare: only the books Matthew, Mark, Luke and Acts make mention of it; exorcism never appears in the Old Testament or in New Testament letters; physical infirmities are far more common.[6] Stanford concludes that for the early church, exorcism played an insignificant role, and that for those who are believers in Christ, demon possession is not even possible.

Simpson, citing Stanford, goes on to contend that assuming demon possession or demonic influence in cases of mental illness is incompatible with Scripture.[7] In light of both the apparent rarity of demon possession in biblical times and the impossibility of demon possession in those who have accepted Jesus as their Lord and Savior, Simpson pointedly asks whether anyone really believes that 25 percent of the population of the United States (the proportion of Americans with a mental illness) is demon possessed. She goes on:

> Automatically asking questions about demon possession distracts us from our calling to minister to people in need. It is harmful and negligent and may discourage a person from receiving critical treatment. . . . Confronting demon possession or demonic influence should not be the starting point for our response to troubled people. If an illness responds to medical intervention, it's a medical problem. And that should be the starting point. If someone displays symptoms of psychological illness, we should not take time to wrestle through questions of demon possession. We should help that person seek and find psychological treatment, walk with the person through the difficult work that will follow and address spiritual issues that linger.[8]

Addiction, like all other mental illnesses, should elicit the same response.

"Addiction doesn't happen to church people." Christian writer and blogger Melody Harrison Hanson can tell you otherwise. "I can't count because it happened so many times, the number of Sundays I spent sitting in church nursing the world's worst hangover, full of shame and self-loathing," Hanson writes.[9] The statistics would suggest she is only one of many churchgoers who show up on any given Sunday struggling with some form of addiction. Christians fall prey to addiction at the same rate as everyone else, so to believe that addiction does not happen to church people is to buy into a great big lie.

Unfortunately, this lie finds ample room to sprout in the landscape that is the contemporary American church. Not unlike the rest of corporate America, many churches have come to believe they are selling a product to prospective consumers, and for this reason, they reveal only an airbrushed image of themselves. For these "attractional" churches—for which church growth and bigger budgets are the most important measures of success—weak, sick and broken people are not good for business.[10] Happy con-

> Christians fall prey to addiction at the same rate as everyone else, so to believe that addiction does not happen to church people is to buy into a great big lie.

version stories about how Jesus has changed lives and helped people live happily, healthily and successfully ever after are a whole lot easier to sell than admissions of struggle or relapse from people with chronic mental illnesses. As Simpson notes, a lot of pastors do not want "the wrong kind of people" to stand in the way of their vision of congregational success.[11]

The biggest problems with this approach are twofold. First, if you are marketing yourself as a group of attractive, put-together people, you will never have an opportunity to love and learn from people in your pews with addiction. They will either avoid your church or, in greater likelihood, fly under the radar and remain at the margins of your community. Your community forfeits an opportunity to experience real, authentic relationships forged in a crucible of brokenness and vulnerability. And recovering addicts in your congregation try to blend in, pretending to be like those nonexistent perfect people.

Second, this way of being church is antithetical to the gospel Jesus proclaims—so much so that a church that exists mainly to attract nice-looking, respectable, successful people is probably not really following Jesus. For one thing, the Jesus we meet in Scripture is rarely if ever calling those sorts of people. His mates are more often than not the poor, the outcasts, the sinners, the prostitutes— "ragamuffins," as Manning termed them. They are the people you might *least* expect a Fortune 500 company to hire.

In a similar vein, the apostle Paul urges the church in Corinth to consider their call, reminding them that not many of them were "wise by human standards" or "powerful" or of "noble birth." That is why the message of the cross can sound so ridiculous, Paul says in 1 Corinthians 1:27-29, which is precisely the point: "God chose what is foolish in the world to shame the wise; God chose what is weak in the world to shame the strong; God chose what is low and despised in the world, things that are not, to reduce to nothing things that are, so that no one might boast in the presence of God."

> If a church takes more pride in being successful than in the message that God and God alone is Savior, that church is contributing to a life-sucking lie.

If a church takes more pride in being successful and having its act together than in the message that God and God alone is Savior, that church is contributing to a life-sucking lie for which Jesus probably has little time. As one theologian framed it and then quoted another, a more "realistic theology of the church must always begin with the frank acknowledgement that . . . 'A basic reality of congregational life is that we are engaged in socially acceptable (indeed socially celebrated) patterns of mutual self-destruction.'"[12]

Sometimes it takes something traumatic like an addiction—something that shatters our protective self-understanding—to open our eyes to this truth and move toward our liberation. Spiritual breakthroughs can come with the kind of discovery writer and journalist Cathryn Kemp made after becoming hooked on prescription painkillers. "I used to think a drug addict was someone who lived on the far edges of society," Kemp writes. "Wild-eyed, shaven-headed and living in a filthy squat. That was until I became one."[13]

Maybe more churches could benefit from a similar awakening.

"Once an addict is born again, she won't relapse." In his final book, *All Is Grace*, Manning pokes holes in this common miscon-

ception. Manning was a popular, sought-after Christian speaker and writer, having written more than twenty books, including the bestseller *The Ragamuffin Gospel*. He was also a recovering alcoholic who relapsed multiple times.

The question Manning says he heard over and over again across the years was how he could relapse after having experienced a conversion to the Christian faith (or what some Christians describe as being "born again"). In Manning's words: "Sometimes [the question] has been asked with genuine sincerity; other times I'm sure it was a loaded Pharisaical grenade: 'Brennan, how could you relapse into alcoholism after your Abba encounters?'" Here is his response in *The Ragamuffin Gospel*:

> It is possible because I got battered and bruised by loneliness and failure; because I got discouraged, uncertain, guilt-ridden, and took my eyes off Jesus. Because the Christ encounter did not transfigure me into an angel. Because justification by grace through faith means I have been set in right relationship with God, not made the equivalent of a patient etherized on a table.[14]

At the end of his life, Manning goes on to say that while he stands by those same words, he believes he can whittle them down to a much briefer answer. How could he relapse after experiencing new life in Jesus? The answer: "These things happen."[15]

The fact that relapses happen yields both a scientific and a scriptural explanation. First, there is the nature of the disease itself: one of its defining characteristics is a high rate of relapse. In Mary's case, this reality meant relapsing four or five times before finding sobriety.

Chronic relapse is pretty typical in cases of addiction. For example, national studies in recent years have placed the "rate of remission" (or relapse) for addiction anywhere between 59 to 82 percent, depending on the year and the study.[16] The high-relapse nature of this disease is no respecter of persons—faith or no faith.

But there is also a biblical and theological way to explain how Manning and many like him fall back into unhealthy patterns and compulsive behaviors after experiencing a genuine conversion. The apostle Paul himself confesses to his own tendency to do the very things he does not want to do and admits to not understanding his own actions: "For I do not do what I want, but I do the very thing I hate," he exclaims (see Romans 7:15-25).

Paul's conundrum sheds light on the questionable actions of a whole cast of shady characters whom God loves and with whom God chooses to be in relationship. Many of us have read their stories in Scripture, from Adam and Eve on. Many of us count ourselves among them: Abraham, Sarah, Rachel and Moses, each with a spotty track record at best. And then come the first disciples, who having seen Jesus in the flesh and having walked and talked with him, fall away from their dearest friend in his moment of greatest need.

Their stories are a reminder that we are all prone to relapses in some form or another—and that, therefore, suggesting to an addict that his relapse is inherently a measure of the genuineness of his conversion is at best unhelpful and at worst a form of spiritual abuse. Such a suggestion fails to take seriously a number of things— among them the narrative of Scripture, the reality that sanctification is never complete in a world marred by sin and the very definition of addiction as a medical disease.

A more helpful and biblically faithful way to frame conversion and a relationship with Jesus is to view them on a much longer continuum that involves multiple experiences of being born again and being awakened anew to God's loving pursuit of us. Entering into a relationship with Jesus may immediately change some but not all of one's old habits. Sanctification is a gradual, ongoing process that can transpire across a whole lifetime and never really ends, at least until death (which some theologians have suggested is itself a final sanctifying process) and possibly not even in eternity (as ancient theologians like Gregory of Nyssa have suggested). A whole lifetime of journeying in God's grace will thus inevitably comprise failures and backsliding—and, with these prodigal moments, fresh experiences of God's power to forgive and redeem broken people.

"Prayer, Bible study and right belief are enough to cure addiction." A September 2013 LifeWay Research survey found that nearly half (48 percent) of evangelicals, fundamentalists and born-again Christians believe that prayer and Bible study alone can help people overcome serious mental illness. This misconception is dangerous because it misconstrues chronic illnesses like addiction as curable, when addiction is actually something one must learn to live with and monitor one's whole life, like diabetes or high blood pressure. In the same way that a diabetic person must learn to check her insulin levels, a recovering addict must develop daily habits of self-care that build resistance to her disease. Doing otherwise can jeopardize her life.

Another problem with this myth is that it overspiritualizes addiction, once again singling out addiction next to other infirmities as more of a spiritual problem than a physical one. That's not to say that addiction does not involve spiritual dimensions just as other sicknesses do—and I will address these later—but that it requires medical treatment just as other chronic illnesses do. To reduce the treatment of addiction to merely praying more and having more faith can actually endanger the health and life of an addict. Yes, God heals—but not always in this life, and certainly not because we have prayed more or been diligent about going to Bible study. God's ways are higher than our ways (see Isaiah 55:8). Furthermore, God uses modern medicine all the time to heal, and he does the same in cases of addiction.

Yet another wrong assumption that undergirds this myth is that addiction is a choice and getting better requires exerting greater willpower. If you believe this myth, you're in good company. A study of the public's views on food addiction and obesity revealed, for example, that approximately one-third of Americans believe food addiction and obesity are a choice.[17]

Nothing could be further from the truth of addicts' lived experiences. "Most alcoholics, for reasons yet obscure, have lost the power of choice in drink" and "are without defense against the first drink," AA's *Big Book* states.[18] Any addict will tell you the same. There is no such thing as choosing to drink only one beer. As the popular saying in recovery circles goes, "One is too many, and one hundred are never enough."

A Stanford professor of psychiatry and behavioral sciences, Dr. Keith Humphreys, who served as a senior White House drug-policy adviser, helps to explain this experience in terms of the biology and neuroscience behind it:

> It's kind of like putting on a lot of weight. Your body changes, and from then on losing weight is way harder than it ever was before you got fat in the first place. Because addiction-associated brain changes are so enduring, a lot of people are going to relapse. So the course of treatment has got to be longer-term than it often is.[19]

So there is usually a limit to how much sheer willpower or prayer or Bible study will accomplish for addicts (without additional interventions). Scripture, too, would suggest that "getting better" when it comes to finding redemption from sin, sickness and the tragedies of this life does not ultimately depend on human "righteousness." Ultimately, there is very little we can do in our own power and apart from the grace of God to make things right. We are actually far more dependent on God and a larger ecosystem of sin and grace than we usually care to admit. Wanting to get better from an addiction can be a first step toward healing, and praying for healing is a commendable part of that process; but rarely are these two things on their own enough to rid a person of addictive behaviors.

When she tells her story, Mary highlights the importance of a desire to quit using as well as her personal experience with prayer. Wanting to get better was the starting point of her journey home from the faraway land of addiction. For a long time, Mary says, "My actual problem was simple: I needed to get to the starting line—that is, I needed to *want* to quit—but I wasn't there, and I couldn't see how to get there."

> So while the church prayed for my miracle transformation, I prayed on my own, too—in between the dope hits—that God would make me want to quit. But the fact is that I didn't want to quit, and I didn't even *really* want Him to make me want to, because I wanted to get high. And so I did. Years later, I got to the starting line, and because I had the desire to quit and the tools I needed, most of my prayers during that time were (and are to this day) prayers of thankfulness, rather than half-hearted pleas for my addiction to just "go away."

Mary's story helps to illustrate how prayer and positive thinking alone are often insufficient to rid a person of addictive behaviors. (And the same might be said of Bible study and having more faith.) Spiritual tools can help in the recovery process, but viewing them as the only thing necessary can endanger that process.

What to Say to Recovering Addicts

This chapter has addressed the popular myths that, for many recovering addicts, pose a stumbling block to receiving God's love in and from the church:

- "Addiction is a sin."
- "Addiction is God's punishment or a sign of God's judgment."
- "Addiction is demon possession."
- "Addiction doesn't happen to church people."

- "Once an addict is born again, she won't relapse."
- "Prayer, Bible study and right belief are enough to cure addiction."

If ever in doubt about what *not* to say to recovering addicts in your midst, a quick review of this list may help. "But what *should* you say to addicts in your midst?" one pastor in our focus group asked. To help me answer that question, I asked Mary what message she would have liked to receive from the church (in contrast to what she did receive). She said, "Unconditional love and acceptance."

> Aside from [my church] not doing what they did do, I would've liked to have been unconditionally loved and accepted. I didn't want to be an experiment on the power of prayer or a candidate for a miracle. If church had been a more peaceful place, less intrusive and domineering; if I could've just sat there quietly, hearing how God loved me and accepted me too; if I had felt safe, if I had not felt I had to "be" or "act" in certain ways in order to gain acceptance—well, I don't know if I would have recovered any sooner, but I would have come back.

On this note, here are some suggestions for what we can and should say to addicts looking (like the rest of us) for unconditional love and acceptance:

You have been made for so much more life and love than what your addiction has taught you to expect for yourself. Remind addicts that their identity and belonging come from Jesus, not drugs, sex or any other unhealthy attachment—and that because this is true, they were made for so much more than putting needles in their veins or dialing hookers. When God has created you and called you "good," when the kingdom of God—a small piece of heaven itself—is within you, why shoot up? Life itself is waiting to be enjoyed and shared for the glory of God, who has your very best in mind. As the ancient church father Irenaeus remarked in the second century, "The glory of God is man truly alive."

God loves you just as you are, regardless of what you've done, are doing or will do. Let addicts know that God loves them unconditionally just as they are—and mean it. Lest you have any doubt about this reality or feel the least bit disingenuous declaring it to be true, remember that Christ died for you while you were still a sinner (Romans 5:8). Jesus did not wait for the human race to get its act together before demonstrating his love for us. The church need not wait either, in loving people with the disease of addiction.

God forgives you—and where you can make amends to the people you have wronged without causing further harm to them or yourself, do so. Leave the rest to God. Tomorrow is a new day. Addicts in recovery may express guilt or regret about decisions they have made when acting out of their place of addiction. Give addicts permission to confess these things confidentially to you—or in a pastoral setting where they feel safe. Assure them of God's mercy and forgiveness, which are new every morning. Encourage them, in the spirit of the twelve steps, to make an honest assessment of their shortcomings and of where they can make amends to those they have wronged.

Welcome! We want you here. Invite addicts to get involved in your congregation and to spend time with God in prayer, Bible study and other forms of spiritual community. Encourage them to see these things as an important part of the solution to their problem but not the only resource available to them. Let them know you are there to support them in finding additional resources for recovery.

Tell me your story. Has God been real to you in it? Invite addicts to share their story with you. Then take a learning posture as you listen, asking them what God has been teaching them in their journey (wherever they are on the recovery spectrum). You may be surprised by what you hear and learn.

You have a chronic disease, and we believe God wants you to find recovery—and so do we. We will walk with you every step of the way, not just on the good days. Because relapse is so common in the recovery process, let addicts know you are in this process with them for the long haul and are aware of how arduous the road ahead will be. Let them know that they will have hard days and may even relapse. And let them know that you want to be in relationship with them no matter what sort of day they are having— and when they are in trouble, you are only a phone call away.

These are just a few of the things one can and should say to people with addiction, rather than the old myths that do more harm than good. Loving addicts really begins here, with a commitment to shelving unhelpful misconceptions so we can better relate to people with addictions as human beings like the rest of us. The truth is that the church needs addicts as much as they need us. Their struggles, like ours, belong to the cosmic recovery story that our prodigal God wants to tell. By listening to and learning from one another's stories, and offering expressions of compassion and understanding and affirmations of God's mercy, we also will journey homeward, both to our prodigal God and to one another.

Discussion Questions

1. Of the myths listed, which one do you think your church is most prone to and why? How do you see this myth play out, either explicitly or implicitly, in your church's culture? What are some ways you might work to dispel this myth in your congregation?

2. Whether or not you struggle with addiction, can you personally identify with any part of Mary's story? If so, what part is it and why?

Section 2

Tools for Creating a Recovery-Friendly Church

four

Cultivating a Culture of Long-Term Sobriety

Before AA we were trying to drink
God out of a bottle.

BILL WILSON
FOUNDER OF ALCOHOLICS ANONYMOUS

THE OTHER BIGGEST QUESTION among the one hundred church leaders I surveyed was a natural corollary to getting an addict into recovery—namely, "How do I help an addict stay in recovery?" And indeed, it is not enough to "arise"; in order to arrive home, prodigal people must turn their face in that direction and begin the long walk of putting one foot in front of the other. Thankfully, with a few key tools at their disposal, churches can help in this process and so arrive home themselves.

Spiritual Resilience and Authentic, Long-Term Relationships

The best predictor of whether a prodigal will stay on a path of sobriety is this: emotional resilience.[1] The capacity to adapt to the inevitable stresses of life is vital to an addict's prospects of full recovery. Thankfully, such resilience is not a genetic trait with which one is born (although some personalities are more naturally resilient); resilience is something that can be taught, formed and "caught" within relationships of care and support. In fact, addiction recovery experts have found that the presence of resilience can be linked to having at least one strong role-model relationship from outside one's family of origin (which may explain the success of the AA sponsorship model).[2]

How, therefore, might churches best help recovering addicts stay on the path toward recovery? The answer lies in cultivating spiritual resilience, which can be the byproduct of a church culture that defines itself in terms of authentic, long-term relationships entrusted to God's care and transformation. Prodigal children's best chances of getting home depend on building reservoirs of connectedness with

> Prodigal children's best chances of getting home depend on building reservoirs of connectedness with God, one another and oneself for when the tough times hit.

God, one another and oneself for when the tough times hit, and churches can help to facilitate this process by fostering relationships characterized by mutual "response-ability," truth-telling, commitment, acceptance, compassion and understanding.[3]

Mutual "response-ability." Antithetical to what many churches might think, their job in relating to addicts is not to be construed merely in "helping" terms, with addicts only being the recipients of that help. There is something inherently hubristic about this assumption—as if the church holds all the answers to recovery and is there to dispense them. Relationships in which there is clearly one helper and one recipient of help (and no exchange of these roles) usually are strictly clinical or professional—and many recovering addicts have these sorts of relationships already in place coming out of a recovery program, such as in the form of a doctor, therapist or recovery coach.

Where the church can most help then is in inviting the mutuality of care that recovering addicts may not be getting elsewhere. The beautiful irony here is that the churches that recognize how recovering addicts can also help them will go the furthest in helping people stay in recovery. Successful recovery, after all, means moving from a place of victimhood and irresponsibility to a place of ownership and response-ability. Addicts must move from passively accepting help as the beneficiary of others' acts of kindness to extending help to others and becoming response-able to the people in their lives. And church communities must move from a position of meeting needs and providing "service" to empowerment and "kinship" in relating to addicts.[4]

Even in an addict's place of greatest need, churches can listen to and learn from him, rather than making him an object of pastoral care or missionary zeal. After all, at the heart of the gospel we proclaim is an earth-shattering claim about reality itself: at the center of existence is a God whose death on a cross and resurrection have transfigured brokenness into gift. The "principle of transfiguration," as Archbishop Desmond Tutu has aptly named it, says that

> nothing, no one, and no situation is "untransfigurable," that the whole of creation, nature, waits expectantly for its transfiguration, when it will be released from its bondage and share in the glorious liberty of the children of God, when it will not be just dry inert matter but will be translucent with divine glory.[5]

And this transfiguration is ongoing. "The texture of suffering changes when we begin to see it as redemptive," Tutu writes, noting that human beings can tolerate suffering but can't tolerate meaninglessness.[6]

One way human suffering thus becomes meaningful is when the lessons learned from it can be shared with others. Mutuality of relationship begins to happen when we invite God's blessings to shine in and through the wounds and fissures we behold in others and ourselves.[7] Addicts—all of us—can experience transfiguration within relationships of mutual care and support.

In contrast, focusing only on the needs of another human being in order to "save" her can greatly impair our vision, obscuring the gifts and contributions of that person. Relating to an addict exclusively in terms of how he should be fixed or saved (rather than as a person made in the image of God who on that ground alone has something to teach us) not only diminishes his own capacity for response-ability but also reduces the capacity of the self-appointed fixer to be attentive to how God is *already* at work.

In addition, the project of fixing is one that the Bible says only God can do; there is only one Savior. And this truth is liberating. The church need not bear the impossible burden of fixing or saving people. Instead, the church can first and foremost set out to build relationships with recovering addicts that are grounded in mutual love and learning. The posture entailed is thus not one of "What do I do to fix their situation?" but rather "What is God already doing in this person's life, and how can I connect with that work?" Is the person in recovery attending a twelve-step group and finding spiritual community there, for example? If so, ask them if you can come along and see for yourself how God's Spirit is at work in their life and the lives of others there. In doing so, you will be building a relationship of mutual trust and care.

Another way to cultivate this mutuality in relationships is by employing what pastor and theologian Matt Russell describes as "theological curiosity."[8] Russell is a founding member of Mercy Street Church in Houston, a spiritual community for recovering addicts and spiritual refugees. When asked to recall how Mercy Street began, Russell says he spent a lot of time in coffee shops listening, learning and asking questions. What he most wanted to know was why so many of these people no longer belonged to a church and what they thought "church" really ought to be. Out of the answers—those that the recovering addicts and spiritual refugees themselves provided—Mercy Street was born.

It took the curiosity of Russell and others—a humble willingness to learn—to initiate these conversations that became the ground for meaningful, long-term relationships. Theological curiosity is therefore about asking where the Spirit of God is already at work in the world.[9] This teachable desire to learn more about God's ways and an attentiveness to God's freeing, restoring and creative work in the world is a necessary precursor to asking how to follow God there.

"If we believe the Spirit of God is happening in the world, our question is not 'What do I do?' but 'What is happening?'" Russell says. "If something is happening, the very life of God, the question is. . . . 'What is happening, and how do I befriend that?'"[10]

By way of illustration, if the God of Exodus, who leads the people of Israel out of bondage, is still at work in the world today, the next question can be, "*Where* is this same God now freeing people in bondage?"[11] If the God of Exodus, who provided manna for his people in the wilderness, is still at work today, the next question can be, "Where are hungry people being fed?"[12] These are the places where the church can go and be transformed by the Spirit of God.

However, Russell says, the church's counterintuitive and counterbiblical tendency is to build mission and ministry programs with the mantra "We've got it. You need it. How about it."[13] The problem with this mindset is that it sets up a false equation between the church and the kingdom of God, so that the church, rather than the world, becomes the center of God's activity—when Scripture would suggest otherwise.[14] In Scripture, the Spirit of God is alive and well, creating, restoring, healing and setting free in the world, which is where the church is invited to follow Jesus and witness to his work.

Your first job in building authentic relationships with addicts is therefore to find ways to learn from the recovering addicts in your midst and in their world, and to let them teach you and share their experience of God's grace with you—even if that grace might be called by a different name or shows up in an AA meeting rather than church. The offshoot of this work will be greater mutual response-ability: as recovering addicts find a new web of relationships in which to practice responsiveness toward others, churches learn how to respond to the work of the Spirit in recovering addicts' lives. This life together thus becomes the seedbed for character reformation and spiritual renewal for both addicts and those who seek to love them.

Truth-telling as "testimony." Authentic relationships that help addicts stay in recovery also entail truth-telling. While this element would seem like a no-brainer, telling the truth in church circles can often be difficult. Professor of Recovery Ministry Dale Ryan, who directs Fuller Seminary's Institute on Recovery Ministry, gives the illustration of the recovering addict who in AA meetings can be honest about the hard, nitty-gritty details of his life but then in church is quick to answer "fine" or "blessed" when asked how he is. Many of us can identify.[15]

Ryan notes that many of us in the church have learned how to give a great testimony, often tying up our faith with a pretty bow only after we have come through a crisis and are able to look back and see God's provision in the rough patches. "It's fine to tell the truth if you're all better now," Ryan explains.[16] Yet we are often terrified to tell the truth about how we are "not better now"—about our wounds and the ways we wound others and the rough edges and incompleteness of our stories. We do not know how to share our sins, doubts and imperfections when we find ourselves in the midst of them.

To be sure, our predilection for deception goes along with being human. In a similar vein, Mark Twain is quoted as saying that "a lie can travel halfway around the world while the truth is putting on its shoes." But prodigal churches are the people doing the hard work of putting on the shoes. Their concern is with living as wholly as possible in reality and representing this reality for others—*being* well, as opposed to only looking well.

There are a number of concrete ways you can encourage truth-telling in your congregation. Consider inviting the often voiceless or marginalized people in your community to share honestly and from the heart, without editing out the hard stuff: the single mother working hard to survive, or the couple reeling from the death of a child, or the recovering addict for whom daily compulsion is a struggle to overcome. There is no "right" testimony, as if in order to be a Christian we must fit our story into a redemptive template that obscures our lived reality. Instead, giving your community permission to tell the truth about themselves and the world they inhabit can be another entrée into authentic relationship that will sustain not just recovering addicts but all of God's wayward children. Sometimes this giving of permission means being the first to ask the hard questions.

Telling the truth can also come from the pulpit, with a willingness to capture the grays and complexities of a life of faith and doubt, sainthood and sinfulness, both in sermons and in leading the weekly prayer of confession.

Leaders can also normalize confession within small groups and support groups, and between accountability partners (in AA, these are called sponsors). Regular opportunities for the sharing of prayer concerns, whether in worship or a weekly prayer meeting or healing service, can also encourage a culture of honesty and inclusiveness of all stories, not just those of the "victorious Christians" in our midst.

Being aware of the kinds of deceptions to which addicts in recovery are uniquely susceptible can also be helpful in creating a climate of greater transparency, vulnerability and accountability. Sensitivity to these potential snares on the road to recovery will better prepare you to help recovering addicts anticipate them and maneuver around them.

One-on-one conversations are the best context for unmasking lies and self-deception for what they are (dangerous cognitive distortions) and replacing them with truths. Some common cognitive distortions used to justify addictive behavior include the following, as relayed in Welch and Shogren's book *Addictive Behavior*, with my italicized suggestions for how to respond:

- "One [drink, hit] isn't going to hurt." *This one hit could cause me to overdose and die.*

- "I am hopeless anyway, so why bother trying to stop?" *I've been promised a future and a hope.*

- "If I do it only once, it will prove that I have self-control." *One is too many, and a thousand is never enough; with one I lose all self-control.*

- "Maybe I'll just hang out with the guys and not drink anything at all." *I'll set myself up for a fall if I do this.*

- "If she wouldn't treat me that way, I wouldn't have to drink." *I do not have to react to the actions of others.*

- "I just need a little something to relax with." *I am capable of relaxing without a substance. I can meditate, listen to music, etc.*[17]

Intentionality of commitment. Intentional commitment says to a recovering addict, "I will help you get home; will you help me, too?" You are, in essence, covenanting to be part of God's work in one another's lives, however that may evolve. You are not covenanting to an agenda or program for how God should work. You are covenanting to a relationship that you have surrendered to God and to the Spirit of God working itself out in one another's lives, and this commitment involves supporting one another in known places of weakness.

Taking the following concrete steps will manifest this intentional commitment:

Invite recovering addicts to share what congregational language or practices trigger or enable their addiction, so you can be sensitive to these things and work to eliminate them in your life together. For example, does the fact that the men's group meets at a pub become an occasion for temptation for the recovering alcoholic in your midst? Do you offer a nonalcoholic option during communion? Or do other elements in your worship service present stumbling blocks? In his autobiography of teenage heroin addiction, Jim Carroll tells the story of a friend who tried to quit his heroin habit by reconnecting with the Catholic church of his childhood. The smell of the church incense, however, was enough to remind him of the sweet odor of heroin—so much so that he left straight from church to go shoot up again.[18]

Ask recovering addicts if they have a plan in place for their recovery and how you can help them stick to it. If they do not have a plan in place to prevent relapse, encourage them to develop one with their sponsor or accountability partner. You now know just how common relapse is among recovering addicts. Especially during the first months back in the real world, recovering addicts can benefit from preparing themselves for the internal and external stresses that often precede relapse. A plan will help a recovering addict prepare for and navigate these various contingencies.

In developing a plan to prevent relapse, an addict can brainstorm all of the various factors in her life that will make sobriety difficult: relational conflicts; old social circles and occasions to drink or use; or unresolved consequences of an addiction, such as snowballing hospital bills or pending drunk driving charges.[19] These external stresses can precipitate a relapse.

So can internal stresses, such as all of the old unhealthy patterns of self-talk that feed addictive behavior: denial, projection and externalization. Having a plan in place with strategies and specific steps to follow when the cravings hit is always a good idea, and church leaders and their communities can gently insert themselves into that plan, making it clear that they understand the dynamics of addiction recovery and want to be part of an addict's recovery.

Encourage the rhythms of recovery in an addict's life by embracing them yourself or by connecting him with others who practice these rhythms. If an addict practices the twelve steps and attends recovery meetings, practice the steps with him or attend a meeting with him every so often. Going regularly is even better. Invitations to deeper life together develop organically within authentic, long-term relationships that embody commitment to one another.

Invite recovering addicts with open arms into the life of your church and its various ministries, demonstrating that you value their contributions as much as those of the person next to them. When I ask clients who have come through my program how the church most helped them stay in recovery, one resounding commonality emerges: clients say that the church provided them with natural outlets for service and ministry and a new web of life-giving relationships.

Unconditional acceptance. In the opening to his book *Addiction and Grace*, Gerald May shares the following conviction:

> After twenty years of listening to the yearnings of people's hearts, I am convinced that all human beings have an inborn desire for God. Whether we are consciously religious or not, this desire is our deepest longing and our most precious treasure. It gives us meaning. Some of us have repressed this desire, burying it beneath so many other interests that we are completely unaware of it. Or we may experience it in different ways—as a longing for wholeness, completion or fulfillment. Regardless of how we describe it, it is a longing for love. It is a hunger to love, to be loved, and to move closer to the Source

of love. This yearning is the essence of the human spirit; it is the origin of our highest hopes and most noble dreams.[20]

If May is right—that a desire for love defines what it means to be human—then helping human beings connect with love itself is not just central to cultivating long-term sobriety among addicts but essential to helping every person in your congregation become more fully human and more fully alive. In other words, the two journeys toward sobriety and fullness of humanity coincide and shape one another—and will depend most fundamentally on the love you are learning to share with God and one another.

> Helping human beings connect with love itself is not just central to cultivating long-term sobriety among addicts but essential to helping every person in your congregation become more fully human and more fully alive.

Are the relationships within your congregation authentic? Are they based on mutual love and support, truth-telling as testimony and intentional commitment? The deepest longing of the human heart, to be loved and accepted not as one should be but as one *is,* resides in an affirmative answer to these questions. Whether we call this universal longing a desire for wholeness or God or love, that longing is there, making us uniquely human. And, in response to this universal longing, the whole meaning of the gospel might be summed up in one simple but powerful declaration: "You are accepted."[21]

The incarnation of unconditional acceptance takes practice.[22] Here are a few suggestions for ways to inculcate it in your midst:

Help people set measurable, daily goals for their spiritual journey. Recognize that setbacks like relapse can belong to the journey toward abstinence (rather than posing a final detour) and need not be feared or dwelt upon. Steer one another away from all-or-nothing thinking about some future spiritual perfection and instead keep your focus on the small, daily victories. Encouraging the living of life "one day at a time" helps. The fact that God's mercies are new every morning means that God's grace can be enough for today, and whatever spiritual assaults or temptations may come in the day ahead, the promise of a new beginning is only a breath away. So encourage the making of spiritual goals that can be achieved within the course of one day— or in some cases one hour at a time—rather than a whole lifetime. In this context, "total abstinence," while still a daunting task, becomes a bit less intimidating viewed through the lens of the here and now of today (rather than against one's entire future).

Practice, practice, practice forgiveness. One man at the end of his life told a pastor I know that he had found an immense sense of release after listing all the names of the people who had wronged him across his lifetime and then intentionally forgiving each of them in prayer, releasing them to God. Forgiveness is not a warm, fuzzy theory; in order to be real, it needs to be put into action and tried deliberately with the help of the Holy Spirit. You can encourage concrete expressions of forgiveness wherever there are opportunities— in worship, sermons and Bible studies on forgiveness, for example. You can engage in relationally based ministries to people groups who have received the message that they are not accepted, like prisoners, the homeless, the mentally ill, addicts and alcoholics, with the goal of asking God to teach you unconditional acceptance for "the other."

Find ways to celebrate even the smallest of victories as milestones. In times of corporate celebration—say, for example, a wedding or anniversary—give room for congregational sharing about the smaller victories in life, those times when as prodigal people you responded to God's love, however small the gesture. The example of AA is instructive. Over the course of one and the same meeting, and with the same gusto, attendees may celebrate one member's fortieth year of sobriety next to another's one week of being clean.[23] During times of corporate prayer and in regular sharing from the pulpit, you can create an environment that comes to see any step in a direction toward home, however small or large, as something worthy of celebration.

Compassion and understanding. Authentic, long-term relationships with recovering addicts can't survive without compassion and understanding. Walking an addict home—helping her stay in recovery—depends on a capacity to suffer with her in her places of pain (*compassion* literally means "to suffer with"). And in this case, compassion requires an understanding of the dynamics of recovery. The more familiar churches are with the physical, emotional and spiritual aspects of recovery and the nature of life after addiction, the more they will tap into their God-given reserves of compassion.[24]

Just as addiction is laden with certain symptoms, so are withdrawal and recovery. In a nutshell, these will involve greatly heightened emotional reactivity, so that even the smallest of issues or stressors can generate a grossly disproportionate response; psychological disturbances like impulsivity, memory loss and confusion; and physical issues such as weight gain, sexual dysfunction and clinically diagnosable conditions like anxiety or depression.

Awareness of these various aspects of addiction and recovery will foster greater understanding of the plight of recovering addicts and ways to be with them in their walk home. Greater understanding breeds greater compassion—and, in turn, more effectiveness at helping recovering addicts take certain steps in their self-care that can alleviate or address the above symptoms. Here are some of those measures:

- Regular psychotherapy to address anxiety and other psychological issues, as well as sexual dysfunction

- Psychiatric oversight for situations involving clinically diagnosed depression or anxiety (or other mental health disorders)

- Regular medical checkups

- Healthy sleep habits, as well as breathing and meditation practices
- Basic organizational habits, such as keeping a to-do list or daily planner that will assist with short-term memory challenges
- Nutritional eating habits and exercise
- Regular involvement in support and recovery groups

Cravings demand a strategy of their own. Churches in authentic, long-term relationship with the addicts in their midst can implement a method known as the Three Rs: recognize, reduce, refocus.[25] First, *recognize* a craving for what it is. When a recovering addict shares a vivid dream or memory associated with his drug of choice or seems to be in a particularly elated or depressed mood, he may be experiencing a craving. Do not be afraid to ask him whether he is.

Then *reduce* the craving by engaging in an activity that interrupts the craving. Often a craving will not last long. An alternative distraction can help here, such as vigorous exercise; eating a nutritious snack; talking with a friend about the craving; meditation or the use of a relaxation technique; or, if the craving is environmentally triggered, disengaging from the tempting situation.[26]

Once the craving is gone, *refocus* on a prior source of attention, without overanalyzing the meaning of the craving.[27] Too much navel-gazing can actually reinforce the power of a craving or misplace the real issue (which is purely a craving). Instead, recovering addicts can be assured that their cravings mean they are on the road to recovery and that the longer they stay on the path of recovery, the more their cravings will diminish in frequency and intensity.

In cases when the Three Rs fail and relapse occurs, churches that are in authentic, long-term relationships with the addicts in their midst will be in an ideal position to steer them back into recovery. They can respond compassionately by

- normalizing the experience of relapse (as something that describes the disease of addiction, thereby removing the shame and stigma)

- offering the assurance that repetition is not failure but another occasion to learn, and then asking what needs to be learned that was not learned before

- praying together for the obsession to lift[28]

- encouraging addicts to see relapse as one more conduit to spiritual growth and stronger long-term recovery

- reminding addicts that rates of relapse are highest (and therefore risks of relapse strongest) within the first year of recovery and then drop significantly after that[29]

These answers to the most common physical and psychological challenges encountered in recovery are not a panacea. There is a reason why those who have been through recovery have often described it as the hardest thing they have ever done. But knowledge of the physical and psychological hurdles of recovery can only enrich churches' efforts to minister compassionately to addicts from within the framework of authentic, long-term relationships.

And I suspect the traits that define these relationships—and that form the genetic sequence of prodigal people—are not just good for addicts in recovery. They are good for all of God's people—and they are good for the world. Mutual response-ability, truth-telling as testimony, intentionality of commitment, unconditional acceptance, compassion and understanding—these can keep us headed in the direction of home.

Rat Park—and the Land of Milk and Honey

Spiritual and emotional resilience, formed in the crucible of a relationship with Jesus and with one another, is the pathway to finding freedom, wholeness and abundant life. These are the outposts of a land that flows with milk and honey. They are the fulfillment of our deepest human longing and an expression of humanity at its best.

And as the pathos-ridden words of one alcoholic illustrate, addiction at its heart is a misguided effort to find the "land of milk and honey": "When I reached a certain point in a drink, I felt as though I was on the edge of a beautiful land. I kept drinking to try to find it, even though I never did."[30]

Churches can help people with addiction stay in recovery by encouraging them to seek the land of milk and honey that will not disappoint them: the kingdom of God. Churches do this work of witnessing to God's *shalom*—the ongoing work of Jesus in the world—through a ministry of word and deed—not just by preaching unconditional grace on Sundays but also by seeking to live it daily in the world.[31] In this way, churches can embrace the reality of the kingdom and its fruit. Love, joy, peace, patience, gentleness, kindness and self-control—these byproducts of a life fully surrendered to God are far more persuasive appeals than the guilt-laden, fear-inducing measures that emphasize judgment over grace and mercy.

> Churches can help people with addiction stay in recovery by encouraging them to seek the land of milk and honey that will not disappoint them: the kingdom of God.

Science itself seems to confirm this claim. Remember those poor rats on crack? They didn't have a chance when their only choice was either heroin or water paired with solitude in a cage. The heroin always won out.

But as one researcher discovered, the plight of those rats took a dramatic turn for the better when they were given a more life-giving alternative to their quick fix in the form of a rats' paradise known as Rat Park.[32] Rat Park was a lush cage where the rats could enjoy delicious rat food, plenty of rat friends and other fun, wholesome stimuli, like bright-colored balls to roll and tunnels to scamper down.

Strikingly, the rats with good lives, those residing in Rat Park, avoided the heroin-laced water, essentially shunning it. They consumed the drugged water at less than a quarter of the rate that the rats in isolation did, and unlike the rats in isolation, none of the rats in Rat Park died during the course of the study period.

Like Rat Park, the kingdom of God is a land that once beheld is hard to trade in for cheap thrills or quick fixes. When congregations begin to participate in what is happening in the kingdom of God, they no longer have time for unfruitful habits. They do not want to drink from ratty, old droppers (pun intended) or wells that run dry.

The same is true for recovering addicts. When the spiritual equivalent of Rat Park is in their midst, they will have less desire for hitting drug-delivering levers. Take TJ, for example. TJ came to inpatient treatment in the fall of 2012 after a short detoxification from alcohol and opiates, including heroin. He was not raised in the church and describes his teenaged years as a time of agnosticism. Eventually, TJ started to drink and experiment with drugs and "this progressively got worse," he recalls. "By age twenty-three, I had crashed my motorcycle; my relationships with friends, girlfriends and family were damaged; and I wanted to check out. I felt as if I was so deep into my using I could never pull myself out."

It was in treatment that TJ says he first really met Jesus—and it was in church that TJ discovered a whole community of people with whom he could share that life-giving relationship.

Now several years sober and with a job in recovery, TJ attributes his ongoing sobriety to active involvement in the church, in addition to AA meetings and working the program daily. For him, weekly, Spirit-filled worship and sermons, the daily application of faith and the twelve steps, and the sense of God's presence in the welcome and fellowship of other Christians—both those in recovery and those "who didn't have such a wicked past as mine"—

were the life-giving alternatives that rendered alcohol and drugs pointless and no longer necessary.

As an example, TJ cites the warm sense of connection he felt upon accepting an invitation to a birthday party from a friend from church:

> I was nervous because I didn't know what to expect. There were about seven or eight of us and the energy was awesome. The women cooked food for us, and we prayed before we ate. We ended up playing games, like board games that you would play with your family at a holiday or something. We had so much fun playing simple games with tons of laughter. They weren't in recovery but they didn't drink. We were like a family that night. . . . I realized that not everyone drinks and uses drugs to have a good time—and that we can have a blast just fellowshipping like "Crazy Christians" (as we were calling ourselves by the end of the night). I've seen the goodness in people at the church. That really impacted me. I've been invited to a special seminar, hung out with missionaries, been at youth services and gotten to know people at church. There are so many ministries to get involved with—over one hundred at the church I attend. . . . They offer Celebrate Recovery. . . . They hold meetings and have community groups to get involved in.[33]

Like Rat Park maybe—but a whole lot better.

Kintsugi and the Art of Broken Pieces

A form of Japanese artwork known as *kintsugi* takes broken ceramics and repairs them with a special lacquer mixed with gold, silver or platinum. The philosophy that undergirds *kintsugi* is that broken parts should not be hidden or thrown away but instead reincorporated into a product that, when finished, will be even more beautiful to behold.

Addiction recovery is like divine *kintsugi*. I have seen this miraculous and creative work of God play out in the lives of many recovering addicts who, like TJ, have discovered they are beloved children of God—maybe precisely because of the brokenness that was there in the first place. And I have the privilege of witnessing clients integrate their experience of brokenness within a life that, in the long haul, will be better for it—more beautiful, more original, more extraordinary to behold. The lesson for churches seeking to help addicts stay in recovery, then, is that such cracks, chips and broken pieces need not be thrown away, ignored or denied, but can be dealt with in the open, in authentic, long-term relationships among recovering people.

I suspect all of us need God's *kintsugi* to be reconfigured in beautiful and original ways.

Discussion Questions

1. How is your congregation investing in authentic, long-term relationships with one another?

2. Of the qualities that define these relationships (mutual responseability, truth-telling as testimony, etc.), is there one that your congregation has already gone a long way in developing? Is there one that your congregation needs to develop more of?

five

Ending the Shame

If we really believe the gospel we proclaim, we'll be honest about our own beauty and brokenness, and the beautiful broken One will make himself known to our neighbors through the chinks in our armor—and in theirs.

FIL ANDERSON
BREAKING THE RULES

NOBODY SETS OUT TO BECOME AN ADDICT. They may find that a few drinks at the bar help numb deep-seated feelings of insecurity that would otherwise keep them from socializing with colleagues. Or that treatment for Parkinson's disease may spike levels of dopamine in the brain—and in turn, a new predisposition for gambling.[1] That first rush of snorting cocaine—of getting high and feeling on top of the world—may seem like an easy escape from a low-grade sense of depression about the way things are, and online porn may appear to be a harmless way to treat a pervasive sense of loneliness and alienation. But, before you know it, you're regularly snorting coke or trolling Craigslist for anonymous hookups. Addiction is never a choice quite like choosing to play the ukulele or hike the Appalachian Trail might be.

Again, addiction is a brain disease, according to an overwhelming consensus in the medical and scientific communities. The American Society of Addiction Medicine (ASAM) defines addiction as a "primary, chronic disease of brain reward, motivation, memory and related circuitry" that "leads to characteristic biological, psychological, social and spiritual manifestations."[2] The disease is characterized by a pathological pursuit of reward or relief by substance use and other behaviors, and like other chronic diseases often entails relapse and remission, as well as the prospect of disability or premature death if left untreated.[3] The latest edition of the American Psychiatric Association's gold-standard textbook for clinicians, known as the *Diagnostic and Statistical Manual of Mental Disorders* (DSM-5) classifies addiction as a mental illness.

Addiction, like other chronic diseases, is never a life aspiration. Take, for example, the story of "Angie." Angie was reared in a mainline church home. Her parents loved her, and she was afforded a good life, playing sports, attending church youth group and excelling academically in high school. She went on to college, got her graduate degree and entered the helping profession. By this time, she had also strayed from her childhood faith.

Then Angie was in a terrible car accident and required prescription pain pills for her rehabilitation. She took them as prescribed but soon found that they gave her energy—an added boost. She kept taking them, citing her pain as the reason, but found that the euphoric effect they had on her helped her get through the day.

Life was easier on pain pills: Angie didn't feel sad, and life challenges were easier to meet. But as her body built up tolerance, she had to take more and more. She then began to doctor shop, and before she knew it was consuming one month of prescribed pain pills in the space of a week. Her work began to suffer, and supervisors stepped in. In shame she admitted that her pill use was out of control. Her supervisor gave her a month of leave, and she went to a traditional treatment program. She stayed sober for several months through her own strength. AA and NA (Narcotics Anonymous) were not for her. Nor did she feel a need for ongoing counseling. One day she found a pill in the pocket of her jeans in the back of the closet. The urge was too much. That one pill sent her in a downward spiral of more guilt and shame, cravings and relapse.

The Problem and Origins of Shame

Because addiction is a disease (albeit with unique contours), talking about its cure in terms of mere choice or the exercise of willpower is not a helpful avenue of discussion.[4] Talking about shame, however, is. That is because shame and addiction are like conjoined twins; they form a mutually reinforcing cycle, so that addressing addiction requires uncovering shame and its tremendous power in the lives of addicts. But what exactly is shame?

The Merriam-Webster dictionary defines shame as "a feeling of guilt, regret, or sadness that you have because you know you have done something wrong; an ability to feel guilt, regret, or embarrassment; or, dishonor or disgrace." The last of these definitions, "dishonor or disgrace," comes closest to a clinical understanding. Whereas guilt entails remorse over specific mistakes made or sins committed, shame affects a person's whole understanding of her self-worth and identity: "I am bad" as opposed to "I did something bad." As Brené Brown puts it,

> Shame and addiction are like conjoined twins; they form a mutually reinforcing cycle, so that addressing addiction requires uncovering shame.

"Guilt is about behavior: 'I made a mistake.' Shame is about self: 'I am a mistake.'"[5] And there are few things more *dis*graceful (that is, grace-denying) than an inner conviction that *I am the mistake.*

Compulsive, repetitive behavior, which changes the neurochemical makeup of the brain over time, often evolves from and feeds on this inherent sense of shame or unworthiness. An initial impulse to take that first hit or click that link to pornographic images can quickly mushroom into a self-imposed exile from oneself, one's God and one's neighbor—because of shame. The same shame that led the first man and woman in paradise to cover themselves in fig leaves and hide from their Creator is one of the biggest reasons why many addicts will never find freedom. As Robin Williams once said, "Cocaine for me was a place to hide." Shame can make hiding seem like the *only* option.

That said, the shame unique to this sickness does not excuse addicts from responsibility for their actions. Like anybody with a medical diagnosis, be it diabetes or high blood pressure, addicts should not be blamed for having their illness; but they can be held accountable for getting better and staying healthy, whether that means taking their medication, seeing a therapist or regularly attending recovery group meetings. Addicts' choices and behaviors, like anyone's, have consequences that they, like everyone, must face.

So healing from addiction first requires uncovering shame and its origins. Former pastor, church planter and recovering sex addict TC Ryan tells the story of his own harrowing journey through the darkness of sex addiction as a minister and offers insights in his book *Ashamed No More: A Pastor's Journey Through Sex Addiction.* He describes various sources of shame: childhood trauma and abuse can contribute to low self-esteem and a sense of inherent unworthiness, and dysfunctional family systems can send the message that misbehaving children should be ashamed of themselves. So can past failures, both those committed by oneself and those suffered at the hands of others.[6]

Over time, such messages can become encoded in the mental scripts addicts play over and over again:

- I'll never measure up.

- I'm not good enough.

- If they only knew just how bad I am, they'd never accept me.

But for Ryan, there is one more source of shame for addicts, one that because of his calling as a pastor he finds "painful to write"— and that's the church. He observes that

> for many folks, the very spiritual community where the message they ought to get is that they are unconditionally loved by God and God's people is a place of moralizing that ends up playing on their vulnerabilities to shame. Instead of love and redemption, the takeaway from Christian churches for far too many people is one of moralizing condemnation. They are told how they ought to behave in a spirit or style that condemns who they are.[7]

The Stigma of Addiction in the Church

I invited a group of clients to share about the messages they received from the church, either implicitly or explicitly. Most of the messages were shaming and impacted the individuals' spiritual identities to the point they thought they didn't belong. Here were their answers:

- I'm the chief of sinners.

- I'm a horrible person because I can't control my drinking.

- I've broken every commandment.

- Addiction is not a disease. It's a sin. I should be able to control it.

- You are doing this to yourself. It's your fault. If you really wanted to, you would stop.

- Go to church more and you'll do better. Pray more. Tithe more. Take Communion more.

- I fell away from God because of the addiction and am not good enough to come back.

- I took Communion as a protection for myself because I was afraid I might overdose and go to hell.

- I don't deserve forgiveness.

It would be impossible to determine how much each of these messages is a projection of the recovering addicts' internalized shame and how much is the real takeaway in congregations, whether directly (from the pulpit and in worship, for example) or more indirectly (from a church culture). The overall impression, though, is that for many of the clients coming I have treated, church was not a safe place because there they felt judged and alienated. There they felt shame.

If the church can be a stumbling block on the path to recovery, can it even be said that the church is helping addicts move beyond their shame? Yes . . . sometimes. Some of our clients—albeit a significantly smaller proportion of them—said they received positive responses from the church before coming through our program. One client said, "I attend a nonjudgmental, accepting congregation where we have recovery groups. I feel very accepted and look forward to going back." Another was quick to admit that "my church could help, but I felt shame because I was putting up a front of sobriety in the middle of a very accepting environment. That was all on me and not from them."

> Americans are more inclined to view addiction as a sign of moral failing than they are other mental disorders, such as bipolar disorder or schizophrenia.

One positive response acknowledged that the church lacks an understanding of addiction: "I could separate the overall message of the gospel from people who didn't understand my struggle."

Based on these findings, it seems safe to assume that in the church addiction remains at least as much of a stigma as among the larger American public. Findings published in the journal *Psychiatric Services* point to a significant discrepancy in how Americans view addiction in relation to other mental illnesses.[8] Americans are more inclined to view addiction as a sign of moral failing than they are other mental disorders, such as bipolar disorder or schizophrenia.

Doing Better Than "No Casseroles"

When she first came to our program after her relapse, Angie was like so many addicts who have internalized that stigma. She had come to see the church of her upbringing as a place of *dis*grace, where her shame would only shout at higher decibel levels. Still, where the church had failed her, there was something irresistibly alluring about a prodigal God who welcomes home broken people. That something was enough to land Angie in a Christian program like ours.

By the grace of God, and with the help of local churches working collaboratively and intentionally with our program to welcome her home, Angie was able to reconnect with this God of love and forgiveness. This God was a far cry from the angry parent who shakes a finger and exclaims, "You should be ashamed of yourself." This God had time to celebrate the present moment as an opportunity to restore what was lost.

During her time with us, Angie began to realize that she wasn't a bad person for being an addict. Nor was God angry with her. She wasn't being punished; she was sick. She reconnected to her faith and today is back in a fulfilling job, has a sponsor, is attending recovery meetings and is involved in a church. Her spiritual life is vital, and she reports being "happy, joyous and free."[9]

Angie's homecoming testifies to the fact that faith-based recovery works. Every day, in stories like hers, I see prodigal children coming home to a God they needed to rediscover as recklessly in love with them. Every day, my staff and I see healing happening before our very eyes: broken lives transfigured by grace. And every day in addiction rehab, humbled, broken people admit their desperation for God's healing touch and a second chance.

Does this kind of experience sound like church—or at least what church *ought* to involve? I asked respondents in my survey of one hundred church leaders how many times in the last year they had been asked for help with an addiction (either a chemical dependency problem like alcohol or prescription drugs, or a process addiction involving food, sex/porn or gambling). Thirty-one percent answered "never," with another 40 percent reporting that they had been approached only "one to two times" in the last year.[10] This finding would suggest that if the great majority of our survey respondents have been asked for help with an addiction only once, twice or not at all in any given year, chances are their congregations are not places of healing from addiction, where those on the path to recovery can know they'll find love and support. But is such an inference fair or accurate?

In her book *Troubled Minds*, Amy Simpson examines lingering church hang-ups around mental illness more generally, with a view to replacing these with healthier, more constructive approaches. She observes that whereas the church is usually quick to organize meals for sick people in its midst, the approximately 25 percent of people in our churches who suffer from some form of mental illness receive no such thing.[11] Simpson goes on to remark, "No wonder several people I talked with called mental illness the 'no-casserole illness.'"[12]

Simpson and her interlocutors make a good point, one that by default would seem to hold true for addiction, too (as a mental illness): if, in American society, addiction often goes untreated, in the church, being addicted won't land you a home-cooked meal from the church caring committee. Instead, most addicts in the throes of their illness will have to count on their local take-out restaurant or the frozen section of the nearest supermarket.

The Shame of a Largely Untreated Epidemic

There is another reason why the term *shame* enters into a discussion of loving the addicts in our midst: it is a disgrace—some would say *shameful*—that addiction in this country and around the world now represents a tragedy of epic proportions and that a looming gap in treating a treatable illness remains. The number of Americans now affected by various forms of addiction (as addicts themselves or as family or friends of addicts) is an indisputable majority. A recent study by the National Center on Addiction and Substance Abuse at Columbia University (CASA Columbia) has found that the disease of addiction now affects more Americans than heart conditions, diabetes or cancer.[13] (This finding exclusively relies on statistics regarding alcohol, nicotine and drug abuse, and would be even more dramatically high if behavioral disorders involving food, sex and gambling were also included.) Then there are the 43 percent of American families who report having at least one alcoholic family member.[14] In other words, addiction, if often hidden, is rampant in American society and could fittingly be called "the elephant in the room."

In a race to keep up with the spread of this epidemic, recovery group options in the United States have proliferated—but maybe not fast enough. Since its founding in 1935, Alcoholics Anonymous (AA) has grown to a global membership of two million, with some two-thirds of those members coming from the United States. Not included in this number are the many groups that have spun off from AA, adopting the twelve-step model for recovery from just about anything, from online gaming to hoarding. While their membership pales in comparison to that of AA, these offshoots represent a significant number of Americans: for example, Narcotics Anonymous (645,000 members); Al-Anon (340,000 members); Co-Dependents Anonymous (11,000 members); and Overeaters Anonymous (50,000 to 65,000 members), to name just a few.[15]

This exponential growth of twelve-step groups has accompanied an unprecedented expansion of the professional addiction treatment industry. Just ten years ago, that industry, encompassing public, private and military facilities, treated 1.1 million patients.[16] Today, the number of patients treated for chemical dependency disorders alone has almost tripled (with the implication yet again that this number would be significantly higher if it also reflected treatment for process addictions).[17] The March 2010 passage of health care reform, which now makes addiction treatment an insured benefit for millions of Americans, has guaranteed that more and more people with addictions will seek treatment.

But will they actually receive it? Despite extensive public awareness about addiction and the increasing accessibility and affordability of recovery and treatment options, a disproportionately large number of Americans with the disease do not get the help they need. The consensus is that only one in ten Americans with a substance addiction receives treatment, in contrast to seven in ten for diseases such as hypertension, major depression and diabetes.[18] *Only one in ten Americans.*

So, in treating the epidemic of addiction, much work is left to do—in the absence of which the increasing recovery gap will remain a downright shame. If the self-declared mission of Jesus is to proclaim good news to the poor, release to the captives and freedom to the oppressed, how might the church join in that mission, better loving the addicts in our midst? How might the church, "the body of Christ," better incarnate the prodigal God it worships?

The Shamelessness of Jesus

I suspect the beginning of an answer lies in getting to know the God Christians proclaim in the person of Jesus. Jesus, like the father in the parable of the prodigal son, doesn't have time for shame. He is far too busy running out to meet people in their places of sin and sickness in order to restore them to *shalom* (Hebrew for "wholeness"). To the adulterous woman about to be stoned for breaking the law (John 8:1-11), Jesus declares his refusal to condemn, sparing her life and setting her free with the words "Go your way, and from now on do not sin again" (v. 11). Whereas the religious leaders equate the value of this woman's life with her sin (the very embodiment of shaming her), Jesus instead comes to her in her mess and in essence tells her just the opposite: "Go and sin no more"; in other words, "You are *not* the bad things you've done; you are better than that, so go and live like it."

Just moments earlier, when the religious leaders bring this woman to Jesus after catching her in the act of adultery, Jesus bends down and silently with his finger begins to write something on the ground. Whatever Jesus writes—and this remains a source of speculation to biblical scholars—is enough to cause each of the woman's accusers to walk away. What might Jesus be writing?

I wonder if Jesus is drawing a line in the sand—a line that illustrates the divide that this woman's sin, her gender and the self-righteousness of the religious leaders have erected. It's a divide that could otherwise be termed *shame*, and Jesus (who alone would be justified in condemning the woman) crosses that line to be with the woman in her place of shame—when all of the religious leaders have themselves walked away.

Some commentators believe that when Jesus wrote in the sand, he was painstakingly cataloging all the secret sins of the woman's accusers. The contemporary equivalent might be a Wikileak exposé cataloging in painful detail all the indiscretions of today's church leaders.[19] At the end, nobody except Jesus has any ground on which to stand.

If this inference by commentators is true, there is an important distinction to draw here between uncovering sin and shaming the sinner. Telling the truth about the ways we fall short does not equate with shame; shame happens when we come to see our transgressions as the sole measure of our value as human beings. In Jesus' economy, telling the truth about one's brokenness—confession—is a pathway to receiving God's healing and restoration. Jesus uncovers the sin of the religious leaders not in order to shame them, but to extend them an opportunity to heal, too, because they, like the older brother in the parable of the prodigal son, are as lost and muddled as the woman Jesus sets free—only in potentially more dangerous and insidious ways.

The Samaritan woman at the well receives a similar blessing from Jesus. Without judgment, he names her past for her: "You are right in saying, 'I have no husband'; for you have had five husbands, and the one you have now is not your husband" (John 4:17-18). The purpose of this honesty is not to deepen an already full reservoir of shame; it is to quench a deep thirst for God's transforming love, in the light of which the Samaritan woman can now share her story, warts and all, without shame.

The same Jesus who spares the adulterous woman's life and draws another out of her hiding place also regularly dines with "sinners and tax collectors"—and shamelessly so, to the outrage of the religious leaders. One of these tax collectors is Zacchaeus, who in his desperation to meet Jesus, climbs up a tree, literally going out on a limb just to catch a peek of Jesus, and he accepts an invitation from this prodigal God: "Zacchaeus, hurry and come down; for I must stay at your house today" (Luke 19:5).

Welcoming Jesus into our homes—and into our churches—begins with acknowledging our brokenness and our need for him. When we honestly and courageously face the chinks in our own armor, we can then glimpse who this Jesus really is and just how much he is rooting for us.

The chinks in our armor are blessed cracks where the light of Jesus can shine through, as the song by Leonard Cohen instructs:

Ring the bells that still can ring
Forget your perfect offering
There is a crack, a crack in everything
That's how the light gets in.[20]

Probably nowhere in the Bible is Jesus clearer about the blessedness of brokenness—as a pathway to God—than in the Sermon on the Mount. "Blessed are the poor in spirit," Jesus says, "for theirs is the kingdom of heaven. Blessed are those who mourn, for they will be comforted" (Matthew 5:3-4). The succeeding list of blessings is a manifesto written by a God who is boldly, unashamedly and totally *for* those who are most in need of God's grace—and know it.

If welcoming Jesus into our home begins by embracing brokenness, wouldn't churches be the first place where this sort of transparency happens? Churches can encourage this vulnerability in at least two ways. First, they can accept the brokenness and suffering in their community, and instead of being surprised by it or pretending it does not exist, they can find ways to talk about it openly and to consecrate it. By consecration, I do not wish to suggest in any way that sin or suffering are good in themselves or that "anything goes" or that all sins and forms of suffering are exactly the same. But I do want to invite a deeper engagement with brokenness, which, by virtue of belonging to the human condition, is operative in your church and in your life together. Addiction is one embodiment of this often hidden brokenness and one way in which your community can begin to tell the truth about the cracks in its façade, in order to ask for God's light to shine through precisely in those places.

> If welcoming Jesus into our home begins by embracing brokenness, wouldn't churches be the first place where this sort of transparency happens?

Just as Jesus is clear that sin is not cause for condemnation, he is clear that suffering is not a manifestation of God's judgment or an indication of moral failing. In the case of the blind man whom Jesus heals, whose condition elicits the question "Who sinned, this man or his parents, that he was born blind?" Jesus refuses any potentially shaming attributions, saying, "He was born blind so that God's works might be revealed" (John 9:2-3).

So the church need not be surprised, baffled or scandalized by the reality of sin and suffering in its midst: the church should expect sin and suffering. And the church can begin to listen to and cry alongside those who suffer, and ask for God's light to shine through in these places of pain and emptiness. It has been said since way back in the second century that the church is a hospital for sinners. *What if we in the church really lived as if we knew this to be true?*

As churches begin to view sin and suffering as the very place where the living God goes looking for hurting people, they can learn to let go of shame. Sometimes this letting go may look more like an old-fashioned exorcism of shame wherever shame rears its head. Here again churches can find a role model in Jesus, who was willing to endure the suffering of the cross but "disregarded" or, as other translations say, "despised" its shame (Hebrews 12:2).

As a very public form of capital punishment, crucifixion was an instrument of humiliation—but Jesus rejects that shame even as he freely and willingly suffers with the rest of us. On the cross, he weds himself to human beings in their sin and sickness: he says yes to us and no to our shame. By openly acknowledging brokenness and standing in solidarity with those who suffer from addiction—or any other form of alienation from God, one another or oneself—the church can join Jesus at the foot of the cross in despising shame.

And when sin and suffering are no longer skeletons in the closet, meant to be hidden away, feared and avoided, but are instead the very stuff of God's redemptive work, shame begins to lose its power.

Shame becomes a piddling, minor character in a great drama about a prodigal God redeeming the world.

Lest there be any doubt, then, in no way is shame ever of God. The Bible says that in the very beginning before sin entered the world, Adam and Eve (in Hebrew *adam* signifies "humankind" and *hawwah*, for Eve, "having life") were naked and without shame. They lived in an open place of vulnerability with one another (metaphorically, nakedness), which was God's intention for them. Paradise was a place of security and vulnerability, but when sin entered the world, that all changed, with fear and shame supplanting security and vulnerability. Then the man and the woman sewed fig leaves for themselves and hid from the Lord. They were now in a state of disconnection from God, one another and their own selves.

Deprogramming Shame

I have tried to show how this abiding problem of human alienation and disconnection finds a remedy in the shamelessness of Jesus. This means that if the church is about encouraging encounters with Jesus, it must also be about the business of eliminating shame and building resilience against it. But how, practically speaking, might your church do this?

To answer that question, let's return one last time to Angie. Angie, like many recovering addicts—and like many in the church, addiction or no addiction—needed a gentle reprogramming of sorts, so that shame would no longer be such an automatic reflex. She needed new habits and coping mechanisms, which our program sought to impart. So, for example, Angie's clinical week with me started first thing on Monday with a "Morning Motivation." During this time, she would meet with peers and a staff member to read from the Scriptures, integrate principles of recovery and spend time preparing for her day in prayer and reflection.

The rest of her morning would be devoted to group therapy addressing psycho-emotional issues like shame that were feeding her addictive behavior. After lunch, she would continue her learning in psycho-educational groups, developing ways to deal with trauma, prevent relapse and integrate the twelve-step model into her daily life, for example. Some days Angie would participate in guided meditation and prayer, which is effective in teaching the addicted brain to slow down. When practiced regularly over time, prayer and meditation can help reprogram the brain.[21]

Other days, Angie would connect with one or more of our in-house recovery professionals, such as our chaplain (for spiritual direction), recovery coach (to prepare for recovery in the real world) or the medical team (to address medical or psychiatric issues that could hamper recovery). In our program, we are intentional about treating the whole person—body, soul and spirit—which means that every one of our clients has the support of a multidisciplinary team including doctors, nurses, psychotherapists and other clinicians, recovery coaches and a chaplain.

Some evenings, Angie would attend an AA/NA meeting in the community. One night a week, she would hear a local clergy person speak about faith and recovery. One night a week she would break bread with peers at a potluck dinner where, led by a staff member, she could converse with other clients about their experiences of faith-based recovery. On weekends she would attend a local church service and be free to make use of the other services we provide, such as leader-facilitated meditation and yoga, dialectical behavior therapy, the gym or excursions to the beach. Meanwhile, with our client care coordinators always on hand, many of them also in recovery themselves, Angie knew she could go to folks who understood her experience and would offer helpful advice.

The point is this: deprogramming from the shame that feeds addiction involves a pretty extensive reprogramming and the support of at least a small caring community. Church can't be a recovery program, nor should it be. But church can be a community in which shame is not welcome and in which people with addiction are intentionally and genuinely invited to share their experiences. Church can consist of shame-free relationships between people who, regardless of where they come from or their struggle, are helping one another "recover" the best life God has for them now.

With this goal in mind, here are some practical ways that you and your congregation can work to end shame in your midst and build shame resilience.

Find ways to normalize the experience of addiction. Shame gains power when those who struggle with addiction start to believe that "If they only knew I struggle with x, they wouldn't accept me." Let parishioners know just how prevalent addiction is and how much they are affected by it: talk about it from the pulpit; invite guest speakers to share their experience and expertise; encourage your parishioners to do the same sort of searching moral inventory that addicts in recovery do, with a view to illuminating addictive behaviors.

Validate feelings of shame while disabusing people of the notion that their shame is warranted. Because they were created in God's image, people with addiction have the same capacity for good; they just have a disease—one that is very treatable; so they don't need to buy into the lie that they are bad or inherently unworthy of God's love. They do need to recognize that their disease only feeds on feelings of shame and can be as strong as those feelings.

At the same time, don't be afraid to help addicts take responsibility for their choices. Disabusing people of shame doesn't mean denying the reality that they have made poor choices or done bad things while under the influence, nor does it mean shielding people from the consequences of their actions. Disabusing people of shame means helping them see that they are inherently better than their actions might say to them and far more loved than they know.

Create safe, confidential settings for honest group sharing.
Shame can't function well in the face of genuine intimacy in community. But genuine intimacy requires safe spaces where people
can share their biggest questions and struggles with one another
without fear. Examples of these sorts of settings might include
"circles of trust" of the kind author Parker Palmer suggests (see the
next chapter); recovery support groups are another—even small
groups, to the degree that they uphold confidentiality and enact key
guidelines around safe, nonjudgmental listening.[22]

Make yourself available for confession. Here Protestants can
learn from Catholics and Orthodox Christians: the sacrament of
confession in Catholic and Orthodox churches is one very effective
way to disable shame. In the absence of a sacrament, Protestant
ministers can still create a version of this rite of confession both in
one-on-one pastoral hours and in congregational worship.

Always keep confidentiality, unless someone's life is in danger
or in known or suspected instances of child abuse or neglect—in
which case, you should immediately report your concerns to law
enforcement authorities or the Department of Human Services. Parishioners need to know that what they share with you really will
stay there—unless, that is, they specifically request that their
problem be added to the church prayer chain.

While pastoral confidentiality would seem like a no-brainer, it
is sadly not always the norm in congregations. Under the cloak
of "prayer concerns," one person's addiction or struggles with
mental illness can suddenly become open public knowledge
before they are ready to share it. The result can be the very thing
you most want to avoid in loving addicts: a shaming effect. When
this happens, you not only lose credibility as a leader, you jeopardize that relationship (and potentially others) by destroying a
parishioner's trust. They and they alone must be able to share
their story first—not you. But by being a confidential prayer and

conversation partner, you can support them in their journey toward freedom from shame and addiction.

Model vulnerability by being honest about your own imperfections and addictive behaviors. This, too, might seem like a no-brainer; but in churches where a senior pastor is often expected to "have it all together" and to have all the answers, and where image often takes center stage, showing vulnerability can seem awfully scary, risky and even taboo. Your willingness to be real about the fact that you are a work in progress and that there is blessedness in this reality will give others permission to do the same with their struggles.

Connect recovering addicts with people who are on the same path. This can mean sending addicts to an AA, NA or Celebrate Recovery group in your area; it also can mean reaching out to someone in your congregation who has found success in recovery and asking her to serve as a mentor to another person with addiction in your congregation (with the latter's permission, of course).

Always extend hope. Addiction doesn't have to be a dead-end street. Instead of being a cause for despair, addiction can be an invitation to opt into a whole new way of life. Addiction is not a failure; it's an opportunity. The breakdown is a signal of a coming breakthrough.

The Whisper Test

In her memoir, Mary Ann Bird recalls the shame she experienced in childhood growing up with multiple birth defects.[23] She was deaf in one ear and had a cleft palate, disfigured face, crooked nose and lopsided feet. These physical impairments, in addition to the emotional damage inflicted by peers, were a constant source of suffering.

"Oh Mary Ann," her classmates would say, "what happened to your lip?" She would lie, saying she cut it on a piece of glass.

One of Mary Ann's worst childhood experiences was the dreaded day of the annual hearing test. That was when the teacher would call each child up, ask him or her to cover first one ear and then the other, and then whisper something like "the sky is blue" or "you have new shoes." This was the so-called whisper test. If the child repeated the teacher's phrase correctly, the child passed the test.

To avoid the humiliation of failing the test, Mary Ann would always cheat, secretly cupping her hand over her good ear so she could hear what the teacher said. But one year Mary Ann was fortunate to have Miss Leonard as her teacher. It was every student's wish to be Miss Leonard's favorite child. She was just that way; she was beloved.

Then came the day of the dreaded hearing test. When her turn came, Mary Ann was called to the teacher's desk. As Mary Ann cupped her hand over her good ear, Miss Leonard leaned forward to whisper seven fateful words.

"I waited for those words," Mary Ann writes, "which God must have put into her mouth, those seven words which changed my life."

Not "the sky is blue."

Not "you have new shoes."

This time when the whisper came, it said, "I wish you were my little girl." Those seven words of love and acceptance changed Mary Ann's life.

Recovering addicts, like all of us, have multiple hidden birth defects. When recovering addicts set foot in church, it's because they, like the rest of us, are hoping to hear a faint whisper that they are worthy of God's love. A whisper that banishes shame, from a God who says, "I wish you were mine." A whisper that changes lives. What are the words that people are hearing from your church?

Discussion Questions

1. Have you struggled with shame? Why or why not? If you haven't really struggled with shame, can you think of one experience in

your life when you did? How did it affect your behavior and relationships?

2. What message(s) would you say your church is currently sending to people with addictions?

six

The Practice of Attentive Listening

At its core, hospitality
is an opening of the heart.

RENÉE MILLER

HOW CAN THE CHURCH BECOME more hospitable to people with addictions? That was the second biggest question among the one hundred church leaders I surveyed. The answer lies in understanding the essence of hospitality and then implementing some key spiritual practices that will deepen and enrich it.

Most fundamentally, hospitality is not about name tags, coffee or donuts for Sunday visitors, or hosting AA meetings in your basement, but rather a posture of welcome: an openness to apprehending the divine image in another human being. This "opening of the heart," as the author Renée Miller defines it, is critical to learning to love— or what the poet William Blake described as the very meaning of existence when he quipped, "We are put on earth a little space, that we may learn to bear the beams of love."[1] Learning to love—being "repossessed by love"—is the essence of recovery, after all.[2]

And the church shows hospitality to recovering addicts when it lives into its identity as a spiritual laboratory of sorts, in which hearts can gradually open to love itself. A more commonly used term to describe the role of the church is that of a *school* for love. The metaphor is fitting: insofar as God is love itself, churches are simply communities learning not just intellectually and doctrinally about that love—which is important, of course—but experientially, through daily rhythms of life that root them more deeply in the very ground of their being (which is this love), by drawing them into greater communion with God and with all creation.[3]

Spiritual exercises are thus only worthy of practice to the degree that they increase one's love of neighbor and self. Many of these practices, like various forms of contemplative prayer, are already familiar as helpful tools for spiritual formation and need only brief mention. Centering prayer, *lectio divina* and yoga—to name just a few such practices—have been helpful to my clients as regular spiritual disciplines, and churches do well to connect with these sorts of offerings. This chapter features some less-familiar practices that—when undertaken even in baby steps—offer great potential for transforming churches into recovery-friendly communities.

The Practice of Attentive, or Redemptive, Listening

In his book *Breathing Underwater: Spirituality and the Twelve Steps*, Franciscan priest Richard Rohr makes the observation that the Western church has traditionally excelled at preaching, teaching and inculcating doctrine, but he says that with the task of forging experientially real spiritual transformation, the church can do better.[4] And recovery is a process of spiritual transformation. So churches seeking to become more recovery friendly—more hospitable to people with addictions—will undertake concrete practices that encourage this spiritual healing and growth.

One such practice is attentive listening, or what Rohr terms "redemptive listening" or "nonviolent communication" (I will use these terms interchangeably). Listening to our own soul and to the stirrings of God's Spirit in our life is certainly important and belongs to a discipline of listening. (Here again, familiar spiritual disciplines for devotional use have a necessary place.) But by redemptive listening, Rohr means the oft-overlooked discipline of listening to one another in ways that build bridges between people rather than further divide them.

Rohr's remarks on redemptive listening come in the context of making amends for addictive behavior that has caused harm to others, as prescribed by step eight of AA's twelve steps.[5] In other words, the act of redemptive listening emerges as an appropriate response to another human being's experience of suffering—and specifically to the pain that we have caused them. But redemptive listening need not happen only within the context of redressing wrongs we ourselves have committed.

Rev. Kelly Carpenter, who pastors Green Street United Methodist Church in Winston-Salem, North Carolina, notes the example of Job's three friends, Eliphaz, Bildad and Zophar, whom he colorfully refers to as "the three stooges of Pastoral Care, the Larry-Mo-&-Curly of Sensitivity, the care-giving trinity from Hell."[6] Carpenter, citing Rabbi Harold Kushner, observes that Job's three misguided friends at least do two things right: they come to Job, refusing to let their own feelings of discomfort about their friend's suffering keep them away; and they sit in silence with Job for a very long time (seven days). They sit in silence because words and explanations— sermonizing—fail when pain and suffering are so palpable and acute. For Carpenter, the capacity to be silent and remain with another human being in the midst of that person's pain is a critical aspect of redemptive listening, whatever the context. The same is true in relating to people with addictions.

Attentive, or redemptive, listening is also the means by which I am able to enter into your story and find places of connection with you, even at points where our stories may dramatically diverge. Nonviolent communication humanizes and dignifies the parties involved, allowing them to tap into God-given reserves of self-empathy, compassion and free mutual connection. Such listening allows both parties to speak and feel heard with respect to their particular feelings and needs.

And this act of listening is indeed a discipline that benefits from practice. On the surface, a person with addiction may seem to have nothing in common with me; listening to her story without jumping to prescriptions for how she should behave or believe (which is often just an extension of how we ourselves tend to behave or believe) demands self-control. Alternatively, a person with an addiction may remind me so much of myself that I am afraid to listen to him for what his brokenness may reveal about those places in my life that feel out of control or hopelessly dark.

Practicing and modeling attentive listening may not come intuitively—especially for pastors trained to deliver and administer the Word of God—but it also does not require a whole course in mediation or conflict resolution; nor does it demand a sophisticated familiarity with the principles of nonviolence that undergirded the civil rights movement in this country. In other words, you do not need to become an expert in order to listen attentively to those in your midst and to encourage the practice in your congregation.

Remember Matt Russell, who appeared in the last chapter as the originator of Houston's Mercy Street? His whole initiative to plant a church for people in need of healing began with the simple act of listening deeply to those same people, many of whom were in recovery from one sort of addiction or another. In these conversations, Russell was not merely a passive recipient. He asked pointed questions that revealed his own heart, and then he actively tuned in to what was being said. He wanted to know what recovery looked like for these folks—and what church might be for them (and what church failed to be for them). The only real agenda, if it could be called that, was to listen carefully to a demographic that looked quite different from the one that typically shows up for worship on Sunday mornings in your average, garden-variety congregation.

Attentive listening has enough of its own agenda, after all: it is inherently redemptive, insofar as its focus is building connections between people (which belongs to the work of a God whose mission is to reconcile all things to himself; see Colossians 1:20). Russell did not show up to listen to strangers in coffee shops in order to sell his church's latest outreach program. He was not there to make a case for why the person on the other side of the table should come back to church—or even to Jesus, per se. But the act of listening was itself an incarnation of the love of Jesus, a way of showing that the feelings, needs and experiences of the person before him mattered to him and mattered to Jesus.

> In listening attentively and in creating opportunities for these listening encounters, you are letting people with addiction know that they matter to you and they matter to Jesus.

In listening attentively and in creating opportunities for these listening encounters, you also are letting people with addiction know that they matter to you and they matter to Jesus. You are letting them know that their story has a place in the larger story of God's people. That in itself is a holy, redemptive enterprise. That is agenda enough.

But something else can happen during the act of listening attentively that can't happen when we are busy talking (or as church leaders, preaching, teaching and offering words of pastoral encouragement). When we listen attentively, we can better hear the subplot of the story that God wants to tell about our lives and those around us. We can begin to connect our story to others' stories and to move out of the suffocating, self-absorbed storylines in which we, like anyone with an addiction, can become stuck.

Knowing what happens in God's story is one thing, but coming to see that we have a part in that story is another. Attentive listening is one way we do this. It can capture and recapture our imagination, firing it with the newness of life that a God who is ever and always making "all things new" extends to those with open, attuned ears (Revelation 21:5). The bigger, better, more spacious story of recovery that God wants to tell using your life and your congregation as writing instruments will become a reality to those who have ears to hear it.

Getting Started

The homework assignment of listening attentively to people with addictions can begin wherever you are in your life together as a community. You may be a church leader with no existing connection to the recovery world. You can start small. Consider doing what one leader did during the announcements section of worship. He invited anyone present who was "friends with Bill W" (immediately familiar language for people in AA) to meet with him after church and share their stories. That initial meeting evolved into a six-month commitment to meet weekly and unpack principles of recovery together. Eventually, that group developed into a recovery ministry.

But you need not meet with this longer-term goal in mind. Your only goal initially can be that of listening to the stories of people in recovery whose struggles and victories have so often remained hidden in the church. And you will be surprised to see how many people respond to your Sunday morning "recovery altar call." People you would never guess to be struggling with an addiction of some form or another may take you up on your offer.

"Every pastor has people in his or her congregation that are in recovery," Pastor Frank Lukasiewicz (who pastors Servant of the

Shepherd Church in River Falls, Wisconsin) assured me. "Most of the time the pastor doesn't know that, because people with addictions don't feel comfortable enough in the church to share it."

A natural question to ask, then, is "How do I encourage enough of a comfort level that people with addictions in our church can respond to an invitation to share their stories with me?" Here are some ideas for preparing an initial, public invitation of this sort:

Reference and be mindful of anonymity. Familiarize yourself with the guidelines for anonymity that undergird AA and other recovery support meetings. (I'd recommend getting a copy of AA's *Big Book* and reading through it, for example.) Expressing your commitment to anonymity will be crucial, especially if your church is beginning with very little connection to the recovery world. People in your church who fall anywhere on the spectrum of addiction recovery will need to be able to trust you.

Adopt a learning posture. Frame your invitation in terms of wanting to learn, see, understand and ultimately serve not just this population but your whole church, as a whole community that (whether or not it knows it) is in recovery.

Choose neutral ground for your meeting place—and don't announce from the pulpit where you'll be meeting for the first time either. Find an environment other than your church office or a Sunday school classroom to conduct this and any other conversations. Coffee shops are often great places for free, easy and unobtrusive conversation, depending on the size of your initial gathering. They are also frequent gathering places for people in recovery.

By meeting in a place like a coffee shop, rather than in your own office, you will be doing a couple of things. You will be making your guests feel more comfortable, since even longtime churchgoers in recovery have come to view church and its associations as a place where they can't share freely about their issue. You will also be helping to normalize and de-stigmatize addiction: you will be sending the message that talking about these matters should not have to be a private, hush-hush affair, in the way that confession with a priest might be, for example. That said, for an initial meeting of this sort, take care not to announce right from the get-go that you will be gathering at your local Starbucks to share journeys of recovery. Simply invite interested folks to come up or contact you after the service, and then take it from there.

Prepare yourself for the fact that you will encounter distrust from this population. And do not be intimidated by this fact. There is usually a tacit understanding within recovery groups that only one addict in recovery can help another. "It takes an addict to know one" so to speak. And many addicts do have hang-ups with the church and have felt let down by God. If you are not in recovery yourself, be prepared to encounter some level of distrust. The way to build trust will be to identify at least one congregant—ideally someone with more than ten years of sobriety, Lukasiewicz suggests—and let this person take the more visible leadership role in these conversations. Your job can then be to give support, be present at the meetings and listen actively and attentively.

Be prepared to share your own story using the language of recovery—and consider how you might make this admission in your invitation from the pulpit. If you are in recovery yourself, by all means mention this fact—not once but often, so that all of your congregants, not just those in recovery, can begin to find points of connection between their story and the language of recovery. If you are not actually in recovery, you can still find ways to bless this language and conscript it in your story.

Frame this initial gathering as a hopeful, even fun, informal conversation with no agenda—and mean it. The subject of sober living (that is, recovery) need not be a killjoy. People in recovery are learning not to take themselves too seriously. When you really mean what you say—that this gathering is an icebreaker of sorts for people in recovery and that your presence there will be only to listen and learn—you and those present can relax and enjoy the time of connecting with one another.

Pray beforehand that God's will be done. A common theme I hear from Lukasiewicz, for example, is the critical and unceasing nature of prayer, accompanied by surrender to God's will. Thankfully, this is not the time for ambitious strategic plans or churchy programmatic solutions. All you need to do is show up having prayed that God's will be done—and then pay attention to what happens next.

Bridging the Great Divide

The practice of listening attentively to people with addictions may look different for churches already hosting AA and other recovery group meetings in their building. Church leaders in these settings face a unique opportunity that is also a challenge: they may have more immediate, natural access to relationships with people in recovery, but often they must bridge an existing separation between that world and the one that exists in Sunday morning worship.

Episcopal priest Lyn Brakeman gives voice to this "great divide." She recalls that in the course of conducting countless phone interviews with churches and inquiring about their already-existing resources for addiction ministry, she heard a common refrain. It went something like this: "We're already taking care of that problem. We have a ministry to [recovering addicts]; we let their groups meet in our basement."[7]

Brakeman remembers the "not-so-subtle separation" she heard in these answers between "us" and "them," and between "their" groups and "our" groups. And while acknowledging (maybe not without some irony) that "the basement strategy of ministry is a charitable use of space for sure," Brakeman is quick to observe that "the strategy disconnects people from the 'other' and also from their own fears and shame"—in essence, the antithesis of hospitality as it is defined in this chapter.[8]

The great divide between the world of AA and the church plagues many church leaders. One minister I spoke with described her sense of helplessness in bridging the gap that exists between the recovery groups that meet in her church and the folks who worship in the sanctuary. She admitted that as a church leader she was hard-pressed to know how to show hospitality to the people who regularly showed up at these recovery meetings, often anonymously, but who never set foot in church.

> The great divide between the world of AA and the church plagues many church leaders.

She is not alone—and her question opens up a spacious room in which to dream about the possibilities for bridging this great divide. Brakeman wonders, and I along with her, whether someone from the downstairs recovery meeting would feel welcome upstairs in the sanctuary, and vice versa:

> I sometimes envision all the people wearing jeans and sneakers who gather regularly in the smoke-filled, coffee-redolent lower rooms of church buildings to laugh, tell jokes, weep, share hell stories and embrace with full-bodied hugs suddenly flooding the upper rooms on Sunday morning. Up there, people wearing suits and Talbot frocks gather regularly in the quiet sanctuary to kneel and pray, look somber, listen to heaven stories, consume little white wafers or bread cubes, sing music we don't hear much on our local radio stations, and do A-frame hugs or shake hands. And what if the reverse was to happen: all the upper room people flooding the lower room?[9]

The answers to these questions are yours to dream about and hopefully enact, but I suspect their articulation begins in a true spirit of hospitality (as openness to love itself)—through the practice of attentive listening. And I wonder if this might be a dream in the heart of God as well.

Brakeman herself offers some concrete suggestions for bridging the great divide, the first being something as simple as starting a conversation in your church. You might consider forming a small group that consists of a few representatives from the AA group that meets in your basement and some church members without a background in recovery who are nonetheless open and spiritually attuned. Your purpose can be getting to know one another and serving as "bridge people" between AA and your church.[10] These bridge people can in turn facilitate further venues for attentive listening between these two groups, maybe, for example, as leaders of "circles of trust" (discussed in the next section).

Alternatively, Pastor Lukasiewicz recommends identifying just one person in your congregation who is in recovery and then asking if you would be able to accompany him or her to a meeting. The same request might also be directed to the contact person for the group; if your church is hosting the meetings, they will be more likely to let you join even a closed meeting of AA, for example, where you could then put some of your questions about becoming a more recovery-friendly congregation before the larger group. Chances are that if you are truly adopting a learning posture and inviting the group's help, they will be delighted to come to your aid in tangible ways as you seek to encourage your congregation in recovery-friendly directions. One principle in AA and twelve-step groups is that of service, after all, and finding recovery through service to others.

If you are attending an AA or other recovery group for the first time, you will want to listen attentively and ask questions that reveal to those present your heart for them and your desire to nurture a more recovery-friendly congregation. Avoid trying to sell your congregation to those present. You can certainly invite the folks there to church on Sunday and describe your lament at the separation between these two worlds and your desire to bridge them. But your approach should once again be understated, not heavy-handed, that of a learner and listener. Those present have something critical to impart about God's redemptive healing work in the world, and the lessons may surprise you.

If your church does not yet host a recovery group like AA, consider hosting one and tapping a few leaders with the vision and call to be bridge people. Or if you are not yet ready to host a recovery support group, you might invite members from a nearby AA or twelve-step group to be part of this getting-to-know-you conversation. This process of attentively listening to those who on the surface seem different from you will at least be one step in the direction of becoming more recovery-friendly.

Circles of Trust and Other Ideas for Church Ministry

In the meantime, church leaders can be equipping their congregation with attentive listening skills by providing opportunities to practice and experience this discipline as a vehicle of spiritual transformation. One very helpful resource is the circle of trust model that Christian author Parker Palmer has developed and replicated for use by small groups. Circles of trust evolved from Palmer's discovery that "a small circle of limited duration that is intentional about its process will have a deeper, more life-giving impact than a large, ongoing community that is shaped by the norms of conventional culture."[11]

Certain basic ground rules govern how these circles function. Participants must be more willing to listen than speak, more quick to withhold judgment than condemn, more eager to learn than to teach and more willing to be changed than bent on changing others.

At the website of the Center for Courage and Renewal, which Parker directs, you can find the following guidelines, along with other opportunities to resource your congregation for the enterprise of attentive listening:

- Be present as fully as possible. Be here with your doubts, fears and failings as well as your convictions, joys and successes, your listening as well as your speaking.

- What is offered in the circle is by invitation, not demand. This is not a "share or die" event! During this retreat, do whatever your soul calls for, and know that you do it with our support. Your soul knows your needs better than we do.

- Speak your truth in ways that respect other people's truth. Our views of reality may differ, but speaking one's truth in a circle of trust does not mean interpreting, correcting or debating what others say. Speak from your center to the center of the circle, using "I" statements, trusting people to do their own sifting and winnowing.

- No fixing, saving, advising or correcting each other. This is one of the hardest guidelines for those of us in the "helping professions." But it is vital to welcoming the soul, to making space for the inner teacher.

- Learn to respond to others with honest, open questions instead of counsel, corrections, etc. With such questions, we help "hear each other into deeper speech."

- When the going gets rough, turn to wonder. If you feel judgmental, or defensive, ask yourself, "I wonder what brought her to this belief?" "I wonder what he's feeling right now?" "I wonder what my reaction teaches me about myself?" Set aside judgment to listen to others—and to yourself—more deeply.

- Attend to your own inner teacher. We learn from others, of course. But as we explore poems, stories, questions and silence in a circle of trust, we have a special opportunity to learn from within. So pay close attention to your own reactions and responses, to your most important teacher.

- Trust and learn from the silence. Silence is a gift in our noisy world, and a way of knowing in itself. Treat silence as a member of the group. After someone has spoken, take time to reflect without immediately filling the space with words.

- Observe deep confidentiality. Nothing said in a circle of trust will ever be repeated to other people.

- Know that it's possible to leave the circle with whatever it was that you needed when you arrived, and that the seeds planted here can keep growing in the days ahead.[12]

Obviously, recovering addicts are not the only people who can benefit from attentive listening in a circle of trust. Circles of trust are for anyone seeking to hear the still, small inner voice that calls them back to who they are as loved and cherished children of God, and attentive or redemptive listening is the means by which we come to hear this voice speak in a more intimate, trusting community and begin to respond. The listening skills taught within these circles of trust can foster our own spiritual transformation while creating a warmer, more hospitable environment for people anywhere on the spectrum of recovery (including those who have yet to recognize their own unhealthy attachments and needs for healing).

Even in venues more traditionally geared for talking, such as preaching, you can model attentive listening for your congregation. Lukasiewicz says he frequently makes his sermons interactive, inviting listeners to share honestly from their experiences. If you are in a congregation in which a good number of people are in recovery (like Lukasiewicz's), this interaction will come easily; it may not be as natural or appropriate in a setting where exposure to the recovery movement is minimal or hard to gauge. However, gradually, with prayer, education and your consistent commitment to grow a recovery-friendly culture, you can arrive at this milestone. And its attainment will speak to the progress you have made in becoming more recovery-friendly as a community. When people begin to share their honest experiences of brokenness and grace during your times of worship—maybe even during your sermon— that will be a sure sign of how far you have come by God's grace. It will be evidence that you are becoming a church that hosts parties for prodigal people.

Creating listening opportunities need not happen exclusively in your one hour of Sunday worship either. One thing I like to do with my former clients, for example, is to invite them back for a monthly alumni dinner. The occasion is much like an informal recovery meeting, but it begins with a simple potluck supper. The alumni (recovering addicts all of them, from those in their first week out of our program to those five or ten years sober) bring whatever food they can, and invariably, there is always plenty of food, from Taco Bell burritos to the finest in comfort-food casseroles. At the potluck dinner, those present are encouraged to be themselves, just as they are, and to share where they are in their journey as it relates to a particular theme, such as hope, honesty or humility. Usually I open the time with a few words of welcome, an introduction to the theme for the night and then a prayer, like the Prayer of St. Francis or the Serenity Prayer.

Like our spread of potluck offerings, the stories heard over the next hour are always more than enough to feed those present with the grace of God. That time together is often more spiritually rejuvenating than some of the best sermons I have heard. Recovering addicts have some of the most powerful, real testimonies you will ever hear. Being in a room full of their stories—in a room of drunks, addicts and self-declared mess-ups sharing their neediness and God's provision—is what Philip Yancey must mean when he likens AA meetings to "grace flowing on tap."

Attentive listening in this context is a matter of drinking up that grace and simply thanking those present for pouring you a cold drink of living water. So find a regular, sustainable way to encourage this wonderfully exciting interaction of mutual sharing and listening, whether in your regular weekly worship or in another fellowship venue. In doing so, you will be encouraging a whole priesthood of believers to love and minister to one another—and to you—by letting a few folks in recovery know that they are seen and heard. If it sounds doable, it should—because it is!

Home Is Where the Heart Is

In her book *Strength for the Journey: A Guide to Spiritual Practice*, Renée Miller unravels the implications of hospitality as an opening of the heart:

> Opening our hearts means we really have to gather others in. Their problems, their dreams, the injustices done to them, the hopes that lie hidden in their souls, the joys that have taken them to heaven's doors—all these become a part of our own hearts when we engage in hospitality as a spiritual practice.[13]

Hospitality to people with addictions is a "gathering in" so that their lives are part of our lives, not enmeshed but conjoined, mutually transformed and blessed for the better. It is a "gathering in" of us and them so that there is only a *we*. This gathering in is the very thing that the prodigal Father does when he invites wandering children—all of us—to the party, calling us from just about every direction we have found ourselves going—east, west and topsy-turvy—to the same joyful feast.[14] Only open hearts *receive* the Father's invitation. Only open hearts are at the feast.

Recovery-friendly communities do not materialize overnight. They are the fruit of spiritual rules of life practiced regularly, both corporately and individually. But their fruition can mean the difference between a place called home and just another pit stop—and between a place at the party and a closed door and clenched teeth. In this sense, home really is where the heart is.

Discussion Questions

1. When was the last time you experienced the essence of hospitality—as an opening of the heart to another—in your congregation? Describe the experience. How did it feel? What was transformative about it?

2. Can you identify with the dilemma of the minister who shared that she doesn't know how to bridge the divide between her church's recovery group and the people who meet for Sunday worship? What in this chapter has been helpful in answering her question?

3. In a small group, try out one of the suggested tips for practicing attentive listening. For example, pick a spiritual theme like trust or hope; then follow the guidelines of a circle of trust, keeping your responses as personally honest and vulnerable as you can but being careful not to share anything that you will regret after a first-time encounter of this sort. Then debrief on your experience. What was it like? Did aspects of the exercise feel uncomfortable? Why or why not?

seven

The Practice of Healing

*There is a difference between curing and healing, and I believe
the church is called to the slow and difficult work of healing. We
are called to enter into one another's pain, anoint it as holy, and
stick around no matter the outcome.*

RACHEL HELD EVANS
SEARCHING FOR SUNDAY

IN ADDITION TO ATTENTIVE LISTENING, churches seeking to
show hospitality to recovering addicts will practice the oft-overlooked
ministry of healing. Here again Rohr offers some insightful observations. He notes that historically the church has spent most of its time
devoted to Jesus' ministry of preaching and teaching, with much less
emphasis given to Jesus' mission of healing.[1] Yet Jesus spends as much
time healing people as he does talking about the kingdom of God.
And Jesus' healing activity on earth is the demonstration and fulfillment of his message about the kingdom of heaven.

Of the dozens of miracles that Jesus performs in the Gospels, an
overwhelming majority concern healing of some kind or another.
Jesus in action is a healing Savior: opening the eyes of the blind.
Exorcising evil spirits. Raising the dead to life. These actions reveal

who Jesus is as God incarnate—a God who wants wholeness and restoration for people. A God whose mission is recovery.

In her book *Jesus Freak*, minister Sara Miles grapples with the implications of this Jesus for those who follow him:

> Jesus calls his disciples, giving us authority to heal and sending us out. He doesn't show us how to reliably cure a molar pregnancy. He doesn't show us how to make a blind man see, dry every tear, or even drive out all kinds of demons. But he shows us how to enter into a way of life in which the broken and sick pieces are held in love, and given meaning. In which strangers literally touch each other, and in doing so make a community spacious enough for everyone.[2]

In a day and age when we are used to hearing televangelists promise miraculous cures for cancer in return for that next donation, talk of healing can make us uncomfortable. Many of us also find it hard to believe that the same Jesus who cast out demons, healed lepers and restored sight to the blind is at work in the world today or in quite the same ways. But I see Jesus healing people just about every day in the world of addiction recovery. He's exorcising old hurts, opening blind eyes, touching the hearts of those whose sickness had convinced them they were untouchable.

So recovery-friendly communities will be as committed to Jesus' healing ministry as to his preaching and teaching, and they will put their commitment into practice.

Celebrating the Small Breakthroughs

Healing in the recovery world most often comes gradually and with much hard work, but such healing is no less miraculous than the sudden disappearance of breast cancer on a mammogram. When Jesus asks his interlocutors which is easier—to cure paralysis or forgive sins—he is gesturing to this reality. He is reminding his listeners of their need for a deeper healing that must take place if they are to find true wholeness, of which physical healing is only a part.

Churches that have opened their heart to people in recovery have the opportunity to be part of that healing process. Pastor Frank Lukasiewicz exclaims that as a pastor he is fortunate in a way that many pastors are not, because he gets to see healing happen just about every day: "Most pastors don't get to see change in front of their eyes. I get to see changes every single day. That's what a spiritual awakening is—even a small change. It doesn't have to be a dramatic blinding light."

> Healing in the recovery world most often comes gradually and with much hard work, but such healing is no less miraculous than the sudden disappearance of breast cancer on a mammogram.

As a case in point, Lukasiewicz shares the story of a young woman, "Sam," who at twenty-three is a meth addict. At the time I spoke with Lukasiewicz, Sam had only just been placed in the care of his congregation one week earlier, when the police dropped her off. Only days earlier, Sam and her boyfriend had had a fight while on meth. (Meth is often a contributing factor in domestic violence.) The police were called, with the result that Sam's boyfriend was carted off to jail, and Sam's two children were taken from her.

With the help of his congregation, Servant of the Shepherd Church (aptly known by the acronym SOS), Lukasiewicz was able to get Sam into detox. After detox, he found a temporary place for her in one of SOS's already full sober houses. Meanwhile, his congregation had also begun visiting Sam's boyfriend in jail.

When I spoke with Lukasiewicz, Sam was only twelve days into her time with SOS, and he described a young woman who was still very scared and distrustful about her new caregivers (the church). "She's waiting for us to zap her with 'you're going to burn in hell because of what you put your kids through.'" But the day before we talked, Lukasiewicz had seen the first glimmers of healing on the horizon when members of SOS took Sam to get her hair cut. "Just her hair cut. That was it. She came back and said, 'You know, maybe this is really a good place for me and maybe my life can change.'"

That flicker of hope was a healing breakthrough. It was one step in the direction of home.

Transformation usually happens in increments, but the incremental nature of recovery makes it no less miraculous. Sometimes we can miss the little healing miracles woven into our daily lives— those small nuggets of blessing that, when multiplied across a lifetime, bear witness to a God who all the while has been stitching us back together. With respect to the healing that is already taking place in our midst, we often can't see the forest for the trees—maybe because we are so obsessed with finding that one ancient, giant sequoia that we miss a whole panorama of fine-looking California redwoods. When we keep looking for that one great miracle that will take our breath away, we can't see the little ones happening every day. It's like looking at before-and-after weight-loss images and wanting to skip to the "after," having no desire to catch the little victories along the way.

In this sense, the job of church leaders can be to illuminate for their members just how many small miracles there are in the ordinariness of a daily journey of sanctification—a journey that is about knowing Jesus and becoming more like him every day. Pastors can be like coaches on the sidelines of a marathon. They can model what smaller, no-less-miraculous acts of healing—like taking an addict to a salon—might look like in that race toward home.

Such healing practices fundamentally require *time*, a scarce commodity for most pastors and thus a somewhat dicey subject to address. But the practice of healing will become a rhythm in your life together when leaders make it a priority and find time to engage in healing practices. The practice of healing is a spiritual discipline after all, so pastors will need to let go of certain activities they have come to view as pastoral duties and outsource these to one or more church members in order to model this spiritual discipline for the congregation. The reality is that, as coaches in the marathon of recovery, pastors must take responsibility for casting a vision of what recovery looks like and modeling the healing practices that go along with recovery.

The good news for pastors is this: when you make time for the practice of healing, you will be refreshed in your calling and reminded of why you do what you do. You probably didn't become a pastor to attend countless committee meetings or, if you are in a small church, to clean toilets. More likely you became a pastor to love and shepherd God's people ("little lambs" as Lukasiewicz likes to call his members). More likely you became a pastor in order to nurture and build up God's people in their calling by participating in their (and your) spiritual transformation (AKA recovery). So your first homework assignment is to free up your schedule so that you have time to practice healing, and then to find ways to connect more deeply during the week (beyond just Sunday morning) with the people you serve.

The story of WordHouse, a church based in Sacramento, California, exemplifies how deep, intimate connections can happen. WordHouse's worship takes place in houses, pubs and coffeehouses, and it begins with those present informally "checking in with one another." The result is that "people are pretty open about their struggles and pain," according to Jeff Richards, an evangelist for the Presbytery of Sacramento who started WordHouse.[3] Divorce, problems at work and other topics (among them, addiction) that often go unmentioned during a traditional church's Sunday worship format are more apt to surface during these relationally focused conversations.

Recovery-friendly churches practice healing when they look for meaningful ways to connect with one another on the journey of faith and then affirm and celebrate the journey's small victories. Recovery-friendly churches are communities of people continually looking for healing however and wherever it occurs, from the big to the small and everything in between. When you affirm and celebrate healing, you look for healing and seek it continually. The hopeful expectation of healing will be in your congregational DNA.

> Recovery-friendly churches are communities of people continually looking for healing however and wherever it occurs, from the big to the small and everything in between.

Most of the time, you will not find your place in this healing work of God in the dazzling acts you might see in a televised miracle service. Instead, the practice of healing can be as simple as taking a scared, shame-filled young woman to the salon and being present for her in the process. Or treating a drug addict who hangs out on your street corner to a burger and the gift of attentive listening. Or attending weekly recovery meetings to be present to your own need for healing and the needs of those around you.

Practicing Healing

Like any other spiritual exercise, healing is worth practicing only if it is increasing love of God and neighbor—that is, if it's helping the one doing the practice to step into others' own recovery. If you are sitting in an AA meeting and only going through the motions of being there, because you are really thinking about going home to get high, you might as well not engage in the healing practice of attending a recovery meeting. Or if you are listening to the strung-out homeless man over a burger without being present to him—without attentively listening to him, because your mind is really on tonight's leadership team meeting and the Sunday bulletin—you might as well not be there. You might as well not engage in that encounter.

Start with your own needs. C. S. Lewis's observation that prayer is transformative primarily because of how it changes the one praying is applicable here. Your practice of healing can and really ought to be as much about your own recovery and about how God is recovering *you*. Your healing practices individually and corporately can begin where you see your own deepest need for healing—when it comes to matters of the heart that bind you and keep you from being truly free to live and move in the grace of God. Start there, remembering that there are plenty of folks out there who may not be walking in your particular shoes, but wear the same brand and struggle with similar challenges. You may not be an addict, for example, but an experience of clinical depression that sensitizes you to your own unhealthy behaviors and your own need for recovery can be the conduit through which to join in the healing that God wants to do in and through your life and the lives of those around you.

Practice attentive listening. If you aren't able to make a clear connection between your own needs for healing and where God may be calling you to practice healing—if, for example, you are not in addiction recovery yourself—go back to the practice of attentive listening to those in your midst who *are* in recovery. Start there. Or join a clergy recovery network in your area (see the appendix). I can assure you that in the act of being truly attentive, God will reveal to you areas where you, too, can experience and practice healing.

Prioritize Jesus' healing ministry and regular opportunities for healing. If healing takes center stage in the drama of God's story, you can let the practice of healing be front and center in your life together as a church—in your worship, in the content of your Bible studies, at your fellowship dinners. Even in your bulletin.

As hospitals for sinners, churches can provide regular opportunities for healing in their midst. They can hold monthly healing services and weekly prayer meetings, during which they can pray for and anoint the sick with oil. They also can make healing prayer available within the context of weekly worship. This practice need not be siphoned off to only a few gifted intercessors—although identifying those with particular gifts in the area of healing can be another important step toward leading your congregation in embracing Jesus' ministry of healing.

Be intentional about inviting those in your midst with addictions and mental illnesses to participate. If you go this route, pay attention to how you talk about healing, too, in the context of addiction and mental illness. The example of Mary in chapter three is an illustration of what to avoid in these settings. Mary became her church's pet healing project, the broken wheel to fix in a whole group of dysfunctional wheels, rather than someone to love, walk with and learn from. And prayers for Mary's healing mostly sought that giant sequoia miracle that would immediately loose her of her chains in one fell swoop. Of course we can and should pray for big miracles, and in some cases they happen. But the harder miracles to pray for are those steady, incremental steps in the direction of home. Pray also and most especially for these things.

Participate in educational offerings. Congregations can also be encouraged to learn more about Jesus' healing ministry and ways to participate through Sunday school classes, retreats and hands-on ministry opportunities. The Pentecostal and charismatic movements have much to teach about spiritual healing practices. Francis and Judith MacNutt and their Christian Healing Ministries, a healing center for prayer ministry and training, are helpful resources. Bethel Church in Redding, California, which offers courses in supernatural healing, is another. But many churches have healing prayer ministries you might connect with in your area.

Or consider a twelve-week preaching series based on the twelve steps, during which you explore the biblical underpinnings of this program for spiritual transformation and invite your congregation to practice a new step each week.[4] They can substitute the word *alcoholism* or *addiction* with whatever issues they are facing. In this way, education about recovery can be put into action in concrete daily steps.

Host a regular recovery service. You might also consider planning a recovery service on some Sunday morning. (Some Christian rehab programs have services that they open up to the community, so you could visit one of these services for ideas.) The service could involve testimonies from recovering addicts, twelve-step readings, prayers for and from those with addictions, and maybe an extended time of laying on of hands for healing and anointing with oil or water. Also, the sacrament of baptism is very powerful for addicts and alcoholics, because it symbolizes rebirth into a life of recovery.

If you are not ready to take this step or your congregation needs more acculturation in recovery, start by simply extending your worship service for those who need healing prayer. Tap your recovery pros and prayer intercessors for this task. Have them available in pairs after worship for anyone desiring prayer support. When you announce this offering to the congregation, be intentional about also using terms like *addiction, mental illness* and *recovery.*

Encourage artistic self-expression and creative forms of worship. Other ideas include opportunities for right-brain exploration and creative self-expression and worship in the form of art, dance, poetry and nature. Recovering addicts may not feel able or ready to share their story in words, but they can on canvas or through the lines of a poem. One recovering addict told me he now belongs to a church where every week during the service someone at the front of the sanctuary is painting on canvas as an act of worship. Encouraging creative modes of self-expression for those who don't feel comfortable sharing their struggles in words is a healing practice.

Talking About Healing

It may go without saying that churches that practice healing *talk* about healing. Talking about healing is an important component of the practice of healing. If the practice of healing is front and center in your life together, talking about it—and *how* you talk about it—will be just as critical. If you are a community that practices healing, the first thing newcomers should see and hear when they show up on Sunday morning is just that. Healing and recovery will be the priority in your congregational language, starting with how leaders speak from the pulpit and extending to your mission statement, your bulletin and even the various "artifacts" newcomers see when they enter your sanctuary. Consider, for example, having copies of the *Serenity New Testament* or *The Life Recovery Bible* in every pew and using these in your worship. Or be sure to have multiple copies of *The Big Book* in your library as well as a whole section of materials labeled "Recovery."

In your bulletin, list general prayer requests for healing—healing for your world and community as well as healing for those struggling with chemical dependency and other addictions. Include prayers for those in your midst with addictions and mental illnesses (being careful to uphold anonymity). And consider including a prayer for healing that individuals can pray in worship and take with them throughout the week.

The Serenity Prayer is a familiar example, as is the Prayer of St. Francis. Or you might personally tailor a prayer that borrows language from *The Big Book* or *The Recovery Bible*. If including a prayer of this sort in the bulletin is not an option, consider incorporating it as an opening prayer in worship.

Take, for instance, the following prayer that concludes one of SOS's worship bulletins:

> Heavenly Father, I am powerless over my addictions and dysfunctions. Grant me today, the ability to turn my troubles, my

will and my life over to Your loving care. I trust in You to completely restore my brokenness into wholeness, insanity into saneness, willfulness into willingness, fear into courage. Lord, lighten my load and free me from all bondage, that I may walk through this day in freedom and in peace.

Form prayers like this one and more extemporaneous, conversational prayers of the kind you might encounter in a weekly healing service are both critical to the practice of healing. Prayer, or talking to God, is one essential incarnation of that practice.

If your church has a mission statement, make sure healing is mentioned in it. For example, the following mission statement appears on the website of Mercy Street Church:

> Our mission is to create a safe harbor for the hurt, the lost, the seeking so that we might experience the radical grace of God!
>
> Our community forms a mosaic of people diverse in our experiences and backgrounds but common in our desire to seek a closer relationship with God. Whether you have faith, struggle with your faith or have lost your faith, Mercy Street opens its doors to people seeking a spiritual roof over their head. A lot of us are involved in recovery from addictions or bad church experiences. Saturday night at Mercy Street is filled with live music, authentic faith journeys and practical messages set in a casual come-as-you-are environment. We extend a gift of Christian community to everyone, no matter what faith, religion, addiction, or experience.
>
> We believe Jesus is our true healer and restorer of all our hurts, pain, afflictions and brokenness. Wherever you are, we will support and love you in your journey.[5]

Do you hear how clearly the themes of healing, addiction and the church as a home for prodigal children come through here? Stating clearly that you are a community for people in recovery and that you exist to be part of Jesus' healing ministry is always a good way to keep yourselves accountable to practicing regular rhythms of healing.

But you do not have to be as explicit in your self-description. You do not even have to use the word *healing*, for that matter, as long as the sentiment comes through. Consider this shorter statement of purpose from SOS: "We lovingly tend to each 'Hurting Lamb' who comes through our doors—no matter what their needs—just as their Shepherd would."

Your talk about healing can extend to the communion table, too. St. Gregory's of Nyssa Episcopal Church in San Francisco is intentional about following Jesus' instructions in Luke 14.[6] "When you give a banquet," Jesus says there, "invite the poor, the crippled, the lame, and the blind. And you will be blessed" (vv. 13-14). The ensuing parable that Jesus tells is about a man who prepares a banquet and invites many guests. When they decline his invitation, the man tells his servant to go out into the streets, alleys and country roads and find others—the sick, disabled and marginalized—who will come to the banquet. St. Gregory's weekly Communion is thus an open table. Those present are not there because they are healthy or sport the right-sounding Christian vocabulary, but because they know they are in search of the Great Physician and are looking to meet him in the act of partaking of his body and blood.

In all these ways—from prayer to mission statements to the Communion table—you can talk about healing. If the job of the church is to mirror God's love and to be, as Lukasiewicz puts it, "Jesus' skin," you will be expressing this hospitality—this opening to love itself—in both word and deed. So talk about healing as you practice it.

Knowing Your Limits and Setting Boundaries

As you practice healing, be sensitive about your own limitations, which comes from knowing your congregation. You need to be aware of who in your congregation is already in recovery and the degree to which your congregation requires further education and equipping in the recovery culture. Participation in addiction recovery is a cross-cultural experience in many ways—so much so that Lukasiewicz describes ministry to people with addictions as a mission field not unlike going to a far-off country. Going on a mission trip without familiarizing yourself with the people, culture and language there would be ill-advised. Besides preparing yourself by learning the language and customs of the particular people group you are hoping to love and serve, you would need to know yourself and honor your boundaries and limitations, too, so that you do not overextend yourself and harm those you seek to serve.

The same is true in ministering to people with addictions. However, they are often very familiar with the Christian religion. Many of them grew up in the church and have been let down by what they experienced there. Many of them are angry with God, and they unleash their anger and suspicion on those who represent God. Those who have grown up in the church and have had a positive experience there are more likely to embrace church as a healing community, but as we saw in chapter five, a great number of addicts associate the church with shaming messages.

Your job as a ministry leader practicing healing is first to learn about the recovery world and to get to know those in your congregation who are in recovery. When in doubt, consult these folks and then, when necessary, refer out to mental health resources in your community, such as therapists, halfway houses or other treatment facilities.

Lukasiewicz recalls a time early in the life of his congregation when things went awry because a few well-meaning, unprepared members of the church—people with little understanding of addicts and addiction—insisted on taking a young woman (we'll call her Lori) into their home. At only nineteen, Lori was hooked on "just about everything—alcohol, cocaine, pot, weed . . . but her main addiction was pills," he says. When Lori came to SOS, she was on a "treatment high": she was enthusiastically spouting the lingo of recovery like a new convert to sobriety, but she was still using drugs.

"If I took her to your home, she'd go into your bathroom and within three or four minutes would look in your medicine cabinet and find the drugs she needed to stay high," Lukasiewicz recalls. "We knew some of this and didn't know how good she was at this—she was that good. . . . Her parents, a wonderful Christian couple, couldn't deal with her anymore and with all the lies and everything else."

What happened next was a lesson in what *not* to do: four couples in the church, none of them in recovery themselves— "normies," as Lukasiewicz likes to call them—decided after praying that they would take care of Lori, despite Lukasiewicz's warnings. They took Lori in and began to try to help her get her life back together—to get a driver's license, look for a job and find a more permanent place to live.

"They didn't know what they were getting into," Lukasiewicz laments. "She burned them and burned them bad. Once she knew the different houses and had moved through all of them, she called a couple of her buddies; a couple robberies took place; she stole cash . . . and [those couples] finally had their fill and couldn't deal with her anymore. . . . Then the people had another meeting and said, 'We can't do this and need to put down restrictions.'"

One lesson here, Lukasiewicz says, is to let the professionals in your church take the lead in reaching people like Lori—those who are familiar with the signs of addiction and with the lies, excuses and manipulations that can go along with addiction. Those working twelve-step programs will be your most effective agents of healing, so invite them to be on the frontlines. Then invite others in your congregation to support them in their work, be it through prayer, hospitality or financial giving.

When the Healing Jesus We Never Knew Meets Us

In his book *The Jesus I Never Knew*, author Philip Yancey recounts a friend's experience while working with the down-and-out in Chicago:

> A prostitute came to him in wretched straits, homeless, her health failing, unable to buy food for her two-year-old daughter. Her eyes awash with tears, she confessed that she had been renting out her daughter—two years old!—to men interested in kinky sex, in order to support her own drug habit. My friend could hardly bear hearing the sordid details of her story.
>
> He sat in silence, not knowing what to say. At last he asked if she had ever thought of going to a church for help.
>
> "I will never forget the look of pure astonishment that crossed her face," he later told me.
>
> "Church!" she cried. "Why would I ever go there? They'd just make me feel even worse than I already do!"[7]

The Jesus we either have never known or are afraid to meet, because of what it might mean for our own transformation, is alive and well in the world of addiction recovery. In that world, the outcasts and the despised, people like sex workers who rent out their kids for a night of getting high, *matter*. They matter to Jesus, and they matter to recovery-friendly churches. When your church becomes a gathering of people that welcomes "the least of these" for what they might teach you about love itself and about your own need for healing, you will have learned how to be hospitable to people with addictions. All you need to do is take a couple baby steps: some prayer and a little practice, for starters. Jesus will lead you the rest of the way home.

Discussion Questions

1. How is your church already practicing and talking about healing? Your brainstorming may surprise you.

2. What do you need healing from? Spend some time asking God to reveal to you where you are soul-sick.

3. How have you met the Jesus who heals in your own life? Share your experience.

Conclusion

Rich and blessed those servants, rather
Than I who see not my Father's face!
I will arise and go to my Father:—
"Fallen from sonship, beggared of grace,
Grant me, Father, a servant's place."

CHRISTINA ROSSETTI
"A PRODIGAL SON"

A STUDENT ONCE ASKED A RABBI, "Why did God create human beings?" The rabbi answered that it was because God loves stories.[1]

The parable of the prodigal God is one such story. In it, the very meaning of human existence comes to life—as a movement toward grace and toward home. In my work with addicts, I have found this story to be one that God likes to tell over and over again.

The characters and contexts may change, and the cadences may vary, but the same general movement is there, and every element in the story seems necessary to this movement: the return of the wayward son to his prodigal father, and before this, the coming to one's senses and the arising, with the distant recollection of home and its familiar warmth and comforting smells, and even earlier the departure from home and the dissolute wandering and reckless self-forgetfulness in a foreign country. All are crucial to an apprehension of grace in a God who loves his children extravagantly.

All are "traveling mercies" of the kind that author Anne Lamott describes in her best-selling book by that name and that the main character in author Marilynne Robinson's latest novel, *Lila*, ultimately must embrace. Lila wrestles with the prospect that a loving God could assign the people she has loved across her life, prodigal children all of them, to an eternal fate in the fiery flames of hell. She decides in the end that "all the tangles and knots of bitterness and desperation and fear had to be pitied"—and "grace had to fall over them."[2]

Grace falls.

Every day in my line of work, I get to see grace falling on the heads of recovering addicts—and on me, too, by extension. Recovering addicts are some of the brightest, most spiritually attuned people I have ever met. In the stranglehold of addiction, they are "frustrated mystics waylaid by spirits," to quote the Swiss psychotherapist Carl Jung, and when they wake up spiritually, they are on fire. Their lives are aflame with what can only be the presence of a God who has come near and heard the cries of those who are poor in spirit.

Strikingly, by and large the church has yet to take notice, or to arise and head in the direction of home, or to leave that small, stuffy room where the older brother is. Almost a century after Bill Wilson founded a fellowship for recovering addicts based on biblically inspired principles for spiritual transformation, the church has remained on the periphery of that new spiritual life sprouting like kudzu.

This book assumes that the issue is not that churches do not want to be part of that new life, but that until now churches have not known *how* to join in. Our survey of church leaders and conversations with pastors suggest this hunch may be correct. In which case, this book has sought to answer your biggest *how* questions and to provide biblical, theological and pastoral tools for loving the addicts in your midst.

Jewish philosopher Martin Buber tells the story of how a rabbi learned to love people.[3] The rabbi was conversing with a group of peasants when one peasant asked another, "Tell me, do you love me or don't you love me?" The other peasant replied, "I love you very much." But the first peasant protested, "You say that you love me, but you do not know what I need. If you really loved me, you would know," to which the second peasant could not respond.

The rabbi concludes that "to know the needs of people, and to bear the burden of their struggles—that is the true love of humanity."

This book has aimed to show that loving the addicts in our midst means knowing their needs and bearing the burden of their struggles, recognizing that their plight is ours, too, because the case can be made on both statistical and existential grounds that the addicts in our midst include our very own selves. One young woman who is quick to mention her affiliation with a recovery group, puts it this way: "Addiction is a first-world problem. Usually when I use that expression 'first-world problem,' I mean it sarcastically. But I'm serious: addiction is an epidemic in this country, and it's not funny."

> If the epidemic of addiction in America is a sobering commentary about the state of our collective soul, the recovery movement bears witness to something else: that the kingdom of the prodigal God is alive and well.

If the epidemic of addiction in America is a sobering commentary about the state of our collective soul, the recovery movement bears witness to something else: that the kingdom of the prodigal God is alive and well outside the four walls of the church—proclaiming good news to the poor, setting the captives free and opening the eyes of the blind.[4]

Whether it comes as a torrential rainfall or one drop at a time, grace is falling just about everywhere I turn in the world of addiction recovery. As Lila said, "The tangles and knots of bitterness and desperation and fear" are coming undone, maybe "because grace [has] to fall on them," and because a prodigal Father can be no other way, even when his children stray.

When I think of falling grace, I think of Elizabeth, who is quick to share how she found a new beginning with the help of Mercy Street Church.[5] Twelve-plus years ago, Elizabeth was in treatment for a third time. Several years before, she had abandoned her three children, who were in foster care. While in treatment, Elizabeth learned that it was her responsibility to find a family member who could assume temporary custody of her two boys—until she was in steady sobriety and parentally fit. The only other option was permanently losing custody of her children. By this time, Elizabeth's daughter was in the care of Elizabeth's sister, who could not take the boys. Elizabeth, who had no other real family to whom she could turn, recalls being worried, scared and in desperate straits upon hearing this news. "I kept praying for help to a God I wasn't sure even existed," she says.

And God came through. In answer to Elizabeth's prayers, a long-lost nephew turned up who agreed to care for Elizabeth's children for the next year, as she stuck with treatment and kept working the program. During this period, God also led Elizabeth to Mercy Street Church.

"I was very, very broken, my soul was shattered, and my heart was empty," Elizabeth recalls. "And those people loved and cared for me, and they believed when I didn't believe. And after a year I was able to be reunited with my children."

The community of Mercy Street sustained Elizabeth during that especially difficult first year of recovery, helping her to reclaim custody of her two boys one year later. And today, as a result, Elizabeth is bold in declaring what she knows to be true about God:

I know that God has carried, protected and saved me many times before that and after; and that his grace and mercy abound and that he can fulfill the desires of your heart and create a future of freedom and restored relationships. His powers are limitless. Just desire him and believe.

Grace is falling.

A pastor friend tells the story of a forty-two-year-old married man struggling with a porn addiction who opened up to my friend about his struggles in the context of a discussion about *The Big Book*'s step 5, which is to admit "to God, to ourselves, and to another human being the exact nature of our wrongs." The man shared he was "on porn every waking moment" and that it was "killing" him.

With my friend's encouragement, the man joined a Christian twelve-step group and is making a comeback—albeit slowly and not without multiple relapses. "But that's okay," my friend says. "He's getting better, and it will take him a while. . . . He struggles with this, yet it is comforting to know that God is working on it. And there is nothing wrong with God's healing: God has a special place and a plan for us, and he's going to take us down that road—and you might struggle with that thing for your whole life. It doesn't mean you don't have a relationship or a purpose; it means it's just there, like Paul's thorn in the side, and that's okay."

Grace is falling.

Yes, the "far-off country" of addiction is as close as my nose and yours. To ignore it is to be as disconnected from reality as the older son in the parable and to pretend that we aren't in a story about a prodigal God: a story with a fall, a rising and a homecoming, at the center of which is love itself.

But to recognize the contours of that near-distant land, to trace their outline across the map of one's soul, is to begin to see this prodigal God a bit more clearly and to arise and turn to him, one prodigal person at a time.

And the celebration will be great.

Discussion Questions

1. What story do you believe God wants to tell about your congregation in relation to the addicts in your midst?

2. Do you agree with the conclusion of the rabbi in Martin Buber's story, that loving people means knowing their needs and bearing their burdens? What is most scary for you about that task?

3. How is grace already falling all around you? Are you part of that movement of God? Do you want to be part of it?

Acknowledgments

✝

THERE ARE MANY PEOPLE TO THANK for making this book possible.

I extend a wholehearted thank-you to the staff of The Recovery Place, and to my colleagues at Elements Behavioral Health (EBH), especially Dr. David Sack, Vera Appleyard, Tiffany Tait and Meghan Vivo. I am grateful to EBH's editorial team for their contributions along the way. Here I extend a special word of thanks to colleague Vaughn Bell, who saw my potential and made it possible for me to author this book. Without her, it wouldn't be here; and without the initiative, ideas and support of this talented group of people with whom I am privileged to work, it would not be what it is.

My editor, Helen Lee, and the wonderful staff of InterVarsity Press also deserve a round of applause. Their anointed belief in this book and their commitment to making it better have been a source of great encouragement.

The following people deserve mention for their help in the research and writing process: Dr. Saskia de Vries, Sean Gladding, Sarah Gombis, Rev. Joan Gray, Rev. Frank Lukasiewicz, Rev. Cec Murphey and Madison Trammel, among others.

Then there are the one hundred church leaders, many of them social media friends and friends of friends, and the Stephen Ministers we heard from, who took time out of their busy schedules as lay and ordained clergy to fill out our online survey and answer our questions. Their responses shaped the content of this book, and I can only express my gratitude. Here I extend a special word of thanks to Deborah Thompson for her help marshaling the feedback of Stephen Ministers from the Atlanta-area network of churches she oversees.

Finally, I wish to thank those whose stories of recovery appear in these pages. Their courage and vulnerability will now be on display for the countless strangers who pick up this book. They are my heroes.

Appendix

Resources for Ministry

Major Forms of Addiction

Important disclaimer: The following list of addictions and their signs and symptoms in no way should be considered clinically exhaustive or sufficient for diagnosing an addiction without the help of an addiction professional. The list is instead intended as an abbreviated introduction to the various addictions and their potential characteristics. Some recovery centers offer free, no-strings-attached assessments for individuals who need help determining whether they or a loved one have an addiction. When in doubt as to whether you or someone you know has a diagnosable addiction, please consult the professionals in your area.

Chemical dependencies (including alcoholism and illicit or prescription drug abuse).

Signs and symptoms:

- frequent tardiness, absenteeism or evading responsibilities at work or school
- frequent health problems
- weight loss
- unusually large or small pupils

- getting drunk or high often

- fatigue, spaciness or poor concentration

- depression or volatile changes in mood

- suicidal tendencies

- patterns of reclusiveness

- using substances to cope with life stressors

    Related reading:

Carnes, Patrick, Stefanie Carnes and John Bailey. *Facing Addiction: Starting Recovery from Alcohol and Drugs.* Carefree, AZ: Gentle Path Press, 2011.

Powers, Jason. *When the Servant Becomes the Master.* Las Vegas, NV: Central Recovery Press, 2012.

Compulsive exercise.

Signs and symptoms:

- excessive guilt or irritability when not able to exercise

- exercising even when sick or fatigued and without rest days

- irregular or absent menstrual periods

- prioritizing exercise before work, family or friends

- overexercising to the point of causing health injuries

    Related reading:

"Exercise Addiction 101," addiction.com, April 6, 2015, www.addiction .com/addiction-a-to-z/exercise-addiction/exercise-addiction-101.

Food addictions.

Signs and symptoms (this should be clinically differentiated from anorexia and bulimia by a health care professional):

- extremes in weight (excessively underweight or overweight) and accompanying health problems

- obsessive-compulsive thoughts and behaviors related to food, such as binge eating or constant dieting, counting calories or weighing oneself

- food cravings, despite being full
- eating much more food than intended
- eating until feeling excessively stuffed
- feeling guilty after overeating, but doing it again soon
- making up excuses
- repeated failures at reigning in eating

Related reading:

Peeke, Pamela. *The Hunger Fix*. New York: Rodale Books, 2012.

Sex and love addictions ("intimacy disorders").

Signs and symptoms:

- preoccupation with sexual fantasy
- obsessive pursuit of casual or non-intimate sex
- use of porn, phone or computer sex or prostitutes
- compulsive and habitual masturbation
- romantic intensity
- prioritizing sex to the exclusion of other activities and despite a negative impact on relationships
- mistaking sex and romance for love
- endlessly searching for "the one"
- dressing seductively to attract attention
- using sex to hold on to a partner
- multiple extramarital affairs
- having sex in high-risk situations
- inappropriate sexual boundaries

Related reading:

Carnes, Patrick. *Out of the Shadows: Understanding Sexual Addiction,*
3rd ed. Center City, MN: Hazelden, 2001.

Carnes, Stefanie. *Mending a Shattered Heart: A Guide for Partners of
Sex Addicts.* Carefree, AZ: Gentle Path Press, 2009.

Weiss, Robert. *Sex Addiction 101: A Basic Guide to Healing from Sex,
Porn, and Love Addiction.* Dublin, OH: Telemachus Press, 2013.

Shopping and hoarding addictions.

Signs and symptoms:

- many unopened or tagged items in the closet
- purchasing things that either are not needed or were not intended
  for purchase in the first place
- shopping as a form of emotional comfort
- experiencing "highs" when shopping and "lows" when not shopping
- attempting to conceal runaway shopping habits
- feeling remorse after shopping
- collecting items that are of little to no value (in the case of hoarding)

Related reading:

"Shopping Addiction 101," addiction.com, April 20, 2015, www.addiction
.com/addiction-a-to-z/shopping-addiction/shopping-addiction-101.

Technology and Internet addictions.

Signs and symptoms:

- technology or Internet use continues to increase
- feelings of depression or anxiety when not online, playing video
  games, etc.
- surfing the web much longer than originally planned
- technology or Internet use has adverse effects on work and family
  relationships and continues despite these negative effects
- unsuccessful attempts to curtail use

Related reading:

"Technology Addiction 101," addiction.com, December 9, 2014, www.addiction.com/addiction-a-to-z/technology-addiction /technology-addiction-101.

Workaholism.

Signs and symptoms:

- burning the candle at both ends all the time
- constantly talking about how much there is to do work-wise
- an inability to turn down projects or new work commitments, even at the detriment of mental or physical health or relationships
- not taking time off
- feelings of anxiety, insecurity or sudden letdown when not working

Related reading:

"Work Addiction 101," addiction.com, www.addiction.com/addiction-a -to-z/work-addiction/work-addiction-101.

Resources for Creating a Church Benevolence Policy

Bagne, Gwen. "Does Your Church Need a Benevolence Strategy?" *Church Executive*, October 2006. www.churchadminpro.com/Articles /Benevolence%20Strategy%20-%20Does%20Your%20Church%20 Need%20One.pdf.

"Benevolence Ministry." *Building Church Leaders.* www.buildingchurch leaders.com/downloads/practicalministryskills/benevolenceministry.

O'Neil, Rod. "Organizing Your Benevolence Ministry." *Building Church Leaders.* www.buildingchurchleaders.com/downloads/practical ministryskills/benevolenceministry/ps81-c.html.

The Twelve Steps of Alcoholics Anonymous

1. We admitted we were powerless over alcohol—that our lives had become unmanageable.

2. Came to believe that a Power greater than ourselves could restore us to sanity.

3. Made a decision to turn our will and our lives over to the care of God *as we understood Him.*

4. Made a searching and fearless moral inventory of ourselves.

5. Admitted to God, to ourselves, and to another human being the exact nature of our wrongs.

6. Were entirely ready to have God remove all these defects of character.

7. Humbly asked Him to remove our shortcomings.

8. Made a list of all persons we had harmed, and became willing to make amends to them all.

9. Made direct amends to such people wherever possible, except when to do so would injure them or others.

10. Continued to take personal inventory, and when we were wrong, promptly admitted it.

11. Sought through prayer and meditation to improve our conscious contact with God *as we understood Him,* praying only for knowledge of His will for us and the power to carry that out.

12. Having had a spiritual awakening as the result of these steps, we tried to carry this message to alcoholics, and to practice these principles in all our affairs.[1]

Books

- *Alcoholics Anonymous: The Big Book.* 4th ed. New York: Alcoholics Anonymous World Services, 2001. *The Big Book,* as it is more popularly known, is a must-read for anyone seeking to understand the recovery mindset and the biblically inspired principles behind it.

- Clinebell, Howard. *Understanding and Counseling Persons with Alcohol, Drug and Behavioral Addictions.* Nashville: Abingdon Press, 1984. Though a bit dated, this book is a thorough and very informative introduction to the pastoral care needs of people with alcohol, drug and process addictions.

- May, Gerald. *Addiction and Grace.* New York: HarperOne, 1988. Written by a Christian psychiatrist, this book remains a trusted resource for understanding addiction as a universal spiritual and physical disease describing the human condition.

- Morris, Bill. *The Complete Handbook for Recovery Ministry in the Church.* Nashville: Thomas Nelson, 1993. This book outlines the nuts and bolts of starting a recovery support group within your congregation.

- Rohr, Richard. *Breathing Underwater: Spirituality and the Twelve Steps.* Cincinnati, OH: St. Anthony Messenger Press, 2011. This book introduces the twelve steps and the gospel principles that underlie them. Questions at the end of the book invite readers to wrestle with the implications of the twelve steps for their own spiritual transformation and are handy for both individuals and small groups.

- Ryan, T. C. *Ashamed No More: A Pastor's Journey Through Sex Addiction.* Downers Grove, IL: InterVarsity Press, 2012. With vulnerability and compassion for people with intimacy disorders, a former pastor tells his own ultimately redemptive story of living with a hidden addiction that afflicts many Americans both in the church and out.

- Simpson, Amy. *Troubled Minds: Mental Illness and the Church's Mission.* Downers Grove, IL: InterVarsity Press, 2013. Because addiction is a diagnosable form of mental illness and often occurs alongside other diagnosable mental disorders, this book is worth a read for anyone seeking a more integrated picture of addiction and mental health. The book's appendix also includes some helpful resources on mental health issues.

Websites

- Addiction.com, www.addiction.com. This online clearinghouse of information on addiction and recovery provides tips on finding treatment and staying sober and the latest insights from expert bloggers on various forms of addiction, from chemical dependencies to intimacy and eating disorders.

- American Association of Christian Counselors, www.aacc.net. The website features a search option to help you find a credentialed Christian counselor in your area.

- Association of Intervention Specialists, www.associationof interventionspecialists.org/about-ais. All members of the association are certified interventionists, and thanks to their online member directory you can identify and contact a trained intervention professional in your area.

- Christian Drug Rehab, www.christiandrugrehab.com. This website connects people with addiction and their families with Christian recovery resources in the form of recovery programs, helpful articles and other materials.

- Christian Recovery International, www.christianrecovery.com. The site includes a wide variety of resources in the way of networking, training and twelve-step materials for churches seeking to become a "safe place for people recovering from addiction, abuse, or trauma." Issues of spiritual abuse are also resourced here.

- National Association for Christian Recovery, www.nacr.org. The resources listed here are especially helpful for pastors.

Organizations

- Alcoholics Anonymous, www.aa.org. Recovery and support groups for people addicted to alcohol.

- Celebrate Recovery, www.celebraterecovery.com. More self-consciously "Christian" recovery support groups for people with addictions.

- Clergy Recovery Network, www.clergyrecovery.com. This network exists to counsel clergy in crisis toward spiritual and organizational health, but its mission to be a place "where ministry professionals find grace and hope" can resource any church leader seeking to find a part in recovery.

- Co-Dependents Anonymous, www.coda.org. CoDA recovery and support groups help men, women and families seeking to recover from dysfunctional relationships.

- Narcotics Anonymous, www.na.org. Recovery and support groups for people with drug addictions.

- National Alliance on Mental Illness (NAMI), http://nami.org. NAMI is a respected source of information and referrals related to issues of mental illness, including addiction. NAMI's FaithNet program specifically resources faith-based communities such as churches with materials for worship services, sermons and other church needs.

- National Eating Disorders Association, www.nationaleating disorders.org. Provides information, referrals, support and prevention resources related to eating disorders.

- Sex and Love Addicts Anonymous, www.slaafws.org. Recovery and support groups for individuals with intimacy disorders.

- SMART Recovery, www.smartrecovery.org. This recovery support group is an alternative to twelve-step groups.

- Substance Abuse and Mental Health Services Administration (SAMHSA), www.samhsa.gov. SAMHSA provides 24-hour, free and confidential treatment referral and information about mental or substance abuse disorders, prevention and recovery. Clergy and churches can also find helpful training resources here.

  - National Suicide Prevention Hotline: 1-800-273-8255

  - National Helpline: 1-800-662-Help (4357)

Christian and Other Treatment Programs

There are a variety of Christian programs throughout the nation. When searching for a Christian program, one must differentiate between a track and a program. A Christian track is where clients are mainstreamed in secular programming and then pulled out for specific Christian or faith-based groups or bible study. A Christian program is where all aspects of programming are infused with spiritual, faith-based principles. When searching for a faith-based program, it's important to verify that there are solid clinical credentials combined with faith-based elements and Christian principles.

Recovery Apps

The Cassava App

This app is meant to be used daily as a way to stay on track in your recovery process. The app locates nearby support groups from a database of more than 150,000 twelve-step and non-twelve-step meetings, monitors your mood and activities, and tracks your daily process. You can download it on iTunes or the Google Play Store.

Notes

Introduction

[1]Tim Keller, *The Prodigal God* (New York: Penguin, 2008), xv.

[2]Henri Nouwen, *The Return of the Prodigal Son: A Meditation on Fathers, Brothers and Sons* (New York: Doubleday, 1992), 38-39.

[3]An estimated 5 percent of Americans are compulsive shoppers (Kimberly Palmer, "Are You Addicted to Shopping?" *U.S. News and World Report,* May 16, 2012, http://money.usnews.com/money/personal-finance/articles /2012/05/16/are-you-addicted-to-shopping); 6 percent exhibit some form of sexual addiction (Ross Rosenberg, "The Emergence of Female Sex Addiction: Understanding Gender Differences," 2011, www.academia.edu/1193969 /The_Emergence_of_Female _Sex_Addiction_Understanding_Gender _Differences); at least 1 percent are pathological gamblers (National Research Council, www.american gaming.org/sites/default/files/uploads /docs/faqs/nrc-pathological_gambling_p._3.pdf); 7.5 percent have eating disorders ("Eating Disorders Statistics," National Association of Anorexia Nervosa and Related Disorders, 2015, www.anad.org/get-information /about-eating-disorders/eating-disorders-statistics; note: the figure given here is actually 24 million Americans, so 24 million out of the total US population of 319 million is 7.5%); and 10 percent have drug or alcohol addictions ("Substance Use and Mental Health Estimates from the 2013 National Survey on Drug Use and Health: Overview of Findings," Substance Abuse and Mental Health Services Administration, September 4, 2014, www.samhsa .gov/data/sites/default/files/NSDUH-SR200-RecoveryMonth-2014 /NSDUH-SR200-RecoveryMonth-2014.htm).

[4]Brené Brown, "The Power of Vulnerability," TED, June 2010, www.ted
.com/talks/brene_brown_on_vulnerability.

Chapter 1: Responding to Addiction

[1]Francis Seeburger, *Addiction and Responsibility: An Inquiry into the
Addictive Mind* (New York: Crossroad, 1993), 5-6.

[2]See *Alcoholics Anonymous: The Story of How Many Thousands of Men
and Women Have Recovered from Alcoholism*, 4th ed. (New York: Alcoholics Anonymous World Services, 2001), 59.

[3]The worksheet is available at www.step12.com/aa-files/4th-step
-instructions-x.pdf.

[4]Edward T. Welch and Gary Steven Shogren, *Addictive Behavior* (Grand
Rapids: Baker Books, 1995), 92.

[5]John Zahl, *Grace in Addiction* (Charlottesville, VA: Mockingbird Ministries,
2012), 106-9.

[6]Patrick Carnes, *Out of the Shadows: Understanding Sexual Addiction*,
3rd ed. (Center City, MN: Hazelden, 2003), 8.

[7]Ashley Casper, "Mummified body found inside hoarder's San Francisco
home," *Las Vegas Review Journal*, April 6, 2015, www.reviewjournal.com
/trending/mummified-body-found-inside-hoarder-s-san-francisco
-home.

Chapter 2: The Intervention

[1]Howard Clinebell offers this tip, and I think it's a good one; Howard
Clinebell, *Understanding and Counseling Persons with Alcohol, Drug and
Behavioral Addictions*, 3rd ed. (Nashville, TN: Abingdon Press, 1984), 352.

[2]Ibid., 306-7.

[3]The parable Jesus tells in Luke 18:9-14 about the Pharisee and the tax
collector is a powerful illustration of how comparing (vs. identifying) is
most fundamentally an obstacle to connecting with God himself.

[4]Francis Seeburger, *Addiction and Responsibility: An Inquiry into the
Addictive Mind* (New York: Crossroad, 1993), 5.

[5]Dr. David Sack, "6 Surprising Traits You May Have in Common with a Drug
Addict," *PsychCentral*, June 9, 2014, http://blogs.psychcentral.com/addiction
-recovery/2014/05/6-surprising-traits-you-may-have-in-common-with-a
-drug-addict.

⁶Edward T. Welch and Gary Steven Shogren, *Addictive Behavior* (Grand Rapids: Baker Books, 1995), 85-86.

⁷Clinebell, 403.

⁸*Detachment* is a term commonly used in Al-Anon. *Release* is the term Clinebell uses in his chapter on counseling family members of addicts. See Clinebell, 412-19.

⁹Ibid., 413.

Chapter 3: Myths About Addiction

¹David Linden, *The Compass of Pleasure* (New York: Penguin, 2011), 7-9.

²Ibid., 58-59.

³The National Institute on Drug Abuse (NIDA) makes the claim that more than half of those who abuse alcohol or drugs are suffering from another mental health issue, like depression, anxiety, bipolar disorder, ADHD or an antisocial personality disorder. See "Drug Abuse and Mental Health Problems Often Happen Together," NIDA, http://easyread.drugabuse .gov/drug-effects-mental-health.php.

⁴Brennan Manning, *All Is Grace* (Colorado Springs, CO: David C. Cook, 2011), 119-20.

⁵Amy Simpson, *Troubled Minds: Mental Illness and the Church's Mission* (Downers Grove, IL: InterVarsity Press, 2013), 138.

⁶See Matthew Stanford, *Grace for the Afflicted: A Clinical and Biblical Perspective on Mental Illness* (Downers Grove, IL: InterVarsity Press, 2008), 32-34, cited in Amy Simpson, *Troubled Minds*, 159.

⁷Simpson, *Troubled Minds*, 159.

⁸Ibid., 160.

⁹Melody Harrison Hanson, "I Was in Love . . . with Vodka, Wine and Gin," *Logic and Imagination* (blog), September 17, 2011, http://logicand imagination.com/2011/09/17/i-was-so-in-love-with-vodka-gin-and -wine.

¹⁰The term "attractional church" arises from the missional church movement. An attractional church is one that, instead of being sent out into the world and joining Jesus in God's mission, prefers to attract prospective attendees to its various services.

¹¹Simpson, *Troubled Minds*, 152.

¹²See Tom Long, *The Witness of Preaching* (Louisville, KY: Westminster

John Knox Press, 2005), 6. Long is quoting Craig Dykstra, "The Formative Power of the Congregation," *Religious Education* 82, no. 4 (Fall 1987): 532.

[13]Cathryn Kemp, *Painkiller Addict: From Wreckage to Redemption—My True Story* (London: Hachette Digital, 2012), 1.

[14]Manning, *All Is Grace*, 177-78.

[15]Ibid., 178.

[16]The Epidemiologic Catchment Area Study of 1980–1984 placed "remission rate" for addiction at 59 percent; the National Epidemiologic Survey on Alcohol and Related Conditions of 2001–2003 at 81 percent; the National Comorbidity Survey of 2001–2003 at 82 percent. Kent Dunnington, *Addiction and Virtue* (Downers Grove, IL: InterVarsity Press, 2011), 25. Here Dunnington is citing Thomas McLellan, quoted in Gene Heyman, *Addiction: A Disorder of Choice* (Cambridge, MA: Harvard University Press, 2009), 66.

[17]Natalie M. Lee, et al., "Public Views on Food Addiction and Obesity: Implications for Policy and Treatment," PMC, September 25, 2013, http://journals.plos.org/plosone/article?id=10.1371/journal.pone.0074836.

[18]Alcoholics Anonymous, *The Big Book*, 4th ed. (New York: Alcoholics Anonymous World Services, 2001), 24; www.aa.org/assets/en_US/en_bigbook_chapt2.pdf.

[19]Bruce Goldman, "Neuroscience of Need: Understanding the Addicted Mind," Stanford Medicine, Spring 2012, http://sm.stanford.edu/archive/stanmed/2012spring/article5.html.

Chapter 4: Cultivating a Culture of Long-Term Sobriety

[1]Kitty Harris, "Recovery Ministry (Part 1): Dr. Kitty Harris with Dr. Virginia Todd Holeman," January 24, 2014, www.youtube.com/watch?v=zM6RXBU4eJU. I'm grateful to Sean Gladding for introducing me to this resource for the church.

[2]Ibid.

[3]One view maintains that the essence of addiction is not one of chemical dependence but rather of isolation. The University of California, Berkeley, philosopher Alva Noë, in adopting the line of reasoning of author and journalist Johann Hari and researchers Bruce K. Alexander and Gene Heyman, says that addiction is most essentially a problem of disconnection and isolation: "Whatever its causes, addiction would seem to be

... a disorder of one's ability to connect to others," Noë writes. "It might be right . . . that we could fix addiction if we could restore in the addict a sense of connection with the world around him or her, and with other people. . . . Addicts are shut off." See Alva Noë, "The Fight Against Addiction: Is Love All You Need?," National Public Radio, March 27, 2015, www.npr.org/blogs/13.7/2015/03/27/395774025/the-fight-against -addiction-is-love-all-you-need?utm_source=facebook.com&utm _medium=social&utm_campaign=npr&utm_term=nprnews&utm _content=20150327.

[4]At Three Strands, entering clients are immediately given chores and are expected to contribute to community life in various ways, the idea being that addicts have duties and responsibilities like anyone else. Matt Russell, "Addiction and Recovery in the Church: Part 1," an interview with Matt Russell, Sean Gladding and Gregg Taylor, by Chris Kiesling, March 15, 2014, www.youtube.com/watch?v=eJVrVg103M4.

[5]Desmond Tutu, *God Has a Dream: A Vision of Hope for Our Time* (New York: Random House, 2004), 3.

[6]Ibid., 75.

[7]Consider 2 Corinthians 4:7: "But we have this treasure in clay jars, so that it may be made clear that this extraordinary power belongs to God and does not come from us."

[8]Russell, "Addiction and Recovery."

[9]Henry and Richard Blackaby first introduced me to this principle of the spiritual life in their *Experiencing God: Knowing and Doing the Will of God* (Nashville, TN: Lifeway Press, 1990).

[10]Russell, "Addiction and Recovery."

[11]Ibid.

[12]Ibid.

[13]Ibid.

[14]Gladding explains that so much of the Gospels is about Jesus' imperative to "seek the kingdom of God" or "enter the kingdom" or "receive the kingdom like a child," and this "kingdom of God" is not the same thing as the church. Russell, "Addiction and Recovery."

[15]Dale S. Ryan, "Christian Recovery Ministry: Dr. Dale S. Ryan with Dr. Stephen P. Stratton, Part 1," February 1, 2014, www.youtube.com/watch ?v=xFR0KwqeS1Y.

[16]Ibid.

[17]Edward T. Welch and Gary Steven Shogren, *Addictive Behavior* (Grand Rapids: Baker Books, 1995), 127-28.

[18]David Linden, *The Compass of Pleasure* (New York: Penguin, 2011), 52.

[19]Ronald McMillin and Chandler Scott Rogers, *Freeing Someone You Love from Alcohol and Drugs* (New York: Penguin, 1992), 141-43.

[20]Gerald May, *Addiction and Grace: Love and Spirituality in the Healing of Addictions* (New York: HarperOne, 1988), 1.

[21]The theologian Paul Tillich develops this theme of total acceptance in chapter 19 of his book *The Shaking of the Foundations* (New York: Charles Scribner's Sons, 1948). The expression "You are accepted" comes from one of Tillich's sermons, which was later developed into an essay and then a chapter in this well-known book. Unconditional acceptance is the healing answer to at least three messages we hear by virtue of being human: "I'm not worthy," "I'm not good enough" and "I'm not loveable." When we practice unconditional acceptance, we counter these shame messages.

[22]The work we do in addiction recovery is at heart incarnational ministry; the first chapter of John—about the Word made flesh—shapes how we approach this task. We are grateful to Dr. Dale Denham for a practical and theological framework for incarnational ministry.

[23]Gladding cites a similar example. See Russell, "Addiction and Recovery."

[24]In clinical work, we call this empathy. Empathy is when we feel with someone; sympathy is when we feel sorry for someone. God-given compassion is empathetic, not sympathetic. Sympathy distances me from you in your pain; empathy connects me with you in your pain so healing can occur.

[25]McMillin and Rogers, *Freeing Someone*, 164-66.

[26]Ibid.

[27]Ibid.

[28]Alcoholics Anonymous, *Twelve Steps and Twelve Traditions* (New York: A. A. Grapevine Inc. and Alcoholics Anonymous Publishing, 1952), 63, 64, 76.

[29]See David Sack in "Drugs Can Become Part of a Lifestyle, Promises' Dr. David Sacks Tells CNN," February 7, 2014, http://www.elementsbehavioral health.com/addiction/drugs-can-become-part-of-lifestyle-promises-dr -david-sack-tells-cnn/.

[30]Howard Clinebell, *Understanding and Counseling Persons with Alcohol,*

Drug and Behavioral Addictions, 3rd ed. (Nashville, TN: Abingdon Press, 1984), 272.

[31]The recovery equivalent to *shalom* is serenity, which is a feeling of well-being even in the midst of trials (or "the peace of God, which surpasses all understanding" to which the apostle Paul refers in Philippians 4:7).

[32]Johann Hari, "The Likely Cause of Addiction Has Been Discovered, and It Is Not What You Think," *The Huffington Post,* January 20, 2015, www .huffingtonpost.com/johann-hari/the-real-cause-of-addicti_b_6506936 .html.

[33]By its own description, Celebrate Recovery is a more explicitly "Christ-based" version of AA's twelve steps.

Chapter 5: Ending the Shame

[1]Researchers from Montreal Neurological Institute (MNI), McGill University and the University of Cambridge have found that Parkinson's disease patients receiving various treatments for their condition develop addictive behaviors such as compulsive shopping, gambling or hypersexuality. See "Addiction: Insights from Parkinson's Disease," *Science Daily,* March 3, 2009, www.sciencedaily.com/releases/2009/02 /090225132341.htm.

[2]See American Society of Addiction Medicine, "Definition of Addiction," www.asam.org/for-the-public/definition-of-addiction. The Institute of Medicine, the National Institute on Drug Abuse, the American Medical Association and the American Psychological Association couch addiction similarly in terms of "brain disease."

[3]See ibid.

[4]The Christian philosopher Kent Dunnington constructively problematizes both the disease model and the choice model, seeking instead to conceptualize addiction as "habit" and conscripting Thomas Aquinas and Aristotle in the enterprise. By embracing a disease model for addiction, we do not wish to imply that this model is perfect or without limitations but to lift up both the consensus of medical science and the merits of this model for treatment and recovery as reasons (among many) for why we believe this model still works and fits within a Christian biblical and theological framework. See Kent Dunnington, *Addiction and Virtue* (Downers Grove, IL: InterVarsity Press, 2011).

[5]Brené Brown, "Listening to shame," TED, March 2012, www.ted.com/talks/brene_brown_listening_to_shame.

[6]See T. C. Ryan, *Ashamed No More: A Pastor's Journey Through Sex Addiction* (Downers Grove, IL: InterVarsity Press, 2012), 77.

[7]Ibid.

[8]Stephanie Desmon and Susan Morrow, "Drug addiction viewed more negatively than mental illness, Johns Hopkins study shows," HUB, Johns Hopkins University, October 1, 2014, http://hub.jhu.edu/2014/10/01/drug-addiction-stigma.

[9]*The Big Book* reads, "We are sure God wants us to be happy, joyous, and free. We can't subscribe to the belief that this life is a vale of tears, though it once was just that for many of us. But it is clear that we made our own misery. God didn't do it." Alcoholics Anonymous, *The Big Book*, 4th ed. (New York: Alcoholics Anonymous World Services, 2001), 133; www.aa.org/assets/en_US/en_bigbook_chapt9.pdf.

[10]Another 15 percent answered "three to five times," and 14 percent answered "more than five times."

[11]Simpson is citing a statistic from the National Institute of Mental Health (NIMH) accepted by most experts that says that "about one in four adults—a little more than 25 percent of Americans ages eighteen and older—suffers from a diagnosable mental disorder in a given year." There is no reason to conclude that in the church this statistic would be any different, or that, if it is different, it is lower; if anything, we would do well to expect that in the church this percentage is actually higher. See Amy Simpson, *Troubled Minds: Mental Illness and the Church's Mission* (Downers Grove, IL: InterVarsity Press, 2013), 33-35. See also "Mental Illness Facts and Numbers," NAMI, March 2013, www2.nami.org/factsheets/mentalillness_factsheet.pdf.

[12]Simpson, *Troubled Minds*, 33.

[13]The report reads, "Addiction affects 16 percent of Americans ages 12 and older—40 million people. That is more than the number of people with heart disease (27 million), diabetes (26 million) or cancer (19 million). Another 32 percent of the population (80 million) use tobacco, alcohol and other drugs in risky ways that threaten health and safety." See "Addiction Medicine: Closing the Gap Between Science and Practice," CASAColumbia, June 2012, www.casacolumbia.org/addiction-research/reports/addiction-medicine.

[14]See Jean Kinney and Gwen Leaton, *Loosening the Grip: A Handbook of Alcohol Information* (St. Louis: Mosby Press, 1995), 21, quoted in Bucky Dann, *Addiction: Pastoral Responses* (Nashville, TN: Abingdon Press, 2002), 9.

[15]See Trysh Travis, *The Language of the Heart: A Cultural History of the Recovery Movement from Alcoholics Anonymous to Oprah Winfrey* (Chapel Hill, NC: University of North Carolina, 2009), 4.

[16]Ibid.

[17]This estimate is based on the latest National Survey on Drug Use and Health produced by SAMHSA and referenced in the introduction. The report concludes that while 22.5 million people over the age of twelve need treatment for substance abuse, only 2.5 million seek it.

[18]See "Closing the Addiction Treatment Gap," Open Society Institute, June 2010, www.opensocietyfoundations.org/sites/default/files/early -accomplishments-20100701.pdf.

[19]For example, a study by Christianity Today's *Leadership Journal* found that at least a third of pastors had viewed online porn in that year alone. Another survey, this one conducted by Barna Group at the request of Proven Men Ministries, found that approximately two-thirds of US men view pornography on a monthly basis and that "the number of Christian men viewing pornography virtually mirrors the national average." See "Pornography Use and Addiction," Proven Men Ministries, www.provenmen.org/2014pornsurvey/pornography-use-and -addiction.

[20]Leonard Cohen, "Anthem," *The Future*.

[21]Andrew Newberg, "How do meditation and prayer change our brains?," Myrna Brind Center of Integrative Medicine, www.andrewnewberg.com /research.

[22]For more on "circles of trust," see chapter 6 and also Parker Palmer, *The Hidden Wholeness* (San Francisco: Jossey-Bass, 2004), 52-57.

[23]I am grateful to Tom Long for introducing me to Leonard Sweet's book and its retelling of Mary Ann's story. In *Witness of Preaching*, 2nd ed. (Louisville, KY: Westminster John Knox Press, 2005), 212-13. Also see Mary Ann Bird, as quoted in Leonard Sweet, *Strong in the Broken Places: A Theological Reverie on the Ministry of George Everett Ross* (Akron, OH: University of Akron Press, 1995), 93.

Chapter 6: The Practice of Attentive Listening

[1]William Blake, "The Little Black Boy," *Songs of Innocence* (Dover, England: Dover Publications, 1971), 41.

[2]Episcopal priest Lyn G. Brakeman uses this expression in formulating a biblical theology of addiction and pastoral care. See Brakeman, "By Love Possessed," in Oliver J. Morgan and Merle R. Jordan, eds., *Addiction and Spirituality: A Multidisciplinary Approach* (St. Louis: Chalice Press, 1999), 195-213.

[3]Theologian Paul Tillich describes God as "the ground of being itself," by which he also means that God can be understood as Being Itself. See Tillich, *Systematic Theology*, vol. 1 (Chicago: Chicago University Press, 1951), 163-72.

[4]Richard Rohr, *Breathing Underwater: Spirituality and the Twelve Steps* (Cincinnati, OH: Franciscan Media, 2011), xvi.

[5]Ibid., 70. Step 8 reads, "Made a list of all persons we had harmed, and became willing to make amends to them all."

[6]Kelly Carpenter, "Praying in Pain," http://greenstreetchurch.org/greenstr -content/uploads/2012/10/PrayinginPain.pdf.

[7]Brakeman, "By Love Possessed," 208.

[8]Ibid.

[9]Ibid., 208-209.

[10]Ibid., 209.

[11]Parker Palmer, *The Hidden Wholeness* (San Francisco: Jossey-Bass, 2004), 52-57.

[12]These guidelines are copied directly from "Circle of Trust Touchstones," Center for Courage & Renewal, www.couragerenewal.org/touchstones. Many of these guidelines are also observed in group therapy and in the various recovery fellowships.

[13]Renée Miller, *Strength for the Journey: A Guide to Spiritual Practice* (New York: Morehouse Publishing, 2011), 41.

[14]As Jesus said, "I tell you, many will come from east and west and will eat with Abraham and Isaac and Jacob in the kingdom of heaven" (Matthew 8:11).

Chapter 7: The Practice of Healing

[1]Richard Rohr, *Breathing Underwater: Spirituality and the Twelve Steps* (Cincinnati, OH: Franciscan Media, 2011), 108.

[2]Sara Miles, *Jesus Freak: Feeding Healing Raising the Dead* (San Francisco: Jossey-Bass, 2010), 105, quoted in Rachel Held Evans, *Searching for Sunday* (Nashville, TN: Thomas Nelson, 2015), 208.

[3]Carol Howard Merritt, "Going smaller and deeper," *The Christian Century,* April 1, 2015, 45.

[4]Alcoholics Anonymous and other twelve-step programs are at heart a spiritually based way of life; the steps are spiritual processes in themselves intended for transformation.

[5]Mercy Street, "Who We Are," www.mercystreet.org/who.cfm.

[6]We are grateful to Rachel Held Evans for this example. See her *Searching for Sunday* (Nashville, TN: Thomas Nelson, 2015), 146-48.

[7]Philip Yancey, *The Jesus I Never Knew* (Grand Rapids: Zondervan, 1995), 147-48.

Conclusion

[1]Thomas Bien and Beverly Bien, *Mindful Recovery: A Spiritual Path to Healing from Addiction* (New York: John Wiley & Sons, 2002), 45-46.

[2]Marilynne Robinson, *Lila* (New York: Farrar, Straus and Giroux, 2014), 260.

[3]See Carol Glass, "Addiction and Recovery Through Jewish Eyes," in Oliver J. Morgan and Merle R. Jordan, eds., *Addiction and Spirituality: A Multidisciplinary Approach* (St. Louis: Chalice Press, 1999), 235. Glass gives her own adaptation of Buber's story.

[4]This refers to Jesus' declaration of his mission in Luke 4:18. Here Jesus is quoting Isaiah 61 but leaves out Isaiah's reference to "the day of vengeance" (v. 2). For prodigals coming home, this is a homecoming to favor rather than to vengeance.

[5]Elizabeth's story can be found among others on Mercy Street's website at www.mercystreet.org/streetstories.cfm.

Appendix: Resources for Ministry

[1]*Alcoholics Anonymous: The Big Book*, 4th ed. (New York: Alcoholics Anonymous World Services, 2001), 59.

About the Authors

Jonathan Benz (MS, Palm Beach Atlantic University) is a clinician, public speaker, ordained minister and certified addictions professional. As a leadership consultant to various agencies he specializes in teaching team leadership, task efficiency, crisis management and conflict resolution to people in the midst of life transitions. He is the author of *Live A Legacy: Spiritual Principles for Strategic Living* and resides in South Florida.

Kristina Robb-Dover is a writer and minister in the Presbyterian Church (USA) and has served in various church and chaplaincy settings. She is the author of *Grace Sticks: The Bumper Sticker Gospel for Restless Souls*. As a featured columnist with the online magazine *Beliefnet*, Robb-Dover posts regularly at her blog, *Fellowship of Saints and Sinners*, and her work has appeared in various publications including *Touchstone*, *The Christian Century*, *Theology Today* and *The Washington Post*. She holds degrees from Yale College and Princeton Seminary.